North America's
GREATEST
Big Game Lodges
and Outfitters

North America's
GREATEST
Big Game Lodges
and Outfitters

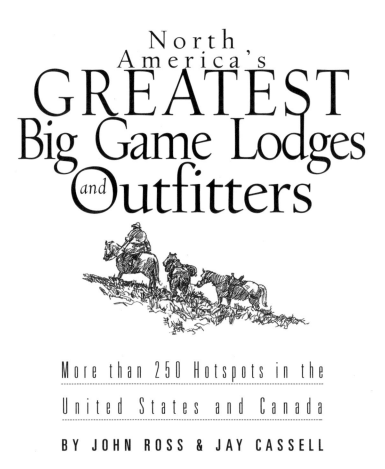

More than 250 Hotspots in the

United States and Canada

BY JOHN ROSS & JAY CASSELL

Printed in the United States of America

DESIGNED BY GRETTER DESIGNS

Maps and Illustrations by R. L. Gretter

Cover Photograph by Andy Anderson

Library of Congress Cataloging-in-Publication Data

EDITED BY KIM LEIGHTON

Published by
WILLOW CREEK PRESS
PO Box 147
Minocqua, WI 54548

Acknowledgments

SOON AFTER MY FAMILY MOVED TO TENNESSEE in the mid-1950s, I joined Boy Scout Troop 30 led by John Kinsey. Mr. Kinsey led us on monthly trips into the Smoky Mountains and down the rivers that drained them. A skilled shot with rifle and pistol, he arranged for us to pick up a few bucks pasting targets when there was an NRA match at the Knoxville Rifle and Pistol Club. Over the years he helped instill in me an abiding love of the outdoors, a deep appreciation for the disciplines of the shooting sports and a healthy respect for firearms, all of which I hope comes through in this book. (John Ross)

My father first taught me to shoot when I was 10. He'd pack up his .38, a .22 and a .177 air pellet gun, and we'd head out to an old gravel pit in Shelter Island, New York, where my family spent the summers. There, he'd line up cans, come back and teach me how to shoot safely and accurately. Later, when I went to summer camp (Forest Lake Camp in Warrensburg, New York, deep in the Adirondacks), I went through the NRA-sponsored course, shooting from prone, sitting and kneeling positions, working my way up to Sharpshooter, 6th or 7th bar. Both my Dad and Forest Lake taught me how to safely use guns, and how to enjoy them. When I got older, I started hunting birds, then whitetails, then larger animals, such as elk and caribou. Throughout my life, I've always had a deep respect and love for the outdoors, and a deep respect and love for the animals I hunt. I don't shoot anything I wouldn't eat, and I make a point of using every part of every animal I take. It's my hope that this book will help you find a lodge or outfitter where you also enjoy the outdoors, and the animals found there. (Jay Cassell)

We've been helped by scores of experienced hunters. Among them have been Jim McCarthy of McCarthy Adventures; Pete Dube of Bear Track Outfitters; Bill Perry of Hidden Creek Outfitters; Peter Fiduccia of the Woods 'N Waters television show; Chris Batin of Alaska Angler (and Hunter) Publications, out of Fairbanks; Thomas McIntyre, of Field & Stream; and Andy Dyess of Pearl River Outfitters in Madison, Mississippi. Frank LaFlesch of the Canadian Embassy in Washington, D.C., and his colleagues in the provinces, especially Siegfried Gagnon of Quebec Tourism, have been extremely helpful, as have the staffs of the state departments of natural resources.

And it's probably not a bad idea (right, guys!) to thank our wives Katie (John's wife) and Lorraine (Jay's wife) for keeping the various wolves at bay while we were married to our computers or engaged in that terribly difficult work of first-hand research known as hunting. Without them, their encouragement, their patience and their love, we would be vastly diminished.

C o n t

e n t s

Introduction

HUNTING IN NORTH AMERICA is changing. Gone are the wild days of pack trips into vast uncharted wilderness. Thanks to GPS we always know where we are (if not where anything else is).

Enlightened game management has brought back record numbers of deer, elk and turkeys where, a generation ago, there were few or none. Lightweight gear and synthetically stocked rifles give us greater range afoot than ever before. We are hunting in a high-tech age.

But it is also an age of uncertainty. Traditional values of honesty and hard work seem to be subverted by the slick spin, get-it-while-you-can crowd. Hunting is an antidote for that. To be alone with a bow, facing a shot that's just beyond range, offers a dilemma. What is the right thing to do? Hunting is a metaphor for life where the results are instant and irrevocable.

For many, where you hunt — the soaring Canadian Rockies, the arid sagebrush plains of the Southwest, or the deep spruce forests of Maine and the Maritimes — is often as important as what you hunt. Terrain, vegetation and climate govern, to a large degree, the movements of game. We've focused on that because those elements, along with what it's like to be in camp and the people with whom you hunt, are true measures of the quality of the experience.

The lodges and outfitters profiled in this book primarily offer fair-chase hunts. You'll find 250 of them whose business is to put you in a position where you are likely to have the opportunity to take the quarry you seek. We did not rate lodges. Tastes are personal. A lodge or outfitter that suits us may not suit you at all. Presented here, then, is a roster of locales where the hunting is better than good, guiding and outfitting services are normally above average and prices are within the range of the large percentage of hunters who travel or who dream of doing so.

John Ross, Upperville, Virginia
Jay H. Cassell, Katonah, New York

1

How To Pick a Lodge or Outfitter

L IKE TO HUNT? OF COURSE YOU DO or you wouldn't be reading this book. Well, finding the right lodge or outfitter is just like hunting. Only, unlike an actual hunt, you're not constrained by reality, at least not at the beginning. There will be plenty of time to face facts and figures later.

In the beginning, let yourself dream. Can you see yourself hunkered down in the aspens on the fringe of a high mountain meadow listening to 800 pounds of angry bull elk crashing your way to fight that interloper who bugled a challenge? How about sitting in a heated shooting box, waiting for a 10-point whitetail to step out into that bean field so you can make that 200-yard shot? Or easing a canoe along the fringe of a blackwater lake where you know a 60-inch plus moose just has to be feeding? Thanks to books, videos, magazines and the Internet, you can plan such adventures from home. Planning a hunt is fun, and thorough planning is the best insurance for a good hunt.

You hold the keys to the success of your hunt. Picking the right lodge or outfitter begins with asking yourself what you want from the hunt. Are you hoping to get an animal big enough to make the Boone & Crockett or Pope and Young record book? Do you want a bragging-size rack to mount in your den or trophy room? Do you want to challenge yourself physically and mentally, just you versus the wilderness? Or are you going into the woods to smooth it, in the words of Nessmuk, the original outdoorsman, who claims we get it rough enough in town? Whatever your motivations, have them clear in your own mind.

A successful hunt, whether or not a tag is filled, strips away the layers of angst we accumulate during our day-to-day lives. For some, a lung-searing, hand-over-hand scramble up a steep slide to that little saddle overlooking the bench where a full-curl bighorn ram is bedded is just the right medicine. For others it's sitting as still as a granite boulder as a black bear edges into the clearing not 25 yards away. Hunting is about rest and rejuvenation. Pick a tonic that will soothe you, and in choosing, to your own self be true.

Want to fly to the best hunting in Alaska? Then pack your gear into a DeHaviland turbo-Otter and head for the bush. In this case, getting there is half the fun.

Texas means good bucks, and this long-tined atypical that Ross took on Krooked River Ranch near Haskell is a fine example of the kind of whitetail that hunters can expect to find.

PACKS.

A teardrop-shaped daypack is a vital piece of every hunter's gear. It'll tote water bottle, sack lunch, emergency kit (space blanket, first aid kit, matches, dry socks, tin cup, instant soup, 20 feet of cord and maybe a tiny portable cookstove) and camera. An external frame pack will be needed in some locales to carry out meat, hide and antlers (most areas require that the antlers be packed out last, meat first). Sometimes packframes are provided by outfitters, other times they're not. It's wiser to ask rather than assume. And if you're on your own, you're on your own!

High hopes are important, but so is reality. The importance of planning a hunt with appropriate expectations cannot be overstated. Expectations, though, are a double-edged sword. Set unrealistically high, they lead to deep disappointment. Too low, they can bring equal disenchantment. No outfitter can guarantee you'll kill a trophy buck. The odds are against you (that's why they're trophies). While we report hunter success rates in some of the profiles, don't read too much into them. Like average college SATs, hunter success rates are of some, albeit limited, use in comparing outfitters. There are too many other factors involved.

On the other hand, you should expect that an outfitter's equipment will be clean and in good repair; that guides will be competent, registered (if required by the state) and highly motivated to put you on game; that pack and saddle stock will be healthy and well suited for the task at hand; that food will be ample and nourishing; and that the hunt will be conducted and billed in the manner promised. Is there a relationship between price and quality? Sure, but it's relative. A $6,000 hunt for Colorado elk isn't the same as a $1,000 Maine deer hunt. Each, however, may be equally enjoyable, and a good time is what you have every right to expect.

The best way to work through your expectations for a hunt is to list answers to the following questions. If you are planning to hunt with a friend, both of you need to do this together. No matter how well you know each other or how long you've hunted together you'll each have different ideas about some elements of the hunt. Working through this together will start you on your way to planning a good hunt.

❖ *What kind of hunter are you?*

Are you a hard-driving type who needs intense physical exercise, or are you more easy-going, intent on savoring the experience. Some deer hunters insist on still-hunting, while others figure they have a better chance at a buck by planting themselves in a tree stand all day. Do you dislike being cold, wet, hungry and bone-weary at the end of the day, or is that all part of the hunt? Does calling in the game fire your imagination, or is spotting and stalking more your style?

❖ *Which is more important: bagging a trophy or a challenging hunt?*

Each of us has his own reason for hunting. Now's a good time to think about yours. The ultimate outcome is, you hope, a great bull or buck with a huge rack and a hunt where you overcame all the difficulties. Such hunts happen. But are you willing to settle for a smaller buck or none at all?

❖ *Which species do you want?*

Antelope, bear, caribou, cougar, coyote, deer, elk, goat, moose, sheep and wolf are all big game. You'll find lots of combo hunts for elk and deer, deer and bear, moose and caribou. Most successful hunters key on one species and may take another if opportunity and licenses permit.

❖ *Where do you want to hunt?*

Lots of hunters return to a favorite locale year after year. Others seek new and different terrain. Does the notion of hunting in the barren tundra of Quebec strike your fancy? Have you seen the awe-inspiring Canadian Rockies? What about Arizona's rimrock country, the gentle lakes and deep woods of Maine, the dark cypress hammocks in Florida, or the rolling hills of the Ozarks? Hunting is a good excuse to explore new country and learn it with an intimacy you can only gain on foot.

❖ *What kind of accommodations will make you happy?*

Is your idea of a hunting camp one of those grand peeled-log lodges of the Adirondacks or a wall tent with a tarp for a floor? Do you prefer full-service accommodations with haute cuisine, vintage wines and daily maid service? Or is a tube tent pitched by a pond in an alpine pass more to your liking? Better animals are found deeper in the wilderness but, for a price, you can have creature comforts too.

❖ *What type of big-game hunting turns you on?*

Blackpowder, bow, handgun, rifle or shotgun? Most outfitters will guide hunters using any legal weapon. But some cater specifically to bowhunters, while others stick strictly to the centerfire rifle crowd. Handgun hunting is permitted in some states but not in Canada. There, however, crossbows may be legal.

❖ *What about the guide's ability to understand and meet your needs as a client?*

Nothing can make or break a hunt more than your relationship with your guide. Obviously you want a guide who knows the country and the game and who'll give 110 percent to get the job done. But you're going to spend a week with this guy or gal. Some guides are well-read, deeply experienced and steeped in the history and tradition of hunting their areas and willing to tell you about it. Others are sphinxes, as silent as a mountain, speaking only to give directions. Outfitters match hunters and guides. If you want a guide with particular qualities, tell your outfitter ahead of time.

❖ *What kind of shape are you in?*

Does climbing a flight of stairs make you huff and puff? What about the last time you actually ran anywhere because you had to? Are you relatively agile? How's your sense of balance? How much can you comfortably carry on your back? How is your eyesight? When was your last physical; and, if you're 40 or older, how about a stress test? While you probably won't need one if you're planning a deer hunt from a stand in the South, a thorough physical is an excellent idea if you're headed for a high-country wilderness hunt. And here's the kicker: Are you really willing to do whatever it takes to get in shape for a physically demanding hunt? If not, consider a different type of hunt.

❖ *How much time and money can you afford?*

A deer doesn't care how much you spend to hunt it, but you do. Big-game hunts are not cheap; airfare, new gear, odds and ends, tips and licenses can easily add an extra $1,500 to the price of the hunt. Hunts for sheep, brown bears and grizzlies can easily top $10,000; first-class hunting lodges charge $5,000 and up per week; outfitted wilderness hunts in the West run between $3,000 and $4,000; deer hunts in the South average about $2,000 per week; and you'll spend more than half that on deer or black bear in Maine or Canada's Maritimes. It's no fun to hunt with one eye on your wallet and another on the calendar. Allowing a few extra travel days for weather delays also makes good sense.

❖ *What will you do with the meat, hide and antlers?*

If you shoot a trophy, what will you do next? Do you want a full shoulder or partial mount? Antlers and skull only, European style? Where in your house or office will you hang the mount? And which taxidermist will you use? And then there's the meat. Most states require that all the meat from elk, deer and moose be packed out with the antlers, the last part of the animal to be removed from the kill site. If you don't want the meat, you can often donate it to a charity, such as Hunters for the Hungry, run by Safari Club International. How much room do you have in your freezer (or how long can you prevail on your neighbors)?

Now that you know what you want, you're ready for the next steps.

❖ ❖ ❖

GATHER INFORMATION

SELECTING AN OUTFITTER should begin a year before your actual hunt. Read the ads in hunting magazines, surf the Web, watch hunting shows on cable TV, talk with friends and colleagues who travel and hunt. With your partner(s), make a preliminary list of possible outfitters. Write, call or e-mail for brochures, a copy of licenses or permits, certificates of insurance, contracts, lists of references and a list of any outdoor sports shows they plan to attend.

Outdoor sports shows are often as crowded as a carnival's opening night. But they do give you the chance to meet and talk with a number of outfitters. Face-to-face conversations are so important, giving you the chance to take a personal measure. Is the outfitter someone with whom you feel comfortable? Is there instant rapport? Is there any a sense of uneasiness? What's the chemistry between you? When you meet at a sports show, if anything gives you pause about the outfitter — demeanor, presentation or whatever — he or she may not be the right one for you. Trust your intuition. After all, not only will you be paying this guy a lot of money, but you'll be living with him, his guides, staff and other clients for a week under conditions that are likely to be fairly primitive and strenuous.

❖ *About booking agents.*

There are two schools of thought about booking a hunt through an agent. On the plus side, agents know many more good outfitters than most of us do. Chances are they have hunted with the outfitters they represent and have inspected their operations. They know something about the clients that each outfitter serves. And they know about the hunting. In most cases, you'll pay the same price for a hunt whether you book through an agent or

do it yourself. (If you book through an agent, the outfitter pays the agent a fee of about 15 percent, but it costs you the same either way.)

On the down side, some agents have exclusive relationships with one or more outfitters. There's a quid pro quo in this. In exchange for being the sole representative of a lodge in, say, the U.S., the agent pledges to provide the lodge with so many guests per year. If an agent is the sole representative, you can bet that his priority is filling those camps with guests. Sure, he wants guests to be satisfied. That keeps him and the lodge in repeat business. But rest assured that he's going to try to sell you on that lodge.

Agents who represent many outfitters have a different perspective. Their bread and butter comes from establishing relationships with clients who may not want to go to the same place year after year. In the main, their job is to help you find the hunting vacation of your dreams and then book it through them. If things go awry on your trip, as they sometimes to do, and you booked it through an agent, you'll have more opportunity for redress than you will if you've booked it directly. Agents are generally current on international travel and airline regulations, and they will provide you with a wealth of practical information that can make your hunt go smoothly.

If you're working with an agent, should you talk directly with your prospective outfitter as well? Yes! And beware of the agent who tries to keep you from doing so. Remember, it's your trip of a lifetime and your $3,000, so you must satisfy yourself that this trip is going to meet your expectations. At the same time, if you're working with an agent who's recommended an outfitter, it's unethical to book the hunt without going through that agent.

The task of selecting an agent is much the same as picking a lodge. We've included a list of some of the best. Call them, ask them about their services, talk with them about their relationships with the lodges they represent, and obtain a list of references, including people who live in your area. Find out if they will be attending any of the outdoor shows in your area, and if so, arrange to meet them in person.

APPROVALS, ENDORSEMENTS & RATINGS

We Americans like to rate things. While no uniform rating system exists for hunting lodges and outfitters, you can get some hints in terms of quality by looking at ratings that do exist. Some tourism agencies in the Canadian provinces rate lodges in terms of service, accommodations and food. Stars are awarded. Call the tourism office in the province you're headed to and ask to see a list of the rankings. The North American Hunting Club (800/922-4868) approves outfitters and lodges based on member reports. Also based on subscriber reports, Don Causey's Hunting Report (305/670-1361) provides custom reports on lodges and regions, but it does not approve or endorse lodges. How valuable are the ratings? They provide useful information, but it should not be the determining factor in your choice of a lodge.

❖ *Making the final choice.*
So, after you've identified several outfitters that appear to meet your criteria, how do you make a final choice? Organize your information, one outfitter per file folder. With your hunting partner(s), spend an evening going over every-

thing. Get out your list of priorities and answers to the questions we discussed at the beginning of this chapter. Grade (A, B, C, etc.) each outfitter on the criteria you set. By the end of the evening, you'll have settled on a handful of possibilities. Check them out thoroughly. Call references, including those who took an animal and those who did not. Call the outfitter association in the state where the outfitter operates and ask if any complaints have been filed. Make similar calls to the state game agency and the regional forest service, if the outfitter operates on public land. They may or may not tell you, but you'll learn some things from their responses. Keep notes of your conversations. And when you're through checking, have your partner(s) over for dinner, open a bottle of good cabernet, kick around what you found out and toast your forthcoming hunt.

GREAT RESOURCES

Whether or not you are a trophy hunter, a number of organizations provide rich troves of information for big game hunters. Among them are:

BOONE & CROCKETT CLUB,
250 STATION DR., MISSOULA, MT 59801; 406/542-1888, FAX: 406/542-0784,
WEB: WWW.BOONE-CROCKETT.ORG
Outstanding descriptions of variations among species (Roosevelt elk vs. Rocky Mountain elk, for instance), habitats and hunting techniques and record books for each, including elk and mule deer; white-tailed deer; sheep, goats and pronghorns; and caribou and moose.

POPE AND YOUNG CLUB,
BOX 548, CHATFIELD, MN 55923; PHONE/FAX: 507/867-4144,
WEB: WWW.POPE-YOUNG.ORG
The club records scientific data on North American big game taken with bow and arrow. Books of special interest include Bowhunting Records of North American Whitetail Deer *and* Bowhunting Big Game Records of North America.

SAFARI CLUB INTERNATIONAL,
4800 W. GATES PASS RD., TUCSON, AZ 85745; 602/620-1220.
Formed as a nonprofit organization to promote good fellowship and communication among sportsmen-conservationists, SCI sponsors wildlife management research, Sportsmen Against Hunger programs and emergency game animal relief programs. The Club also records trophy animals taken by members worldwide.

BUCKMASTERS,
BOX 244022, MONTGOMERY, AL 36124-4022; 1 800/240-3337.
Buckmasters, a group dedicated to the pursuit of ethical hunting, the spirit of fair chase and to the conservation of wildlife for future generations, publishes Buckmasters magazine, which provides

AN OUTFITTER'S TIP

GETTING YOUR

TROPHY HOME.

If you anticipate having your trophy mounted, find a taxidermist in your area and whose work you admire and who has experience with the game you are hunting. Most outfitters will prepare antlers and package hides for shipment home (the cost, you'll bear, of course). Some will recommend taxidermists that they use for their own mounts (ask to see samples and prices before making a commitment). In many cases, you'll have better luck using a good taxidermist who lives in your area. If you shoot a trophy, you'll have to make decisions about what kind of mount you want before the animal is skinned. Before you go on a trophy hunt, have in mind the place where you'll hang the mount when you get home.

AN OUTFITTER'S TIP

SHIPPING MEAT HOME.

Having friends over for a dinner of broiled caribou steaks, wild cranberries and a good cabernet is one of the finest pleasures of the hunt. But it's a long way from Ungava to Atlanta. Getting the meat home safely is critical. One option is to have it butchered, wrapped, frozen, and then packed in waxed boxes for the return trip home. You'll have to pay about $75 extra per box for the additional luggage, and if you're on a small plane and it's over the weight limit, something is going to be taken out of the baggage compartment for later shipment. Jay has found that airlines will usually make sure that the meat is shipped home with you, opting instead to remove your duffels first. He's had this happen to him, and has never lost a duffel; they usually show up a few days later, courtesy of the airline.

If you don't want to run the risk of your luggage getting separated from you, you can also have the meat butchered, wrapped and shipped overnight in waxed boxes or plastic foam containers to your home. Your outfitter will, or should know, what's best, and you might check with the references he gave you to see how their meat (and hide and antlers) survived the trip. Once home, you can butcher the meat yourself (if you bone roasts and chops) or have a local butcher finish the job.

solid hunting information for serious whitetail hunters; and Buckmasters Whitetail Trophy Records, *a full-credit scoring system that does not deduct anything from the rack of a deer.*

ROCKY MOUNTAIN ELK FOUNDATION,
BOX 8249, MISSOULA, MT 59807-8249; 800/225-5355,
WEB: HTTP://WWW.RMEF.ORG
The Foundation's mission is to ensure the future of elk and other wildlife by conserving, restoring and enhancing natural habitats. Projects funded by the foundation include research, management, habitat improvement, conservation education and habitat acquisition. RMEF publishes an excellent magazine, Bugle, *and books of interest to elk hunters.*

FOUNDATION FOR NORTH AMERICAN WILD SHEEP,
720 ALLEN AVE., CODY, WY 82414-3402; 307/527-6261,
WEB: WWW.IIGI.COM/OS/NON/FNAWS/FNAWS.HTM
Dedicated to promoting and enhancing increasing populations of indigenous wild sheep on the North American continent, to safeguarding against the decline or extinction of such species, and to funding programs for professional management of those populations, the FNAWS is a nonprofit organization. Its quarterly publication, Wild Sheep, *is an outstanding magazine for sheep and goat hunters, with hunting and conservation news and more.*

AND A WORD ABOUT MAPS

Successful hunters know the terrain they're hunting. And nothing can give you a better look at the lay of the land than topographic maps. You can order United States Geological Survey (USGS) maps from a variety of sources or look at them in map repositories associated with the major universities in your state.

Two companies are now offering products that bring topographic maps of most of the country to your home computer. One of the handiest aids is Topo USA by DeLorme (Two DeLorme Dr., Box 298, Yarmouth, ME 04096; 207/846-7058, Web: www.delorme.com). On four CDs, this is a searchable atlas of the whole country. Type the name of a mountain, a stream, a tiny town in the back of nowhere, and, presto, there's your map, contour lines and all. And you can print it!

You can also purchase USGS maps on CD from Maptech (655 Portsmouth Ave., Greenland NH 03840; 888/433-8500 Web:www.maptech.com).

PREPARING FOR YOUR HUNT

In an ideal world, all of us would be totally prepared for our hunts. We'd all be in perfect physical condition, we'd all be excellent shots with bow or firearm and we'd all be knowledgeable woodsmen, able to help our guides and outfitters whenever needed. But that's not the case. We know it and, more important, so do the outfitters. Few are the hunters who, upon booking a hunt, begin a rigorous training program to improve their stamina, strength, flexibility and marksmanship.

Just how fit you need to be varies from hunt to hunt. A sheep hunter in British Columbia needs to be in better condition than one whose plan is to sit all day in a tree stand in the Mississippi Delta. Building cardiovascular capacity through jogging, hiking or vigorous walking with a 15-pound knapsack will definitely help. Try to set aside an hour every couple of days to work out. Muscular flexibility is also essential if you're going to climb through blowdowns and boulders to reach the place from which you'll shoot. It also doesn't hurt to work on your mental conditioning. Doing your exercises when you're pressed for time or are tired is a great start.

Being able to shoot your rifle or bow accurately is essential to hunting success. The number of hunters who go afield with rifles they've seldom shot or shot just once a year, right before the opening of the season, is amazing. No wonder they miss. The key to good marksmanship is simple: practice! First, of course, you must have a rifle that suits the game you're hunting: a .30-06 for whitetails, perhaps; a .270 for antelope; a .338 Win. Mag for elk or bear; and so on. Stock fit is important. Wearing the clothes you'll wear during your hunt, raise the rifle to your shoulder. Does the recoil pad catch on your jacket? Do you have to reach for the trigger? Is the scope crooked, or too close to your eye? If the gun doesn't fit you, take it to a gunsmith and have the stock altered. Your big game rifle should fit you as well as your shotgun. Mounting a scope can be done at home with a few basic tools. But if you don't have time, a gunsmith can do it for you. Get the rifle bore-sighted at the same time. Now, buy ammunition that's appropriate for the game you're after. A 150-grain bullet fired from a .30-06 might be fine for open-country whitetails, but you might want 165 or even 180 grains if you're hunting deep woods. Try several different brands to see which your rifle shoots best. Or better still, develop your own handloads.

Next, go to the range and practice. If you anticipate shooting at ranges of 50 to 100 yards, then practice at those distances. Shoot not only from a benchrest, but also from prone, kneeling, sitting and offhand positions; anything to simulate what you might encounter afield. If you plan to use a bipod or shooting sticks, practice with them as well. Keep at it until you start placing bullets in consistent groups: From a supported position

AN OUTFITTER'S TIP
SLEEPING BAGS

Down, long the staple for backpackers because of light weight, retains moisture like cotton. If you want to carry a down bag because of its easy packability and light weight, look for a bag with high loft, but which compresses into the smallest package. Otherwise, consider a slightly bulkier bag filled with Dacron, Hollofill or another synthetic. If you will be hunting in a region where it gets below freezing, you'll be thankful for the extra warmth.

Most outfitters provide a foam mattress, but few offer pillows. If you sleep with one at home, add a pillowcase to your gear. You can stuff it with clothing or towels to make a pillow.

such as prone or with a bipod, strive for one- to two-inch groups at 50 or even 100 yards if you're shooting a light caliber, such as a .243. With something heavier, such as a .300 Weatherby Mag, three-inch groups at 100 yards are fine. (If you think you may be taking shots longer than 100 yards, consult ballistic charts for details on precisely how high your point of impact above the bull's-eye should be at 100 yards, or better yet, hie yourself to a 200- or 300-yard range.)

If you've bought a new rifle, break in the barrel properly. After each shot, run a cleaning patch through the bore for maybe the first 10 shots. Then you can back off a bit on the cleaning. When testing ammo in your rifle, fire the first shot, clean and dry the bore with solvent and patches, let the barrel cool for two or three minutes, then fire the second, clean it again, and so on. Five three-shot groups are enough to verify the performance of the ammo in your rifle. After each three-shot group, let the barrel cool for 20 minutes or so. Once you've settled on ammo that works, buy (or hand-load) 100 rounds. Then, once or twice a month, head for the range and practice shooting. You'll be surprised at how accurate and confident you'll become.

Bowhunters, of course, should also practice, although the routine is somewhat different. Always practice with the bow you're planning to take on your hunt, not a different one. Use the same weight arrows, too. If you're planning to hunt deer in Illinois with, say, Easton XX75 camo arrows, size 2213, then practice with those arrows at home. If you anticipate shots at 30 yards, practice at that yardage (although anything beyond 40 is pretty unrealistic for most people). Your draw weight should be comfortable, and probably not much less that 58 pounds for most hunting situations. If you're hunting grizzlies or other game that might bite back, then go with heavier draw weights.

❖ *A couple of keys to practicing with a bow:*

◆ ◆ ◆

DON'T OVERDO IT. When Jay practices, he goes into his yard and shoots six arrows. Then he stops for the day. The next day he shoots six more, then stops. And so on. His theory is that the more you shoot, the more tired your arms get; and the more tired your arms, the less accurate you will be. Which, in turn, will destroy your confidence. Stick to four or six a day; you'll gradually build up your arm muscles and confidence. And remember, it's the first shot that counts, not the 25th.

◆ ◆ ◆

TRY TO SHOOT FROM DIFFERENT ANGLES. If you're going to be still-hunting, practice shooting uphill, downhill, on level ground and so on. If you're only going to be hunting from a tree stand, practice shooting out of a tree stand in your yard, if possible. If that's not possible, shoot at a target from your garage roof, or from atop your stone barbecue pit (Jay does this), deck or whatever works. Also, wear clothing that is similar to what you'll be wearing on your hunt. If you're going to be hunting trophy white-tails in Saskatchewan while wearing thick clothing, heavy gloves and a face mask, it will do you no good to practice while wearing a t-shirt and pair of shorts.

◆ ◆ ◆

PRACTICE WITH YOUR BROADHEADS AT A TARGET MADE SPECIFICALLY FOR BROADHEADS. You don't have to do this all the time, as broadheads are pretty expensive to use up in practice sessions. But broadheads are aerodynamically different from field tips; they fly different-ly, and are affected by breezes and winds. Especially when the date of your big hunt begins to approach, put aside the field points for your broadheads (make sure your broadheads weigh the same as your field points, 125 grains, for example, and that that weight is what you really want for your hunt). Only practice in a safe area, of course. When you first start shooting with broadheads, you'll see that your groupings may be all different and that you're not hitting where you aim. Keep practicing. It'll come.

◆ ◆ ◆

Travel Tips

T WO HUNTERS RETRIEVED their baggage at the airport in Sheridan, Wyoming. The first, we'll call him Pete, wrestled a wheeled suitcase, a bulging frame pack with sleeping bag attached and a heavy metal rifle case out of the luggage area. He carried an over-stuffed carry-on across his shoulder. The other hunter reached for a hard rifle case and a large but obviously not-quite-full duffel bag; that was it. Where was the frame pack? In the duffel bag. Same with his sleeping bag. Outfitters dread the Petes of this world — all that stuff and so little space in a packhorse's pannier. When it comes to gear for the traveling hunter, going light and right is the only way.

The essentials. When packing for a hunt, ask yourself: What are the most important items I must, and I mean MUST, not be without?

THE BASICS

IF YOU'VE TAKEN CARE of the essentials, you'll survive your trip and most likely won't go broke. But what about luggage, clothing and traveling hunting gear?

MEDICATIONS & PRESCRIPTION GLASSES

Lay in an emergency supply of medications. Carry one supply with you, pack the other in your luggage. Be sure to have current copies of prescriptions. In addition to prescription sunglasses, you should take a spare pair of glasses and extra sets of contact lenses, if you use them.

MONEY

Traveler's checks, ATM cards and credit cards have pretty well reduced the need for cash on the road. But not with outfitters. For any outstanding balance due for the hunt, carry a money order or a certified check. While guides prefer cash for tips, give them a check. That way you have a record of your expenditure. If you're hunting in Canada or Mexico, carry the equivalent of $100 (U.S.) in local currency, and another $300 in traveler's checks. Take only two or three credit cards (American Express, MasterCard or Visa). In addition, stash $200 in emergency cash and traveler's checks and a list of all your credit cards (card numbers and phone numbers if you have to cancel them) in a place separate from where you carry your main funds. That way you won't be out of luck if your wallet is lost or stolen.

IDENTIFICATION

Even though it's not required, if you're traveling to Canada or Mexico, get a passport. If you don't have one, apply when you pay the deposit for the hunt. If you neglect to get a passport, a photo ID, such as a driver's license and your birth certificate will suffice. Also, make a list of any medical conditions and allergies and keep it with your identification. A copy of your identification should be cached with your emergency money.

AIRLINE TICKETS

Outfitters with sophisticated operations will offer to assist in booking your flight, but you may do better to have the outfitter tell you where and when to arrive, and then book the flights yourself. Sometimes a travel agent can get you a good deal, but again, you can sometimes do better yourself. It depends, mainly, on whether you're willing to spend the time to do it. Advance-purchase tickets can save you a bundle, but not if the no-refund, no-alteration policy is so strict as to limit flexibility in the case of missed connections due to weather, primarily on the return leg of your trip. Beware of connections that are too tight — less than an hour — particularly at international airports. Though baggage may be checked through, you'll have to take it through customs yourself. When entering or leaving Canada or Mexico, two hours between planes isn't too much. Booking agents have shepherded thousands of clients through the intricacies of international travel. If you're new to the traveling hunter game, they can be a big help.

Tickets do get lost or stolen. Make two copies of your ticket before leaving home. Keep one with your packet of emergency cash, the other folded in your wallet. If your ticket vanishes mysteriously, the copy will help you cancel the ticket and may help secure a replacement. And don't carry your ticket sticking out of a travel bag. Sure, it's convenient, but it's also easily swiped.

INSURANCE

Outfitters book far in advance and require payment of up to 50 percent to hold a reservation. In some cases the balance is due in advance, others want it on arrival. In any event, you will have contracted for services; should you not be able to make the trip, you'll be liable for the full cost. If you cancel more than 90 days in advance, there's a fairly good chance that the lodge or outfitter will be able to fill the space. (Each has its own refund policy. Check them out thoroughly.) Travel insurance is available, too. Should illness, accident or a death in the family prohibit you from making the trip, travel insurance will pay up to the full amount of your obligations. Available coverage varies extensively among insurance companies, as do premiums. However, you can expect to pay about 5 percent of the total coverage, or roughly $350 for a policy worth $6,500.

While we're on the subject of insurance, if you're traveling to another country, you'll want to check with your medical insurance carrier to determine coverages. If you're stricken with an acute medical problem while in the bush, will your insurance pay for air evacuation to the closest hospital? It's also a good idea to determine the applicability of automobile insurance and loss/theft provisions of homeowner's or business insurance in Canada or Mexico.

BAGGAGE

Add it up: hunting boots, heavy and light hunting clothes, raingear, sweaters, hats, gloves, socks, long underwear, sleeping bags, binoculars, flashlight, camera, rifle, etc., etc., etc. None of it's light and most is bulky. Take only what you need. Most outfitters provide lists. Follow them religiously. Space on horse-back is minimal, and your partner in a spike camp will probably forgive you if you don't dress for dinner. Unfortunately, hunters are obvious prey for baggage thieves. For bags that you check, use tough, nondescript, soft-sided luggage. Put your name, address and phone on a luggage tag outside and inside each bag.

Checked baggage does get lost. In your carry-on, pack things you absolute-ly cannot do without: medications, extra glasses, Gore-Tex hat (wear the parka and one of your two pairs of boots), mini-shaving kit, camera, gloves, flashlight, a Ziploc bag with two pairs of heavy socks and lightweight Polypro long under-wear, a woolen or fleece shirt and sweater, and wool hunting pants plus your brand-new Swarovski 10x50 binoculars. All this, stuffed into a large waterproof kit bag, such as the one from Orvis, weighs about 20 pounds and slings comfort-ably over your shoulder. It fits in most overhead bins and can be shoved under most seats. Leave cotton clothing at home.

Also consider wearing a fannypack for extra supplies. It's unobtrusive and secure, and you'll soon forget you're wearing it, but you'll be glad you've got it.

THE TRAVELING RIFLE

When traveling with your favorite .270 or .338, there are a couple of tenets to live by. First, your firearm must be in an airline-approved, locking, hard gun case. It cannot be loaded, the bolt should be removed and stored in the case, and you cannot store the ammunition in the same case.

When traveling with his Ultralight Arms .30-06, for example, Jay does all of the above. He also tapes a business card inside his Doskocil gun case, and he carries a roll of duct tape to the airport. Why? Most major airports will not let you check your guns curbside anymore. Rather, you will have to get in line with the other ticketed passengers (leave yourself enough time!) and declare the gun to the agent at the desk. The agent will probably ask you to step into a back room, open the case, and demonstrate that the firearm is not loaded. He or she will then slip your signed declaration form into the case and ask you to lock up the case so it may be placed on the conveyor belt along with the rest of your lug-gage. The tape is for the locks. Over the years, Jay has had a few bashed open by handlers. The tape protects the locks, and a few wraps around the whole case keeps everything closed even if a lock comes undone.

Time was that takedown rifles were a no-no. When reassembled, they seldom shot where they did before you took them apart. But with the advent of pillar bed-ding and synthetic stocks, the game has changed for the better. John's traveling rifle is a Winchester Model 70 in .30-06 with a factory synthetic stock. As long as he tightens the trigger guard screws to the same torque, the rifle shoots to the same point of impact, no matter how often the barreled action is removed from the stock.

For about $100, a gunsmith cut the 24-inch barrel to 21 inches and lopped two inches off the forearm so that each piece is less than 30 inches in length. These fit in a locked and padded hard case designed for a takedown shotgun, and the whole works slips inside a duffel bag, out of sight from airport thieves. (Orvis and Cabela's currently market special concealment duffel bags for this very purpose.)

Winchester offers its own version of a takedown rifle, as does H-S Precision. Both employ similar technology. The barrel with forearm attached screws into the receiver, which is bolted to the buttstock. SIG Arms imports two takedown rifles. The first, the Blaser, utilizes a pillar-bedded barrel into which the bolt locks when the action is closed. The second, the SIG SHR 970, is also a swap-barrel rig, but the barrel slides into the action and is clamped in place with a pair of set-screws. Accuracy with these rifles is quite good, about an inch at 100 yards. Takedown systems are bound to wear over time, and thus accuracy after 3,000 rounds or so may deteriorate. But it won't change much between your final practice session on your home range and when you sight in with the outfitter (an absolute must, whether you're carrying a takedown rifle or not) before the hunt. Tuck a collapsible cleaning rod, a vial of solvent, brush, jag, a dozen patches and appropriate screwdrivers and wrenches in a little kit and carry it with you.

Depending on where you are going to be, you may also want to stash a soft rifle case in your duffel. It all depends on whether weight is a consideration in your hunt.

NOTE: If you are traveling to Canada or Mexico, register your rifle with U.S. Customs before leaving the country. You may do this on the day you travel, but you may find it more convenient to visit a customs office a week or two before your hunt. If you have them, bring bills of sale for each firearm you plan to use. The process takes very little time, but it's essential.

THE TRAVELING BOW

Taking a cased bow through an airport can be pretty amusing. Jay has had more than a few people ask what type of instrument he was carrying. An oboe? Some type of keyboard? A mandolin?

No matter what other travelers may think is in your case, it's your bow, your only bow on the trip, and it had better be stored safely, in a hard, airline-approved case. Jay stores his Golden Eagle compound bow in the case, along with his arrows (broadheads are removed and stored elsewhere). To further protect the bow, he lines the inside of the case with socks, Polarfleece long underwear and other soft articles of clothing. He also puts a business card inside the case, and tapes the outside of the case (including the locks) with duct tape. (You can do this before you go to the airport, as no agent has ever asked him if the bow was loaded, at least not yet!)

As with a gun, carry the appropriate tools you may need to make field repairs. Take an extra bowstring and know how to install it, and carry an extra release. (Ever wonder what would happen if your release broke when you're somewhere off in the tundra, hundreds of miles from the nearest bow shop?)

• • •

Vital Statistics

ALONG WITH EACH PROFILE of a lodge or an outfitter, there's a list of handy data. Accurate as this book may be, some things may have changed since this writing. Check the lodge, outfitter and state or province department of game for the latest information.

We've compressed a great deal of information into the Vital Statistics column. A few notes may help you decipher our shorthand.

• • •

❖ GAME/ARM/SEASONS: SEASONS vary by species, game management area and type of arm. And each state and province defines legal hunting arms somewhat differently. For example, in-line muzzleloaders may be legal during the blackpowder season in one state but not in another. Same applies to crossbows in archery seasons. For convenience, we've lumped rifle, handgun and shotgun under centerfire.

• • •

❖ RATES: Booking a fishing trip is fairly straightforward. But hunting is a different story. Often the price tag varies for each species, and even that changes. Some outfitters charge more for trips when deer, for instance, are in the peak of the rut. Others who are com-

Some lodges, such as Echo Canyon Guest Ranch near La Veta, Colorado, offer first-class accommodations with lodges of log and glass, fine cuisine, and bedrooms with private baths. Elk, deer and lion hunters who stay here have topnotch hunting, but don't have to rough it.

mitted to managing a herd for trophy deer will charge a higher fee if you shoot one that is below the minimum. Other outfitters add a premium charge if you kill a buck or bull with a huge rack. In the case of some goat and sheep hunts, if you shoot a ram, you'll pay a fee in addition to the price of the hunt. Most hunts are based on two hunters per guide. If you want your own guide, you'll have to buy his or her time (Yes, there are women guides out there, and some very good ones at that!). The prices we've given in the book are for the 1998-99 season, and they provide a basis of comparison. Most Canadian outfitters are now quoting rates in U.S. dollars.   CND denotes prices in Canadian dollars.

❖ ❖ ❖

❖ CONFERENCE GROUPS: A few lodges and outfitters combine business with pleasure and offer facilities conducive for corporate team-building or performance incentives. But don't expect much in the way of phone and fax connections, or, heaven forbid, data. And remember, in places where the hunting is best, cell phones don't work.

❖ ❖ ❖

❖ GUIDES: Keep in mind that the great guy you talk to at the sports show and later by phone probably will not be your guide. Guides are seasonal employees. Tips for good service are always appropriate and expected.

❖ ❖ ❖

❖ Preferred Payment: Many outfitters run cash operations. Generally, personal checks are fine for deposits but, aside from those few outfitters who take credit cards, they'll want cash on the barrel when you show up for the hunt. Certified and traveler's checks give you a measure of protection.

❖ ❖ ❖

❖ Other Activities: In a few instances, fishing overlaps big game seasons. Bring along a pack rod and some lures or flies. They don't weigh much. If you nail your buck, bull or boar early in your hunt, you can always fish.

❖ ❖ ❖

❖ Contact: If this were a perfect world, addresses, phone and fax numbers, and Web and e-mail addresses wouldn't change. But they do. If you're having trouble reaching an outfitter or lodge in this book, call information as a last resort.

❖ ❖ ❖

Jay Cassell took this trophy 4 x 4 mulie with his .270, high on a grassy plain hunted by BearTrack Outfitters of Buffalo, Wyoming. Cassell also took a 14 1/2-inch pronghorn on the same trip.

CANADA EAST

MANITOBA, NEW BRUNSWICK, NEWFOUNDLAND/LABRADOR, NOVA SCOTIA, ONTARIO, PRINCE EDWARD ISLAND, QUEBEC

WITH THE exception of a thin rim of cities along the southeastern coast, up the St. Lawrence River and on the vast plains of southern Manitoba, eastern Canada is a land of deep forests and innumerable lakes. Bear and moose roam the woods of the southern interior. On the island of Newfoundland you'll find huge herds of woodland caribou. Looking for trophy whitetails in an unpressured, natural environment? Check out Quebec's Anticosti Island at the mouth of the St. Lawrence. And while you may find fewer deer in the forests and abandoned farmlands of New Brunswick, bucks grow large here and carry heavy racks. Big antlers are also the main draw where Manitoba's grainfields begin to give way to timber. To the north, the climate becomes increasingly too harsh for deer and then for moose and bear. Forests and soils thin, evolving into tundra and the land of the great migrating herds of Quebec-Labrador caribou. In the main, the lands of eastern Canada are not ruggedly demanding, success rates on caribou are very high and wilderness hunts are generally less expensive than those of the provinces to the west.

Lodges:

MANITOBA
1 DUCK MOUNTAIN OUTFITTERS

NEW BRUNSWICK
2 GUIMAC LODGE AND CAMPS
3 MIRAMICHI INN
4 NORTH VIEW HUNTING & FISHING FISHING LODGE
5 NORTHERN OUTDOOR LODGE

NEWFOUNDLAND
6 BIG RIVER CAMPS
7 MT. PEYTON OUTFITTERS
8 NORTHERN LABRADOR OUTDOORS LTD.
9 OWL'S NEST LODGE
10 RAY'S HUNTING & FISHING LODGE
11 STEEL MOUNTAIN LODGE
12 TUCKAMORE LODGE & OUTFITTERS
13 VICTORIA LODGE
14 STEWIACKE VALLEY OUTFITTERS

ONTARIO
15 CRAWFORD'S CAMP
16 HUBER'S LONE PINE LODGE LTD.
17 MATTICE LAKE OUTFITTERS

QUEBEC
18 AIR MELANÇON
19 ARCTIC ADVENTURES
20 CLUB EXPLO-SYLVA
21 JACK HUME ADVENTURES INC.
22 NORPAQ HUNTING & FISHING ADVENTURES

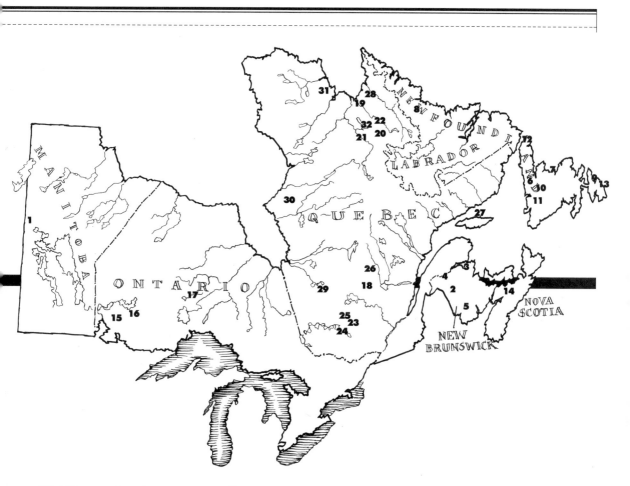

References:

Northern Ontario
Outdoor Guide
by Shawn Perich
and Gord Ellis
Outdoor News Publications
3410 Winnetka Ave. North
New Hope, MN 55427; 612/546-4251

Resources:

Department of
Natural Resources
Box 22, 200 Saulteaux Crescent
Winnipeg, Manitoba R3J 3W3, Canada
204/945-6784
or 800/214-6497
or
Tourism Manitoba
21 Forks Market Rd., Winnipeg MB
R3C 4T7 Canada at 204/945-3777 or
800/665-0040
Web: www.gov.mb.ca/natres

Department of
Natural Resources & Energy
Fish & Wildlife
Box 6000, Fredericton, NB, E3B 5H1
Canada; 506/453-2440
Web: www.gov.nb.ca

Department of
Natural Resources
Box 698, Halifax, NS, B3J 2T9
Canada; 902/424-6609
Web: www.gov.ns.ca/natr

Ministry of Natural Resources
Information Center, 900 Bay St.
Toronto, ON M7A 2C1, Canada
416/314-2000; 800/667-1940
Web: www.mnr.gov.on.ca

Fish & Wildlife Division,
Department of Technology
and Environment
Box 2000, Charlottetown, PE, C1A
7N8, Canada; 902/368-4683
Web: www.gov.pe.ca

Ministere de l'Environment,
Department of
Recreation, Fish and Game
Box 88, 675 Boule. Rene-Levesque Est
Quebec, QC G1R 4Y1, Canada
800/561-1616
Web: www.mef.gouv.qc.ca
or
Tourisme Quebec
1010 Sainte-Catherine Ouest, Rm 400
Montreal QC H3B 1G2, Canada
800/363-7777
Web: www.tourisme.gouv.qc.ca

[C A N A D A   E A S T]

Duck Mountain Outfitters

M i n i t o n a s ,   M a n i t o b a

Hunt the hinterland between forest and the barren ground.

VITAL STATISTICS:

Game/Arm/Seasons:
BLACK BEAR:
Bow, centerfire, muzzleloader:
Late Apr. through mid-June and late Aug. through late Sept.
DEER:
Bow: Late Aug. through early Nov.
Centerfire, muzzleloader: Early through late Nov.
Rates:
BEAR $1,900/6 days
DEER $2,500/6 days
Accommodations:
MODERN HOME
NUMBER OF ROOMS: 5, SHARED BATH
MAXIMUM NUMBER OF HUNTERS: 8
Meals:
Home cooking
Conference Groups: Yes
Guides: Included
Gratuity: Hunter's discretion
Preferred Payment:
Cash, check
Other Activities:
Biking, bird hunting, boating, fishing, swimming, wildlife photography
Getting There:
Fly to Swan River and you'll be picked up.

Contact:
Les Nelson
Duck Mountain Outfitters
Box 99
Minitonas Manitoba
R0L 1G0, Canada
204/525-4405

SOME DEER CAMPS are hard-charging affairs run with pseudo-military precision; others are more laid back, more in keeping with the words of Nessmuk, that quintessential outdoor writer of the turn of the last century who believed that you go into the woods to "smooth it" because you get it "rough enough in town." Such is the case with Duck Mountain Outfitters, which has exclusive rights to hunt some 2,000 square miles north of Duck Mountain Provincial Park.

A land of gently rolling terrain carpeted by mixed coniferous and hardwood forests with grassy meadows and patches of wetland bog along watercourses draining numerous lakes, the region provides some of the best bear and deer habitat in the province. For almost 20 years Les Nelson, head of Duck Mountain Outfitters, has been guiding hunters in this area. Bear hunting is his first love. He's divided his hunting region into four 500-square-mile sections. In each area, Les maintains 30 to 40 active baits, some of which are used by as many as 20 bears. No more than four hunters are permitted in each area, and often there are only two. Only 20 permits per year are offered for each area, thus hunting pressure is relatively light. An average bear will run close to 300 pounds here, and 30 percent of those taken are color-phase bears. Both spring and fall bear hunts are scheduled.

When it comes to whitetails, Les ferries his hunters to heated stands that are 20 to 30 miles back in the bush where boreal forest begins to give way to barren ground. Stands overlook meadows or game trails. Racks on these whitetails can be massive, scoring upwards of 150. Atypicals are not uncommon here. Normally, two hunters share a guide, but one-on-one hunts can be arranged.

Home base for Duck Mountain is literally "home," a modern 5,000 square-foot residence where Les and his family live. Sturdy meals of meat, chicken and stews prepared by Les' wife are accompanied by fresh breads, pastries and rolls. You won't lose any weight on this trip.

Guimac Lodge and Camps

Hartland, New Brunswick

Trophy bucks roam across the border from Maine.

VITAL STATISTICS:

Game/Arm/Seasons:
BLACK BEAR:
Bow: Early through mid-Sept.
Centerfire, muzzleloader: Oct.
DEER:
Bow: Early through mid-Oct.
Centerfire, muzzleloader:
Late Oct. through late Nov.
Rates:
BEAR, $825/5 days
DEER $875/5 days
Combo $925/5 days
Accommodations:
FRAME CABINS WITH OUTPOST TENTS
MAXIMUM NUMBER OF HUNTERS: 16
Meals: Family-style
Conference Groups: Yes
Guides: Included
Gratuity: 10%
Preferred Payment:
Cash, Visa, check
Other Activities:
Biking, bird hunting, bird watching,
boating, canoeing/rafting, fishing,
golf, wildlife photography
Getting There:
Fly to Bangor, Maine, and rent a car
or the lodge van will collect you for
$90 round-trip.

Contact:
Ralph Orser
Guimac Lodge and Camps
RR #4
Hartland, New Brunswick
E0J 1N0, Canada
506/375-4711
Fax: 506/375-8599
e-mail: triton@nbnet.nb.ca
Web: www.orser.hartland.nb.ca/guimac

EAST OF THE ST. JOHN RIVER town of Hartland rises a low band of hills. Soil here is too thin to farm anything but trees. Dense forests of fir and spruce roll across the countryside, broken here and there by abandoned farms. It's the kind of cover that harbors healthy populations of deer and bear, woodcock and grouse. In the woods rise the headwaters of the north and south branches of the Becaguimac, a river with a bit of a reputation for brook trout in the upper mileage and smallmouths lower down. On the banks of the river, about 14 miles out of town, is the lodge and its 12 frame cabins run by the Orser family since 1933.

Whitetails are the draw in these camps come fall, but the hunting is anything but easy or predictable. Guides continually scout the region in the upper drainages for sign. With 4WDs or ATVs, hunters are driven to the most promising areas. Starting with a stand overlooking an old kitchen orchard, a hunter may sit and watch until the sun clears the treetops. Still-hunting then occupies the day, with a break for lunch at the lodge or a sack lunch (pack your own) as preferred. Evening finds hunters on stands, watching travel routes from bed to feeding areas. Normally one guide directs the efforts of three hunters, though for an extra $150 per week a private guide can be employed. Bucks that come out of this country are large, with heavy bodies and racks of 8-points-plus. But they are wary and not everyone brings home a trophy.

Bear, too, are a staple of Guimac Lodge and Camps. With baits in both spring and fall seasons, archers and rifle hunters use either ground or tree stands (bring your own), depending on terrain. Quiet patience is the key to success here. Smoking, nibbling on candy or sucking soda pop alerts bears to a hunter's presence. Even though conditioned to feeding at a bait, a bear sensing such foolishness on the part of a hunter will wait until the hunter leaves the stand before coming to the bait. Average bears run in the 200-pound class.

When hunting this area in the fall, it's a good idea to pack along a rod and a box of lures, and maybe a 20 gauge for grouse and woodcock. Not that they're needed to fill the larder, because ample stews, roasts and fresh baked breads and pies take care of that. It's just that fishing for fall brookies is one of the outdoors' finer delights, and the bird hunting's so good it's hard not to give them a whirl.

Miramichi Inn

R e d   B a n k ,   N e w   B r u n s w i c k

For bear, salmon and a bevy of redheads you'll love the rest of your life.

VITAL STATISTICS:

Game/Arm/Seasons:
BLACK BEAR:
Bow, centerfire, muzzleloader: Mid-May through mid-June

Rates:
BEAR $1,500/5 days

Accommodations:
LOG LODGE
NUMBER OF ROOMS: 8; 6 WITH PRIVATE BATH
MAXIMUM NUMBER OF HUNTERS:6

Meals:
Outstanding regional fare with a flair

Conference Groups: Yes

Guides: Included

Gratuity: Hunter's discretion

Preferred Payment:
Cash, check

Other Activities:
Bird hunting, fishing

Getting There:
Fly to Fredericton and rent a car.

Contact:
André Godin
Miramichi Inn
1100 Halcomb Rd.
Box 331
Red Bank, New Brunswick
E9E 2P3, Canada
506/836-7452
Fax: 506/836-7805

SK XAVIER LE BRETON. He knows about the bears here, this man. Guide for a handful of years, hunter for a lifetime, Xavier owned a large sporting-goods store until the call of the woods overcame him. Now you'll find him, come early April, scouting and setting up baits for André Godin's Miramichi Inn. "You have to have two, maybe three times as many baits as you have hunters, that's the way," says André. André's the boss, but he gives Xavier a long, long leash. Why not? Success rates are high on mature black bears. "We don't shoot the little ones," André grins, "and sometimes, eh, (a shrug and a twinkle of the eye) we don't shoot the big ones. But some bear come back to the baits every year." Most of the bears taken are between 5 and 7 year's old, weighing between 150 and 200 pounds.

Meat from this size bear is ideal for cooking a la André. Brown a roast in a Dutch oven on top of the stove and season it as you like (a little fresh garlic and black pepper is good). Add two cups of brewed black tea, a dash of Worcestershire sauce and enough water for the vegetables (onions, carrots and potatoes) you'll add later. Bake in the oven for three to five hours depending on the size of the roast. Add raw vegetables in the last hour. Serve with early green peas, Parker House rolls and French red wine.

André and Xavier hunt about 800 square miles west of Red Bank where the Little Southwest Miramichi becomes tidal. Spring bear hunting is a gentlemanly affair. You may fish a bit in the morning, and then reach your stand by mid to late afternoon. Then it's a matter of sitting and watching. The trick is not to shoot the first bear you see. While the season opens in late April and runs into the last week in June, the best hunting is from mid-May into mid-June.

The Miramichi Inn is one of the few hunting and fishing lodges in New Brunswick to earn a four-star rating from Canada Select. The lodge is of honey-toned log situated on the bench overlooking the river. Several rooms have private baths, and the layout of the place ensures just the right balance between privacy and the family touch that André and wife Susan provide. Three times a day the focal point is the paneled dining room with the fireplace in the corner. The talk will be of bear and salmon, but also of grouse and woodcock and André's kennel of steady Irish Setters you'll gun over if you're ever lucky enough to be there come autumn.

North View Hunting & Fishing Lodge

P l a s t e r   R o c k ,   N e w   B r u n s w i c k

Close to the Maine border, Canada runs out of roads and into scads of bear.

WHERE THE ST. JOHN RIVER defines the border between New Brunswick and Maine, the names of the towns are French — Ste.-Anne-de-Madawaska, Bellefleur, Grand-Sault. But there, the border plunges straight south, the river wanders a bit to the east and the names of the towns become English. Roughly 20 miles southeast of Grand-Sault is the village of Plaster Rock, headquarters for hunting whitetails and bears in northwestern New Brunswick. Habitat is ideal. Working farms provide green pasture grasses and crops; stands of spruce and fir along stream drainages offer seclusion; and hardwood ridges of beech yield a bit of a mast crop. East of Plaster Rock, few public roads invade the forest where logging operations produce plots of woods in various stages of regeneration. Terrain, while thick with vegetation and occasionally swampy and boggy, is not excessively high or difficult. It's easy to negotiate for hunters who are in reasonable shape.

From tree stands or ground blinds, hunters watch bears coming into active baits in the spring. Stands are at varying distances from the baits, providing opportunities for bow as well as rifle hunters. North View has exclusive rights to private acreage, so there's virtually no competition. An average spring bear runs about 250 pounds. By the time the fall bear hunt rolls around two months after the close of the spring season, bears have gained about 20 percent more weight. Fall bear season overlaps rifle season for deer.

If you're looking for a sure thing, bet your money on a spring bear hunt. More than eight out of 10 are successful. Success rate drops considerably for whitetails, running in the vicinity of 25 to 40 percent. You'll hike into the woods before dawn to reach a spot where you can sit and watch crossings or rubs. Later in the day you'll still-hunt the ridges, and when evening comes, you may work the edge of a field. Deer are reasonably big, dressing out at 200 pounds-plus with 6- and 8-pointers dominating. The normal pattern calls for one guide to serve three hunters, but for an additional $60 per day, you can have a guide to yourself. For deer hunting, this may be well worth it. Hunters stay in the modern log lodge or in a log cabin nearby. All rooms have private baths, and the food is much more than ample.

VITAL STATISTICS:

Game/Arm/Seasons:
BEAR (SPRING):
Bow, centerfire, muzzleloader:
May through June
BEAR (FALL):
Bow: mid-Sept.
Centerfire, muzzleloader:
Mid through late Oct
WHITE-TAILED DEER:
Bow: Early through late Oct.
Centerfire, muzzleloader: Late Oct.
through late Nov.

Rates:
From $1,200/5 days

Accommodations:
LOG CABINS
NUMBER OF ROOMS: 5 with private bath
MAXIMUM NUMBER OF HUNTERS: 15

Meals:
Roast beef, pork chops, chicken

Conference Groups: No

Guides: Included

Gratuity: $50 to $100

Preferred Payment:
Cash, check, credit cards

Other Activities:
Antiquing, biking, bird hunting, bird watching, boating, canoeing/rafting, fishing, golf, skiing, swimming, waterfowling, wildlife photography

Getting There:
Drive or fly to Presque Isle, Maine, and rent a car.

Contact:
Wayne DeLeavey
North View Hunting &
Fishing Lodge
Box 593
Plaster Rock, New Brunswick
E0J 1W0, Canada
506/356-7212

[C A N A D A   E A S T]

Northern Outdoor Lodge

S t .   G e o r g e ,   N e w   B r u n s w i c k

*On the fringe of the Bay of Fundy,
hunt moose, deer and bear.*

ITH ITS TIDES that rise to 70 feet, the highest in the world, the Bay of Fundy is thought of most often as a summer vacation haven. In saltwater, there's flounder, cod, mackerel and bluefish. Smallmouths inhabit the streams that drain the interior, which rises abruptly and sometimes spectacularly from the cold green-blue bay. Undulating hills capped with spruce, fir, hemlock, maple and birch roll northwesterly toward Mt. Pleasant, the highest point in Charlotte County. Thin soils support rich patches of blueberries and cranberries. Along river valley's, dairy farmers eke out their living as they have done for centuries. Here you'll find ample herds of whitetails, black bear and a few moose.

A relative newcomer to the hunting lodge scene, Bruce Hanley chose his territory well. Located on the Fundy shore, the simple log-faced lodge and the forests and farms that surround it benefit from a moderate climate. Despite occasionally heavy, wet snows, deer and moose can find ample food throughout winter. The result: good racks. A typical deer here will be an 8-pointer with thick bases and nice symmetry that will score in the 130s. Moose carry spreads of 40 to 50 inches. Moose hunting in New Brunswick is by draw and only 100 or so licenses are offered to nonresidents. The three-day season at the end of September is short. If you're lucky enough to get drawn, your chances of bagging a trophy run about 50 percent. Deer hunts have no quota (no Sunday hunting). A three-week bow season opens in October, and Bruce places hunters in trees or portable stands where shots average 20 to 35 yards. Rifle season runs from late October into the third week of November. Here, too, hunting is from stands.

For bear hunting, Bruce runs a 110-mile route through winding back roads of sand and occasionally gravel. Baits are three to four miles apart. At any given time, only a third of his 25 to 30 baits will be hunted. That helps ensure success. Average bears weigh about 200 pounds. Spring bear hunting is generally better than fall, but bears tend to be smaller. A maritime-area black bear will gain 25 to 30 percent of its body weight during the summer. A bowhunter himself, Bruce caters to archers and says that the two-week season in early fall offers fine opportunities for shots of 15 to 20 yards. That's taking your bear up close and personal.

VITAL STATISTICS:

Game/Arm/Seasons:
BLACK BEAR:
Bow: Mid to late Sept.
Centerfire, muzzleloader: Spring, May through late June; Fall, Oct.
WHITE-TAILED DEER:
Bow: Early through late Oct.
Centerfire, muzzleloader: Late Oct. through late Nov.
MOOSE:
Bow, centerfire, muzzleloader:
Late Sept.
Rates:
BEAR $1,250/5 days
WHITE-TAILED DEER $1,150/5 days
MOOSE $1,550/5 days
Accommodations:
WOOD FRAME LODGE
NUMBER OF ROOMS: 4, SHARED BATHS
MAXIMUM NUMBER OF HUNTERS: 8
Meals:
Substantial home cooking
Conference Groups: No
Guides: Included
Gratuity: $50
Preferred Payment:
Cash, check
Other Activities:
Fishing, bird hunting, bird watching, wildlife photography
Getting There:
Fly to Saint John and the lodge van will pick you up for $50 round-trip.

Contact:
Bruce Hanley
Northern Outdoor Lodge
RR 4
St. George, New Brunswick
E0G 2Y0, Canada
888/588-2327
Fax: 506/755-9802

Big River Camps

P a s a d e n a ,   N e w f o u n d l a n d

Three old-time camps where caribou and moose abound.

VITAL STATISTICS:

Game/Arm/Seasons:
BEAR, CARIBOU, MOOSE:
Centerfire, muzzleloader: Mid-Sept. through late Oct.
Rates:
From $2,850/7 days
Accommodations:
FRAME AND LOG CABINS
NUMBER OF ROOMS: 3
MAXIMUM NUMBER OF HUNTERS: 4
Meals:
Roasts, turkey, chops
Conference Groups: No
Guides: Included
Gratuity: $100
Preferred Payment:
Cash, check, credit cards
Other Activities:
Fishing, wildlife photography
Getting There:
Fly to Deer Lake and you'll be met by a representative of the outfitter.

Contact:
Bob or Edith Skinner
Big River Camps Inc.
Box 250
Pasadena, Newfoundland
A0L 1K0, Canada
709/686-2242
Fax: 709/686-5244
Web: www.huntcamp.com/outfitters/big-river.html
off-season: 561/734-8065

LIKE THEIR CARIBOU, Newfoundland and Labrador are united yet separate. Newfoundland is the island that lies at the mouth of the Gulf of St. Lawrence. Labrador shares its boundary with Quebec, running north toward the Arctic. The two are governed jointly as a single province. Barren ground caribou, large mammals of 800 pounds and more, roam the tundra of northern Labrador and points west. The woodland caribou of Newfoundland are smaller, more compact animals weighing 500 pounds or so. Strategies for hunting woodland caribou are very different than those for their northern cousins. You'll see a dozen of the latter for every one of the former. With the caribou of the tundra, you'll glass a number of bulls before taking the trophy you want, generally at ranges in excess of 100 yards. But with woodland caribou, you may see a half-dozen good bulls during a week's hunt. Approaching them is not generally a problem. Woodland caribou graze into the wind. If you come up on them downwind, you can get very close.

Moose, of course, are another story. As they say: Big old bulls didn't get that way by being dumb. Solitary and somewhat sedentary, moose feed early and late, holing up in heavy timber or thickets during the day. On Newfoundland, an 800-pound moose with a 45-inch spread is a pretty good bull. The most successful hunters find those low, boggy areas in the muskeg where moose feed, create a ground blind downwind and sit and wait. Patience pays. Bears may also be taken, but bruins are definitely lowest on most hunters' priority list.

Bob Skinner, one of the pioneers of outfitting in Newfoundland/Labrador, runs three hunting camps. They're found on Middle and White Bear lakes and Burnt Pond, about 30 miles due north of Burgeo, on the island's south coast. Terrain around the camps is not difficult, but it's no walk in the park. Muskeg and a nefarious foot-grabbing ground cover called tuckamore makes getting about some areas dicey. Timber is thick in places and in others the land rises as barren hills. Most hunting is one-on-one here. Two hunters may share a guide if they wish, but provincial law requires nonresidents to be guided. The success rate on woodland caribou is close to 100 percent, and 80 percent on moose. Unlike some lake-cabin camps, you'll have a cook as well as a guide. So all you have to do is the hunting.

[C A N A D A   E A S T]

Mt. Peyton Outfitters

B i s h o p s   F a l l s ,   N e w f o u n d l a n d

There's fodder for body and soul at this log lodge near the sea.

VITAL STATISTICS:

Game/Arm/Seasons:
BLACK BEAR:
Bow, centerfire, muzzleloader: June
CARIBOU, MOOSE:
Bow: Late-Aug. through mid-Sept.
Centerfire, muzzleloader: Mid-Sept. through Nov.

Rates:
BEAR $1,750/6 days
CARIBOU $2,800/6 days
MOOSE $2,350/6 days
Combo hunts $4,200/6 days

Accommodations:
MODERN LOG LODGE
NUMBER OF ROOMS: 6
MAXIMUM NUMBER OF HUNTERS: 18

Meals:
Newfoundland cuisine

Conference Groups: Yes

Guides: Included

Gratuity: $100

Preferred Payment:
Cash, check

Other Activities:
Wildlife photography

Getting There:
Fly to Gander and you'll be met.

Contact:
Don Tremblett
Mt. Peyton Outfitters
Box 463
Bishops Falls, Newfoundland
A0H 1C0, Canada
709/258-6374
Fax: 709/258-6394

D
RAINING A HUGE AREA of central Newfoundland, the Exploits River tumbles down a heavy set of rapids before becoming tidal below Bishops Falls. Five miles east is Mt. Peyton, a gentle 1,400-footer, but high enough to provide sparsely forested ridges favored by woodland caribou. Some of the land around the mountain, prior to 1998, was not hunted by nonresidents. And though convenient to hundreds of seacoast hamlets north of Gander, the area gets little resident hunting pressure. The result is caribou that generally score better than 300 on the Boone & Crockett scale. You'll hunt with one guide, spotting and stalking, working into the wind, ever alert for movement of a small herd.

Numerous logging roads lace the country and you'll walk them slowly, peering into the lush forest, hoping to catch a glimpse of a feeding bull. That you'll see moose is beyond doubt; you can expect to see a dozen or more during your six-day hunt. Most shots are taken at 150 yards or less, making a .30-06 ideal for this country. Practice shooting offhand before you come. You'll be surprised just how fast a startled moose can run. Moose hunting also requires good knee-high rubber boots (or breathable stocking-foot waders worn under a loose-fitting pair of soft jeans and boots you don't mind soaking).

For spring bear, the name of the game is hunting from tree stands over bait. Don Tremblett, head of this outfit for the past dozen years, is adamant about hunters shooting bruins of 250 pounds or greater — only. To shoot bears of lesser size is to jeopardize successive generations. Hunting is normally from tree stands 50 yards or so from active baits. Bowhunting stands may be as close as 15 yards.

Accommodations are provided in Mt. Peyton's log lodge, located on a bench near the mountain. You'll either hike from the lodge or ride various conveyances with your guide into the areas you'll hunt for the day. Three hunters will share a room and all rooms share common shower facilities. Bring your own sleeping bag and personal gear, but don't worry about the chow. You'll dine on seafood, meat, pasta and home-baked breads of your dreams.

Northern Labrador Outdoors Ltd.

Torngat Mountains, Labrador

Where caribou is king and bear a friend of the court.

VITAL STATISTICS:

Game/Arm/Seasons:
CARIBOU, BEAR:
Bow, centerfire, muzzleloader: Aug. through Oct.
Rates:
From $1,825/7 days
Accommodations:
TENT CAMPS
MAXIMUM NUMBER OF HUNTERS: 6 PER CAMP
Meals:
Caribou, steak, fish
Conference Groups: Yes
Guides: Included
Gratuity: $250
Preferred Payment:
Cash, check
Other Activities:
Bird hunting, fishing, waterfowling, wildlife photography
Getting There:
Fly to Goose Bay and catch an air shuttle at no additional charge.

Contact:
Harvey Calden
Northern Labrador Outdoors Ltd.
Box 89
Jay, ME 04239
1-888/244-7824
Fax: 207/897-6892

LABRADOR NARROWS to a thin sliver north of 60° and the famous Torngats mark the boundary with Quebec's Ungava Bay country. Brutally barren yet beautiful, the Torngats rise rocky and gray from forests of stunted fir. Valleys are tufted with stands of scrub and tundra grasses, and here and there, fast, bright, clear rivers race from glacial lakes down to fjords and thence to the cold sea.

Caribou is the primary game here, but scores of black bears work berry flats along the rivers. Like their cousins in Alaska, these bears fish for char and spawning salmon. A typical trophy runs 250 pounds or so. If you want one, the bear are here for the taking. However, in the camps run by Harvey Calden of Northern Labrador Outdoors, the focus is on the bulls of the Koroc Herd. The Koroc group does not migrate in the same way that other bands of the George River herd do. Instead, they move within the area between the mountains and the sea. Hunting is a question of spotting and stalking. On average, a hunter will look at a dozen bulls before deciding which one to take. Success rates are near 100 percent on bulls scoring 350 or so.

This is big country, and even though the Koroc herd does not migrate, it does wander about. Harvey spends a good deal of time flying the area searching for concentrations of reasonable bulls. Then he and his troops will move spike camps, consisting of wall-tents serving two hunters and their guide into likely areas. He operates several camps, but generally they'll never be within eight to 10 miles of each other. Also available are hunts for migrating caribou.

Along with caribou and black bear is some of the world's best fishing for arctic char. August is the best time for char, which happily coincides with the opening of caribou and bear seasons. Okay, sure, you're paying for the hunting, but grilled char with a little of that rosemary you slipped into your duffel sure has a way of brightening up a camp menu.

*There just isn't an easy way to move one of Anticosti's
big bucks out of the island's woods, unless you have a guide from a
fine camp such as SEPAQ's Jupiter 12 to lend a hand.*

Owl's Nest Lodge

St. John's, Newfoundland

With 120,000 moose, you're sure to find one you like.

WITH A DOZEN LODGES south and west of the little town of Buchans at the end of Provincial Highway 370, Owl's Nest Lodge offers bear, caribou and moose hunts in remote wilderness. You'll fly from Buchans via fixed-wing or rotary aircraft to log or frame outpost cabins and from there spend a full six days hunting. The landscape is not as challenging as that of the Northern Peninsula around Gros Morne Park, but just west of Buchans rises 1,500-foot Notched Mountain. Scores of brooks and ponds, many unnamed, drain this area, offering numerous grassy bogs close to stands of spruce and fir, favored cover for moose and bear. Ridges are more open, offering grazing to wandering woodland caribou.

Estimated at 120,000 head, Newfoundland's moose population is one of the largest in North America. Antlers generally spread about 40 inches-plus with handsome shovels. While rifles are the weapon of choice for moose, Owl's Nest offers a special two-week season for archers in early September. Still-hunting is the most effective strategy, though spotting from a boat or canoe and planning a stalk can also work. Caribou hunting is similar, with still-hunting getting the best results. Bear hunters have the option of hunting over bait, though some score after searching out sign and then sitting or standing patiently (very patiently). Bear are also seen from boats, offering a bit of spot-and-stalk hunting. High rubber boots are essential for hunting pond drainages.

Newfoundland is one of those places where you can take more than one bear, caribou or moose. If you see a larger bull later in your hunt, you can harvest it for no more than the cost of a second license. And, similarly, if you want to split a moose, for instance, with a partner (nobody has freezer space for an entire moose), two can hunt on one license provided that only one moose is shot. And from this camp there's a reasonable chance for a "Newfie" grand slam. Here one guide serves two hunters and there's a cook in every camp. Fly-outs to extremely isolated sites for hunting out of spike tent camps can also be arranged.

VITAL STATISTICS:

Game/Arm/Seasons:
BLACK BEAR:
Bow: Late-Aug. through mid-Sept.
Centerfire, muzzleloader: Spring, June; fall, mid-Sept. through Nov.
CARIBOU, MOOSE:
Bow: Late-Aug. through mid-Sept.
Centerfire, muzzleloader: Mid-Sept. through Nov.

Rates:
BEAR from $1,350/6 days
CARIBOU, MOOSE from $2,500/6 days

Accommodations:
FRAME AND LOG CABINS
MAXIMUM NUMBER OF HUNTERS: 4 TO 12 DEPENDING ON CAMP

Meals:
Wild game, fish, turkey

Conference Groups: Yes

Guides: Included

Gratuity: $50 to $300

Preferred Payment:
Cash, Visa, MasterCard, check

Other Activities:
Bird hunting, boating, canoeing/rafting, fishing, snowmobiling, waterfowling, wildlife photography

Getting There:
Fly to Gander and be met by the lodge van.

Contact:
Ronald D. Parsons
Owl's Nest Lodge
Box 2430 Station C
St. John's, Newfoundland
A1C 6E7, Canada
709/722-5100 or
709/368-9013
Fax: 709/722-0808
e-mail: owlsnest@webpage.ca
Web: www.webpage/ca.owlsnest

Ray's Hunting & Fishing Lodge

H o w l e y ,   N e w f o u n d l a n d

Dense populations of caribou and moose, with manageable terrain.

VITAL STATISTICS:

Game/Arm/Seasons:
BLACK BEAR:
Bow: Early through mid-Sept.
Centerfire, muzzleloader: June;
mid-Sept. through Nov.
CARIBOU, MOOSE:
Bow: Early through mid-Sept.
Centerfire, muzzleloader: mid-Sept.
through Nov.
Rates:
BLACK BEAR from $2,000/7 days
CARIBOU, MOOSE from $3,000/7
days
Combinations from $3,500/7 days
Accommodations:
MODERN LODGE OR TENT CAMP
MAXIMUM NUMBER OF HUNTERS: 8
Meals:
Family-style
Conference Groups: No
Guides: Included
Gratuity: $100 to $200
Preferred Payment:
Cash, traveler's check
Other Activities:
Bird hunting, bird watching, boating,
fishing, wildlife photography
Getting There:
Fly to Deer Lake and you'll be
picked up.

Contact:
Ray Broughton
Ray's Hunting & Fishing
Lodge
Box 31
Howley, Newfoundland
A0K 3E0, Canada
709/635-3628
e-mail:
s.v.broughton@nis.sympatico.ca
Web:
www3~ns.sympatico.ca/sv.broughton

FORMED DURING THE SAME COLLISION of continental plates that pushed up the Appalachians, Newfoundland is a ribbed highland that tilts to the east. At 2,651 feet, Gros Morne Mountain, hard by the west coast, is the highest point on the island. Though its location at the mouth of the Gulf of St. Lawrence should suggest otherwise, Newfoundland is buffeted by massive and bitter cold fronts that sweep out of the arctic. Native vegetation reflects the bitter climate. Most of the province is forested with balsam fir and black spruce mixed with paper and yellow birches, plus a wide variety of hardwood shrubs. Fires and erosion have produced barrens favored by small woody plants.

An abundance of browse and the presence of bogs makes this prime habitat for moose. Not native to the island, a pair of moose were released in the vicinity of Howley in the late 1800s. Now more than 150,000, about three per square mile, roam the island. So large is the herd that the Inland Fish and Wildlife division occasionally has to advertise for hunters to help control crop damage caused by hungry moose. These bulls are smaller than those of the mainland. But each year at Ray's Hunting camps east of Howley, a number of bulls with spreads in excess of 40 inches are taken. Hunting from stands, calling, and spotting and stalking are all productive tactics. The success rate is close to 100 percent.

Newfoundland also has the largest population of woodland caribou in North America, and each year Ray's hunters do almost 100 percent on these as well. These herds see very little pressure from local hunters. Still-hunting into the wind through cut-over country is probably the most effective manner for taking a caribou here. Chances of a trophy are reasonably good. Newfoundland bulls dominate the Boone & Crockett listings. Black bear hunting over baits in both spring and fall is also quite good. Black bears seem larger here and perhaps more predatory than those in other parts of the country. A typical spring black bear here will run 250 pounds, and fall bears normally exceed 350. Because the population is very high on the island, hunters are encouraged to take two bears.

Plentiful game is only part of the reason why success rates are high at this lodge. The other is that most guides work with one hunter and, on average, guides have 10 years of experience. Hunts are staged from Ray's main lodge at the north end of Grand Lake and from a tent camp 20 miles farther into the bush. Not only are all hunts guided, but there's a first-class cook in each camp.

Steel Mountain Lodge

St. George's, Newfoundland

Altitude and location make all the difference.

VITAL STATISTICS:

Game/Arm/Seasons:
CARIBOU, MOOSE:
Bow: Late Aug. through mid-Sept.
Centerfire, muzzleloader: Mid-Sept. through mid-Oct.

Rates:
CARIBOU, MOOSE $3,300/7 days
Combo $4,800

Accommodations:
WOOD-SIDED LODGES
NUMBER OF ROOMS: 4 TO 8
MAXIMUM NUMBER OF HUNTERS: 4

Meals:
Roasts, chicken

Conference Groups: No

Guides: Included

Gratuity: Hunter's discretion

Preferred Payment:
Cash, check

Other Activities:
Bird watching, boating, wildlife photography

Getting There:
Fly to Stephenville and catch the bush aircraft.

Contact:
Benedict F. Alexander
Steel Mountain Lodge
Box 10
St. George's, Newfoundland
A0N 1Z0, Canada
709/647-3373
Fax: 709/647-3373

RUNNING THE LENGTH of the western coast of Newfoundland are the Long Range Mountains, a chain of rounded highlands with peaks that climb to 2,600 feet. From bottoms where alders and spruce choke flowages, dark timber fringes the waterways and climbs low hills. But it rapidly becomes sparse, unable to withstand the persistent cold winds off St. Lawrence Bay. Soon the forest gives way to scrub and blueberry barrens and muskeg before grading into tundra similar to that of northern Quebec. Altitude makes all the difference. So too, of course, does location. With three remote fly-in camps — Alexander, Benabbey and Princess — hunters are dispersed into areas where they'll rarely see another. Princess lodge, located beneath the highest of the southern end of the Long Range Mountains, has a reputation for producing excellent caribou. The lodge sits in the path of a major north/south migration route. A good caribou will have main beams of 33 inches-plus, long top palm points and 25 to 30 points. Most hunting is spotting and stalking, and virtually all hunters harvest a good animal. Caribou are also hunted out of Alexander and Benabbey camps in the Flat Bay drainage. You'll find moose with 36- to 40-inch spreads, and the success rate is in the neighborhood of 90 percent. What you won't find here is bear hunting. If you see one during a caribou or moose hunt, you're welcome, if you have a permit, to take it. But bears are purely incidental to the main quarry of these camps.

You'll reach these camps via floatplane or chopper from Stephenville, the gathering spot for Steel Mountain's clients. Each of the insulated wood-sided camps has hot and cold running water, showers, bedrooms for up to four hunters and quarters for guides and the camp cook. You'll walk or boat from camp to the area for the day's hunt and work your way back to camp as dusk falls.

Tuckamore Lodge & Outfitters

M a i n   B r o o k ,   N e w f o u n d l a n d

Handicapped hunters (and all others) will find a special friend here.

VITAL STATISTICS:

Game/Arm/Seasons:
BLACK BEAR:
Bow: Early through mid-Sept.
Centerfire, muzzleloader: June; Sept.
CARIBOU, MOOSE:
Bow: Early through mid-Sept.
Centerfire, muzzleloader: Mid-Sept.
through Nov.
Rates:
BLACK BEAR from $1,500/6 days;
$5,000/6 days (trophy)
CARIBOU from $3,250/6 days
MOOSE from $3,100/6 days
Combinations from $5,950/6 days
Accommodations:
SCANDINAVIAN LODGES
NUMBER OF ROOMS: 9 WITH PRIVATE BATH
MAXIMUM NUMBER OF HUNTERS: 8
Meals:
Elegant regional cuisine
Conference Groups: Yes
Guides: Included
Gratuity: $50 to $120
Preferred Payment:
Cash, Visa, check
Other Activities:
Bird hunting, bird watching,
canoeing/rafting, fishing, skiing,
snowmobiling, wildlife photography
Getting There:
Fly to St. Anthony or Deer Lake and
you will be met.

Contact:
Barb Genge
Tuckamore Lodge &
Outfitters
Box 100
Main Brook, Newfoundland
A0K 3N0, Canada
888/865-6361
or 709/865-6361
Fax: 709/865-2112
e-mail:
Tuckamore.Lodge@thezone.net
Web: www.tuckamore-lodge.nf.net

WHAT'S A TROPHY BLACK BEAR? How does 720 pounds with a 21 7/8-inch skull sound? Good enough for Boone & Crockett. And for the hunter who killed it, the bear was, indeed, the trophy of a lifetime. Every lodge has a story like this, you say. Well, this hunter was physically challenged. "He was crippled up," says lodge owner Barb Genge. "He could walk half decent, but we had to hoist him into the tree." Tuckamore doesn't make a "thing" about hosting handicapped hunters. They just do it. The second question you ought to be asking about now is how you get 720 pounds of black bear out of the woods?

Trophy bear is something of a specialty at Tuckamore, a first-class lodge on Southwest Pond near the tip of Newfoundland's northern peninsula. Barb's opened two areas, one on White Arm Pond and the other on Sail Pond, which had not been hunted for generations. She has exclusive rights to this territory and allows no more than five hunters (normally it's two or three per year) to hunt it. You'll pay a hefty price: $5,000 for a five-day hunt. On the other hand, you get to come back for each of five years until you harvest the bear you want. Whether you hunt over bait is up to you, as is your choice of ground blind or tree stand. Now, if bubba bear does happen by your stand and you decide he's the one, you can return the following year for a week of Atlantic salmon fishing or to hunt bear in a nontrophy area for free.

Spring and fall bear are not the only game in this town. Woodland caribou and moose roam the hills and bogs of this high, forested plateau. In 1996, a wildlife survey showed about 7.7 moose per square kilometer, and a similar caribou survey two years later estimated 8,000 in Area 76, which is now being managed for trophy bulls. For the past 25 years, Area 76 had been closed to hunting. A good moose will have a 40-inch spread and a caribou, 48 inches. Hunting is normally one-on-one and you ride from the main or remote lodge to the general area where you'll hunt in a 4WD.

As you might suspect, this is not your usual hunting camp. Barb runs a pair of lodges, Scandinavian-style inns, really, where all you need to bring is your toothbrush, hunting gear and distilled spirits of your choice. Guest rooms have private baths, there's a sauna to soothe aches, and menus feature the likes of crab au gratin appetizer, grilled T-bones or spare ribs and strawberries and ice cream for dessert.

Victoria Lodge

Hunt in the land of the original "Red" Indians.

VITAL STATISTICS:

Game/Arm/Seasons:
BLACK BEAR:
Bow: Early through mid-Sept.
Centerfire, muzzleloader: Spring,
June; Fall, Sept. through Oct.
CARIBOU, MOOSE:
Bow: Early through mid-Sept.
Centerfire, muzzleloader: Mid-Sept.
through Nov.

Rates:
BLACK BEAR from $1,650/6 days
CARIBOU from $3,010/6 days
MOOSE from $2,795/6 days
Combinations from $2,900/6 days

Accommodations:
FRAMED LODGE AND CABINS
MAXIMUM NUMBER OF HUNTERS: 6 TO 8

Meals: Salmon steaks, turkey, beef

Conference Groups: No

Guides: Included

Gratuity: $50 to $100

Preferred Payment:
Cash, check, money order

Other Activities:
Bird hunting, bird watching, boating,
canoeing/rafting, fishing, skiing,
snowmobiling, swimming,
waterfowling, wildlife photography

Getting There:
Fly to Deer Lake and you'll be met.

Contact:
Dave Evans,
Victoria Lodge
6 Birmingham St.
St. John's, Newfoundland
A1E 5C8, Canada;
709/745-1048
Fax: 709/745-5452
e-mail:
victoria.outfitters@thezone.net

FROM VICTORIA LAKE, a narrow river pushes northeast through the boggy spruce bottoms of central Newfoundland until it eventually spills into Red Indian Lake. Throughout Europe "Red" Indian is a common phrase used to describe all the aboriginal peoples of North America. In fact, the appellation got its start when John Cabot discovered Newfoundland in 1547 and encountered the Beothuks, the native people who smeared their bodies with ochre as protection from blackflies and perhaps for religious reasons as well. They were hunters and gatherers and lived in the vicinity of the lake and the lodge. Though the last died in 1827, when you hunt this land you can still see where they camped.

Hunting is done from the lodge on the bank of the river. You and your guide can walk through the spruce forest breaking out into the barren highlands on the flanks of 1,000-foot Hungry Hill. This is prime grazing ground for woodland caribou, and a herd of about 700 remains in the area around the lodge all year. Hunter success runs close to 100 percent. With boats you'll run upriver, moving ashore in your knee-high rubber boots through country rich with moose. Because of its fine swamps and nearby stands of thick timber, the moose population is also quite high. Nine out of 10 hunters take bulls, a third of them trophies of 40-inch or better racks. Caribou and moose hunts match one hunter with a guide; for bears the ration is 2:1. Bears are hunted spring and fall and over baits or not. It's your choice. Often moose and caribou hunters take a bear along the way and pay an additional fee.

Dave Evans, who's owned the lodge for a decade, is something of a specialist when it comes to bowhunting. And there's nothing he likes better than helping clients take a "Newfie" grand slam — bear, caribou and moose, all with broadheads. Of course, he doesn't look down his nose at hunters who tote other arms of choice. Guests stay in his comfortable cabins for two, colored ochre like the Beothuk, and dine on steak and turkey in the great room, where a fire warms the hearth. Some spring hunts coincide with salmon season so be sure to bring a rod.

Stewiacke Valley Outfitters

B r o o k f i e l d ,   N o v a   S c o t i a

A lovely farm family offers good deer hunting at a price that can't be beat.

VITAL STATISTICS:

Game/Arm/Seasons:
BEAR:
Bow, centerfire, muzzleloader: Mid-Sept. through early Oct.
DEER:
Bow: Early Sept. through late Oct.
Centerfire, muzzleloader: Late Oct. through early Dec.
Rates:
BEAR $900/5 days
DEER $650/5 days
Accommodations:
FRAME LODGE
NUMBER OF ROOMS: 4, SHARED BATH
MAXIMUM NUMBER OF HUNTERS: 8 TO 10
Meals:
Roast beef, chicken, turkey
Conference Groups: No
Guides: Included
Gratuity: Hunter's discretion
Preferred Payment:
Cash, check
Other Activities:
Bird hunting, fishing
Getting There:
Fly to Halifax International and rent a car, or arrange for the lodge to pick you up for an additional $25.

Contact:
David Kennedy
Stewiacke Valley Outfitters
RR #3
Brookfield, Nova Scotia
BON 1C0, Canada
902/673-2023
Fax: 902/673-2023

LUSH FORESTS OF FIRS and spruce inter-mixed here and there with maple and poplar flow over the low hills of this gentle island like a thick loden sea. Large farm fields, pasture for dairy and beef cattle, turn tawny gold in early autumn, and through the farms runs the Stewiacke, a river to which Atlantic salmon are returning. You can catch browns in the river in the fall, and a prudent archer who ventures into this country will pack along a fly- or spinning rod.

For 25 years, Dave Kennedy has been guiding hunters on his 3,000-acre farm and those of his neighbors. He also hunts provincial and crown lands. Because the woods are so dense with underbrush, Dave prefers that clients hunt from tree or tripod stands, but not all are willing to do so. These Dave guides personally, and after two days of busting through the bush, those who once favored still-hunting are delighted to sit on a stand. Some stands overlook rubs, scrapes and trails, but most provide views of treelines and adjoining pastures. A typical deer dresses out at 200 pounds and will carry a 6- or 8-point rack. Six out of 10 hunters go home with venison.

There's no spring bear hunting in Nova Scotia, and Dave is limiting his fall hunts, which are over bait, to the two weeks at the end of September. A 250-pounder is about average, and hunting is, of course, a late-afternoon affair. During the morning you have a choice of chasing trout, pheasants or grouse. Accommodations are provided in a large remodeled garage with four bedrooms and two baths on the top floor and a large paneled lounge downstairs.

Crawford's Camp

Sioux Narrows, Ontario

A primitive land where only blackpowder firearms or bows are allowed.

VITAL STATISTICS:

Game/Arm/Seasons:
BEAR:
Bow, centerfire, muzzleloader:
Spring, mid-Apr. through mid-June;
Fall, Sept.
DEER:
Bow, centerfire, muzzleloader:
Mid-Oct. through mid-Nov.
MOOSE:
Bow, muzzleloader: Mid-Oct.
through mid-Nov.
Rates:
BEAR from $785 (Canadian)/7 days
double occupancy
DEER from $800 (Canadian)/7 days
double occupancy
MOOSE from $1,085 (Canadian)/7
days double occupancy
Accommodations:
CABINS OR TENT CAMPS
MAXIMUM NUMBER OF HUNTERS: 4 PER
TENT CAMP
72 MAIN CAMP
Meals:
Self-catered
Conference Groups: No
Guides: $75 (Canadian) per day
Gratuity: $100 (Canadian)
Preferred Payment:
Cash, MasterCard, Visa, check
Other Activities:
Biking, bird hunting, bird watching,
boating, fishing, swimming,
waterfowling, wildlife photography
Getting There:
Fly to International Falls and meet
the van from the camp ($100 round-
trip for four).

Contact:
Bob Rydberg
Crawford's Camp
Box 330
Sioux Narrows, Ontario
P0X 1N0, Canada
888/266-3474 or
807/226-5646
Fax: 807/226-5196

WHAT LOOKS, at first glance, to be a large island in the midst of Lake of the Woods is, in fact, the huge Aulneau Peninsula attached to the mainland by a thin isthmus west of the little town of Crow Lake. A low, rolling, rocky land smoothed by glaciers and dotted with myriad lakes and ponds gouged out by their passing, the Aulneau is home to one of the few public hunting reserves set aside for primitive weapons. Leave your centerfire at home. Here you'll hunt moose and bear, and maybe one day elk, the old-fashioned way with blackpowder, bow or crossbow.

Named for Father Jean Pierre Aulneau, a Jesuit priest who explored the area in the 1730s, the peninsula's forests of spruce and fir were stripped in the late 1800s and early 1900s, leaving a dense second growth of poplar, birch and scrub oak mixed with stands of spruce, white pine and cedar. Elevations are not high. Though the terrain is rugged, it breaks for a number of grassy meadows and bogs. There is no better habitat for moose, and the peninsula boasts one of the largest populations per square mile in Canada.

Crawford's Camp, located a few miles east of the peninsula at Sioux Narrows, hunts about 500 square miles of the Aulneau. After a thorough briefing on the lay of the land and patterns of animal movement, hunters are provided maps and ferried by boat or floatplane to tent camps on the peninsula. Each camp is a single wood-floored wall tent with an airtight stove and propane cooking range. Guides are not generally used, though they may be obtained by special arrangement. In an effort to control the burgeoning population, each hunter is allowed one bull and one calf, although party hunting, where two hunters share a tag, is permitted as well. Muzzleloading, both in-line and traditional, is much more effective than archery for taking moose; it's difficult to get close enough with a bow to make a fatal shot on a bull moose. The one exception may be during the rut in mid-October when it's possible to work a bull with a call. Bulls with spreads in the 50-inch range are not at all uncommon.

Along with moose hunting, Crawford's Camp offers bear hunting with conventional weapons on the Aulneau, deer hunting from stands, wolf hunts and some duck hunting. These hunts are run from a string of wooden lakefront housekeeping cottages that stretch for a quarter mile along the shore.

[C A N A D A   E A S T]

Huber's Lone Pine Lodge Ltd.

D r y d e n ,   O n t a r i o

What if A.J. were a moose hunter?

VITAL STATISTICS:

Game/Arm/Seasons:
BEAR:
Bow, centerfire, muzzleloader: Sept.
DEER:
Bow, centerfire, muzzleloader:
Mid-Sept. through early Oct.
MOOSE:
Bow: Mid through late Sept.
Centerfire, muzzleloader: Early
through mid-Oct.

Rates:
BEAR $1,475/6 days
DEER $1,225/6 days
MOOSE $2,500/9 days

Accommodations:
LOG LODGE
NUMBER OF ROOMS: 44 WITH SHARED BATH
MAXIMUM NUMBER OF HUNTERS: 5 TO 10

Meals: German cuisine

Conference Groups: Yes

Guides: Included

Gratuity: $100

Preferred Payment:
Cash, check, credit card

Other Activities:
Antiquing, bird hunting, bird
watching, boating, fishing, golf,
waterfowling, wildlife photography

Getting There:
Fly to Dryden International and take
the lodge van for $35 round-trip.

Contact:
Walter Huber
Huber's Lone Pine Lodge Ltd.
Box 546
Dryden, Ontario
P8N 2Z2, Canada
1-800/665-2257
Fax: 807/938-6651
e-mail:
whuber@dryden.lakeheadu.ca
Web: www.hearland.on.ca/hubers

SOME YEARS BACK, A.J. McClane conjured up a list of the top 99 fishing spots in the world and listed Wabigoon Lake, at Dryden, in the top 30. Had he been a moose hunter, he might have listed it as number one. Why would a fishing camp deserve such accolades? For the last decade at least, Huber's clients have been 100 percent successful on moose with good racks of 40-inch-plus spreads. Huber's hunts more than 120 square miles of prime terrain, low brush, boggy stream channels and thick timber. But the hunts have a decided difference.

On most lake-based camps, you'll boat the shore, looking for moose on the bank. Here, you may do some of that, but the main game is to scoot up the lake before dawn and to land near a snowmobile trail. You'll still-hunt down the trail until you find a bull moose. Snowmobile trails? Right. There are more than 250 miles of them lacing the area where Huber runs his hunts. In the winter these are frigid paths of ice and snow, but come summer they green up with lush and succulent grasses and the tender shoots of young trees. Moose graze on the trails, and come fall, during the rut and the weeks before, they'll travel the trails rather than the thick woods. Who said they were dumb? Seasons are short, with 10 days in September for archers and 10 days in October for centerfire guys.

You'll also find deer here, bucks that run in the 6- to 8-point range, with live weights of 250 to 300 pounds. Bring your own stand and pick one of two dozen sites over scrapes, rubs or trail crossings. Huber restricts the harvest to no more than a handful of hunters, and slots are booked at least a year, sometimes more, in advance. Along with hunting from stands, stalking and limited drives also produce. And, in a large area about 20 miles away from the lake, he runs fall bear hunts. Fall bear and moose seasons overlap with grouse and duck hunting; lots of hunters drive up with retrievers kenneled in their trucks.

Hunters stay in the base lodge, a lovely compound in a green glen by the lake. Dark firs rise around the quaint log-sided cabins, each with its own private bath. With a chef who is flown in each year from Munich, there's little doubt about the quality of the cuisine.

Mattice Lake Outfitters

Armstrong, Ontario

Where the dawn patrol takes the moose.

WEST OF THE NORTHERN TIP of Lake Nipigon is the little town of Armstrong that's served both by rail and an all-weather highway, Route 527. Armstrong is headquarters for Mattice Lake Outfitters, its numerous camps on lakes Mojikit, Ogoki, Short and Whitewater. The camps are about a 45-minute flight in a De Havilland Beaver.

Best known for wonderful pike and walleye angling in spring and summer, these camps become the special province of a select group of moose hunters who are wise enough to book at least a year in advance. For three or four weeks (depending on weather) beginning in mid-September, Mattice offers self-catered, self-guided hunting for moose with racks in the 48-inch range. In some respects, the weather plays a big role. During warmer years, the harvest is down, but three of four days of sub-freezing nights will trigger the rut and improve hunter success, which is normally better than 50 percent.

The drill is this: Early in the morning (dawn is best) you and your buddy will pull a little life into the 9.9-horse kicker on the back of your boat and begin to cruise the shore. If and when you spot a moose, you'll cut the motor and head toward shore. If it's a good bull, you may shoot from the boat. (Shooting a moose from a boat that's under power is illegal.) Or you may run aground and try to stalk him. If you're fortunate enough to be hunting during the rut, calling will work. But Don Elliot advises that you buy tapes and practice, practice, practice. Otherwise, you'll be bleating in the wind.

Mattice Lake Outfitter's camps are modern and of log construction, with propane refrigeration and solar-charged batteries for electric lights. Bring your own food and sleeping bags. The resident camp manager can help with an appropriate tip about moose locations. And while you're there, of course, to hunt, don't forget that as lake temperatures drop, pike and walleye move up in the water column and feed aggressively. A well cast fly, spoon or plug may bring you a 25-pound northern.

VITAL STATISTICS:

Game/Arm/Seasons:
MOOSE
Centerfire, muzzleloader:
Mid-Sept. through mid-Oct.

Rates:
$1,550/7 days

Accommodations:
MODERN LOG CABINS
NUMBER OF ROOMS: 2
Maximum Number of Hunters:
4 to 6

Meals: Self-catered

Conference Groups: Yes

Guides: Included

Gratuity: Hunter's discretion

Preferred Payment:
Cash, Visa, check

Other Activities:
Bird hunting, boating, canoeing/rafting, fishing, wildlife photography

Getting There:
Fly to Thunder Bay and rent a car.

Contact:
Don or Annette Elliot
Mattice Lake Outfitters,
Box 157
Armstrong, Ontario
POT 1A0, Canada
807/583-2483
Fax: 807/583-2114
e-mail: mattice@cancom.net
Web: www.matticelake.com

Air Melançon

S t e . - A n n e - d u - l a c ,   Q u e b e c

Ride Beavers and Otters to remote hunting camps on secluded lakes.

VITAL STATISTICS:

Game/Arm/Seasons:
BLACK BEAR:
Bow, muzzleloader, centerfire:
Mid-May through June
MOOSE:
Bow, muzzleloader, centerfire: Late
Sept. through mid-Oct.
Rates:
BEAR from $720/4 days
MOOSE from $660/7 days
Accommodations:
FRAME CABINS
MAXIMUM NUMBER OF HUNTERS:
4 TO 6 PER CABIN
Meals: Self-catered
Conference Groups: No
Guides:
$100 per day additional
Gratuity:
Hunter's discretion
Preferred Payment:
Cash
Other Activities:
Fishing
Getting There:
Drive to Ste.-Anne-du-lac, Quebec.

Contact:
Francine Melançon-Milot
Air Melançon
2 chemin Tour-du-lac
Ste.-Anne-du-lac, Quebec
J0W 1V0, Canada
819/586-2200
Fax: 819/586-2388
e-mail: air-melancon@ireseau.com
Web: ireseau.com/air-melancon.html

MORE THEN 40 YEARS AGO, Réal Melançon began exploring lakes in the highlands of central Quebec and opened his flying service to carry anglers to the best walleye, brook trout and pike fishing he found. Over the years he established 33 tidy cabins on 18 lakes in the territory between Ste.-Anne-du-lac, about 125 miles northwest of Montreal, and Reservoir Gouin in the central part of the province. On his trips, he noted the best habitats for moose and bear. And, come hunting season, he uses his fleet of four Beavers, a turbo-Otter and a Cessna 185 to ferry hunters to isolated cabins where the only other hunting pressure comes from the members of your party.

For moose, Réal prefers the majestic landscape of the Moselle, a rolling highland pocked with lakes between low ridges that spans more than 125 square miles between the Gatineau River and the Coucou River. Hunters take a 30-minute flight from the base at Ste.-Anne-du-lac to one of 18 camps where they are on their own for a week. With aluminum boat and motor you'll scout the shoreline of your lake or you'll hike cleared trails and find the boggy areas where moose are feeding. Still-hunting is a favorite tactic in these parts.

Air Melançon also runs spring bear hunts over baits in the Moselle. Active baits are established before you fly in to your camp. All you have to do is hike to the site, climb into the tree stand and outlast the blackflies, mosquitoes and no-see-ums. A typical bear will run about 250 pounds and most hunters are successful. A little farther north and to the east is the Sauterelle, a second destination for moose hunters. In this trio of lakes set among a maze of rugged wooded hills, hunters choose from four exclusive hunts. Moose average about 800 pounds and spreads of about 40 inches can be expected. Quebec requires two licenses to harvest a moose, meaning that you've got someone to share the fun of packing out the meat and rack.

Air Melançon's camps are clean frame cabins. More than half have running water and indoor showers. You'll fly-in your own sleeping bags and grub (perishables can be purchased at a grocery in Ste.-Anne-du-lac). All camps have gas refrigerator/freezers (most have two for, uh, beverages) and stoves, a woodstove with plenty of firewood and boats (14-foot Lunds) with 6.5- or 8-horse outboards. And, while cooks and guides are not really needed here, both are available at some camps if desired.

Arctic Adventures

B a i e   d ' U r f e ,   Q u e b e c

When you hunt caribou with Bobby Snowball, you're a member of the family.

VITAL STATISTICS:

Game/Arm/Seasons:
CARIBOU:
Bow, centerfire, muzzleloader: Mid-Aug. through late Sept.

Rates:
From $2,100

Accommodations:
PLATFORM TENTS
MAXIMUM NUMBER OF HUNTERS: 8 PER CAMP

Meals:
Hearty steaks, roasts, fish

Conference Groups: No

Guides Included

Gratuity: Hunter's discretion

Preferred Payment:
Cash, check

Other Activities:
Bird hunting, fishing

Getting There:
Fly to Kuujjuaq and meet the bush plane.

Contact:
Stephen Aston
Arctic Adventures
19950 Clark Graham,
Baie d'Urfe, Quebec
H9X 3R8, Canada
800-465-9474 or
514/457-9371
Fax: 514/457-4626
e-mail: arcticad@total.net
Web: www.archcadventures.ca

For almost 40 years Arctic Adventures has been guiding hunters in the area around Ungava Bay. The quarry, of course, are Quebec Labrador caribou, listed as a distinct classification by Boone & Crockett. Initially, one herd centered in the George River drainage attracted most of the attention. But changing migration patterns prompted by limited food for a rapidly growing herd forced the caribou to extend beyond their old range. Now a small, nonmigratory herd is found in the northeasternmost corner of Quebec. Known as the Koroc Herd, named for a major river that flows into Ungava Bay two watersheds north of Port Noveau Quebec, these animals have the reputation for making Safari Club International and Pope and Young, as well as B&C records. Across the bay is the Leaf River Herd, which calves north on the peninsula but migrates toward the Koksoak and its major tributary, Riviere aux Melezes, before the rut.

Arctic Adventures operates camps that are placed to intercept migrating caribou. Bobby's Camp, named after its Inuit manager Bobby Snowball, is on Lake Kakiattukallak, 120 miles west of Kuujjuaq in the midst of the massing ground for the Leaf and George River herds. This is a full-service operation staffed by Bobby and his family and neighbors. All have grown up in this area and they have an intuitive understanding of the ways of migrating caribou that puts archers and rifle hunters on record-book-quality bulls. With one guide for every two hunters in camp, the odds are heavily in your favor. Similar services are offered at Willie's camp on the Melezes.

Along with the full-service lodges, Arctic Adventures also runs a series of self-guided camps staffed by a pair of Inuits who know the region. Located on land owned and managed by Native Peoples, the areas around these camps are exclusively hunted by Arctic Adventures, an arm of the native corporation. Sited because of the presence of migrating herds, camps contain platform tents for up to eight hunters, a full kitchen and dining tent, hot showers, generators and enough food to founder a battalion. There's a motorboat and an ATV for hunters' use. The camp staff will provide helpful suggestions, but when it comes to guiding, cooking and care of game, you're on your own.

[C A N A D A   E A S T]

VITAL STATISTICS:

Game/Arm/Seasons:
CARIBOU:
Bow, centerfire, muzzleloader:
Aug. through Sept.
BLACK BEAR:
Bow, centerfire, muzzleloader:
Late Aug. through Sept.
Rates:
From $3,250/5 days semi-guided
Accommodations:
PERMANENT AND TENT CAMPS
MAXIMUM NUMBER OF HUNTERS: 12
Meals:
Excellent (whether you or they cook!)
Conference Groups: No
Guides: Depends on package
Gratuity: $25 to $200
Preferred Payment:
Cash, check
Other Activities:
Bird hunting, fishing, wildlife photography
Getting There:
Fly to Montreal and Explo-Sylva takes over from there.

Contact:
Michel Threlfall
Club Explo-Sylva
4101 Radisson
Montreal, Quebec
H1N 3T6, Canada
514/254-6345
Fax: 514/254-6159
e-mail: explo@explosylva.com
Web: www.explosylva.com

Club Explo-Sylva

M o n t r e a l ,   Q u e b e c

To get a bull, save a buck and take the bus.

THE LITTLE TOWN of Caniapiscau on the reservoir with the same name is headquarters for the sprawling Threlfall operation, which runs 23 camps (at last count) in the region between Riviere Serigny to the east, Lac Maricourt to the north and Petite Baleine (Little Whale) to the west. Accommodations vary from plywood cabins at some locations to snug tents in others. All sites feature camp kitchens, secure meat and rack storage houses, generators and hot water. You can fly into these camps directly from Montreal, but it's possible to save $400 by riding the Caribou Express, a 28-passenger bus that makes the run from Montreal to Caniapiscau. No Greyhound bus this! A steward serves drinks and meals as you roll northwest through the heavy spruce forests of the south into northern subarctic tundra. Once in Caniapiscau, you'll hop an Otter to reach your final camp.

In this area, the George River and Leaf River herds mingle. Hunter success rates on bulls scoring between 300 and 450 Boone & Crockett points have run about 96 percent over the past decade. The trick, if there is one, to a productive caribou hunt is staying downwind of the herd you're hunting. While not abnormally sensitive to noise and with notoriously poor vision, caribou do detect even the smallest movements. Slow and steady does it when you're stalking. Hunting from Explo-Sylva's camps is a matter of boating to a likely location and then making a short hike to a stand where you'll watch a crossing. At some of the camps you can cast to Arctic char, Atlantic salmon, brookies and lake trout if you hunt before the end of the first week in September. Black bears become legal in late August, and an $87 permit allows you to harvest one if the opportunity presents. However, only 5 percent of the hunters in this area see black bears.

Explo-Sylva's packages? At the low end is a non-guided housekeeping plan where each hunter is allowed 50 pounds for food in addition to 60 pounds of luggage. You and your party of six will handle all your own camp chores with the assistance of a camp steward. On the other end is a first-class seven-day trip with one guide for two hunters, with guided fishing on the side. And there are variations in between.

Jack Hume Adventures Inc.

Lachute, Quebec

Follow the trail of the golden typewriter to record caribou.

ALL OF THE TOP outdoor writers have been there — Boddington, Lawrence, Wooters and Carmichel — and their yarns tell only a little of the Jack Hume story. For more than 25 years, Jack's been guiding in the George River herd's range in subarctic Quebec. In the glory days, his camps in the drainage of the George were almost a sure bet for hunters seeking trophy caribou. But that changed with the routes of these big migratory deer. Faced with declining success rates, he shifted gears, abandoned the concept of fixed camps and moved west 100 miles into the flowages of the Caniapiscau, Delay, Pon's and Serigny rivers. The seasons have been good to this operation. It's not unusual for racks taken at these camps to wind up in Boone & Crockett's annual top 20.

With his son Richard taking over the day-to-day operations, Jack no longer actively guides clients. But he does spend much of his time during the season piloting his black-and-gold-striped Cessna over the endless tundra, looking for bands of roving caribou. His mission: get hunters to where the caribou are massing. And as he sees patterns develop, he moves hunters and camps into areas to intercept the flow. From these camps, you'll hunt on foot or from large freighter canoes. And hunting here is not a competitive sport. Guides (generally one for every two clients) set comfortable paces. Hunt as hard or as easy as you want. After all, it's your hunt.

As this is being written, Jack's main camps are found on the Caniapiscau and Pon's rivers, and on Ronald's Lake near the Delay. Here you'll find heated plywood cabins, hot and cold water and flush toilets. A chef is on hand to fatten you up and you and your partner will share a guide who'll help you walk off the calories. You'll bring your own sleeping bag, towels and other personal gear. He also runs a string of outpost camps. While facilities are similar to his main digs, outpost camps are generally staffed by a guide-cum-caretaker. You buy your own food and do your own cooking, housekeeping and scouting (with lots of helpful advice). A deluxe version of the outpost camp, which includes food, a chef and up to two guides is also available. This may be the best bet with all the comforts of the main camps but located out where caribou have seen few hunters. Along with caribou, there's also black bear during the last week of August and char and lake trout through the first week of September.

Norpaq Hunting and Fishing Adventures

S t e .   A u g u s t i n ,   Q u e b e c

A score of camps cover the movements of the migratory herds.

VITAL STATISTICS:

Game/Arm/Seasons:
CARIBOU:
Bow, centerfire, muzzleloader:
Aug. through Sept.
BLACK BEAR:
Bow, centerfire, muzzleloader:
Last week in Aug.
Rates:
From $2,250/6 days (unguided)
Accommodations:
TENTS
MAXIMUM NUMBER OF HUNTERS: 4 TO 12
DEPENDING ON CAMP
Meals:
Wholesome fare
Conference Groups: No
Guides: Varies with package
Gratuity: $150 to $200
Preferred Payment:
Cash, Visa, check
Other Activities:
Bird hunting, bird watching, fishing, wildlife photography
Getting There:
Fly to Schefferville and catch the floatplane to your hunting area.

Contact:
Jean or Pierre Paquet
Norpaq Hunting and Fishing
Adventures
Box 88
Ste. Augustin, Quebec
G3A 1V9, Canada
800/473-4650
Fax: 418/872-4652
Web: www.promosit.qc.ca/norpaq

THREE HERDS — Koroc, George River and Leaf River — comprise the caribou population of the Ungava Peninsula, that northernmost territory in Quebec. Nonmigratory, the Koroc herd occupies the slender tip of Quebec between Ungava Bay and the Torngat Mountains on the Labrador border. To the south, below the 58th parallel, is the George River Herd, which every fall moves west from highlands near the provincial boundary, streaming toward the interior. The third, the Leaf River, summers on the land between Ungava and James bays, moving southeast with cold weather toward the lower interior.

Norpaq operates a score or more of camps throughout the region frequented by the George River Herd. Norpaq is headquartered in a long, low, red-roofed log lodge beneath the pines overlooking the George River, 120 miles or so northeast of Schefferville. Norpaq also hunts a large section of the Whale River drainage and a broad area around Lac Châteauguay, 120 miles west of Schefferville. Hunters have the option of selecting a variety of packages ranging from System 3, which includes one guide per two hunters, food and a camp cook to System 1, a less expensive do-it-yourself option where you and five of your buddies sling your own hash and fathom the ageless mystery of migrating caribou with the aid of a sole camp manager. You'll stay in canvas tents stretched tightly over frames and floored with wood. Bring your own sleeping bag and booze, and food too, if you have chosen System 1.

In the midst of the two-month caribou season is a one-week season for black bear. If you're of a mind, you can also chase ptarmigan, but weight restrictions make packing along a shotgun somewhat questionable. A flyfishing pack rod or spin rod doesn't weigh much, though, and Arctic char, brook trout and lakers are there to be had.

You'll hunt on foot, occasionally using canoes and boats, over open tundra. The terrain is not steep. It's open and windswept, but when the wind dies, be prepared for a mosquito or two. Shots are generally at least 100 yards and more likely 200. Good rifles include the 7mm mags and the big .30s. Binoculars are a must, as are Sorell or Maine guide-style boots with rubber bottoms, felt liners and waterproofed leather uppers. Odds are you won't walk distances more than a mile or so. Gore-Tex or other breathable raingear is essential, as is Polar Fleece sweaters and gloves.

O'Sullivan Lake Lodge

M a n i w a k i ,   Q u e b e c

*Prime pelts from a springtime boar,
and maybe a tackle busting pike on the side.*

VITAL STATISTICS:

Game/Arm/Seasons:
MOOSE:
Bow: Early through mid-Sept.
Centerfire, muzzleloader: Mid-Sept.
through mid-Oct.
BEAR:
Bow, centerfire, muzzleloader: Mid-May through June
Rates:
From $750 (Canadian)/7 days
(self-catered)
Accommodations:
CABINS
MAXIMUM NUMBER OF HUNTERS: 40
Meals: Home cooking
Conference Groups: No
Guides:
Included or not depending on package
Gratuity: $100
Preferred Payment:
Cash
Other Activities:
Bird hunting, fishing
Getting There:
Fly to Ste.-Anne-du-lac and take the bush shuttle.

Contact:
Stanley Gagnon
O'Sullivan Lake Lodge,
50 Aqueduc
Maniwaki, Quebec
J9E 3A2, Canada
819/449-3109
Fax: 819/449-7394
e-mail: gagnon@travel.net.com
Web: www.travel-net.com/~gagnon

SURROUNDED BY THICK FORESTS of fir and pine, O'Sullivan is one of a dozen lakes in the 96 square miles leased by Russell and Stanley Gagnon who manage the lodge located near La Verendryne Provincial Reserve. During the summer, the lodge caters to anglers and is earning a reputation for pike of 30 pounds and more. You'll also find walleye and a few brook trout, and the fishing season overlaps with bear season in the spring and moose hunting in fall.

In eastern Canada, bear hunting follows a formula. Depending on the severity of winter, bears leave their dens in late April or early May. Pelts are in prime condition, with no rub spots, and little hair loss. Weights, though, are down; a black bear can weigh 25 to 30 percent more in the fall than in the spring. During the first few days after leaving the den, a bear will eat fresh grasses to purge its system. Then it becomes ravenous and anything from grubs to ground squirrels is fair game. That's the best time to hunt bear over bait. The Gagnon's typically run 30 to 40 baits, placed in areas where scat and tracks show high activity. Stands are close enough, within 35 yards or so, to allow archers a sure shot. Others are better suited to rifle hunters. Often, more than one bear will visit a bait. Normally, the later the hour, the larger the bear.

O'Sullivan offers three packages for bear hunters. Top of the line is a week in the modern cabins with all meals, guide, skinning and freezing of hide and meat, and a boat and motor. Additional guide service is available if needed. You can customize your package by limiting the number of days, foregoing boat and motor, and doing your own cooking.

The same options exist for fall moose hunting. You and your partner (remember, it takes two licenses to hunt a moose in this region) will share a guide and boat to those little boggy ponds or shallows on the lakes where moose, the largest of North America's deer family, feed. Getting out early is as important as hunting in the gathering dusk. At midday, after your box lunch, you may stretch out in a sunny, soft, mossy spot and snooze. Spotting from the canoe or boat, still-hunting along logging roads or calling during the rut are the most effective tactics. The moose population in this area is generally on the upswing. Archers have the first crack when the season opens in early September. Two weeks later, the centerfire and muzzleloading crowd takes over. Here it's legal to take one bull or one calf, but no cows.

Pavillon Richer

M a n i w a k i ,   Q u e b e c

More than 100 square miles of exclusive ground for moose and bear.

VITAL STATISTICS:

Game/Arm/Seasons:
MOOSE:
Bow, muzzleloader, centerfire:
Mid-Sept. through mid-Oct.
BEAR:
Bow, muzzleloader, centerfire:
Mid-May through June
Rates:
From $898 (Canadian)/7 days
(European Plan)
Accommodations:
FRAME, LAKESIDE CABINS
MAXIMUM NUMBER OF HUNTERS: 46
Meals:
Hearty fare or self-catered depending
on the plan you choose
Conference Groups: No
Guides: $125 (Canadian)
Gratuity: Hunter's discretion
Preferred Payment:
Cash, traveler's check
Other Activities:
Bird hunting, bird watching, boating,
fishing, waterfowling, wildlife
photography
Getting There:
Fly to Maniwaki Airport and rent a
car.

Contact:
Raymond Richer
Pavillon Richer
110 Cavanaugh
Maniwaki, Quebec
J9E 2P8, Canada
819/449-1613
e-mail: pavillon.richer@atreide.net
Web: ppp.atreide.net/pavillon.rich-
er/defaulta.htm

THE TRICK TO FINDING good bear and moose hunting in Quebec is to locate an outfitter who has exclusive rights to a sizable chunk of real estate. Private territory is important: an outfitter, working with Provincial officials can manage game populations to ensure that guests will have a reasonable chance to harvest a quality animal. So it is with Pavillon Richer, about 250 miles northwest of Montreal on the edge of Lake Echouani near La Vérendrye Provincial Réserve. Raymond Richer and his wife Gisèle run a lodge with 16 closeby cabins and 30 others scattered through their 135 square miles of prime hunting country.

With more than 70 active baits, there's a reasonable chance that you'll take a bear here. Typically, bears average 185 pounds, though many are larger and at least one, a massive old boar scoring 21 points-plus, qualified for Pope and Young, Boone and Crockett, and Safari Club International records. It was taken at 45 yards with a single arrow. The season in these parts runs from mid-May through the end of June. Generally, hunters arrive in camp the day before their week begins and spend the afternoon and evening scouting the baits with one of Richer's guides. Some stands are better suited for archers, others for rifle hunters and a few are screened and insect-proof. Think of it. Bear hunting without blackflies. Three out of four hunters bag bears and, screened blinds not withstanding, everyone gets bug bitten.

On Richer's acreage are 42 lakes of which Echouani is the largest. Boggy flowages that feed and drain the lakes are prime habitat for moose that typically carry 35- to 38-inch racks. During the rut, which runs from mid-September to early October, grunting into a birch-bark megaphone moose call is quite effective. A bull moose, ever unpredictable and especially so when on the make, is liable to crash right into your stand, allowing time for little more than a hasty shot. Because calling is an art which most moose hunters haven't mastered, more of these huge creatures are taken by still-hunting along miles and miles of logging roads or by motor boating quietly along lake shores. About 35 percent of Richer's clients harvest moose, an average that is better than it sounds. In this area only one moose is allowed for every two licenses.

Pavillon Richer offers hunters a pair of options: stay in a cabin near the main lodge and eat in the warmly paneled dining room overlooking the lake, or transport and prepare your own chow at one of the cabins located on other nearby lakes. Guides are available, but not included.

Poirier Fish and Game Territory Inc.

M a n i w a k i ,   Q u e b e c

Amid scores of lakes are riparian zones so loved by moose.

VITAL STATISTICS:

Game/Arm/Seasons:
BEAR:
Bow, centerfire, muzzleloader:
Mid-May through June
MOOSE:
Bow, centerfire, muzzleloader:
Mid-Sept. through mid-Oct.
Rates:
BEAR from $275 (Canadian)/3 days
MOOSE from $1350 (Canadian)/
7 days
Accommodations:
CABINS
NUMBER OF ROOMS: 28
MAXIMUM NUMBER OF HUNTERS:
BEAR 15
MOOSE 24
Meals: Self-catered
Conference Groups: No
Guides: Extra
Gratuity: Hunter's discretion
Preferred Payment:
Cash, check
Other Activities:
Bird hunting, bird watching, fishing,
swimming, wildlife photography
Getting There:
Fly to Ottawa, rent a car and drive to
the lodge.

Contact:
Frank Poirier
Poirier Fish and Game
Territory Inc.
Box 294
Maniwaki, Quebec
J9E 3C9, Canada
819/449-3032
Fax: 819/449-3453

BIG GAME IN ZONE 12 of central Quebec means bear in the spring and moose in the fall, and this outfitter leases exclusive hunting rights to about 125 square miles of prime country centered on Lac Delaney, 125 miles northwest of Ottawa. You'll find more than 100 named lakes, a bunch without monikers and a maze of interconnecting streams. Low gravel hills, some of which are drumlins, eskers and moraines left by wasting glaciers, provide relief. Spruce and firs predominate, though clear-cut areas are regenerating deciduous trees and new green growth.

Spring bear means hunting over active baits, typically placed in barrels and screened by stands of two or three thin trees. Hunters using their own tree stands or ground blinds position themselves where they can have a clear view of the bait and an area roughly 25 yards on either side. Archers will find cover within 25 yards of baits; rifle hunters need not be so close. On average, shots are little more than 50 yards. Any centerfire rifle of 7mm or larger bore wearing a low-power scope will do fine. Bears range from 150 pounds to 500 pounds, and one out of every four hunters is successful.

The average is better on moose, hunted from mid-September to mid-October. In zones where moose hunting is authorized, the bag limit is one moose per two hunters. That makes it a team effort. At Poirier Fish and Game, groups of two or more are allocated an area of one square mile or more. The best terrain is swamp bordered by heavy timber. Calling works best. And while a moose may not answer, the odds are that he'll come to investigate. Hunters will also scout the edges of small lakes and still-hunt logging roads through the forest. Normally, guides are not used at this camp, though for an additional $500 to $700 (Canadian) one can employ a guide who will have spent three or four days scouting an area before you arrive. About half of the groups that come here to hunt moose go home with enough meet to fill their freezers and those of all their relatives.

Ross wanted a bear for the table and not necessarily for the wall. Stephan, the friendly bearmeister of Pourvoirie Barrage Gouin in Quebec, set the author up over bait that this four-year-old bruin had been frequenting. One well-placed shot resulted in roasts and filets that rival fine pork or beef on the table.

Sprawling on a gravel bluff above the river, André Godin's Miramichi Inn near Red Bank is known for fine spring bear hunting in New Brunswick's big woods. In fall, you'll find grouse and woodcock hunting, plus late runs of Atlantic salmon.

Pourvoirie Barrage Gouin

St. Marc des Carrieres, Quebec

What's surf and turf Quebec style?
Walleye and bear.

VITAL STATISTICS:

Game/Arm/Seasons:
BEAR:
Bow, centerfire, muzzleloader: Mid-May through June
Rates:
From $995 (Canadian)/5 days
Accommodations:
FRAME CABINS, LODGE
NUMBER OF ROOMS: 25
MAXIMUM NUMBER OF HUNTERS: 6
Meals: Canadian/American with a continental flair
Conference Groups: Yes
Guides: Included
Gratuity: Hunter's discretion
Preferred Payment:
Cash, check, credit card
Other Activities:
Bird watching, boating, canoeing/rafting, fishing, swimming, wildlife photography
Getting There:
Drive via Montreal or fly in via a bush charter service at an additional charge.

Contact:
Francois Beaudoin
Pourvoirie Barrage Gouin
CP 610
St. Marc des Carrieres,
Quebec G0A 4B0, Canada
819/666-2332
off-season:
418/268-8900
Fax: 418/268-8210
e-mail: pourvoirie@barrage-gouin.qc.ca
Web: www.barragegouin.qc.ca

RÉSERVOIR GOUIN, about 200 miles due north of Montreal, is the third-largest lake in Quebec. On the left abutment of the dam sits Ghislain Beaudoin's lodge, Pourvoirie Barrage Gouin. Ten red and white cabins, each with a full kitchen and private bath are scattered around the main lodge with its five bedrooms, restaurant and store. Facing the lake, the lodge is primarily known for its excursions for walleyes; Gouin is one of the most prolific walleye fisheries in the world.

Surrounding the reservoir is a vast spruce forest. If you ride Max Air or another bush plane outfit up from Montreal, you'll see that the forest is checkered with clearcuts and parcels in various stages of regrowth. Timber companies are farming trees up here as, in similar manner, Ghislain and his family are farming bears. The difference is that timber companies plant seedlings, and Ghislain relies on nature to restock the 40-square-mile area he hunts. Each season he harvests 15 or so bruins from a population that exceeds 100 mature adults. Each year he matches the number of bear hunters with what he believes the bear population can sustain, and in that manner the bear population remains in balance. Bears leave their dens in April or early May, purge their systems and begin to feed. At this time of the year, coats are thick and silky, and the bears are lean. Over the summer they'll up their body weight by 25 to 30 percent. Baits consisting of barrels of stale pastries are set out in locations where scat and tracks indicate bear traffic. Hunters use tree stands or hastily constructed ground blinds. Some stands are within 35 yards, close enough for archers. Others range between 75 and 100 yards, depending on the vagaries of terrain. In late afternoon, Ghislain's head guide ferries hunters to within a mile or so of their stands. After walking in, oh so quietly, hunters sit, arrange headnets so blackflies and no-see-ums can't get in, and wait. Smaller bears, whose meat is the most tender, lean, and flavorful, generally reach the bait first. Larger, older bears arrive at dark. Whether you shoot a bear is up to you. If you do, the outfitter's staff will skin and prepare the hide and rough butcher and freeze the meat.

Bear hunting over bait is strictly an activity for spring afternoons. That leaves mornings free for walleyes or brook trout, found in isolated mountain ponds. And after dark, after a meal of crisp green salad and walleye cheeks and a white burgundy or Bordeaux, take your rod and cast for walleyes in the pool below the dam. It is the perfect way to end an evening.

[C A N A D A   E A S T]

SEPAQ

A n t i c o s t i ,   Q u e b e c

More than 120,000 whitetails inhabit this island in the mouth of the St. Lawrence.

VITAL STATISTICS:

Game/Arm/Seasons:
WHITE-TAILED DEER:
Bow, centerfire, muzzleloader: Sept. through Nov.

Rates:
$1,395/4 days

Accommodations:
FARMHOUSES OR LOG LODGES
NUMBER OF ROOMS: 4 TO 6 PER LODGE
MAXIMUM NUMBER OF HUNTERS: 8 TO 12 PER LODGE

Meals: Exquisite cuisine

Conference Groups: Yes

Guides: Included

Gratuity: Hunter's discretion

Preferred Payment:
Cash, check, credit cards

Other Activities:
None during hunting season, but salmon fishing in summer

Getting There:
Fly to Port Menier and you'll be met.

Contact:
Gilles Dumaresq
SEPAQ-Anticosti
801 Chemin St. Louis
Bureau 125
Quebec, Quebec
G1S 1C1, Canada
800/463-0863
Fax: 418/682-9944

WHEN JACQUES CARTIER sailed into the Bay of St. Lawrence, he had no idea that the big island at the head of the bay was prime whitetail habitat. How could he have known? He named it Assomption, but a decade later it was referred to as Isle d' Anticosti, a name apparently taken from naticosti, a native peoples' word for "where bears are hunted." Were it not for chocolatier Henri Menier, who leased the 3,066-square-mile island to develop its timber resources, we might think of it as a place of bears instead of that peerless reserve of massive whitetails. That the deer survived, let alone thrived, is one of those weird and happy coincidences of nature. Menier had no idea that the island lacks nut-bearing trees when he brought in his whitetails. But they, ever adaptable, took to lichens and protein-rich seaweed and went forth and multiplied.

Today their population is estimated to be in excess of 120,000. Two deer, either bucks or does can be harvested, and the hard part is holding out for a buck of 8 points or more. Terrain is not at all difficult. The island is essentially a highland, part of the Côte-Nord region, broken here and there by rivers. Coniferous trees, firs, spruce and larch, dominate. But here and there are stands of birch and poplar and bogs that turn lush with fresh grasses in early summer.

SEPAQ, a crown corporation, operates a 1,700-square-mile (more than half the size of the island) reserve where access is limited to guests who stay in one of the five lodges or 20 housekeeping cabins. On average, each guest during the season from September through November has eight-square miles to hunt. One guide serves four hunters, and included is a 4WD, crew-cab pickup, an ATV and horses, if you're so inclined. More experienced hunters may seek little more than general direction from the guide, while first-timers will receive personal attention. A typical hunt spans four days. You'll spend the first two glassing and passing up deer that you'd ordinarily shoot back home. During the last two days, the heat's on. Will you find that 8-point-plus wall-hanger? All depends (on the weather as much as anything else). Be prepared for cold, damp and snow anytime from October on. Guests in the lodges live well. Meals are definitely first class, with shrimp and oysters followed by smoked salmon and wines of good vintage to match. And all of this costs much less than one would think. Though bigger deer are being taken in Manitoba, it's no wonder that this is a popular spot booked as much as two years in advance.

Silak Adventures

S u t t o n ,   Q u e b e c

The Inuit know the ways of migrating caribou.

VITAL STATISTICS:

Game/Arm/Seasons:
CARIBOU
Bow, Muzzleloader, Centerfire:
Late Aug.-Sept.
Rates:
$3,400/6 days
Accommodations:
PLATFORM TENTS
MAXIMUM NUMBER OF HUNTERS: 9
Meals:
Native char, steaks, pasta, veggies
Conference Groups: Yes
Guides: Included
Gratuity: Hunter's discretion
Preferred Payment:
Cash, check
Other Activities:
Bird hunting, fishing, wildlife
photography
Getting There:
Fly to Montreal, rent a car and drive
to the camp.

Contact:
Jacques Dery
Silak Adventures
1108 Jordan
Sutton, Quebec
JOE 2KO, Canada
800/461-5444 or
514/538-5244
Fax: 514/538-5244

GRAY OVERCAST GLOWS AS THE DAY brightens and the low hills across Lake Ballantyne from the camp of canvas wall tents takes on its own definition in drab olives and rusts. The wind stirs the lake into a sheen like antimony floating in a pot of molten bullet metal. Breakfast and coffee is down, riding comfortably above your belt.

Your Inuit guide knows where they are going, these caribou from the Leaf River Herd. Heading southeast, they'll mingle with the fringe of the George River Herd moving west from the barren highlands along the Labrador border. He grounds the freighter canoe and you clamor ashore, grateful for your high, felt-lined rubber boots. Daypack slung over your right shoulder, and your rifle, muzzle down, over your left shoulder for a quick shot, swings under your arm comfortably as you start up the low hill. Your binoculars bounce on your chest.

The terrain isn't high or steep in this region due west of Kuujjuaq. The three-mile walk from the shore to a little rise overlooking a trail heaved and softened by permafrost is relatively easy. "They'll come," says your guide. "Sit. Here, sit." And you do. You can't outwalk a caribou, but it's possible to outflank them–if the guide is good. Yours seems to be. Already three nice bulls are in camp. Each of you can harvest two caribou. For you one, one with a record spread, will do the job.

For this trip you've brought your 7mm Remington Magnum. You debated: the .30-06 would have been ample, but for the trophy, a longer shot might be necessary and distances here in this country of no landmarks are deceiving. John Adams, who with Jacques Dery founded Silak a decade ago, had suggested the flatter shooting cartridge. He got no argument from you. Nor did you kick much when he suggested the base camp with its wooden cabins rather than one of his half-dozen outpost camps. Cost was about $700 more per week but worth it. The guide makes all the difference, though maybe next year you'll hunt on your own from one of the tent camps. Your mind is thinking of next year, when you catch the rhythmic sway of antlers working along the stream at the base of the next hill. You glass. The third bull looks really good. Sliding into sitting position, you place the crosshairs just aft of the shoulder. You don't even hear the report of the rifle, the way you never do with a well-placed shot. The bull is down, and you're tempted to light that Cuban you bought in Montreal. Later. The aroma might foul your partner's chances.

Tamarac Air Service Ltd.

C l o v a ,   Q u e b e c

Ride the rails to the floatplane base, then fly in for moose and bear.

VITAL STATISTICS:

Game/Arm/Seasons:
BEAR:
Bow, centerfire, muzzleloader:
Mid-May through June
MOOSE:
Bow: Early through late Sept.
Centerfire, muzzleloader: Late Sept.
through mid-Oct.
Rates:
MOOSE from $450/7 days (4-person minimum)
BEAR from $800/7 days (no minimum)
Accommodations:
LOG CABINS
MAXIMUM NUMBER OF HUNTERS: 4 PER CABIN
Meals: Self-catered
Conference Groups: No
Guides: Included
Gratuity: Hunter's discretion
Preferred Payment:
Cash, MasterCard, Visa, check
Other Activities:
Fishing
Getting There:
Fly to Ottawa and rent a car, or take the train from Montreal.

Contact:
Jean Blanchard
Tamarac Air Service Ltd.
Poste Resante
Clova, Quebec
G0X 3M0, Canada
819/662-3300;
off-season:
3955 Laurier
St. Hyacinthe, Quebec
J2S-3T8, Canada
514/223-1298
Fax: 514/773-9795
e-mail: tamarac@hy.cgocable.ca
Web: www.tamarac.qc.ca

YOU CAN TAKE THE TRAIN, you can take a plane or you can drive. All roads lead to Clova, a whistle-stop on the Canadian Northern's cross-country line where 0-752, one of Quebec's rural gravel roads, terminates after leaving Réserve Faunique La Vérendrye, a long 125 miles to the south. There you'll find Jean Blanchard's seaplane base for Tamarac Air. His main business is ferrying folks to guest cabins on Reservoir Gouin and Lac Hèbert, a pair of world-class walleye fisheries. He'll also swing down to Montreal or Ottawa to pick up sports, though hunters may find baggage restrictions somewhat limiting: 300 pounds total, including the hunter. (They get lots of tall, thin Americans, Jean's wife laughs.)

Hunters fly up to this neck of the woods for bear in the spring and moose in fall. Expressly for hunters, though anglers do use them in the summer, Jean operates four to six camps in Panama, 10 miles northwest of Clova. Bear hunting, from 60 stands overlooking active baits, kicks off in the mid-May and continues through June. Aside from a guide who shows you baits that suit your choice of firearm and who maintains the baits, you're pretty much on your own. Cabins hold from two to eight hunters, one of whom ought to be fairly good with a skillet and another with the SOS pad. The menu, of course, is as infinite as your imagination and will to haul it in. Terrain is moderate, not steep. Clear-cutting and regenerating forest provide a variety of habitats sprinkled with boggy ponds and tannin-black brooks. Once you take your bear — and three out of four hunters do — one of Jean's staff will skin, rough-butcher and freeze it for your trip home.

The story's similar for moose. You'll hunt from the comfortable camps with indoor toilets in Panama or Gouin, with or without a guide. As is usual in this region, it takes two licenses to harvest a moose. Normally that means you and your buddy. How do you decide who shoots it? Flip a coin. Once bagged, there's enough meat for a small army. Tamarac Air will freeze the meat and prepare the rack for the trip back home. Calling during the rut is the most successful approach, but much can be said for sitting at the edge of the woods watching a brace or two of game trials that lead to a pond. The cabins are accessible by truck as well as aircraft.

Umiujaq Outfitters

Radisson, Quebec

Caribou migrations are moving west, and that's where you'll find Greg Bonecutter.

VITAL STATISTICS:

Game/Arm/Seasons:
CARIBOU:
Bow, centerfire, muzzleloader: Mid-Aug. through late Sept.
Rates:
From $2,195/5 days
Accommodations:
PLATFORM TENTS WITH RIGID ROOFS
MAXIMUM NUMBER OF HUNTERS: 12
Meals:
Self-catered except at Deception Bay
Conference Groups: No
Guides: None
Gratuity: $50
Preferred Payment:
Cash, check
Other Activities:
Fishing, snowmobiling
Getting There:
Fly to LaGrande Airport, or drive to Radisson, Quebec.

Contact:
Greg Bonecutter, Sr.
Umiujaq Outfitters
Drawer 36
Letart, WV 25253
304/895-3297
e-mail: caribou@citynet.net
Web: www.cariboucountry.com

IF YOU'RE LOOKING FOR a quality caribou hunt but are leery of all the folks hunting out of Schefferville and points north, you might want to check out Umiujaq Outfitters. Greg Bonecutter, a West Virginian with two decades of north country guiding experience, has opened three camps about 100 miles east of James Bay and 300 miles north of Radisson. Caribou in these parts are elements of the Leaf River Herd and they grow to reasonably good size. A typical bull will score between 350 and 450 Boone & Crockett points. And in 1997, 35 of the 115 bulls harvested at his Lac Minto Island camp toted green-scored racks that qualified for Pope and Young. Archery is something of a specialty here, but firearms hunters are accommodated with equal ease. You'll find 12 hunters in each camp, but archers and rifle guys are usually on speaking terms, because here they seldom hunt the same areas.

Lac Minto is the headwater for Rivière aux Feuilles, the Leaf River. Overlooking the lake is a 15x28-foot bunkhouse that sleeps 12 and a nearby 16x20-foot kitchen and dining lodge. The next watershed south is drained by Rivière Nastapoca, where a pair of bunkhouses sleeps six hunters each. This camp is served by a full kitchen and dining lodge, and a generator provides light and power for charging VCR batteries. The third camp, on Deception Bay of Lac Minto, is similar to the camp on Nastapoca. Operations at the three camps are very similar except that at Lac Minto food and a cook are provided.

The camps are staffed by a pair of caretakers—campmen as Greg calls them—but otherwise you'll find no guides. And when it comes to caping, salting and preparing your rack for the trip out, you'll receive lots of good advice, but the work is up to you. For some hunters, that may seem a disadvantage, so used are well-heeled sports to having the work done. But honoring the game includes preparing the trophy and packing the meat for the long trip home.

While you can fly commercially to Radisson, where the base camp is located, the community is also served by a paved two-lane highway. Most clients drive there, meet Greg and then fly to the camps in Cessna turbo-prop Caravans. Along with caribou, there are brook trout and lakers. So bring a rod and have a ball!

[C A N A D A   E A S T]

Ungava Adventures

P o i n t e   C l a i r e ,   Q u e b e c

*Where the hunter who chills out
takes the best caribou.*

VITAL STATISTICS:

Game/Arm/Seasons:
CARIBOU:
Bow, centerfire, muzzleloader:
Aug. through Sept.
BLACK BEAR:
Bow, centerfire, muzzleloader:
Late Aug. through Sept.
Rates:
From $3,250/5 days (semi-guided)
Accommodations:
PERMANENT AND TENT CAMPS
MAXIMUM NUMBER OF HUNTERS: 6 TO 8
Meals: Steaks, fish
Conference Groups: Yes
Guides: Depends on package
Gratuity: 5% of trip cost
Preferred Payment:
Cash, check
Other Activities:
Fishing
Getting There:
Fly to Montreal and catch the flight to
Kuujjuaq included in your package.

Contact:
**Sammy Cantafio
Ungava Adventures
46 St. Anne St., Suite 3A
Pointe Claire, Quebec
H9S 4P8, Canada
514/694-4424**

AGENTS:
**Cabela's Outdoor Adventures
308/254-3658
Jim McCarthy Adventures
717/652-4374
Kidder Safaris Co.
616/791-1400**

SLOWING DOWN IS HARD. You know just how it is. Take this hunt. You've been hustling to get all your gear together, the rifle sighted in, travel plans organized and then changed (always happens right after you book the flights). Miracle of miracles, your baggage was not overweight, you cleared customs and you made the last connecting flight to Kuujjuaq. So did your luggage. You're on a roll! You hooked up with Sammy Cantafio, who runs Ungava Adventures, and the flight to the camp at Weymouth Inlet above the Koroc River was a breeze. Fueled by too much coffee and a brace of killer pastries, you're raring to go. The guide puts you on the flank of a low, almost brushless hill, and below you is a thin creek and a path where caribou pass, screened by scrubby willows. You've been sitting there, bug-eyed with excitement, and here comes a string of caribou, just like the guide said they would. Wow! Look at the third one from the left. Good points on the palmated tops. Shovels look big. He's a huge bull, bigger than any whitetail you've ever seen. So you raise your rifle and finger the trigger. But remember, patience in hunting, as in love, is a virtue. You don't have to shoot the first best bull to come over the rise. Let him pass. Chill out. Eat an apple. Hey, you're hunting, not gutting out the daily grind.

Hunting with Cantafio, you'll see lots of good bulls and it's not a bad rule of thumb to spend the first and second days of your five-day hunt checking out the countryside and scoping the bulls. He operates three base camps: Weymouth Inlet for the Koroc (nonmigratory) Herd; Helen's Falls for the George River Herd; and Wolf Lake Camp for the Leaf River herd. In addition, he runs a number of mobile camps southwest of Kuujjuaq, where caribou from the Leaf and George River herds mingle late in the season. Base camps feature hard-sided cabins; the mobile camps use platform tents. Clients in the permanent camps benefit from one guide for every two hunters. Hunts from the mobile camps are semi-guided. And with the mobile hunts, you can save $300 by doing your own cooking.

The limit is two caribou per hunter plus bear, ptarmigan and fish (brook trout, Arctic char and lake trout). One of the oldest and most respected outfitters in the Ungava region, Cantafio began guiding hunters in 1954. Along with his operations in Ungava, he offers spring bear hunts on Quebec's north shore and moose in Newfoundland.

Whale River Lodge

Where a degree of latitude makes all the difference.

VITAL STATISTICS:

Game/Arm/Seasons:
CARIBOU:
Bow, centerfire, muzzleloader: Aug. through Sept.
BLACK BEAR:
Bow, centerfire, muzzleloader: Late Aug. through Sept.
Rates:
From $3,400/7 days
Accommodations:
RUSTIC CABINS
NUMBER OF ROOMS: 2/6-PERSON CABINS PER CAMP
MAXIMUM NUMBER OF HUNTERS: 12
Meals:
Solid and satisfying with fresh breads and pastries
Conference Groups: No
Guides: Included
Gratuity: Hunter's discretion
Preferred Payment:
Cash, MasterCard, Visa, check
Other Activities:
Bird hunting, fishing, waterfowling
Getting There:
Fly to Schefferville and catch the floatplane at Squaw Lake.

Contact:
Alain Tardif
Whale River Lodge
Box 370
St. Henri, Quebec
GOR 3E0, Canada
1-800-463-4868
Fax: 418/882-0140
e-mail: cariboui@globetrotter.net

ALAIN TARDIF'S CARIBOU operations straddle the 57th parallel as it swings across northern Quebec in the area known as Ungava. With camps near Lac Ministibi on the Labrador border, Rivière à la Baleine (Whale), a major tributary of Rivière aux Mélèzes (Larch) and Rivière aux Feuilles (Leaf), Alain's reach spreads like four fingers across some of the very best caribou hunting in North America.

Pick your site based on the kind of hunting you want. Frontier Camp, on the border, sits on a high, clear, sandy spit overlooking the lake. You'll climb into a deep freighter canoe each morning, and your guide runs you and your partner along the bank to a trail that leads to a good stand from which to glass passing caribou. You may walk a little, but not much. Or you may prowl the shore, looking for caribou crossing shallow streams that flow into the lake. Then you'll land and plan your stalk. Camps on the Whale and the tributary to the Larch are similar, but the water is smaller and you're more apt to run upriver, beach the canoe, hike into the barren hills to sit and spot, and then plan your approach to a band of migrating caribou. Hunting on the Leaf is largely a matter of riding 30 to 40 miles up- or downriver to crossings in active use. The Leaf River Herd is gaining a reputation for producing the trophy animals with multi-pointed, palmated tops and heavy bez tines and shovels. You'll pay a premium to hunt on the Leaf, but it's worth it. Alan keeps tabs on caribou migration via radio reports from his camps and by scouting from the air. If trophy animals aren't migrating past your camp, he'll move you to one where bulls are more plentiful.

Accommodations are much better than average at these camps. Beds in heated cabins for six are firm, and there's always a convenient wash house with hot showers and flush toilets. In the dining lodge you'll be served steaks, chicken and hearty caribou stew. Hunts include transportation from Montreal, overnight in Schefferville, flights in and out of camp, meat preparation and packaging, guiding (four hunters per guide is the norm, two-on-one and one-on-one service is available), transport of meat and one split set of antlers and your caribou permit. If you're hunting prior to September 7, pick up a fishing license. And if your hunt begins after August 25, you may want to buy a bear tag as well. One never knows what's going to walk out of the brush.

CANADA WEST

ALBERTA, BRITISH COLUMBIA, NORTHWEST TERRITORIES, SASKATCHEWAN, YUKON TERRITORY

THE WESTERN provinces of Canada have it all. Jagged, glacier-capped mountains born as volcanoes line the coast of British Columbia. To the east, along the border with Alberta, soar the Canadian Rockies, thrust skyward by colliding continental plates. In between are deep green valleys where hunters find elk, moose, mountain lion and black and grizzly bear. As elevation increases and timber thins, the country is the domain first of mule deer, then of sheep and mountain goats. Only hunters hardy enough to climb in the thin air of such high elevations will get a chance at these monarchs. Whitetails are found in the lower valleys and across the mountains, on the high prairies of Saskatchewan, where the world-record typical whitetail, scoring 213 5/8, was taken by Milo Hanson near Biggar in November 1993.

Lodges:

ALBERTA
1 ANDREW LAKE LODGE AND CAMPS
2 EAGLE RIVER OUTFITTING
3 SHEEP CREEK LODGE

BRITISH COLUMBIA
4 BEAVERFOOT LODGE
5 CHILCOTIN HUNTING ADVENTURES
6 INDIAN RIVER RANCH GUIDES & OUTFITTERS LTD.
7 MACKENZIE TRAIL LODGE
8 SCOOP LAKE OUTFITTERS LTD.
9 SILENT MOUNTAIN OUTFITTERS INC.

NORTHWEST TERRITORIES
10 GANA RIVER OUTFITTERS

SASKATCHEWAN
11 BAIT-MASTERS HUNTING CAMPS GREEN LAKE, SASKATCHEWAN
12 GLEN HILL'S TROPHY EXPEDITIONS
13 MAKWA RIVER OUTFITTERS

YUKON
14 DICKSON OUTFITTERS LTD.
15 TROPHY STONE SAFARIS LTD.

Resources:

DEPARTMENT OF ENVIRONMENTAL PROTECTION
Petroleum Plaza, South Tower
9915 108 St.
Edmonton, AB T5K 2G8 Canada
780/944-0313
Web: www.gov.ab.ca/env/

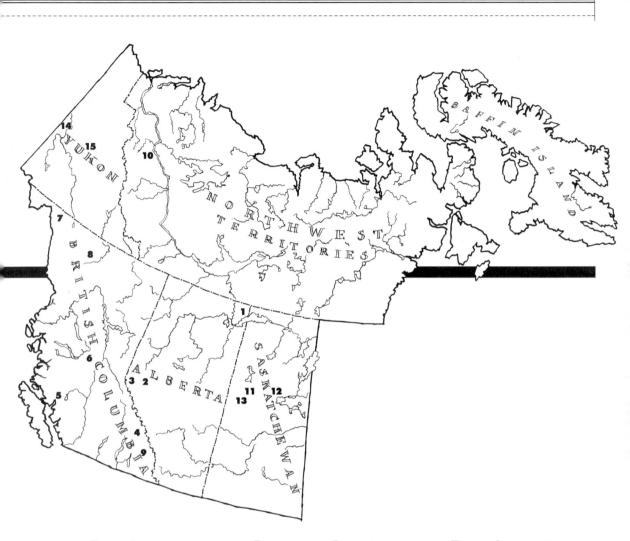

Travel Alberta
300—10155 102nd St.
Edmonton AB T5J 4G8 Canada
800/661-8888
www.explorealberta.com

Ministry of Environment
Wildlife Branch
PO Box 9374
Station Provincial Gov't.
Victoria, BC V8W 9M4, Canada
250/387-9731
Web: www.env.gov.bc.ca
or
Tourism British Columbia
865 W. Hornby St.
Vancouver BC V6Z 2G3 Canada
604/660-2861 or 800/663-6000
Web: www.travel.bc.ca

Department of Resources
Wildlife and Economic
Development, Government of the
Northwest Territories
Box 2668, Yellowknife
Northwest Territories
X1A 3P9, Canada
web: www.rwed.gov.nt.ca
867/873-7184
or
NWT Arctic Tourism,
PO Box 610, Yellowknife NT
X1A 2N5; 800/661-0788
Web: www.nwttravel.nt.ca

Saskatchewan Environment
and Resource Management
524-3211 Albert St.
Regina, SK S4S 5W6, Canada
306/787-2931
Web: www.gov.sk.ca/govt/environ/

Tourism Saskatchewan
500-1900 Albert St.
Regina SK S4P 4L9 Canada
www.sasktourism.com

Department of
Renewable Resources
Fish & Wildlife Branch
Box 2703
Whitehorse, Yukon Territory
Y1A 2C6, Canada
867/667-5715
Web: www.gov.yk.ca/
or
Tourism Yukon
Box 2703, Whitehorse
Yukon Territory Y1A 2C6, Canada
867/667-5340
www.touryukon.com

[C A N A D A   W E S T]

Andrew Lake Lodge and Camps

E d m o n t o n ,   A l b e r t a

Where moose racks go 50-inches-plus,
this place is worth the trip.

VITAL STATISTICS:

Game/Arm/Seasons:
BLACK BEAR:
Bow, centerfire, muzzleloader: May through June
MOOSE:
Bow, centerfire, muzzleloader: Late Sept. through early Oct.
WHITETAIL and MULE DEER:
Centerfire: Nov.
Rates:
BEAR from $2,750/7 days
DEER from $3,250/6 days
MOOSE from $4,250/7 days
Accommodations:
CABINS, TENTS OR MOTELS
MAXIMUM NUMBER OF HUNTERS: 6
Meals: Solid Canadian cooking
Conference Groups: Yes
Guides: Included
Gratuity: 10 to 20%
Preferred Payment:
Cash, MasterCard, Visa, check
Other Activities:
Bird watching, boating, canoeing/rafting, fishing, wildlife photography
Getting There:
Fly to Fort Smith, NWT, and catch the bush plane (no charge).

Contact:
Glen Wettlaufer
Andrew Lake Lodge
and Camps
Box 5846, Station L
Edmonton, Alberta
T6C 4G3, Canada
780/464-7537
Web:
www.cantravel.ab.ca/andrew.html
Off-season:
780/872-5272.

WITH 5,000 SQUARE MILES of largely unhunted real estate tucked away in the northeasternmost corner of Alberta, Andrew Lake Lodge and Camps operates a very successful program for moose and bear hunters. And far to the south, in the foothills of the Rockies, the lodge stages deer hunts for both mulies and whitetails. Just how isolated is Andrew Lake? The closest you can drive is Fort Smith on the Slave River and then you must hop an aircraft to make it the last 60 miles. Reaching Fort Smith by car isn't all that easy either. The one road to town comes south from the Northwest Territories.

Andrew Lake's claim to fame is its trophy northern pike, walleye and lake trout. But around its swampy shore, the low hills between scores of named lakes and hundreds of ponds that aren't and the swift little blackwater rivers that connect them is some of the finest moose and bear habitat in all of Canada. Moose are hunted three ways: spot and stalk (often from a boat but also from ATVs); calling during the rut in October; and from stands overlooking rut pits. A typical bull will carry a 50-inch spread. Success on moose runs about 60 percent.

Bear thrive in this area as well, and hunters are permitted to harvest two each season. Spotting and stalking is the preferred method of bear hunting, but many hunters opt to shoot over baits. Running the Slave and Salt rivers in 16- to 18-foot aluminum V-hulled boats allows hunters to scan spruce and birch along the banks, looking for bears moving through the brush. When you see a bear, you'll run ashore and begin your hunt. Bears average 19 to 20 inches, and most hunters take two. Some will use a bow on the first and a muzzleloader on the second; others will harvest an eating-sized black first, and then spend their remaining time looking for a trophy light-phase bear.

Accommodations for moose or bear hunting may be in the main lodge or in tent camps, depending on where most game activity is occurring.

Deer — 150 score or better — are hunted in the eastern slopes of the Foothills region around Rocky Mountain House and Sundre, about 40 miles west of Red Deer. Largely hilly forest cut with logging roads, the terrain is not steep but it is inaccessible. You'll ride an ATV into prime country — a blend of forests and open parks. This is strictly a rifle hunt. After the hunt, there's a hot shower in your motel room and then dinner in town.

Eagle River Outfitting

Whitecourt, Alberta

Surely this corner of Alberta is a candidate for paradise.

VITAL STATISTICS:

Game/Arm/Seasons:
BLACK BEAR, WHITETAILS, MULE DEER, MOOSE, ELK:
Bow: Late Aug. through mid-Sept.
Centerfire, muzzleloader: Mid-Sept through late Nov.
SPRING BLACK BEAR:
Bow, centerfire, muzzleloader: Apr. through May

Rates:
Fall from $3,000/7 days
Spring from $2,800/6 days

Accommodations:
CABINS OR TENT CAMPS
NUMBER OF ROOMS: 4 WITH PRIVATE BATH
MAXIMUM NUMBER OF HUNTERS: 6

Meals: Hearty mountain fare

Conference Groups: No

Guides: Included

Gratuity: 10% of package

Preferred Payment:
Cash, check, credit card

Other Activities:
Antiquing, bird hunting, bird watching, boating, canoeing/rafting, fishing, golf, skiing, snowmobiling, swimming, waterfowling, wildlife photography

Getting There:
Fly to Edmonton and pay $120 for the round-trip transfer to the lodge.

Contact:
Reg R. Williams
Eagle River Outfitting
Box 164, Station Main
Whitecourt, Alberta
T7S 1N4, Canada
403-778-3251
Fax: 403/778-6601

I T'S CALLED THE "FOOTHILLS," that range of ridges and low hills that climb from the prairies to the tortured peaks of the Canadian Rockies on the border this province shares with British Columbia. The foothills are perhaps Alberta's most diverse habitat. Lodgepole pine and barren rock cap the higher elevations, but lower down the slopes are stands of poplar and willow and spruce and fir that open to grassy parks. Sinuous rivers twist through sometimes boggy bottoms often spotted with lakes and beaver ponds. Elsewhere, rivers flow fast and hard, crashing and cascading through gorges and around house-sized boulders. While a good deal of foothills is given over to pasture, much is owned by the province and managed for timber, oil and gas, and mining.

You'll find moose, elk, whitetails, mule deer, black and grizzly bear, wolves and sheep in the foothills region, and there's no better headquarters for hunting this section than Whitecourt, where the McLeod River joins the Athabasca about 90 miles west-northwest of Edmonton. Whitetail bucks in this area average about 200 pounds and mule deer run a little heavier. A typical elk will score 300 or so and tip the scales at 600 pounds. The big guys in river-swamp terrain are moose. Racks usually span about 44 inches, not bad for critters weighing 1,100 pounds or more. You'll also find black bears and a very few grizzlies in the Foothills. Despite a huge difference in size blacks (Ursus americanus) are occasionally confused with grizzlies (Ursus arctos). Why? Light color-phase black bears are reasonably common. A large black bear will go 400 pounds, about half that of a mature grizzly.

Reg Williams and his Eagle River Outfitting has been working the area around Whitecourt for 20 years. His specialty is moose and elk, but he and his staff do well on whitetail and mule deer. His clients stay in modern guest houses with private baths, kitchens and electricity on the banks of the McLeod River, or in mobile tent camps. It all depends on the quarry. His tent camps tend to be smaller than those down in the U.S. Two- or three-person wall tents are the rule. And in brush camps, guests as well as guides pitch in on cooking, cleaning and firewood chores. Normally only four hunters share a camp, although sometimes there are fewer, and once in a while the number grows to six.

[C A N A D A   W E S T]

Sheep Creek Lodge

G r a n d e   C a c h e ,   A l b e r t a

Deep in the Alberta wilds you'll hunt huge elk, mule deer, moose and bear from this very special lodge.

VITAL STATISTICS:

Game/Arm/Seasons:
ELK:
Bow, centerfire, muzzleloader: Mid-Aug. through Sept.
Rates:
$300 (Canadian) per day
Accommodations:
LOG CABINS
MAXIMUM NUMBER OF HUNTERS: 4
Meals: Family-style
Conference Groups: No
Guides: Included
Gratuity: 10%
Preferred Payment:
Cash, check, money order
Other Activities:
Bird hunting, canoeing/rafting, fishing, riding
Getting There:
Fly to Grande Prairie, rent a car and drive to the lodge.

Contact:
Vic Stapleton
Sheep Creek Lodge
Box 195
Grande Cache, Alberta
T0E 0Y0, Canada
403/827-2829
Fax: 403/827-4838

THE ROAD NORTH from the new old town of Grande Cache is a good road, Vic Stapleton, owner of Sheep Creek Lodge, will tell you. It's made of hard-packed and well-graded gravel. But to reach his lodge, you soon leave the good road, descending in to a creek which you'll follow for a quarter mile before wallowing up the other side. Not to worry, though, Vic's jeep hasn't been stuck badly yet.

Across the creek on a floodplain sits the lodge, a cluster of rustic cabins set in a grove of aspen on a low bench that overlooks the river. Your first thought is that time has somehow warped you back into a small mining town. The windows of each cabin are small-paned glass. Broad front porches invite one to sit. Bells on the horses, ranging free in the woods, jingle as they amble into the clearing at the sound of the vehicle. Inside each cabin are antique washstands, comfortable beds, woodstoves and oil lamps. Curtains are pert and pretty. You light the stove in your cabin and put on a kettle of water, which you'll want when you wash for dinner.

Behind the house rises a mountain. A short hike up through the aspens brings you to a narrow footpath that ascends a steep grassy slope. You climb for half a mile, traversing the hill until you reach a copse of trees. From there you can look out across the valley of Sheep Creek as it flows out of the northern end of the Willmore Wilderness. Behind you the mountain rises at a more gentle rate, then climbs steeply through heavy timber that thins and vanishes well below the summit. This is Stapleton's backyard. It's where he takes a few elk and mule deer hunters — archers mainly, but also rifle hunters. If you can make the first steep climb to the copse of trees, you can climb all over this pocket of beauty and ferret out an elk that may score 350 Boone & Crockett points or better.

Maybe two or three times a season, Stapleton runs very personal hunts for elk, and occasionally mule deer, whitetails, bear, moose or wolf. He's assisted by two guides who've worked with him for nearly a decade and who know the land and respect it as much as he does. You'll hunt on horseback if that's what's required to get you into the area where game is most active. But mostly you'll clamor over the mountains on foot, spotting, listening, stalking, and sucking great draughts of air so clean and pure that it makes your heart sing. And maybe that's why his hunters always return.

Hunting the Chilcotin Mountains of south-central
British Columbia is a lot easier than it was when
Col. Townsend Whelen explored it around the turn of
the last century. Whelen had to make do with a
canvas tent instead of this all-season lodge.

Bait-Masters in Saskatchewan is known as much
for its excellent deer hunting as it is for delicious hearty soups
that have everyone asking for recipes.

Beaverfoot Lodge

G o l d e n ,   B r i t i s h   C o l u m b i a

Hidden behind Yoho National Park, this is the place to be for goats, moose and mulies — and more.

VITAL STATISTICS:

Game/Arm/Seasons:
BLACK BEAR:
Bow: Spring, mid-May through early June; fall, mid-Sept. through mid-Oct. Centerfire, muzzleloader: Mid-Sept. through mid-Oct.
GRIZZLY BEAR:
Centerfire, muzzleloader: Mid-May through early June
COUGAR:
Bow, centerfire, muzzleloader: Mid-Nov. through mid-Jan.
MULE DEER:
Bow, centerfire, muzzleloader: Mid-Sept. through mid-Nov.
ELK:
Bow, centerfire, muzzleloader: Mid-Sept. through mid-Oct.
MOUNTAIN GOAT:
Bow: Sept. through Oct. Centerfire, muzzleloader: Mid-Sept. through early Nov.
SHIRAS MOOSE:
Bow, centerfire, muzzleloader: Late Oct. through early Nov.
WOLF:
Centerfire: Mid-Sept. through June

Rates:
BLACK BEAR $2,500 (Canadian)/10 days
GRIZZLY and BLACK BEAR combo $6,500 (Canadian)/10 days
MOOSE $4,500 (Canadian)/10 days
MULE DEER $2,500 (Canadian)/10 days

Accommodations:
LOG LODGE, OUTCAMPS
NUMBER OF ROOMS: 11
MAXIMUM NUMBER OF HUNTERS: 6
Meals: Home cooking
Conference Groups: Yes
Guides: Included
Gratuity: $200 to $300 (Canadian)
Preferred Payment:
Cash, MasterCard, Visa, check
Other Activities:
Bird watching, canoeing/rafting, fishing, riding, snowmobiling, swimming

Getting There:
Fly to Calgary and the lodge van will meet you.

Contact:
Don or Patsy Wolfenden
Beaverfoot Lodge
Box 1560
Golden, British Columbia
V0A 1H0, Canada
604/344-7144
Web: www.beaverfootlodge/index.htm

FROM THE LODGE, a long pasture still green despite the gold of the aspens slopes a quarter-mile down to the Beaverfoot River. Pines edge the pasture like centurions on parade, and beyond them rise the Ottertail Mountains. So steep and high are they that from where you sit on the front porch you must crane your neck to see the glacier-capped crest. Don Wolfenden, owner and guide extraordinare, tells you to look to the left over the highest ridge of trees on the mountain. That's where he sees a white goat moving slowly over the face of the mountain. You can't see the goat without the aid of the spotting scope on the tripod. So you get up and take a look and sure enough, there it is.

Beaverfoot Lodge is set in a little tuck of land between Yoho National Park to the east and the last high range of mountains before you drop down into the Columbia River valley. Vast sheets of sedimentary rock have been tipped vertically, making mountains that soar like no others. The high slopes are the special province of goats, which Don would rather hunt than any other game. Elk and mule deer roam the high forests near the timberline. A little lower, but not always as much as you'd like to think, is the range of Shiras Moose. Grizzly, black bear, cougars and wolves prowl the stream drainages. Mountain goats, Shiras moose and mule deer bring the most clients to the Beaverfoot.

If you hunt here, the odds are you'll be successful. There are two reasons for that. First, you're going to do your part and get yourself in shape beforehand. If you don't, it's a waste of a wonderful opportunity, because Don will climb right along with you, guiding you up the mountains and into those little places where goats and elk play. Second, if you're not up to it, Don will know immediately and tailor a hunt that accommodates your abilities. Don operates a pair of cabins in the highlands between Yoho and Kootenay parks, and he places satellite tent camps where he needs them. Don's horses are trail savvy and easy to ride. And food, whether in the main lodge or at a tent camp, is solid, simple and scrumptious.

Chilcotin Hunting Adventures

G o l d   B r i d g e ,   B r i t i s h   C o l u m b i a

The favorite haunt of a
famous gun scribe.

VITAL STATISTICS:

Game/Arm/Seasons:
BLACK BEAR:
Bow, centerfire, muzzleloader:
Spring, May through mid-June; Fall,
Sept. through late Nov.
GRIZZLY BEAR:
Bow, centerfire, muzzleloader: May
through mid-June
MOOSE:
Bow, centerfire, muzzleloader: Early
Oct. through late Nov.
MOUNTAIN GOAT,
CALIFORNIA BIGHORN SHEEP:
Bow, centerfire, muzzleloader:
Sept. through Oct.
COUGAR:
Bow, centerfire, muzzleloader:
Mid-Nov. through mid-Feb.

Rates:
BLACK BEAR from $2,200/7 days
GRIZZLY BEAR from
$10,500/14 days
COUGAR from $3,400/7 days
MULE DEER from $2,500/7 days
MOOSE from $3,500/7 days
MOUNTAIN GOAT from
$4,500/7 days
CALIFORNIA BIGHORN SHEEP
from $12,500/14 days

Accommodations:
LOG CABINS, TENT CAMPS
MAXIMUM NUMBER OF HUNTERS: 6
Meals: Hearty and healthy
Conference Groups: Yes
Guides: Included
Gratuity: $100 to $400
Preferred Payment:
Cash, check, credit card
Other Activities:
Biking, bird hunting, bird watching,
boating, fishing, skiing, swimming,
waterfowling, wildlife photography
Getting There:
Fly to Vancouver International and
rent a car, or the lodge van will pick
you up for $100 each way.

Contact:
Kevan Bracewell
Chilcotin Hunting Adventures
Gun Creek Rd.
Gold Bridge
British Columbia V0K 1P0
Canada
250/238-2274
e-mail:
chilcotin_holidays@bc.sympatico.com
Web: www.chilcotinholidays.com

I N 1901, A LIEUTENANT in the national guard resigned his commission and hopped the train to Ashcroft in British Columbia's Chilcotin Mountains. Once there, he plunked down $25 for a saddle horse and another $30 for a pair of packhorses. He loaded them with as much grub and gear as they could safely carry, slipped his new Winchester .30-30 into its scabbard, mounted his horse and headed up the Bridge River Trail on the way into a nine-month odyssey. When he returned, Townsend Whelen was no longer a nimrod. He went on to an illustrious career in the Army and became one of the leading experts on hunting firearms of the 20th Century. Along with a host of writings, he left us with the .35 Whelen, essentially a .30-06 necked up to .35 caliber that packs enough wallop for the bears, moose, sheep and mule deer he found in this rugged, isolated plateau.

The Chilcotins make up a southern portion of the Coast Range, that brutally steep string of serrated glacier-capped peaks that defines the west coast of British Columbia. The jumping off place is Gold Bridge, a small town where Gun Creek meets the Bridge River four and a half hours by car from Vancouver. Of this wilderness, about 2,000 square miles are the exclusive province of Chilcotin Hunting Adventures. The region, in the rain shadow of the Coast Range, is relatively dry, but not arid. Among the rounded peaks, California bighorns and mountain goats are hunted, and up here you'll also find good mule deer with spreads to 24 inches. In the lower elevations and in hundreds of grassy valleys between heavily forested ridges there are moose averaging 45 inches, grizzly (24-inch skulls), black bears of six-plus feet, and cougar.

Hunts are conducted from the year-round lodge on Gun Creek or from spike camps high in the sandy shale mountains. Horses carry hunters as far as the trail permits, then it's up to shanks mare. Normally you'll hunt with one guide for sheep, cougar or grizzly, unless you prefer to share a guide with another hunter. One-on-one hunting offers the best odds for success. Hunter success rates vary, of course, but most hunters get shots at trophy animals, and many (more than half) send a trophy to the taxidermist.

[C A N A D A   W E S T]

Indian River Ranch Guides & Outfitters Ltd.

A t l i n ,   B r i t i s h   C o l u m b i a

A successful hunt is merely mind over matter.

VANT A TROPHY? The key to success, according to Jamie Schumacher, owner of Indian River Ranch, is physical and mental conditioning. To get horns of bragging quality, you have to hike with a pack of 25 pounds or more and a rifle that is seven pounds plus. That's the only way to reach the oldest and wariest sheep, goats and to some degree, caribou. Start a fitness program the day you book a rigorous hunt. By the time you're ready to depart for the wilderness, you'll be in shape for the physical challenges of the hunt. Schumacher insists on physical conditioning, and he also believes that mental conditioning is important. How long can you stand to be cold, wet, tired and maybe hungry? Sure, adequate clothing and careful packing can mitigate these factors, but you have to be prepared to tough your way through unexpected challenges if you're going to harvest that trophy.

For more than a dozen years, Schumacher has been guiding hunters out of Indian River Ranch. Located on Gladys Lake in extreme northwestern British Columbia, he guides hunters for sheep, goats, moose, caribou and bear in 3,000 square miles of the northern Cassair Mountains. Terrain here is varied. High peaks of bare rock and talus provide difficult yet fulfilling hunts for stone and Fannin sheep and goats. Sheep sport 37-inch curls and billies typically sport 9-inch horns. To find trophies, you'll ride out of a spike camp as far as the horse will take you. The remaining distance is up to you. Hunting in alpine terrain is a matter of spotting, stalking and climbing. Lower down you'll find woodland caribou in the 360-point class. While the climbs aren't as strenuous as those for sheep and goats, you'll get a good workout. Moose and bear inhabit the lowest terrain. Schumacher tries to shoot nothing smaller than moose with 50-inch spreads or bear that go six feet for blacks and 7 1/2 for grizzlies.

This is a small, custom and intimate operation. Seldom will there be more than four to six hunters in camp at any given time. Usually one guide serves one hunter, but two hunters can share a guide (at substantial savings) if special arrangements have been made. Cabins and camps will be of log or canvas, depending on location.

VITAL STATISTICS:

Game/Arm/Seasons:
BLACK BEAR, GRIZZLY BEAR:
Bow, centerfire, muzzleloader:
Spring, mid-Apr. through mid-June;
Fall, Sept. through late Oct.
CARIBOU:
Bow, centerfire, muzzleloader: Mid-Aug. through mid-Oct.
MOOSE:
Bow, centerfire, muzzleloader: Mid-Aug. through mid-Nov.
MOUNTAIN GOAT:
Bow, centerfire, muzzleloader: Aug. through mid-Oct.
STONE SHEEP:
Bow, centerfire, muzzleloader: Aug. through late Oct.

Rates:
BLACK BEAR from $1,500/10 days
GRIZZLY BEAR from $8,500/10 days
CARIBOU $5,500/10 days
MOOSE from $6,200/10 days
MOUNTAIN GOAT from $4,600/10 days (two-on-one)
STONE SHEEP from $13,000/14 days

Accommodations:
LOG CABINS OR TENTS
MAXIMUM NUMBER OF HUNTERS: 6
Meals: Caribou, moose, sheep
Conference Groups: Yes
Guides: Included
Gratuity: $100
Preferred Payment:
Cash, certified check
Other Activities:
Boating, canoeing/rafting, fishing, wildlife photography
Getting There:
Fly to Juneau, Alaska, or Whitehorse, Yukon Territory, and catch a bush shuttle (about $300 additional round-trip).

Contact:
Jamie Schumacher
Indian River Ranch
Guides & Outfitters Ltd.
Box 360
Atlin, British Columbia
V0W 1A0, Canada
250/651-7747

MacKenzie Trail Lodge

Tsacha Lake, British Columbia

A river runs the length of this marvelous land of moose.

VITAL STATISTICS:

Game/Arm/Seasons:
MOOSE, MULE DEER, BLACK BEAR:
Bow: Early through mid-Sept.
Centerfire, muzzleloader: Mid-Sept.
through mid-Nov.
Rates:
From $3,500/7 days
Accommodations:
LOG LODGES
NUMBER OF ROOMS: 2 TO 6
MAXIMUM NUMBER OF HUNTERS: 6
Meals: Salmon, steak, turkey
Conference Groups: Yes
Guides: Included
Gratuity: $200
Preferred Payment:
Cash, check, credit cards
Other Activities:
Bird hunting, bird watching, boating,
fishing, waterfowling, wildlife
photography
Getting There:
Fly to Vancouver and catch a charter
to the lodge for $255 additional
round-trip.

Contact:
MacKenzie Trail Lodge
27134 NW Reeder Rd.
Portland, OR 97231
888/808-7688 or
503/621-3416
Fax: 503/621-3551

THIS LODGE on the Blackwater River boasts some of the finest wild rainbow trout fishing in the world, and it offers outstanding opportunities to harvest Canadian moose, black bear and mule deer. However, if you go to look it up on a map, you may not be able to put your finger on it. The Blackwater is also known as the West Road River, perhaps from the early days when explorers paddled up its runs and through its many lakes, looking for a way across the mountains and down to the Pacific. It's this string of lakes and the long, narrow, grassy meadows through which its tributaries flow that makes hunting at MacKenzie Trail Lodge so successful.

Lodge guides have been hunting in this 90-mile-long valley for more than 30 years. They have exclusive rights to 800 square miles and the Blackwater flows right down the middle. Moose is the primary quarry at MacKenzie Trail. Most hunt from boats, working along the shoreline. Others climb low hills studded with thin pines to glass the verdant meadows below. A typical moose will carry a spread in the high 40s to mid-50s, and every year a few in the 60-inch-plus range are harvested. On average hunters fill their tags within their first three days in camp. The rest of the time they hunt 4x4 and bigger mule deer and, because winter comes early to interior British Columbia, mule deer are often found very near moose habitat. Bear, too, are on the menu here. Sightings are very common, and about 15 percent of those seen are cinnamon, brown or very rarely, blonde. A 300-pounder is typical, but some have gone better than 600 pounds.

The lodge operates a dozen log-cabin camps for hunters, each staffed with a cook and a guide or two, depending on the size of the hunting party. On average, you'll only find two to four hunters in the camps. Clients get lots of personal attention. When the flying weather's good, the fleet of four Beavers ply the skies over the river, ferrying hunters here and there. Pilots are always on the lookout for game and provide the kind of constant airborne intelligence that spells success. More than eight out of 10 hunters take moose and about half collect all three species. Since most of the hunting is from boats with very little walking required, MacKenzie Trail welcomes physically challenged hunters as long as they can get about via wheelchair or braces.

*Follow Vic Stapleton up the hill behind his camp on
Sheep Creek in Alberta and you never know what you'll
find. This big shed came from a bull elk that's
now growing a bigger and better rack.*

Scoop Lake Outfitters Ltd.

Kelowna, British Columbia

Hunt sheep and elk in the grandeur of British Columbia's Serengeti.

AT THE FAR END of the Rocky Mountain trench, a stunning 300-mile valley west of the high peaks, lies a wide upland of plateaus, broad valleys and mountains of 8,000 feet and more. It is an ideal land in which to hunt sheep, goats, moose, elk and bear, both grizzly and blacks. The region, known as British Columbia's Serengeti, is relatively dry. Winds from the Pacific climb the St. Elias and Boundary ranges, losing moisture as precipitation on the western slopes and leaving the Cassair Mountains, where Scoop Lake Lodge is located, in a rain shadow.

Don't get the wrong idea, however. Lusty stands of white spruce, sub-alpine firs and occasionally aspen climb the flanks of the mountains. Here the forest is broken by occasional parks. Dark timber and grassy meadows provide habitat for elk running in the 330 Boone & Crockett class. Above, the timber thins and vanishes, replaced by alpine grasslands and barren rock interspersed with patches of matted brush. You'll find Dall and Stone sheep here as well as goats. Stone sheep usually carry 38x14-inch horns, and goats are respectable 9-inchers. The broad intermountain region is characterized by muskeg and black spruce bogs where drainage is poor. Where it's drier, willow and birch predominate. Moose, grizzly and black bear, and wolves are common in the lowlands.

For more than 25 years, Darwin and Wendy Cary have been running their lodge on Scoop Lake, which sits at the base of the highest and most rugged mountains in the region. With 10 cabins (bring your own sleeping bag), four base camps and more than a dozen satellite camps all of log or rough-hewn board, Darwin provides his hunters with lodging that's a cut above most tent-based operations. During your hunt, you'll have the exclusive services of a single guide, though hunters can team up with a single guide by special request. You'll ride, fly, or four-wheel to the outpost camp from which you'll hunt. The season begins here with Stone sheep in August and continues into mid-October, when bitter arctic winds bring snow that makes getting around very difficult. The best time to visit depends on the species you're hunting.

VITAL STATISTICS:

Game/Arm/Seasons:

BLACK BEAR, GRIZZLY BEAR:
Bow, centerfire, muzzleloader: Spring, May; Fall, Sept.

ELK:
Bow, centerfire, muzzleloader: Sept. through mid-Oct.

MOOSE:
Bow, centerfire, muzzleloader: Mid-Aug. through mid-Oct.

MOUNTAIN GOAT:
Bow, centerfire, muzzleloader: Late Aug. through early Oct.

STONE SHEEP:
Bow, centerfire, muzzleloader: Aug. through mid-Oct.

Rates:
BEAR, ELK from $6,000/10 days
MOOSE from $6,500/10 days
MOUNTAIN GOAT from $4,600/10 days (two-on-one)
STONE SHEEP from $9,500/12 days (plus $5,000 trophy fee)

Accommodations:
LOG CABINS
MAXIMUM NUMBER OF HUNTERS: 12 TO 20
Meals: Hearty home-style
Conference Groups: No
Guides: Included
Gratuity: 5 to 10%
Preferred Payment:
Cash, certified check
Other Activities:
Biking, bird-watching, boating, canoeing/rafting, fishing, swimming, wildlife photography
Getting There:
Fly to Watson Lake, Yukon Territory, and catch the bush plane to the lodge for an additional $480.

Contact:
Darwin or Wendy Cary
Scoop Lake Outfitters Ltd.
5615 Deadpine Dr.
Kelowna, British Columbia
V1P IA3, Canada
250/491-1885
e-mail:
scooplake@mail.okanagan.net
Web: www.okanagan.net/scooplake

[C A N A D A   W E S T]

Silent Mountain Outfitters Inc.

C r a n b r o o k ,   B r i t i s h   C o l u m b i a

Fine elk and goats in the shadow of the Canadian Rockies.

VITAL STATISTICS:

Game/Arm/Seasons:
BLACK BEAR:
Bow, centerfire, muzzleloader: Mid-May through mid-June
GRIZZLY BEAR:
Bow, centerfire, muzzleloader: Late April through late May
COUGAR:
Bow, centerfire, muzzleloader: Dec. through Jan.
MULE DEER:
Bow, centerfire, muzzleloader: Mid-Sept. through mid-Nov.
WHITE-TAILED DEER
Bow, centerfire, muzzleloader: Late Oct. through mid-Nov.
MOOSE:
Bow, centerfire, muzzleloader: Late Oct. through early Nov.
MOUNTAIN GOAT:
Bow, centerfire, muzzleloader: Mid-Oct.

Rates:
BLACK BEAR from $2,500/7 days
GRIZZLY BEAR $8,000/10 days
COUGAR $2,800/7 days
DEER from $2,885
ELK from $2,975/7 days
GOAT $5,250/10 days
MOOSE $4,500/10 days

Accommodations:
LOG CABINS
NUMBER OF ROOMS: 5, SHARED BATH
MAXIMUM NUMBER OF HUNTERS: 4 TO 5

Meals: Family-style

Conference Groups: No

Guides: Included

Gratuity: Hunter's discretion

Preferred Payment:
Cash, certified check

Other Activities:
Fishing, wildlife photography

Getting There:
Fly to Calgary or Spokane and meet the lodge van ($150 additional round-trip).

Contact:
Dieter Bohrmann
Silent Mountain Outfitters Inc.
Box 808, St. Main
Cranbrook, British Columbia
V1C 4J3, Canada
250/489-2335

THE CANADIAN ROCKIES is a vertical land. Vast beds of sedimentary rock are turned on their edges, which tower to 10,000 feet and more. Four of Canada's national parks straddle the border: Jasper and Banff, the larger and better known pair, are located in Alberta; Kootenay and Yoho are in British Columbia. On virtually any day's drive through these parks you'll see elk and sheep, possibly bear, and maybe goats high up on the talus and ledges. There's no hunting in the parks, but to the west the story is different. The Columbia River rises at the base of the west flank of the Canadian Rockies, flows north to Kinbasket Lake and then south toward the U.S. In between are the Purcell Mountains, which contain Canada's Glacier National Park and the Bugaboos, a provincial alpine recreation area.

From a pair of log cabins, Silent Mountain sits on 1,000 square miles north of the Bugaboos and south of Glacier. Cedar and hemlock cover the lower slopes which grade into spruce and fir and ultimately sub-alpine tundra on the crests. Elk are very abundant in this region as are black and grizzly bears and bighorn sheep. You'll also find moose, goats and mule deer, and a few small populations of caribou. Via ATVs, 4WDs, and horses Dieter Bohrmann and his guides transport hunters from the cabins up into areas that are only hunted once or twice a season. Elk in the 6x6 range are a mainstay of this operation, followed by bear. Licenses for black bears are available over the counter, but those for grizzlies are limited. Dieter hunts goats (nine inches plus is average) but not sheep. Valleys and the low hills in them yield Shiras moose with spreads between 45 and 55 inches. Higher up you'll find mulies, typically 22-inch 4x4s. Hunts are typically one-on-one. By prior arrangement, you can share a guide with a friend and receive a reduction in price.

While summer weather in this, the southern end of the Rocky Mountain Trench, is reasonably predictable, fall weather is not. Soundless waterproof clothing is a must for quiet stalking. Two pairs of eight-inch boots, Gore-Tex or not, are also essential. A waterproof hat is also a very good idea. You'll need your sleeping bag, of course, and a pillow case. Don't forget a pair of fingerless woolen gloves.

Gana River Outfitters

Norman Wells, Northwest Territories

Hunt sheep and caribou in the Mackenzies, where game is plentiful and people are not.

VITAL STATISTICS:

Game/Arm/Seasons:
CARIBOU:
Bow, centerfire, muzzleloader: Late July through late Sept.
MOOSE:
Bow, centerfire, muzzleloader: Early through late Sept.
STONE SHEEP:
Bow, centerfire, muzzleloader: Mid-July through early Sept.

Rates:
CARIBOU from $3,500/5 days
MOOSE from $6,000/10 days
STONE SHEEP from $7,500/12 days

Accommodations:
WOODEN CABINS AT LODGE, TENTS IN THE BUSH
MAXIMUM NUMBER OF HUNTERS: 10

Meals: Wild game

Conference Groups: No

Guides: Included

Gratuity: Hunter's discretion

Preferred Payment:
Cash

Other Activities:
Bird hunting, fishing, wildlife photography,

Getting There:
Fly to Norman Wells, Northwest Territories, and take the shuttle plane to the lodge (return fare of $550 Canadian is extra).

Contact:
Bill McKenzie
Gana River Outfitters,
Box 4659
Quensel, British Columbia
V2J 3J8, Canada
250/992-8639

FROM GREAT SLAVE LAKE, the Mackenzie River slices northwest toward the delta at Inuvik where it flows into the Beaufort Sea. To the east of the river rise the Norman Mountains and to the west, beyond a band of kettle lakes and low spruce bogs, are the rugged 8,000-foot-plus Mackenzie Mountains. Game is plentiful in the Mackenzies and people are not. That makes for ideal hunting for Alaska-Yukon moose, mountain caribou and Dall sheep.

Moose and caribou frequent river valleys and are hunted during the first two weeks of September via raft floats on major tributaries flowing from the west into the Mackenzie. Just you and a guide will spend eight days on the river, scanning banks for moose with racks of at least a 60-inch spread. Nothing smaller will be taken. Often mountain caribou are seen along the river and for an additional $2,000 you can harvest a trophy bull of 370 points or better. You and the guide will share camp chores, but he'll paddle the raft. Moose and caribou can also be hunted on foot or with ATVs from Gana River Outfitter's main camp on Palmer Lake.

While the float trip is a great deal of fun, the meat-and-potatoes of this outfit are its high-mountain hunts for sheep and caribou and the occasional moose that wanders a bit from its normal range. From the trailhead, you'll ride deep into the Mackenzies, climbing toward the treeline and your outpost tent camp. On foot, you'll gain more elevation, spotting and stalking, always searching for that ram with a 40-inch curl, or a caribou that tops 425 points. You may hunt glaciers; caribou seem to favor their coolness as a defense against ever-present blackflies. (Take note!) Horseback hunts are run from July 15 into the third week of September, when weather becomes a bit dicey. Wolf and wolverine are also available.

Trophies taken on the hunts are fully caped, salted, wind-dried and prepared for shipment to a taxidermist. Meat is packaged for shipment as well. The cost of shipping trophies and meat is borne by the hunter as is the price of round-trip airfare from Norman Wells to Palmer Lake, about $550 Canadian. The outfitter provides hunting licenses, but hunters must purchase a species permit and pay export fees for game taken during the hunt.

[C A N A D A   W E S T]

Bait-Masters Hunting Camps

G r e e n   L a k e ,   S a s k a t c h e w a n

Hunt with an expert in an area famed for record-book whitetails.

VITAL STATISTICS:

Game/Arm/Seasons:
BEAR:
Bow, centerfire, muzzleloader: Mid-April through mid-June
DEER:
Bow: Late Aug. through late Oct.
Centerfire: Early Nov. through early Dec.
Muzzleloader: Early Sept. through late Oct.
MOOSE:
Bow: Late Sept. through early Oct.
Centerfire, muzzleloader: Late Sept. through mid-Oct.

Rates:
BEAR $1,750/5 days
DEER from $1,750/5 days (archery); $3,000/5 days (centerfire)
MOOSE $3,000/5 day

Accommodations:
LOG CABINS
MAXIMUM NUMBER OF HUNTERS: 4 PER CAMP

Meals: Wonderful wild rice dishes
Conference Groups: No
Guides: Included
Gratuity: Hunter's discretion
Preferred Payment:
Cash, check
Other Activities:
Bird hunting, bird watching, boating, fishing, golf, waterfowling, wildlife photography
Getting There:
Fly to Saskatoon, rent a car and drive to the lodge.

Contact:
Brian Hoffart
Bait-Masters Hunting Camps
Box 99
Green Lake, Saskatchewan
S0M 1B0, Canada
306/823-2084
Fax: 306/823-2147

YOU AND YOUR GUIDE are crouched in the ground blind, both well doused with scent-killing potions. In a clearing about 20 yards away stands a buck. Only this buck is a decoy with a movable tail. The guide rattles a set of aged antlers once, then a little longer, twisting the tines against each other for full effect. You hear the crashing in the brush, the chop-chop-chop-chop of a deer walking fast. To your left there's another, and in a moment they both burst into the clearing hell-bent on doing significant damage to each other. You draw, and as the larger of the two, a 6-pointer, pauses, you slowly relax your arm and lower your bow. Watching two bucks duke it out isn't something you see every day.

And it's not an everyday occurrence when you hunt with whitetail guru Brian Hoffart, who runs Bait-Masters Hunting Camps on Green Lake with his wife Sylvia. These are nice folks who've been in the business for 15 years and who, a few years ago, expanded their log lodge. Whitetails are Hoffart's love, and he'd rather rattle up bucks than do most anything else. Hunters shoot from tree stands, shooting boxes and heated stands — whatever works in this boreal forest a couple hundred miles north of Saskatoon. Rattling works into December, when the snow filters down through the leafless woods. A blessing, the snow lets hunters see much farther in the woods. Typical bucks fall into the 140s with an occasional 150 or so. Hoffart hunts deer out of the lodge at Green Lake and two other camps: one at Hillyer Lake, 45 miles north, and the other at Cowan Lake, 18 miles east. Both are Hudson Bay-style log cabins complete with electricity and sauna and staffed with a guide and a cook.

When he's not hunting deer, Hoffart runs bear hunts over bait both fall and spring. Over the years, he's added two to the Boone & Crockett books and six to Pope and Young. Moose are also available, called up out of the willow swamps onto ridges of jack pine where a hunter waits. Because the number of licenses is limited, Hoffart takes bowhunters one year and rifle hunters the next. These are nice-sized bulls, with spreads ranging from 38 to 42 inches. In the off-season, the Hoffarts host anglers at their lodge, and in late summer they gather wild rice from the shallows of nearby lakes. Sylvia's wild rice soup — 2 cups of cooked wild rice; diced onion, celery, fresh mushrooms (wild are best), and green pepper sautéed in butter until tender; chicken broth; 1 cup flour for thickening; and a cup of whipping cream—has never known a left-over jar. If you're lucky, she'll have it simmering the night you arrive.

Glen Hill's Trophy Expeditions

Saskatoon, Saskatchewan

Come up and stay for a while, relax and harvest a big buck.

VITAL STATISTICS:

Game/Arm/Seasons:
BEAR:
Bow, centerfire, muzzleloader:
Spring, May through June; Fall, Aug. through Sept.
DEER:
Bow, centerfire, muzzleloader: Nov. through Dec.
Rates:
BEAR from $1,495/5 days
DEER from $2,095/6 days
Accommodations:
LOG LODGE, CABINS OR REMOTE CAMPS
MAXIMUM NUMBER OF HUNTERS: 8 TO 10
Meals: Scrumptious home-style cooking
Conference Groups: Yes
Guides: Included
Gratuity: $200
Preferred Payment:
Cash, cashiers check
Other Activities:
Bird hunting, bird watching, fishing, golf, swimming, waterfowling, wildlife photography
Getting There:
Fly to Saskatoon and the van from the lodge will meet you.

Contact:
Glen Hill
Glen Hill's Trophy Expeditions,
1529 East Heights
Saskatoon, Saskatchewan
S7J 3B4, Canada
306/374-3223
Fax: 302/374-3223
e-mail: trophies@sk.simpatico.ca
Web: www.sasktrophies.com

RISING IN THE PRAIRIE pothole country east of Edmonton, Alberta, the Saskatchewan River cuts down through flat grain fields and grasslands, following a leisurely course across the province that bears its name. Near Prince Albert, the river enters a changing landscape. Vast farms of open fields begin to give way to stands of heavy dark spruce and fir, the fingers of the boreal forest poking southward. Game thrives in these seams between environments. Whitetails find excellent feed in open fields at night and return to the dense woods at dawn.

As the name states, Glen Hill specializes in trophy deer. Saskatchewan is home to the 'Dakota' strain of white-tailed deer, which yields large racks on heavy-bodied deer. The largest typical antlers have measured 188 while the best nontypicals have topped 214. Hunters can realistically expect to harvest a buck scoring 140 or better. Essentially Glen offers two packages: a six-day or an 11-day hunt. Choosing the latter increases your chance for a record-book buck. You'll hunt from stands or ground blinds, with perhaps a bit of still-hunting. Bow seasons begin in October and continue until the first of November. That's when regular firearms season opens. The rut generally begins in early November.

With more than 25 years of experience as a guide, Glen is also highly regarded for his bear hunts. Conducted in an area where he has the only permit, Glen delights in finding big and old bears. The largest so far weighed 606 pounds. Brown color-phase bears comprise about half of the population. Spring bears run a little smaller (260 pounds) than fall bears (300 pounds) and both bow and rifle hunters share equally high success rates. Accommodations are provided either in charming log cabins around the lodge or in a remote camp, depending on where the action is best and the kind of hunting experience you want.

[C A N A D A   W E S T]

Makwa River Outfitters

M a k w a ,   S a s k a t c h e w a n

VITAL STATISTICS:

Game/Arm/Seasons:
BEAR:
Bow, centerfire, muzzleloader: Mid-Apr. through mid-June
DEER:
Bow: Late Aug. through late Oct.
Centerfire: Early Nov. through early Dec.
Muzzleloader: Late Aug. through early Dec.

Rates:
BEAR $1,800/6 days
DEER $2,500/6 days

Accommodations:
LOG LODGE
NUMBER OF ROOMS: 3
MAXIMUM NUMBER OF HUNTERS: 8

Meals: Meat and potatoes with vegetables

Conference Groups: No

Guides: Included

Gratuity: Hunter's discretion

Preferred Payment:
Cash, check

Other Activities:
Bird hunting, golf, wildlife photography

Getting There:
Fly to Saskatoon, rent a car and drive to the lodge.

Contact:
Ken Dopko
Makwa River Outfitters
Box 89
Makwa ,Saskatchewan
S0M 1N0, Canada
306/236-4649
Fax: 306/236-4716

The land of trophy whitetails beckons hunters who not only want deer, but bears and waterfowl as well.

PICTURE SASKATCHEWAN as a tableland tilted to the east. Its great rivers rise in the Canadian Rockies in Alberta to the west and flow through the province into Hudson Bay. The northernmost portion of Saskatchewan is tundra, which southward grades into boreal forest. Pines and spruce blanket most of the land, broken by clear-cuts. Thin rivers drain hundreds of lakes and ponds lying in areas left by melting glacial ice. It is a land of big whitetails, heavy black bears and abundant waterfowl.

Since the early 1990s, Ken Dopko and his wife Kathy have been guiding and hosting hunters. One of the Kopko's four guides works with each pair of hunters, driving out daily from their comfortable log lodge in Makwa, a small town southeast of Makwa Lake Provincial Park, to exclusive hunting areas half an hour away. The quarry is white-tailed deer, hunted from heated tree stands, a dozen miles or more by all-terrain vehicle from the nearest gravel road. Stands overlook trails that run from bedding to feeding areas, the edges of cut-over woodlots, or boundaries between swamp and forest. As the season progresses into the rut, calling and rattling techniques can really pay off. Bucks in this area score into the 140s and higher. Winter comes early to west-central Saskatchewan. Blustery winds and driving snow brings the season to a close in early December.

The abundance of lakes and ponds makes this a duck and goose hunter's dream. If you book early in the season, you'll find that waterfowling coincides with deer hunting. Bring along a 12-gauge and boxes of non-toxic No. 1s and 4s. And plan to spend some time lying in a blind after the deer hunting's done. Bear season opens in mid-April, but the hunting doesn't really get good until a month later. By then, boars are out of their dens and feeding aggressively at baits. Color-phased bears — particularly blondes and chocolates — are reasonably plentiful. Typical bears run 250 pounds.

If you hunt with Makwa River Outfitters, you can leave your sleeping bag and towels at home. Everything except gun, ammo and personal gear is provided. Two or three hunters share rooms and a common bath in the lodge that's adjacent to the main house. Dinners are family affairs skillfully prepared by Kathy. But when it comes to breakfast you're the cook. You'll find everything in the fridge, just where Kathy said it would be.

Dickson Outfitters Ltd.

Whitehorse, Yukon Territory

One of the oldest outfitting operations in Canada can put you into prime bear, moose and sheep country.

VITAL STATISTICS:

Game/Arm/Seasons:
BEAR:
Bow, centerfire, muzzleloader: May
MOOSE:
Bow, centerfire, muzzleloader: Mid-Aug. through mid-Oct.
SHEEP:
Bow, centerfire, muzzleloader: Late July through mid-Sept.
Rates:
BEAR $8,000/14 days (plus $3,500 kill fee)
MOOSE $7,500/9 days
SHEEP: $8,000/10 days
Accommodations:
LOG LODGES
MAXIMUM NUMBER OF HUNTERS: 3 PER CAMP
Meals: Hearty hunting chow
Conference Groups: No
Guides: Included
Gratuity: 5 to 10%
Preferred Payment:
Cash, check
Other Activities:
Bird hunting, bird watching, boating, fishing, swimming, waterfowling
Getting There:
Fly to Whitehorse and ride up in the van from the lodge or fly up for $600 (Canadian) additional.

Contact:
David Dickson
Dickson Outfitters Ltd.
Box 9130-29 Wann Rd.
Whitehorse, Yukon Territory
Y1A 4A2, Canada
867/633-5456

LOOKING FOR an experienced outfitter who knows the real estate? Try Dave Dickson; his grandad started the operation in the early 1900s. Today, it's one of the oldest continuously owned family outfitting concerns in Canada.

Terrain here is varied. To the west rises Beaver Mountain, a 6,000-footer with barren peaks that wear patches of snow year-round. To the east are the braided channels of the White River, which floods with melt-water runoff from the Wrangell Mountains farther west. Between the two are the foothills and thick forests that thin as elevation increases. In all, the area that Dickson hunts encompasses 3.5 million acres, or 5,500 square miles. And he's the only outfitter licensed to guide nonresidents here.

The season begins in May down in the river bottoms for grizzly, when boars have left their dens. Typical grizzlies will run about 500 pounds or so with skulls greater than 20 inches and hides squaring seven feet or better. Hunts are typically conducted from boats. You'll see bears feeding on salmon in the river or digging for roots. Archers are as successful as rifle hunters. Black bears and wolves are also fair game on these hunts.

Fall hunts open in late July for Dall sheep. You'll hunt them high on the rocky talus of the mountains, glassing and stalking and glassing again. The best hunting is in August, soon after the season opens, when sheep are still following summer patterns. A typical ram will carry 35- to 37-inch horns, with exceptional heads going to 41 inches. Most hunters are successful, with only three in the past 30 years going home without trophies. Key, of course, is physical conditioning and the ability to make a clean shot out to 350 yards. Some hunters add moose — the average spread runs about 60 inches — to their fall hunts. Riding boats or horses, you'll work the river bottoms and low timber. Grizzlies can also be taken in the fall. All hunting is based on one guide for each client.

Dickson operates a pair of log base camps. The first — primarily for bear and moose — is a little way from the Alaska Highway, and the second — the sheep camp — is up on Tchawsahmon Lake. To reach the latter you'll fly in or ride horseback. Both camps are staffed by cooks, feature hot showers and include a separate cabin for guides. And, depending on the dictates of the game you're hunting, you may hole up in a spike camp somewhere up in the mountains. If you intend to hunt in this neck of the woods, it's best to begin planning 18 months in advance. Floatplanes are normally scheduled a year ahead of time.

[C A N A D A   W E S T]

Trophy Stone Safaris Ltd.

W h i t e h o r s e ,   Y u k o n   T e r r i t o r y

The Yukon's golden triangle for sheep, caribou and moose.

VITAL STATISTICS:

Game/Arm/Seasons:

CARIBOU:
Bow, centerfire, muzzleloader: Mid-Aug. through mid-Oct.

GRIZZLY BEAR:
Bow, centerfire, muzzleloader: Spring, May; Fall, late Aug. through late Oct.

MOOSE:
Bow, centerfire, muzzleloader: Late Aug. through late Oct.

STONE SHEEP:
Bow, centerfire, muzzleloader: Late-July through early Sept.

Rates:
CARIBOU $6,900/12 days
GRIZZLY BEAR $9,400/11 days
MOOSE $7,400/11 days
STONE SHEEP $14,000/12 days

Accommodations:
FRAME, LOG AND TENT CAMPS
MAXIMUM NUMBER OF HUNTERS: 6

Meals: Wild game

Conference Groups: No

Guides: Included

Gratuity: $500

Preferred Payment:
Cash, check

Other Activities:
Biking, bird hunting, boating, fishing

Getting There:
Fly to Whitehorse and take the air shuttle ($475 round-trip).

Contact:
Curt Thompson
Trophy Stone Safaris Ltd.
Box 9176-29 Wann Rd.
Whitehorse, Yukon Territory
Y1A 4A2, Canada
875/668-6564
Fax: 867/668-6564
Web:
www.web-workshop.com/trophystone/

FROM LITTLE SALMON, the Pelly River flows down the course of the Tintina Trench, a geologic zone where two continental plates are in the process of colliding. Over millennia, the forces pressuring the plates have pushed up a number of small mountain ranges — Glenlyon, Anvil, Wilkinson and Tatchun Hills. None of these are particularly high, at 4,500 to 6,000 feet. But when the climate is as cold and dry as the Yukon's, it takes very little elevation to create those rugged habitats favored by Stone sheep. And that's why Curt Thompson sought out this triangle of the Yukon, a land of 4.5 million acres bounded by Faro on the east, Carmacks on the south and Pelly Crossing on the north.

A Beaver or Otter will fly you to Curt's base camp about 120 miles north of Whitehorse. Once there, you'll head off by horse for locales where sheep have been spotted. You may hunt out of a tent camp with wood floors, stoves and other creature comforts. Or you may shoulder your pack and head for the high ridges, overnighting in a mountain tent and drinking your coffee to the hissing of a little gas stove. A typical Stone in this neck of the woods will carry a 39-inch curl. To bag one, you'll need a flat-shooting rifle and you'll have to be in pretty good shape.

On the low, sparsely forested ridges are easier hunts for mountain caribou, a larger cousin of the woodland but smaller than the Quebec-Labrador branch of the family. A typical bull will score 390. Alaska/Yukon moose also inhabit this country, and you can't count on them to be found along lakes and rivers, which abound. Often they're high on the ridges in the same terrain as caribou. That's one of the reasons most of Curt's hunters carry both tags. A grizzly tag is also nice to have. While serious hunting for grizzlies occurs during the fall dog salmon run along the Yukon near Minto, you never know when you may run into one feeding on a kill. Spring hunts for grizzlies are also available.

ALASKA

I T'S NOT SO MUCH the steepness of the land that makes hunting in Alaska so arduous, though there's enough up and down to satisfy anyone. It's the climate that makes life interesting. Not that it's always bitter cold. The Yukon and Northwest Territories are more frigid. Alaska's fall and spring hunting seasons are times of transition. Massive fronts deliver inches of wet snow one day, only to be followed by warm breezes that turn everything to mush. The Alaskan brown bear, the largest and most dangerous game in North America, is hunted in the arc that swings from the southeastern panhandle around to the Aleutians. This is one place where a .375 H&H might come in handy. Moose — 60-inchers and up — as well as Dall sheep, mountain goats and caribou are all hunted throughout the state. And while a few outfitters may run pack trains, distances are so great that tundra-wheeled Super Cubs are the conveyance of choice for ferrying hunters into the wilderness, where most trophies can be found.

Lodges:

1 AAA ALASKAN OUTFITTERS, INC.
2 AFOGNAK WILDERNESS LODGE
3 ALASKA BROOKS RANGE ARCTIC HUNTS
4 ALASKA NORTH COUNTRY ENTERPRISES
5 ALASKA REMOTE GUIDE SERVICE
6 ALASKA TROPHY SAFARIS
7 ALL ALASKA OUTDOORS LODGE
8 AUSTIN'S ALASKA ADVENTURES
9 CHRIS GOLL'S RAINBOW RIVER LODGE
10 JAKE'S ALASKA WILDERNESS OUTFITTERS
11 KICHATNA GUIDE SERVICE
12 LAZER'S GUIDE SERVICE
13 LOST CREEK RANCH
14 MORRIS HUNTING COMPANY
15 NORTH AMERICAN
16 NORTHWARD BOUND
17 PIONEER OUTFITTERS
18 STEPHAN LAKE LODGE
19 WESTWIND GUIDE SERVICE
20 ZACHAR BAY LODGE

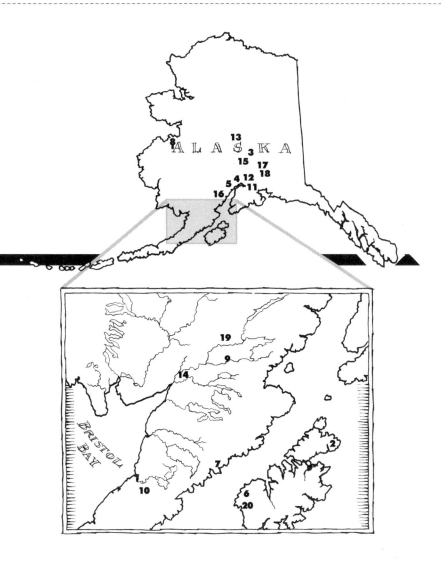

References:

HUNTING IN ALASKA:
A COMPREHENSIVE GUIDE
by Christopher M. Batin
Alaska Angler Publications
Box 83550, Fairbanks, AK 99708
907/455-8000

HUNT ALASKA NOW
— SELF-GUIDING FOR
TROPHY MOOSE & CARIBOU
by Dennis Confer
Wily Ventures Publishing
2509 Kilkenny Circle, Anchorage, AK
99504; 907/338-3099

Resources:

ALASKA DEPARTMENT
OF FISH AND GAME
Box 25526, Juneau, AK 99802
907/465-4100
web.www.fishgame.state.ak.us.

[A L A S K A]

AAA Alaskan Outfitters, Inc.

C o o p e r   L a n d i n g

With three different camps, this outfit offers hunting for brown bear, Dall sheep, mountain goats and caribou.

VITAL STATISTICS:

Game/Arm/Seasons:
BROWN BEAR:
Bow, centerfire, muzzleloader: Mid-Oct. and mid-May
MOOSE:
Bow, centerfire, muzzleloader: Mid-Sept.
CARIBOU:
Bow, centerfire, muzzleloader: Sept. through Oct.
DALL SHEEP:
Centerfire: Mid-Aug.
GOAT:
Centerfire: Early Sept.
Rates:
Brown bear from $8,950/10 days
Caribou from $3,125/7 days
Sheep from $8,250/10 days
Accommodations:
FRAME AND TENT CAMPS
MAXIMUM NUMBER OF HUNTERS:
14
Meals:
Moose, caribou and salmon
Conference Groups: No
Guides: Included
Gratuity: 5%
Preferred Payment:
Cash, personal check
Other Activities:
Fishing, wildlife photography
Getting There:
Fly to Pilot Point, Alaska, and take the air taxi for $150 round-trip.

Contact:
Brent Jones
AAA Alaskan Outfitters
Box 707
Cooper Landing, AK
99572-0707
907/595-1522
Fax: 907/595-1542
Web: fordinfo.com/aaa/alaska

WHILE the accommodations may not be five star, AAA's three camps put hunters in the midst of prime habitat for brown bear, caribou, moose and sheep. And over the past decade this outfit has earned a reputation for putting bowhunters onto big bears: five of Pope and Young's top 10 were taken by AAA hunters. So dedicated are the folks at AAA to hunter success that if a hunter fails to get a chance at a bear on a 16-day spring hunt, owner Brent Jones will provide a hunt at no charge the following season.

Most of the bears are taken from the camp on the Dog Salmon River that flows into Ugashik Bay just west of the Alaska Peninsula Wildlife Refuge. The river rises in the ice fields of Mt. Kialagvik and Mt. Chiginagak and rapidly descends into a braided channel that winds through a long flat bowl choked with stunted alder and lush grasses—bear cover at its best. A 10-foot brown taken in 1997 scored more than 27 inches. The camp itself is a modest collection of frame cabins (two for guests, a dining hall, shower, cabin and numerous outbuildings) tucked in the brush off a flat that serves as a runway. But each year it produces a number of fine moose including a 58-inch Pope and Young bull that scored 190. Rifle hunters typically connect with 60-inch or better bulls. Caribou averaging 390 points are also a staple of AAA. From the camp on the Dog Salmon, owner Brent Jones and his guides hunt more than 700 miles of excellent cover including some 170 miles of Pacific Coast across the Shelikof Strait from Kodiak Island.

For Dall sheep, Jones shifts operations to Bryson Bar Camp on the Chitina River between the Saint Elias Mountains to the north and the Wrangell-Saint Elias Preserve to the south. The mountains tower 5,000 feet above the camp and their slopes of outcrop and talus are home to both sheep and goats. The camp's 14-year average for sheep is 37.5 inches, while goats run in the 9-inch range. Both are respectable in anyone's book.

AAA's third camp is on Otter Lake in the Nushagak-Mulchatna area. The terrain here is moderate; grassy uplands climb gently from creek bottoms and flats thick with brush and berry bushes. Caribou score 370 or better; moose in the 66-inch range; and black bear, 18 inches plus. Set among the spruce near the lake is the semi-permanent tent camp.

Afognak Wilderness Lodge

S e a l   B a y

Hunt for huge brown bears on famed Afognak Island.

A WELL-APPOINTED, luxurious lodge on the mountainous and densely forested Afognak Island in the Kodiak Island group at the entrance to the Gulf of Alaska, Afognak Wilderness Lodge offers a variety of spring and fall hunts. Brown bear hunts run in April and May, while fall bear hunts occur in mid-October into November. Guided or unguided hunts for Sitka black-tailed deer and guided hunts for Roosevelt elk are also available in the fall, with deer starting as early as August and elk beginning in September.

This is fun hunting in a truly rugged part of the wilderness. If you're in decent physical shape and can shoot straight (go with a .338 Win. Mag. for bear, something a bit less for elk, perhaps a .270 or 7mm for deer), your chances of success are excellent. Most years, hunts out of the lodge have a 95 percent success rate on bears, 60 to 75 percent on elk, and 100 percent success on deer and sea ducks. Perhaps this explains why owners Roy and Shannon Randall get so many repeat customers, and why the lodge is consistently rated one of the best in North America.

The lodge itself has a cozy living room with fireplace, six guest rooms, plus four modern but rustic cabins. Meals run the gourmet gamut, with salmon, halibut, crab, shrimp, venison, elk, pork and ribs all served. And after dinner, head to the communications "center," where you can contact your office by phone or fax, work on a computer, copy documents or just plop down and watch some television after a long day in the field.

VITAL STATISTICS:

Game/Arm/Seasons:
BROWN BEAR:
Bow, centerfire, muzzleloader: Spring, mid-Apr. through mid-May; Fall, late Oct. through mid-Nov.
ELK:
Bow, centerfire, muzzleloader: Late Sept. through late Nov.
SITKA BLACKTAIL DEER:
Bow, centerfire, muzzleloader: Early Aug. through late Dec.

Rates:
BROWN BEAR $10,500/10 days
ELK $3,200/6 days
SITKA BLACKTAIL DEER $450 per day

Accommodations:
MODERN CABINS
NUMBER OF ROOMS: 6
MAXIMUM NUMBER OF HUNTERS: 12

Meals:
Salmon, halibut, crab, venison, elk, chicken, pork

Conference Groups: Yes

Guides: Included

Gratuity: $50 to $100

Preferred Payment:
Cash, MasterCard, Visa, check

Other Activities:
Antiquing, bird-watching, boating, fishing, hiking, swimming, waterfowling, wildlife photography

Getting There:
Fly to Kodiak and take a floatplane to the lodge for an additional charge.

Contact:
Shannon Randall
Afognak Wilderness Lodge
Seal Bay, AK 99697
907/486-6442
Fax: 907/486-2217
Web: www.afognaklodge.com

[A L A S K A]

Alaska Brooks Range Arctic Hunts

F a i r b a n k s

The oldest outfitting operation in the state can put you onto a variety of game.

ESTABLISHED 35 YEARS AGO, Alaska Brooks Range Arctic Hunts (ABRAH) is the oldest Brooks Range guide/outfitter operation in existence. Offering hunts not only in the Brooks Range but in interior Alaska and the Alaska Range as well, ABRAH can give a hunter exactly the type of experience he or she is looking for.

In the Brooks Range, hunters hunt from either Timber Lake Base and/or spike camps in Game Unit 25A, an exclusively assigned area in the Arctic National Wildlife Refuge. This is the most remote, primitive, least-explored and least-hunted part of Alaska. The mountains are low here, making the hunting fairly easy for hunters not in the best of shape. Dall sheep, grizzly, trophy caribou, moose, wolf and wolverine are all available.

In interior Alaska, hunters booking with ABRAH hunt in units 20B or F or 21B, depending upon the species hunted. These are primarily river float-hunts, although backpack hunts are also available. If you're looking for trophy moose in the 50-inch range, this is the place.

For brown bear hunts, the camp staff will meet you in game unit 9A or B on the Alaskan Peninsula, in the Aleutian Range.

No matter what you're hunting, plan on packing at least a .270, and something heavier for bear. Sight your rifle in for 200 yards dead on, and know how to use it. The average single-species hunt is eight days, including arrival and departure days, although brown bear hunts on average usually take a few more days. Hunts are two hunters per guide, though one-on-one hunts may also be arranged. When you consider that guides who work for owners Eugene Witt Sr. and Jr. have an average of 15 years service with ABRAH, you can rest assured you're going out with someone who knows the country and the game.

Lodging is in tents, no matter where you hunt. And the food is good, no matter which of the three areas you go to, with meat and potatoes, stews, hash and casseroles all offered. If you need special dietary considerations, simply let the Witts know in advance. They'll take care of you.

VITAL STATISTICS:

Game/Arm/Seasons:
GRIZZLY:
Bow, centerfire, muzzleloader: Late Aug. through late Sept.
DALL SHEEP:
Bow, centerfire, muzzleloader: Early Aug. through mid-Sept.
MOOSE:
Bow, centerfire, muzzleloader: Early through late Sept.
CARIBOU:
Bow, centerfire, muzzleloader: Early Aug. through early Sept.
BROWN BEAR:
Bow, centerfire, muzzleloader: Spring, May; Fall, Oct.
BLACK BEAR:
Bow, centerfire, muzzleloader: Mid-Aug. through late Sept.

Rates:
GRIZZLY $7,300/8 days
DALL SHEEP $6,900/8 days
MOOSE $7,000/8 days
CARIBOU $4,000/8 days
BROWN BEAR $9,000/8 days
BLACK BEAR $2,500/ 8 days

Accommodations: TENTS
MAXIMUM NUMBER OF HUNTERS: 6

Meals: Stews, casseroles, chow mein, chili, vegetables, dessert

Conference Groups: No

Guides: Included

Gratuity: $25 to $50

Preferred Payment:
Check, money orders

Other Activities:
Antiquing, bird hunting, boating, bird watching, canoeing/rafting, fishing, hiking, waterfowling, wildlife photography

Getting There:
Fly to Fairbanks International Airport, Homer, Arctic Village, Bettes, and take a charter flight to the base camp.

Contact:
Eugene M. Witt & Son
Alaska Brooks Range Arctic Hunts
455 3rd Ave., Apt. 512
Fairbanks AK 99701-4743
907/452-8751
e-mail: ett@ptialaska.net

Alaska North Country Enterprises

Big Lake

Hunt with one of the state's premier guides for big bears, moose and sheep.

VITAL STATISTICS:

Game/Arm/Seasons:
BROWN BEAR:
Bow, centerfire, muzzleloader:
First half Oct. and early Apr.
GRIZZLY:
Bow, centerfire, muzzleloader:
Last half Sept.
MOOSE:
Bow, centerfire, muzzleloader:
Mid-Aug. through mid-Sept.
CARIBOU
Bow, centerfire, muzzleloader: Oct.
DALL SHEEP:
Bow, centerfire, muzzleloader:
Mid-Aug. through mid-Sept.
GOAT:
Bow, centerfire, muzzleloader:
Sept. through Oct.

Rates:
BROWN BEAR from $7,500/10 days
CARIBOU from $2,250/7 days
SHEEP from $7,500/10 days
MOOSE from $6,500/10 days ($2,500 unguided)

Accommodations:
MOUNTAIN TENT CAMPS
MAXIMUM NUMBER OF HUNTERS
1 OR 3

Meals:
Steaks and stews, with freeze-dried meals for backpacking

Conference Groups: No
Guides: Included
Gratuity: $100 to $500
Preferred Payment:
Cash, certified check
Other Activities:
Wildlife photography
Getting There:
Fly to Anchorage and be met by Frank and his Super Cub.

Contact:
Frank Dinello
Alaska North Country
Enterprises
Box 520712
Big Lake, AK 99652
907/373-1207

WHAT WOULD an Alaskan outfitter do without a Super Cub? Ask Frank Dinello, who commutes to and from work in his tundra-tired Cub. From his home on Big Lake outside of Wasilla, Frank fires up his Piper and flies down to Anchorage to pick up a client. Then, depending on the season, he heads down the Alaska Peninsula for bear or up into the grassy river bottoms and foothills of the Talkeetna Mountains for moose. Some commute.

When you book a guided hunt with Alaska North, you get Dinello, his 10-year store of knowledge about the game in Alaska's bush country, his gear, his considerable skill as camp cook and, of course, his Cub. Together, you and he will pick a likely area, fly in, set up camp and hunt. During the course of the 10- to 15-day hunt, you'll follow the game until you get your trophy. Accommodations are lightweight mountain tents. Food in the bush is often freeze-dried, as weight out here is at a premium. You'll bring your own sleeping bag and pad, a sturdy pack and mesh game bags for hides and meat.

While you may hunt from only one camp, odds are that you'll be constantly on the move, hiking and glassing until you find an animal you want. Being in good physical condition is a must for these hunts. You'll carry your own gear and pack out the game to the landing site. Good boots — ankle-fitted hip boots if you're hunting moose in the swamps — are critical. This is one-on-one hunting at its best, and hunter success runs more than 90 percent. Dall sheep run to 37 inches or so; goats to 8 inches-plus; moose in the 50s; and brown bears to around 9 feet. Grizzlies run a bit smaller.

Along with his guide program, Frank offers unguided moose hunts from drop camps. You and two partners will be flown into prime hunting territory along with all the gear you'll need to set up camp. You're responsible for bringing your own food, sleeping bags and packs. Frank will give you general information about where moose are moving in the area, and then it's up to you. Weather permitting, he'll check back in the middle of your 10-day hunt and pick you up at its conclusion. Is this a good deal? Hunter success rate is roughly 50 percent. If you're a good hunter who's reasonably fit, this option is well worth considering.

Alaska Remote Guide Service

Wasilla

Spring hunts for trophy brown bear; fall hunts for 60-inch-plus moose.

VITAL STATISTICS:

Game/Arm/Seasons:
BROWN BEAR:
Centerfire: Sept. through Oct.;
Mar. through May.
MOOSE:
Centerfire: Mid-Aug. through mid-Sept.

Rates:
BROWN BEAR $11,700/14 days
MOOSE from $8,000/10 days

Accommodations:
WALL TENTS
MAXIMUM NUMBER OF HUNTERS: 2 OR 3

Meals:
Lasagna, turkey, freeze-dried meals in spike camps

Conference Groups: No
Guides: Included
Gratuity: $100 to $500
Preferred Payment:
Cash, certified check
Other Activities:
More hunting
Getting There:
Fly to Anchorage and catch an air charter to camp ($300).

Contact:
Wayne Kubat
Alaska Remote Guide Service
Box 874867
Wasilla, AK 99687
907/376-9568

HUNTERS LOOKING FOR trophy brown bears — nine-footers and occasionally better — need look no further than the snow-covered ridges north of Cook Inlet. For more than a dozen years, Wayne Kubat has specialized in hunting the big bears just as they're coming out of their dens in March to feed. Their coats at this time are in full winter prime: deep, lush and the color of English toffee. If you want a bear-skin rug, March through early April is the time to get it.

Hunters and their guides are flown to a base camp in famed Game Management Unit Number 16, in a ski-equipped Super Cub. Comfortable and well-equipped, this camp of wall tents serves as headquarters for the two-week hunt. You'll leave camp by snowmobile long before dawn. When you get close to an area known to hold bears, you'll stash the machine, strap on snowshoes and head out, spotting and stalking as you go. If all goes well, you'll find a fresh moose kill on which bears are feeding. Then it's a matter of wind, weather and waiting. Rifle hunters can usually get to within 100 yards of a bear, while archers must creep to within 40 yards or less. Success on these hunts nears 100 percent.

Kubat also offers fall hunts in the same area. Bears at this time are feeding on salmon, berries and ground squirrels, and you don't have to deal with snow. While these hunts can yield a trophy, the real attraction now is trophy moose of 60 inches or better. Moose hunting begins in late August and usually takes place above timberline. On these 10-day hunts, the drill is stalking and calling with Kubat's "Bull Magnet," a modern call based on a traditional design. Hunters can also take black bears, wolves and wolverines in the fall.

Alaska Remote conducts mostly rifle hunts, and recommends one guide per hunter unless the clients are in good physical condition and hunt well together. For brown bear and moose, Kubat recommends at least a .300 Winchester Magnum with partition bullets, sighted dead on at 200 yards. For black bear, a .30-06 will do the job.

Alaska Trophy Safaris

Chugiak

Hunt Kodiak bears and Dall sheep in this special part of Alaska.

VITAL STATISTICS:

Game/Arm/Seasons:
KODIAK BEAR:
Centerfire, muzzleloader: Apr. through May, Nov.
GRIZZLY BEAR, BLACK BEAR, MOOSE:
Centerfire, muzzleloader: Sept.
CARIBOU:
Centerfire, muzzleloader: Aug. through Sept.
DALL SHEEP:
Centerfire, muzzleloader: Aug.
Rates:
GRIZZLY from $7,500/10 days
BLACK BEAR from $3,450/5 days
CARIBOU/BLACK BEAR from $6,950/10 days
DALL SHEEP from $8,950/10 days (two hunters)
MOOSE from $7,950/10 days
Accommodations:
LOG LODGE OR TENT
MAXIMUM NUMBER OF HUNTERS: 4
Meals:
Anything desired
Conference Groups:
Yes
Guides:
Included
Gratuity:
$500
Preferred Payment:
Cash, personal check
Other Activities:
Fishing, bird hunting, waterfowling, hiking, bird watching, wildlife photography.
Getting There:
Fly to Anchorage and rent a car, or catch the flight to Kodiak.

Contact:
Dennis Harms
Alaska Trophy Safaris
Box 670071
Chugiak, AK 99567
907/696-2484

IS A GRIZZLY DIFFERENT from a brown bear? What about a Kodiak? It depends whether the biologist you ask is a "lumper" or a "splitter." Lumpers, so-called because they tend to lump species together, will tell you they're all the same bear. Splitters contend that because of hàbitat and diet, the bears have evolved into different critters. For must of us, this makes little difference. Sure, brown bears that live along Alaska's coasts are bigger than their inland brethren, the grizzly. Kodiak bears, restricted to the islands, are Alaska's biggest browns.

Dennis Harms has made a specialty out of hunting big bears on Kodiak Island in the Anakulik River drainage and across the Shelikof Strait in the Alaska Range. Bears in these territories average 10 feet, with skulls in the 26- to 28-inch neighborhood. Several trophies taken by Harms' clients have qualified for Boone & Crockett and Safari Club International lists. Grizzlies taken from the Alaska Range are a bit smaller than those from Kodiak. The best hunting is in the spring, but very good bears are also taken in the fall. There's no place where the bear hunting is better than along the salmon streams of Kodiak.

If big bears are Harms' first love, Dall sheep have to be his second. From his base camp of hand-hewn log in an unnamed valley in the Alaska Range, clients ride horseback up the rugged canyons favored by rams. A good one will better the 38-inch full curl that is standard in these spots. Depending on weather and the vagaries of wandering sheep, hunters may fly from the base lodge to spike camps and hunt the high ground from there. The success rate on sheep in this outfit is better than 90 percent.

The lodge in the Alaska Range is also headquarters for grizzly, moose and caribou hunters. Harms offers two packages for moose hunters — standard fare for bulls averaging 60 inches, and a trophy hunt for big boys with racks topping 65 inches. Hunter success on trophy moose runs about 80 percent. Caribou are normally hunted from horseback in this part of the state, and the bulls are good, usually scoring in the 380s. For hunters seeking even better bulls, there's an optional trip to a spike camp on the Mulchatna River north of Iliamna. The Mulchatna herd is one of the best in Alaska.

If you've booked into the lodge on the Ayakulik, you'll enjoy it. It's endorsed by Orvis and offers fishing for king, coho, chum, pink and sockeye salmon, steelhead and Dolly Varden. The Mulchatna is also known for its king salmon fishing. Life, sometimes, is very hard.

[A L A S K A]

All Alaska Outdoors Lodge

S o l d o t n a

A luxurious lodge that offers guided and unguided flyouts for moose, caribou and black bear.

VITAL STATISTICS:

Game/Arm/Seasons:
MOOSE:
Bow, centerfire, muzzleloader: Sept.
CARIBOU:
Bow, centerfire, muzzleloader: Aug. through Sept.
Rates:
MOOSE $2,095/7 days
CARIBOU $1,595/5 days
MOOSE/CARIBOU combo $3,195//10 days
Accommodations:
MODERN LOG LODGE
NUMBER OF ROOMS: 4
Maximum Number of Hunters: 16
Meals:
Meal packages are offered at an additional cost
Conference Groups: Yes
Guides: No
Gratuity: Hunter's discretion
Preferred Payment:
Cash, check
Other Activities:
Bird hunting, bird-watching, fishing, golf, hiking, waterfowling, wildlife photography
Getting There:
Fly to Anchorage, rent a car and drive to the lodge or take a commuter flight to Kenai where you will be met by a representative of the lodge.

Contact:
David Williams
All Alaska Outdoors Lodge
Box 208
Soldotna, AK 99669
907/262-6001
Fax: 907/262-1349
e-mail: info@allalaska.com
Web: www.allalaska.com
off-season:
1108 North Country Club
La Porte, TX 77571
281/470-1353
Fax: 281/470-6770

HUNTING ALASKA is every big game hunter's dream. To get out in the wilderness—no posted signs, no other hunters within miles, but with game galore—if you're a serious hunter, you couldn't ask for more.

All Alaska Outdoors Lodge can make it happen for you. Offering guided and unguided hunts, All Alaska will put you up in one of their two luxurious lodges in the Soldatna area for the first night. Then you fly out to the western slopes of the Alaska and Aleutian ranges for moose, caribou or black bear. Or, if you prefer, All Alaska will set you up on a moose/caribou combination river float trip in the Bristol Bay area. This is a September hunt, where you drift silently through pristine wilderness, trying to call rutting bulls out of the thickets, into bow or rifle range; or you may wish to beach your neoprene raft, get out, and glass some of the low hills for caribou. If you spot the bull you want, then it's a question of stalking ahead of the moving herd and into range.

No matter what type of hunt you choose, All Alaska prides itself on its two luxurious lodges. The Log Lodge, nestled in the woods high on a hill overlooking beautiful Longmere Lake, has private porches that provide spectacular views of the gorgeous sunsets. This lodge has four suites, each with a private bath, fully equipped kitchen, a dining area, living room, plus TV/VCR and maid service. Longmere Lake Lodge, only 150 yards away, is a traditional lodge with a shared Alaska great room, fully equipped kitchen, and bright and airy dining room. Branching out from the social area are five private, beautifully decorated guest rooms, each with its own private bath and TV. Meal options are many, ranging from going into town each day to the quaint restaurants in Soldatna to having the lodge buy your supplies each day so you can do your own cooking.

Austin's Alaska Adventures

St. Michael

Dogsled for grizzlies and moose in an off-the-beaten-path part of Alaska.

VITAL STATISTICS:

Game/Arm/Seasons:
GRIZZLY BEAR:
Centerfire: Spring, early Apr. through mid-May; Fall, early Sept. through early Oct.
MOOSE:
Centerfire: Mid-Aug. through late Sept.
CARIBOU:
Centerfire: Mid-Aug. through Sept.
Rates:
GRIZZLY BEAR $8,500/10 days
MOOSE $5,500/10 days
CARIBOU: $2,500/6 days
Accommodations:
RUSTIC LOG LODGE
NUMBER OF ROOMS: 3
MAXIMUM NUMBER OF HUNTERS: 4
Meals:
Steaks, ribs, chicken, salmon, king crab
Conference Groups: No
Guides: Included
Gratuity: Hunter's discretion
Preferred Payment:
Cash, check
Other Activities:
Bird hunting, bird-watching, boating, fishing, hiking, waterfowling, wildlife photography
Getting There:
Fly to St. Michael and be transported to the lodge via boat at no extra charge.

Contact:
Jerry or Clara Austin
Austin's Alaska Adventures
Box 110
St. Michael, AK 99659
907/923-3281
Fax: 907/923-3272
e-mail: jaustin79@aol.com
Web:
www.alajlcan.com/austin/hunting.html

OWNER JERRY AUSTIN has been guiding hunters for brown bear, moose and caribou for nearly 30 years, centering his operations in Units 18, 21 and 22 in western Alaska. Hunts are primarily by walking, boating, ATV, dog team or snow machine, depending on the species hunted and time of year.

Bears are Austin's specialty. Many clients return from a hunt here saying they've never seen so many bears. With so many moose and caribou in the area, bears never go unfed around here. Perhaps the best time to hunt them is April or May, when North Slope grizzlies typically move from their alpine denning areas to the flood plain. Snow still covers the ground, but snowmobiles or, better, dogsleds will get you to the hunting area. (Austin should know a thing or two about dogsleds from his 18 Iditarod finishes!) Bears of 20-plus (skull) inches are in prime condition in early spring, with guard hair that is long and shiny. It pays to be in shape when hunting these critters, for they range far and wide and can lead you into some God-awful country. Finding a den, then glassing and stalking are the preferred methods of hunting. Just make sure you know how to judge bear size from a distance. You don't want to hike five miles and set up an ambush only to discover that the bear you're after isn't big enough. Success rates for Austin's camp have been running 100 percent the past few years, so just take your time and wait for the griz you want.

Moose also run large in this area. Float-hunting is a preferred method, although calling during the rut in September is an ideal way to take a 60-inch plus bull. What's more exciting than having an enraged bull charge out of an alder thicket, answering your call, and fully intent on ripping you to pieces?

Barren ground caribou can be tough, too. In many ways, hunting them is more a matter of finding the herd than anything else. But you still have to judge a bull from a distance, execute a stalk to get within range, and pull it off without spooking the herd.

Austin's lodge is a handsome, well-run affair, hard by the mouth of the Golsovia River, which feeds into Norton Sound. It's right outside the historic Russian/Yupik Eskimo village of St. Michael. Austin also runs a number of tent camps, so hunters can get out into the backcountry where the game is. Meals at the lodge consist of steak, roasts, ribs, salmon, chicken and king crab; hearty fare that will fuel you for the following day.

Chris Goll's Rainbow River Lodge

Iliamna

Here you'll find big bears, caribou and fishing on the side.

VITAL STATISTICS:

Game/Arm/Seasons:
BROWN BEAR:
Bow, centerfire, muzzleloader:
Mid-May
GRIZZLY:
Bow, centerfire, muzzleloader:
Mid-Apr. through mid-May
MOOSE:
Bow, centerfire, muzzleloader:
Aug. through Sept.
CARIBOU
Bow, centerfire, muzzleloader:
Aug. through Sept.

Rates:
BROWN BEAR from $9,000/9 days
CARIBOU from $4,000/7 days
Combo MOOSE/CARIBOU from
$8,500/7 days

Accommodations:
TENTS IN SPIKE CAMPS, WITH A NIGHT OR
TWO AT THE MAIN LODGE POSSIBLE
NUMBER OF ROOMS: 6
MAXIMUM NUMBER OF HUNTERS: 16

Meals: Steak, prime rib,
halibut, salmon

Conference Groups: Yes

Guides: Included

Gratuity: 5-10%

Preferred Payment:
Credit card, personal check

Other Activities:
Fishing, bird hunting, waterfowling,
rafting, swimming, boating, hiking,
bird watching, wildlife photography

Getting There:
Fly to Iliamna or Dillingham and you
will be ferried to the lodge or spike
camp by private aircraft.

Contact:
Chris Goll
Chris Goll's Rainbow River
Lodge
Box 330
Iliamna, AK 99606
907/571-1210
Fax: 907/571-1210
(Nov. through May):
Box 1070
Silver City, NM 88062
505/388-2259
Fax: 505/388-2261

THE NAME OF THIS LODGE, of course, says fishing in a big way. Hard by the Copper River in Alaska's Iliamna country, Goll's snug and secluded cabins of cedar (all with private baths) and gourmet meals served in the contemporary, cathedral-ceilinged log lodge only seem to make the fishing better. Big rainbows are ravenous here in the fall and succumb to virtually any reasonable pattern.

Most folks know the lodge for its angling, but a select few have also sampled its outstanding bear, caribou and moose hunting. Each hunter has a private guide, and Goll maintains three private big game concessions. That means no other hunters or guides are competing for your trophy.

Bears are the prime quarry. Clients hunt grizzlies in the mountainous interior of the state — the specific area will vary depending on populations — within an hour flight from the lodge. Working out of spike camps, hunters hike, often on snowshoes, into active denning areas. At this time of the year, mid-April to mid-May, the grizzlies are emerging from hibernation and are beginning to feed.

In mid-May the action shifts to the rugged river valleys of the Alaskan Peninsula where Kodiaks — the largest carnivore in North America — are on the move. These hunts are less arduous. Super Cubs and Beavers, Alaska's workhorse bush aircraft, ferry hunters into areas where bears are active. Then on foot, or frequently by jet-powered boat or raft, clients search for a bear that they want. The drill is the same in October, only by then Kodiaks have fattened up on berries and salmon. Generally, fall bears are bigger than spring bears, but spring bears have deeper, lusher coats.

In addition to bear, Chris offers an August/September hunt for barren ground caribou in the mountain meadows above Iliamna. As with spring grizzly, hunts are conducted from comfortable spike camps. Along with caribou, hunters frequently take moose and occasionally brown bear and wolves. This is also the peak of the season for Copper River rainbows fat with salmon spawn. Take a fly-rod and plan a couple of extra days for fishing. Or pack a 12 gauge along with your rifle and have a go at waterfowl and ptarmigan.

Jake's Alaska Wilderness Outfitters

A n c h o r a g e

For trophy brown bears, look no farther than master guide Jake Gaudet.

VITAL STATISTICS:

Game/Arm/Seasons:

BROWN BEAR:
Bow, centerfire, muzzleloader: May and Oct.

GRIZZLY AND BLACK BEAR
Bow, centerfire, muzzleloader: May and Aug.

MOOSE:
Bow, centerfire, muzzleloader: Sept.

CARIBOU
Bow, centerfire, muzzleloader: Mid-Aug. through mid-Oct.

DALL SHEEP:
Centerfire, muzzleloader: Mid-Aug. through mid-Sept.

Rates:

GRIZZLY BEAR from $7,500/10 days
BROWN BEAR from $10,500/15 days
CARIBOU from $3,950/7 days
DALL RAM from $7,800/10 days
(each for two hunters)
MOOSE from $7,800/10 days

Accommodations:

TENT CAMPS

MAXIMUM NUMBER OF HUNTERS: 12

Meals: Fresh meats, vegetables, fruits and homemade desserts

Conference Groups: Yes

Guides: Included

Gratuity: $200 to $500

Preferred Payment:
Credit cards, personal check

Other Activities:
Fishing, bird hunting, waterfowling, rafting, hiking, camping, wildlife photography

Getting There:
Fly to Anchorage, McGrath, King Salmon or Dillingham, depending on where you're hunting, and take a private air shuttle into camp (no charge).

Contact:
Jake Gaudet
Jake's Alaska Wilderness Outfitters
Box 104179
Anchorage, AK 99510
907/522-1133
e-mail: jakesawo@alaska.net
Web: jakesalaska.com/

JAKE GAUDET IS A GUY who gets around. For 25 years, he's been checking out bear, caribou, moose and sheep hunting in the 49th state, and he's come up with three or four locations where quality game is plentiful and other hunters are not.

When hunting and Alaska are mentioned in the same breath, bears immediately come to mind. After scouting numerous areas over the years, Gaudet settled on the Becharof National Wilderness Refuge, which lies northwest of the Aleutian Range and just south of Katmai National Park. This is bear country with a capital "B."

From state-of-the-art tent camps pitched in remote river valleys, clients — only four per year — have their pick of brownies moving down the slopes and along the streams. Typical trophies are in the 10-foot range, and hunter success verges on 100 percent. Not only is the camp first class — meals include fresh fruits and vegetables along with steak and salmon — but volcanoes and glaciers make the scenery absolutely stunning. And, of course, there are salmon for those with the good sense to bring a fishing rod.

For caribou and trophy moose, Gaudet takes hunters into an exclusive area in the Innoko National Wildlife Refuge, a vast glacial plain of kettle ponds amid kame ridges. Clients hunt from boats on the Innoko, a tributary of the Yukon, or on foot in high alpine meadows. Moose in the bottoms typically carry racks with spreads in the mid-60s. During the rut, they can be called to within 15 yards; archer success is 100 percent. Caribou from the Kuskokwim and Mulchatna herds run in the 300-point class, and the wide-open countryside is perfect for glass-and-stalk hunting. Black bear and grizzlies are found in the berry patches in the high, open meadows. Accommodations are tent camps staffed by an ever-present major domo whose culinary skills are beyond reproach.

Dall sheep, the most elusive of Alaskan trophies, roam the high, barren ridges of the Talkeetna Mountains north and east of Anchorage. Grizzly and black bear face little pressure in this rugged area, and during spring hunts clients will see half a dozen or more shootable bear. In the fall, sheep, bear and moose are in season. Hunters fly into tent base or spike camps, depending on species and weather, then walk and glass the ridges searching for the perfect boar, bull or ram.

[A L A S K A]

Kichatna Guide Service

C h u g i a k

This guide service hunts prime game country on an exclusive basis.

VITAL STATISTICS:

Game/Arm/Seasons:

MOOSE AND CARIBOU:
Bow, centerfire, muzzleloader: Early-Sept. through early-Oct.

GRIZZLY:
Bow, centerfire, muzzleloader: Mid-Aug. through late Sept.

KODIAK BEAR:
Bow, centerfire, muzzleloader: Late-April through mid-May

KODIAK BEAR and SITKA BLACKTAIL:
Bow, centerfire, muzzleloader: Late Oct. through mid-Nov.

DALL SHEEP:
Bow, centerfire, muzzleloader: Mid to late Aug.

Rates:
MOOSE $7,250/10 days
CARIBOU $4,950/7 days
GRIZZLY $7,950/10 days
KODIAK BEAR from $9,750/9 days
DALL SHEEP $7,250/12 days
SITKA BLACKTAIL $4,250/6 days
Combo hunts available

Accommodations:
WALL TENTS, LOG CABIN
(DEPENDING ON LOCATION)
NUMBER OF ROOMS: 1 IN CABIN
MAXIMUM NUMBER OF HUNTERS: 6

Meals:
Game, chicken, steak, pork chops

Conference Groups: No

Guides: Included

Gratuity: $100 to $500

Preferred Payment: Cash, check

Other Activities: Fishing

Getting There:
Fly to Anchorage, and rent a car

Contact:
Harold (Zeke) Schetzle
Kichatna Guide Service
Box 670790
Chugiak, AK 99567
907/696-3256
Fax: 907/694-2200
e-mail: kitchatna@corecom.net,
Web: www.corecom.net/kichatna

ESTABLISHED AND RUN by master guide/outfitter Harold "Zeke" Schetzle since 1974, Kichatna Guide Service offers hunts ranging the length of Alaska, from the tundra country of the northern Brooks Range to the forested south-central Alaska Range Mountains to Kodiak Island in the Gulf of Alaska.

Schetzle's hunters hunt Dall sheep in the northern part of the Brooks Range, above the Arctic Circle, and in the Arctic National Wildlife Refuge, for which Kichatna has an exclusive permit. These are backpack hunts, with hunters sleeping in wall tents at the base camp. Make sure you take a good pair of 10x50X binoculars on this hunt to judge the rams before you hike high up in the scree and talus where the big ones live.

In the Alaska Range, where Schetzle has a concession to operate in the Denali National Preserve, hunters go after Dall sheep as well as caribou. Schetzle calls these hunts "challenging," which means you better be in good shape and able to accurately shoot a flat-shooting rifle such as a .270 loaded with 150-grain bullets.

Elsewhere in the Alaska Range, hunters who sign up with Kichatna can go one-on-one with a guide after moose, brown/grizzly bears, caribou and black bears. Two different base cabin sites are here. And the main lodge even has a sauna for those whose muscles ache after a day of slogging through tough brambles.

Heated wall tents are available to hunters who venture down to Kodiak after trophy brown bears (April through May and September through November) and Sitka blacktails. Mountain goat hunting is also available on a permit basis here. And don't forget to take along a flyrod, as the action on Dolly Varden can be hot in the fall.

The food is basic but hearty, with dinners centering around game meat, chicken, pork chops and steaks. Heart-healthy meals are also available for those who wish.

Lazer's Guide Service

Palmer

Personalized service is what Lazer's is all about.

VITAL STATISTICS:

Game/Arm/Seasons:
BROWN BEAR:
Bow and centerfire: May and Oct.
GRIZZLY BEAR:
Bow and centerfire: Sept.
DALL SHEEP:
Centerfire: Aug. and Sept.
SITKA BLACK-TAILED DEER:
Bow and centerfire: Oct. and Nov.

Rates:
BROWN BEAR $8,500/10 days (two-on-one hunting)
GRIZZLY BEAR $5,900/10 days (two-on-one hunting)
DALL SHEEP $6,500/10 days (two-on-one hunting)
SITKA BLACK-TAILED DEER $1,695/10 days (unguided); $2,995/10 days (guided)

Accommodations:
TENTS
MAXIMUM NUMBER OF HUNTERS: 5

Meals: Hamburgers, spaghetti, vegetables, fruits

Conference Groups: No

Guides: Included

Gratuity: $100

Preferred Payment:
Deposit check or cash, balance in cash

Other Activities:
Bird hunting, sightseeing

Getting There:
Fly to Anchorage and be met by van from Lazer's Guide Service. Fly to Kodiak or King Salmon and take shuttle flight to camp for $150 from Kodiak and $350 from King Salmon.

Contact:
David L. Lazer
Lazer's Guide Service
HC5 Box 6877
Palmer, AK 99645-9612
907/745-3006
Fax: 907/745-3006
off-season:
416 Luther Rd.
Johnstown, PA 15904
814/269-4929

IF YOU'RE LOOKING for a personalized, one-on-one or two-on-one hunt, then look no further than Lazer's Guide Service. David Lazer has been in the guiding business for almost 30 years, and he knows his stuff. He personally guides both bow and rifle hunters for trophy brown bears from seven to 10 feet (you can hunt them in May or October), grizzlies from six to eight feet (September) and full-curl (36 inches) Dall rams (in August or September). Lazer will also guide for blacktails that may run 150 to 175 pounds, with 4x4 racks. Hunters can also hunt these cousins of the mule deer on their own, with Lazer helping to set them up and point them in the right direction.

Lazer recommends that rifle hunters use at least a .270 for sheep, and a .30-06 for deer and bears. Especially with the big bears, many hunters prefer something with a bit more stopping power, such as a .300 Win. Mag. or .338 Win. Mag.

Camp consists of comfortable wall tents, no matter what part of Alaska Lazer may take you to. (He also runs trips in Mexico for deer and in Russia for big game. Contact him directly for information on those hunts.) Food in camp is straightforward and good, with breakfasts of eggs and pancakes, sandwiches for lunch, and anything from spaghetti to meat or fish for dinner.

[A L A S K A]

Lost Creek Ranch

E u r e k a

Hunt moose, caribou, rams, grizzlies and black bear from this remote dude ranch.

VITAL STATISTICS:

Game/Arm/Seasons:
GRIZZLY:
Bow, centerfire, muzzleloader: May and Sept.
BLACK BEAR:
Bow, centerfire, muzzleloader: Mid-May through mid-June
MOOSE:
Bow, centerfire, muzzleloader: Sept.
CARIBOU
Bow, centerfire, muzzleloader: July through Sept.
DALL RAM:
Centerfire, muzzleloader: Aug.

Rates:
GRIZZLY from $4,500/10 days
BLACK BEAR from $1,500/5 days
CARIBOU from $2,500/7 days
DALL RAM from $5,000/14 days
(each for two hunters)
MOOSE from $5,500/10 days

Accommodations:
LOG LODGE OR TENT
MAXIMUM NUMBER OF HUNTERS:
4 PER CAMP

Meals:
Alaskan fare (game and fish)

Conference Groups: Yes

Guides: Included

Gratuity: Hunter's discretion

Preferred Payment:
Cash, MasterCard, Visa,
personal check

Other Activities:
Fishing, bird hunting, bird watching, hiking, horseback riding, waterfowling, wildlife photography

Getting There:
Fly to Fairbanks and the ranch staff will collect you for the trip to the lodge.

Contact:
Les Cobb
Lost Creek Ranch
Box 84334
Fairbanks, AK 99708
907/672-3999
e-mail: AlaskaLCR@aol.com
Web: members.aol.com/alaskaLCR

I**N THE OLD DAYS**, the trail left Eureka, climbed a dome by the same name and then settled down into the Minook Valley following the creek north for 25 miles to Rampart, on the Yukon. A shortcut to that great river highway, the trailhead is roughly 150 miles north of Fairbanks. Now a gravel track that passes for a good road in these parts, a century ago it carried prospectors and authors such Jack London and Rex Beach (read *The Barrier* if you can find a copy). When his riverboat was caught by early ice, the saloon-keeping former marshal, Wyatt Earp, was forced to winter in this once booming town.

Twenty-five years ago, Les and Norma Cobb chucked the trappings of contemporary civilization and headed up the trail as far as they could drive and homesteaded a section on the upper waters of Minook Creek. There they built a log lodge, opening what may be the northernmost dude ranch in the U.S. Spring and fall are high hunting seasons. Grizzlies in the 800-pound range generally scoring 8 inches or better, and black bear of 275 pounds or so are the main attractions in spring. Caribou with 300-point racks kick in during July. Dall sheep averaging 38 points-plus become legal in the second week of August, and when they go out of season, moose with 60-inch spreads become legal.

This is a straightforward, no-frills operation. Guests hunt out of the main lodge for black bear and use tent camps located near the Yukon in the mountains of the North Slope for grizzly, caribou, moose and sheep. Here, your ATV is a horse or, if you're working the myriad islands and channels of the Yukon, a boat. Most hunting is one-on-one, which is a real advantage. Most of Cobb's guides have been with him for more than 10 years.

Headquarters for the operation is the low, rambling ranch that offers a variety of accommodations from a two-bed cabin, a second cabin of four beds, or the bunkhouse, which sleeps an even dozen (assuming that nobody snores). Meals are basic and family-style, featuring game, salmon and halibut. It's not a bad idea to bring a rod; Dolly Varden, grayling, salmon and trout run in the Minook. Also pack along a bathing suit. A soak in the Cobb's hot spring just might ease those sore muscles.

Morris Hunting Company

Anchorage

Hunt the Iliamna region for bear, moose, caribou and sheep.

VITAL STATISTICS:

Game/Arm/Seasons:
BROWN BEAR:
Bow, centerfire: Late Apr. through late May
MOOSE:
Bow, centerfire: Early through mid-Sept.
CARIBOU:
Bow, centerfire: Early Aug. through late Oct.
BLACK BEAR:
Bow, centerfire: Year-round
SHEEP:
Bow, centerfire: Mid through late Aug.

Rates:
BROWN BEAR from $8,000/10 days
MOOSE $7,000/10 days
CARIBOU from $3,500/10 days
BLACK BEAR offered as a combination hunt
SHEEP $7,000/10 days

Accommodations:
WALLED TENTS AND 1 CABIN
NUMBER OF ROOMS:
2 IN CABIN
MAXIMUM NUMBER OF HUNTERS: 12

Meals:
Wild game steaks, stews

Conference Groups: No

Guides: Included

Gratuity: $200 per animal

Preferred Payment:
Cash, cashier's check, money orders

Other Activities:
Wildlife photography

Getting There:
Fly to Iliamna and be met by a representative of the outfitter.

Contact:
Steven L. Morris
Morris Hunting Company
Box 190342
Anchorage, AK 99519
907/243-4868 or
907/571-1478

OFFERING HUNTS for grizzly and brown bear, moose, caribou and sheep, registered guide and outfitter Steven Morris runs his brown bear hunts on the Alaska Peninsula and grizzly hunts in the Alaska Range. Caribou hunting is done in the Mulchatna River drainage, while moose and sheep hunts take place in varying game management units in the Iliamna area.

Morris is a hard worker, and he and his assistant guides put forth every effort to get you the game animal you want. (Only caribou hunts may be unguided if you're not an Alaska resident.)

Many of Morris' hunts are based out of a large, modern cabin in Iliamna. The company also has a wall-tent camp west of Iliamna from which many of the brown bear (spring and fall), moose and caribou hunts take place. Morris also owns property on the coast of Cook Inlet, home to brown bears that average eight and a half feet.

Caribou hunting along the Mulchatna is the least difficult of all the hunts. Morris will fly you in, help you set up your tent camp, then either guide you to a trophy bull or leave you on your own. The Mulchatna herd is huge and growing, and your chances of filling a tag are extremely high. (You can buy up to five tags.)

The toughest hunt is the sheep hunt, which requires that you're in good physical shape. These hunts involve lots of glassing. And if you see a Dall ram that you like, be prepared for some heavy climbing over steep scree slopes and across icefields. Getting a nice ram is very possible in this region, if you're up to the task.

No matter what you hunt — and brown bear hunting is no piece of cake, especially in the spring when you may have to deal with snowy conditions — you can relax at the cabin at the end of the day, watching television, reading a book, then dining on wild game and salmon.

North American Wilderness Adventures

Big Lake

Do-it-yourself moose hunts in the Matanuska-Susitna Valley.

VITAL STATISTICS:

Game/Arm/Seasons:
BLACK AND GRIZZLY BEAR:
Bow, centerfire, muzzleloader:
Mid-Aug. through mid-Sept.

Rates:
$1,195 per person

Accommodations:
MODERN YET RUSTIC CABIN
NUMBER OF ROOMS: 4
MAXIMUM NUMBER OF HUNTERS: 8

Meals:
Self-catered

Conference Groups:
No

Guides:
Not available

Gratuity:
Hunter's discretion

Preferred Payment:
Cash, check

Other Activities:
Fishing, bird hunting, bird watching, wildlife photography

Getting There:
Fly to Anchorage and the lodge van will meet you at the airport.

Contact:
**Woody Main,
North American Wilderness Adventures, Inc.
c/o Lake Anna Lodge
Box 521865
Big Lake, AK 99652**
off-season:
**RD 1, Box 501A
Brookville, PA 15825
814/849-7040**
e-mail: nawa@penn.com
Web: www.tulipcom.com/nawa

FOR DO-IT-YOURSELF HUNTERS, there's a rustic lodge tucked back on a little lake named Anna in the heart of the Matanuska-Susitna Valley of south-central Alaska, about two hours by car north of Anchorage. For a shade less than $1,200 each, you and seven of your buddies will have eight days to track down moose. You'll guide yourself. The camp manager will tell you where moose have been sighted, and otherwise point you in the right direction.

Are there moose here? Of course. This is Game Management Unit 14A, which consistently has the largest moose harvest per square mile in Alaska. Here, the Matanuska flows though a broad glacial river valley dotted with scores of kettle ponds. To the north rise the Talkeetna Mountains, perpetually ice-capped. Moose frequent the river bottoms, where dense thickets of alder and swamp provide almost impenetrable cover. During the month-long season, the most popular weeks are the last two, because the leaves are off the trees and you can see what you're hearing. Hunters who schedule trips for early September have the opportunity to hunt black bear as well. These are bear of 300 pounds-plus with glossy, black pelts in their prime.

North American Wilderness Adventures does not employ guides. Advice from owner Woody Main, a sheaf of topo maps, and boats and ATVs will get you where you're going. Then it's strictly up to you. Self-guided hunting can save you big bucks, but hunter success rates are lower than on guided hunts. And there are more apt to be hunters from other camps in your area. It's a trade-off. But if the hunt is as important as meat in the freezer and budget is a consideration, then North American Wilderness Adventures may be a good place to begin.

The lodge itself is a three-story cabin set in the trees by Lake Anna. Not only does the lodge have everything you need (bedding, towels, etc.), you'll arrive to a kitchen fully stocked with steaks, turkey, chicken, fresh vegetables, fruits, condiments and important stuff, such as cookies. Bring your own liquor, if you're so inclined. Also slip a fishing rod into your duffel, as nearby streams are loaded with salmon and Dolly Varden.

Northward Bound

C h u g i a k

The Lake Clarke region offers moose, caribou, sheep and bear in the midst of incredible wilderness.

VITAL STATISTICS:

Game/Arm/Seasons:
CARIBOU:
Bow, centerfire, muzzleloader:
Early-Aug. through Oct.
MOOSE:
Bow, centerfire, muzzleloader:
Early through late Sept.
DALL SHEEP:
Bow, centerfire, muzzleloader:
Early Aug. through late Sept.
GRIZZLY:
Bow, centerfire, muzzleloader:
Early Sept. through late May
BLACK BEAR:
Bow, centerfire, muzzleloader:
No closed season

Rates:
CARIBOU $3,400/6 days
MOOSE $6,950/9 days
DALL SHEEP $7,500/customized
hunt, approximately 6 days
GRIZZLY $7,500/12 days (spring only)
BLACK BEAR $1,000 extra in
conjunction with any hunt

Accommodations:
RUSTIC LOG LODGE
NUMBER OF ROOMS: 8 WITH PRIVATE BATH
MAXIMUM NUMBER OF HUNTERS: 14

Meals:
Meat, fish, potatoes

Conference Groups: Yes
Guides: Included
Gratuity: Hunter's discretion
Preferred Payment: Check

Other Activities:
Antiquing, bird hunting, bird watching, canoeing/rafting, hiking, skiing

Getting There:
Fly to Anchorage and take the air shuttle to the lodge for $600 round-trip.

Contact:
Jim Harrower
Northward Bound Stoney River Lodge
13830 Jarui Dr.
Anchorage, AK 99515
907/345-2891
Fax: 907/345-4674
e-mail: harrower@alaska.net

HUNTING AN AREA that covers more than 1.5 million acres in the heart of Alaska — the Lake Clarke National Park Preserve — Northward Bound can put hunters in prime moose, bear, sheep and caribou territory. The hub of the activity is Stony River Lodge, which is modern and complete, including laundry, sauna and showers. Most hunters spend little time there, however, using it as a stopping-off point on their way to one of the 30 spike camps operated by Northward Bound. These camps vary from cozy cabins and frame shelters to Indian-style teepees, wall tents and fly camps.

Most hunting consists of a lot of walking and climbing, so being in good physical shape should be priority if you want to improve your odds for success. If you don't mind sleeping in a spartan fly camp, near spots where your guide has seen trophy bear or moose, then your chances of success are even greater. Some of the easier hunting is reserved for older hunters or those with physical limitations, but that sure doesn't mean the quality of the animals is sub-par. In this part of Alaska, a 60-inch moose is just as liable to walk out in front of a canoe-bound hunter as in front of a backpacking hunter.

Moose and caribou are the backbone of the operation, and most hunts involve one or both of these animals. But according to owner Jim Harrower, sheep hunts in this region are becoming more and more popular, with some 10- and 12-year-old trophy Dall sheep being taken every year.

Harrower's outfit also takes some outstanding grizzlies each year, which have won many awards in the Alaska Professional Hunters Association annual competition.

[A L A S K A]

Pioneer Outfitters

T o k

Hunt sheep, bear and moose in the southeastern panhandle.

VITAL STATISTICS:

Game/Arm/Seasons:
BLACK AND GRIZZLY BEAR:
Bow, centerfire, muzzleloader:
Late Apr. through June and
Sept. through mid-Oct.
MOOSE:
Bow, centerfire, muzzleloader: Sept.
DALL RAMS:
Centerfire, muzzleloader:
Mid-Aug. through mid-Sept.
Rates:
GRIZZLY from $7,500/10 days
DALL RAM from $9,900/10 days
MOOSE from $6,900/10 days
Accommodations:
TENT CAMPS OR WOODEN CABINS
MAXIMUM NUMBER OF HUNTERS:
4 PER CAMP
Meals:
Home-style cooking
Conference Groups: No
Guides: Included
Gratuity: $300 to $1,000
Preferred Payment:
Cash, traveler's checks
Other Activities:
Icefishing, bird hunting, hiking,
glacier walks, wildlife photography
Getting There:
Fly to Fairbanks and take 40-Mile Air
to Chisana ($575 per charter).

Contact:
Terry Overly
Pioneer Outfitters
Box CZN
Tok, AK 99780
907/734-0007
Fax: 907/734-7433
e-mail:
pioneer-outfitters@worldnet.att.net

EVER GET THE FEELING that some guys have "been there and done it?" Well, when it comes to the Wrangell-St. Elias National Park and Preserve area at the top of Alaska's southeastern panhandle, Terry Overly knows his way around. For 35 years he's been guiding clients after sheep, bear and moose in the jagged, rocky peaks and thick alder valley's of Game Management Unit 12.

From his base camp at Chisana, shadowed by 6,800-foot Euchre Mountain, Overly hunts a 3,600-square-mile area that butts up against the park boundary beyond which no hunting is allowed. Game flow in and out of the protected area provides a steady supply of healthy, trophy animals.

Sheep season kicks off around August 10 and continues to September 20 or so. From comfortable cabins and tents, depending on which camp's in use, you ride out in the morning, climb the ridges and glass and stalk. That's the key. If you move too often, you won't see sheep or they will see you. Either way you lose. This is a game where patience pays off in trophy horns. The average set is a 35-inch curl with a 13-inch base. Sometimes fate deals hunters spectacular rams of 38 inches or better, but other times the state average is 32 inches. Such is luck, a factor every bit as important in sheep hunting as physical conditioning and shooting skills.

Whether it's spring and bears are eating old berries or digging out ground squirrels near the glaciers, or fall when you may find them lower, in areas frequented by moose and caribou, the drill is the same — hours of glassing while the bears do the moving. Grizzlies in these parts run a good seven feet, and black bear average about six feet. Moose are also on the agenda here. Early in the fall season, they'll be in the river bottoms. Come the start of the rut in the mid-September, the bulls will begin to climb. In search of prime bulls — the average is about 57 inches — Overly's clients hunt from horseback through vast stands of timber.

Stephan Lake Lodge

E a g l e   R i v e r

Made famous by "Sports Afield" magazine's Russell Annabel, the Talkeetnas offer bear, moose and sheep, all of trophy quality.

VITAL STATISTICS:

Game/Arm/Seasons:
GRIZZLY AND MOOSE:
Centerfire: Aug. through Sept.
BROWN BEAR:
Centerfire: Spring, Apr. through May;
Fall, Oct. through Nov.
SHEEP:
Centerfire: Early Aug. through early Sept.
BLACK BEAR:
Centerfire: July through Sept.
SITKA BLACK-TAILED DEER:
Centerfire: Oct. through Nov.
Rates:
GRIZZLY, MOOSE, SHEEP
$7,000/7 to 12 days
BROWN BEAR $10,500/7 to 12 days
BLACK BEAR $2,800/7 to 12 days
SITKA BLACK-TAILED DEER
$2,800/7 to 12 days
Combination hunts are also available
Accommodations:
MODERN LOG LODGE
NUMBER OF ROOMS: 7
MAXIMUM NUMBER OF HUNTERS: 14
Meals:
Roasts, ham, chicken, homemade desserts
Conference Groups: Yes
Guides: Included
Gratuity: Hunter's discretion
Preferred Payment:
Cash, MasterCard, Visa, check
Other Activities:
Bird hunting, canoeing/rafting, fishing, hiking, waterfowling, wildlife photography
Getting There:
Fly to Anchorage International Airport and take the air taxi to the lodge at no additional cost.

Contact:
Jim Bailey
Stephan Lake Lodge
Box 770695
Eagle River, AK 99577
907/696-2163
Fax: 907/694-4129
e-mail: bbailey@servcom.com
Web:
www.AlaskaOne.com/stephanlake

OUTFITTER JIM BAILEY has been guiding in Alaska for more than 20 years and knows his stuff as well as anyone. Bailey operates out of two areas: Game Management Unit 13 in the Talkeetna Mountains and Susitna drainage, for grizzly bear, moose, Dall sheep and black bear; and Game Management Unit 8, on Kodiak Island, for brown bear and Sitka black-tailed deer.

The lodge is 130 air miles from Anchorage, on the shore of Stephan Lake in the middle of the Talkeetnas. Grizzlies, in particular, are plentiful in this area, generally running seven to eight feet, with the occasional nine-footer taken. Big black bears are abundant too, as are moose. Moose here usually average 60 to 70 inches, several of which have made the Boone & Crockett book, and most have made the Safari Club record book. Dall sheep are also in this part of the Talkeetnas, an area made world famous in the 1950s and 1960s by Sports Afield magazine's long-time writer Russell Annabel.

Hunters after big brown bear in the spring — a time when they are fresh out of their dens, with coats heavy and in prime condition — should try Bailey's operation on Kodiak Island. You have to be in decent shape, as hunting for bear means hiking the three major canyons surrounding camp. The country is generally rolling, mountainous and laced with alder patches and cottonwoods. Snowy conditions are always possible here in the spring, especially at the beginning of the season, April. Bear and black-tailed deer are also available in the fall on Kodiak.

If you choose to stay at Bailey's lodge at Stephan Lake, be prepared for a treat. With a large living area, a dining room that overlooks the lake, private baths and seven guest rooms, you'll feel pampered after a long day in the woods. Guests may also stay at several rustic outlying cabins, or tent spike camps situated where the game is. And if you get what you're after, make sure you have a fishing rod, as salmon and trout abound in both the lake and its outlet stream.

[A L A S K A]

Westwind Guide Service

E a g l e   R i v e r

Guided or unguided hunts for black bear, caribou and moose.

VITAL STATISTICS:

Game/Arm/Seasons:
BROWN BEAR:
Bow, centerfire, muzzleloader: Apr. through May and Sept. through Oct.
MOOSE:
Bow, centerfire, muzzleloader: Sept.
CARIBOU:
Bow, centerfire, muzzleloader: Aug. through Oct.
BLACK BEAR:
Bow, centerfire, muzzleloader: May through June and Aug. through Sept.

Rates:
BROWN BEAR from $7,000/10 day (guided)
CARIBOU from $3,200/7 days (guided)
Combo MOOSE/CARIBOU/BLACK BEAR from $8,500/7 days (guided); $1,900/8 days (unguided)
Various combinations on request

Accommodations:
Tents in spike camps with a night or two at the main lodge possible
NUMBER OF ROOMS: 6
MAXIMUM NUMBER OF HUNTERS: 10

Meals:
Chicken, pork chops, spaghetti, wild game/fish

Conference Groups: Yes
Guides: Optional
Gratuity: 5 to 10%
Preferred Payment:
Cash, personal check
Other Activities:
Fishing, hiking, wildlife photography
Getting There:
Fly to Iliamna and catch the air taxi for $350 per hunter round-trip.

Contact:
Tony Lee
Westwind Guide Service
Box 771224
Eagle River, AK 99577
907/745-2047
e-mail:
westwind/nayco@bigfoot.com
Web:
www.alaskaoutdoors.com/Westwind

OUTFITTER Tony Lee offers you two basic choices: You can hunt with a guide or without for black bear, caribou and moose. If you choose a guided hunt, you get the full attention of someone who knows the country and the habits of the game and who takes the lead on all those lovely chores around camp — not the least of which is caring for your trophy and meat once you've done your part. On guided hunts success rates for caribou reach the high 90s; moose, the mid-80s; and bear, mid-70s, with spring producing the better animals.

In a drop-camp hunt, you stay in the same kinds of tents and eat the same chow, only you're on your own. Tony or one of his minions will check on you every other day. It's up to you to find your bull or boar and decide whether the next one that comes along is likely to be better. On the other hand, there's no one to make you feel guilty if you miss. And if you connect, guess who's gonna pack out the kill? Archers seem to do particularly well in drop camps, with success rates verging on 100 percent.

No matter which way you go, you'll hunt in the Mulchatana area about 100 miles north of Lake Iliamna. Lee's Super Cub, the airborne jeep of the Alaskan bush, will land you in the midst of this great rising plain where other hunters are few or none. Depending on the program you select, you'll hunt for a week or more, stalking brown bear of eight to nine feet in the spring and again in the fall. Moose in the 60-inch range is a September song in this drainage, and caribou (350 Boone & Crockett) and black bear (6-foot average) are good in the fall. Black bear are also hunted in the spring. The top Pope and Young and Safari Club International velvet caribou came from one of Lee's camps.

Lee makes no bones about it: Conditioning is everything. While this land is not vertical, it's rough and thick. Hunters should feel very comfortable hiking four or five miles per day. Hunters headed for drop camps should be able to pack out 700 pounds of meat in several trips.

Hunts begin at the main camp where there are four cabins of modern design. Generally speaking, you'll find only four to six hunters in camp at any given time, though Lee can take up to 10 if pressed. Guided fishing for rainbows, some of them 30-inchers, is also available for an additional fee.

Zachar Bay Lodge

Kodiak

This is the do-it-yourselfer's ideal Sitka blacktail hunt.

HEN MARTY EATON retired after 20 years as a fisheries biologist with the Alaska Fish and Game Department, he and his wife Linda followed their dreams by turning an abandoned salmon cannery into Zachar Bay Lodge.

The idea wasn't as crazy as it might sound. The cannery — located on the green slopes above Zachar Bay on the southwestern coast of Kodiak Island — included a number of cabins and a main dining hall for the workers. The bay has excellent fishing, while brown bears and Sitka black-tailed deer inhabit the ridges surrounding the bay.

After fixing up the cabins and dining hall, the Eatons opened the lodge in 1989, when six hunters rented cabins. They've been specializing in unguided Sitka black-tailed deer hunts ever since, renting the cabins to hunters from the season opener in mid-October until its closure in mid-December. Alaskan residents may also rent the cabins for unguided bear hunts.

There are three cabins available: Lookout House will house three people; Superintendent House will accommodate six; and Delta House can hold 10. Each cabin has gas stoves and cooking utensils. Boat transport is provided to hunters who want to try different parts of the island. And what an island it is! The land rises dramatically from the beach, going almost straight up to elevations higher than 2,500 feet. Covered with dense grasses, alder, birch and cottonwood, along with the bushes and berry species typical of alpine vegetation, this is prime deer habitat. Hunters have to be in shape to get up those cliffs, but if that's where the deer are, that's where you have to go. Just be careful of the bears, especially after you shoot a deer. Bears in this part of the world know that a rifle shot means there's a dead blacktail around, and they'll come running!

Hunters supply their own gear and food when renting a cabin at Zachar. This is the perfect hunt for do-it-yourselfers. Just make sure to reserve early, as the good word on Zachar's is getting out.

VITAL STATISTICS:

Game/Arm/Seasons:
SITKA BLACK-TAILED DEER:
Bow, centerfire: Mid-Oct. through mid-Dec.

Rates:
Sitka blacktail deer $65 per day
(all hunts are unguided)

Accommodations:
3 RUSTIC CABINS
NUMBER OF ROOMS: 8; 6 w/PRIVATE BATH
MAXIMUM NUMBER OF HUNTERS: 19

Meals:
Cook for yourself

Conference Groups: No

Guides:
All hunts are unguided

Gratuity:
Hunter's discretion

Preferred Payment:
Cash, American Express, Discover, MasterCard, Visa, check

Other Activities:
Bird hunting, bird watching, fishing, hiking, wildlife photography

Getting There:
Fly to Kodiak and take a shuttle flight for $75 one way or take a charter flight for approximately $350.

Contact:
Martin or Linda Eaton
Zachar Bay Lodge
Box 2609
Kodiak, AK 99615
1-800/693-2333
907/486-4120
907/847-2333
Fax: 907/486-4690
e-mail: zbay@ptialaska.net
Web:
www.ptialaska.net/~zbay/zbay.htm

THE EAST

CONNECTICUT, MAINE, MASSACHUSETTS, NEW HAMPSHIRE, NEW JERSEY, NEW YORK, PENNSYLVANIA, RHODE ISLAND, VERMONT

ONE-THIRD of the U.S. population lives in these nine states, yet most are clustered around the great coastal cities and on navigable rivers. Folks from other parts of the country are really surprised by the vast farms, fields and forests so close to cities such as New York, Boston and Philadelphia. Still-hunting, standing and driving for whitetails are the main events here, and opening day of the season can be crowded. In the old days, savvy hunters would hike deep into the woods the night before opening day and sleep curled up in a blanket so they'd be ready the next morning when other hunters pushed deer their way. Today, many hunters either belong to traditional deer camps or lease private lands. Others hunt the vast stretches of public land found throughout the area from New York's Adirondack Mountains to Pennsylvania's Alleghenies. Still others stay at a lodge or hire an outfitter and trek off into huge stretches of wilderness. Thanks to changing habitat and careful management, deer populations are increasing dramatically throughout the region, particularly on public lands in and near suburban centers. Black bears are also hunted, as are moose — if you are lucky enough to win the draw — and coyotes.

Lodges:

MAINE

1 ALLAGASH GUIDE SERVICE

2 CEDAR RIDGE OUTFITTERS

3 CONKLIN LODGE AND CAMPS

4 FOGGY MOUNTAIN GUIDE SERVICE

5 GENTLE BEN'S HUNTING & FISHING LODGE

6 NELSON L. COLE AND SON

7 NORTHERN OUTDOORS

8 PINE GROVE LODGE

9 RED RIVER CAMPS

10 STONY BROOK OUTFITTERS

PENNSYLVANIA

11 BIG MOORE'S RUN LODGE LTD.

References:

A GUIDE TO HUNTING PENNSYLVANIA WHITETAILS
by Tom Fegely
B&T Outdoor Enterprises, Box 518 Coopersburg, PA 181036.

THE MAINE ANTLER AND SKULL TROPHY CLUB RECORD BOOK
by Dick Arsenault. RR #5, Box 190 Gorham, ME 04038.

NORTHEAST HUNTING GUIDE: A MODERN APPROACH TO FINDING GOOD HUNTING IN OUR CROWDED REGION
by Jim Capossela
Stackpole Books, Cameron and Kelker Streets, Box 1831, Harrisburg, PA 17105; 800-READ-NOW

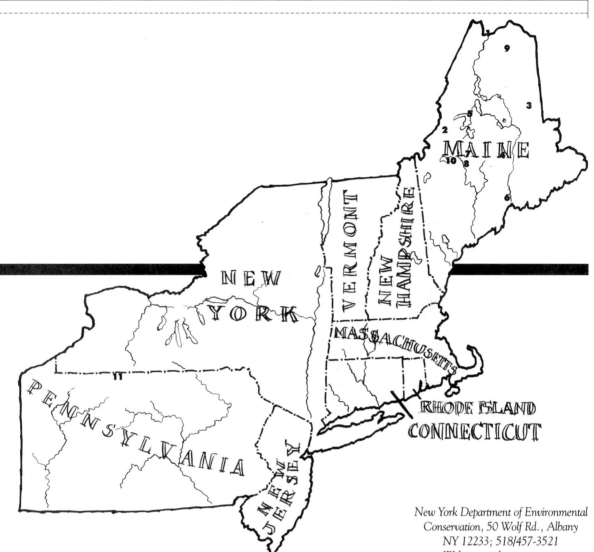

New York Department of Environmental Conservation, 50 Wolf Rd., Albany NY 12233; 518/457-3521
Web: www.dec.state.ny.us

WHITETAIL STRATEGIES
by Peter J. Fiduccia, Gotcha Products Inc., Box 64, Bellvale, NY 10912
914/986-0326.

Resources:

CONNECTICUT DEPARTMENT OF ENVIRONMENTAL PROTECTION, WILDLIFE DIVISION
79 Elm St., 6th Floor, Hartford, CT 06106; 860/424-3011

MAINE DEPARTMENT OF INLAND FISHERIES AND WILDLIFE
284 State St., Station #41, Augusta ME 04333; 207/287-8000
Web:
www.state.me.us/ifw/homepage.htm

MASSACHUSETTS DIVISION OF FISHERIES AND WILDLIFE
100 Cambridge St., Room 1902 Boston, MA 02202; 617/727-3155
Web: www.state.ma.us/dfwele

NEW HAMPSHIRE FISH AND GAME DEPARTMENT
2 Hazen Dr., Concord, NH 03301 603/271-3422, Fax: 603/271-1438
Web: www.wildlife.state.nh.us

NEW JERSEY DIVISION OF FISH, GAME AND WILDLIFE, INFORMATION & EDUCATION DIV.
PO Box 400
Trenton, NJ 08625-0400 609/292-9450,
Web: www.state.nj.us/dep/fgw

PENNSYLVANIA GAME COMMISSION, 2001 Elmerton Ave., Harrisburg, PA. 17110-9797; 717/787-4250
Fax: 717/772-2411
Web: www.pgc.state.pa.us

RHODE ISLAND DIVISION OF FISH AND WILDLIFE
Oliver Stedman Government Center 4808 Tower Hill Rd., Wakefield, RI 02879-2207; 401/789-8281
Web: www.state.ri.us/dem

VERMONT FISH AND WILDLIFE DEPARTMENT
103 South Main St., Waterbury, VT 05676; 802/241-3700
Web: www.state.vt.us/anr

Allagash Guide Service

A l l a g a s h ,   M a i n e

Where "B" equals bear
and brook trout.

VITAL STATISTICS:

Game/Arm/Seasons:
WHITETAILS:
Bow: Sept.
Centerfire: Nov.
Muzzleloader: Dec.
BEAR:
Sept. through Oct.

Rates:
WHITETAILS from $450/6 days
BLACK BEAR from $850/6 days

Accommodations:
MODERN LOG AND WOOD LODGE,
WILDERNESS TENTS
NUMBER OF ROOMS: 25, ALL WITH PRIVATE
BATH
MAXIMUM NUMBER OF HUNTERS: 25

Meals:
Beans, gingerbread pancakes, pork chops and turkey

Conference Groups: No

Guides: Included

Gratuity: 5 to 10%

Preferred Payment:
Cash, check

Other Activities:
Bird hunting, bird watching, canoeing/rafting, fishing, snowmobiling, waterfowling, wildlife photography

Getting There:
Fly to Presque Isle, rent a car and drive to the lodge or take the lodge van for $80.

Contact:
Sean Lizotte
Allagash Guide Service
RR 1, Box 131D
Allagash, ME 04774
207/398-3418
e-mail: allaguide@ainop.com
Web: www.maineguides.com

U P HERE, THE A.B. DEGREE stands for Allagash Bear — black bear that is — and the Allagash is the place to hunt them. Big territory, this 2.8-million-acre tract runs from Baxter State Park west and then north to the confluence with the St. John, and it's home to legions of black bears. In fact, Wildlife Management Unit 2, which covers the core of Allagash Guide Services 200,000 acres, accounts for about 30 percent, or about 600, of the state's annual black bear harvest. The most successful tactic is baiting, of course, but the most fun is hunting bears with hounds. From 14-foot high tree stands and ground blinds you'll hunt over baits that are electronically monitored to ensure that the bait is, indeed, active.

Should you score early, put down the rifle and pick up the fishing rod. The first two weeks of fall bear season coincides with the best time to fish Maine's trout waters. Telemetry gets into the act with dogs as well. Each is fitted with high-tech tracking equipment, which vastly simplifies the task of finding dogs and bear when the latter has been treed. Most bear hunters stay in the lodge but a few opt for the comfortable and complete wall-tent camp on the St. John River. The camp includes a full-time guide and a cook who, given the right conditions, will even wash the dishes.

You'll find big deer in these deep woods, where bucks of 6 to 12 points are not uncommon. The habitat here is forest plots in various stages of clear-cut regeneration, which supports about 15 deer per mile. The last few weeks of the season generally hunt better than the first weeks. Early, deer are beginning the rut, but later they become more concentrated in areas where there's good browse. During years when beechnut mast is abundant, whitetails will work hardwood ridges as long as they can. In other years, you'll find them clipping hardwood browse or working over patches of lichens and mushrooms. The secret to getting one of Maine's big whitetails? "Do the time," according to Sean Lizotte, owner of the guide service. Hunters willing to put in 10 to 12 hours per day simply see more deer than their friends who give up after six or seven. Tree stands and ground blinds provide the cover. You keep your eyes open and do the shooting.

Cedar Ridge Outfitters

J a c k m a n ,   M a i n e

Located in a remote corner of a remote state, Cedar Ridge has a lock on trophy deer, bear and moose.

VITAL STATISTICS:

Game/Arm/Seasons:
BLACK BEAR:
Bow, centerfire, muzzleloader: Sept.
MOOSE:
Bow, centerfire, muzzleloader:
Second week of Oct.
WHITE-TAILED DEER:
Bow: Oct.
Centerfire: Nov.
Muzzleloader Late Nov. through early Dec.

Rates:
BLACK BEAR $950/6 days (guided)
MOOSE $1,450/6 days (guided; 2 people, 1 moose)
WHITE-TAILED DEER from $750/6 days (guided)

Accommodations:
CABINS
NUMBER OF ROOMS: 14
MAXIMUM NUMBER OF HUNTERS: 40

Meals:
Roast pork, turkey, homemade baked goods

Conference Groups: No
Guides: Included
Gratuity: $50 to $100
Preferred Payment:
Cash, MasterCard, Visa, check

Other Activities:
Biking, bird hunting, boating, canoeing/whitewater rafting, fishing, hiking, skiing, waterfowling, wildlife photography

Getting There:
Fly to Bangor.

Contact:
Debbie or Hal Blood
Cedar Ridge Outfitters,
Box 744
36 Attean Rd.
Jackman, ME 04945
207/668-4169
Fax: 207/668-7636
Web:
www.maineguide.com/Jackman/Cedar.html

JACKMAN, MAINE, located in the northwestern corner of the state, just 15 miles from the Quebec border, is in a remote area of steep mountains and pristine lakes. Because of this remoteness, the area receives little hunting pressure — and consequently produces trophy deer and bear on a regular basis. In fact, one out of every six deer taken by Cedar Ridge hunters weighs more than 200 pounds dressed and is 4 1/2 years old. The bear population is healthy, too, with bears of 200 pounds common, and some more than 300 pounds are taken every year.

"We focus on trophy-class deer, bears and moose (if you're lucky enough to draw a tag)," states owner Hal Blood. "But don't be misled into thinking that everybody gets a trophy, or even hunts for one. It's just that we have a good average."

Early-season bowhunts for deer involve rattling and calling, while hunts later in the season are mostly still-hunts. One or two hunters and a guide head into the thick cedar and hardwood forests off the eastern slopes of the White Mountains, moving quietly, glassing ahead, watching trails and grown-over clearcuts to jump a big buck from his bed or catch him while he's making his daily rounds. Depending on the terrain, some hunters post in ground stands. Others track deer if there's snow on the ground (there usually is). But the stealthy still-hunter usually is the one who connects here.

Moose calling works early in the season, but they are also still-hunted or stalked after being glassed in swampy areas. Bear hunting is done over bait in September at Cedar Ridge's more than 50 stations, with bows, rifles and muzzleloaders all legal weapons. Hal Blood hunts bears in almost 100 square miles of exclusive territory, so harvests can be controlled and bear numbers managed carefully.

The six beautiful, newly built housekeeping cabins at Cedar Ridge have all the modern conveniences and are just five minutes from town, down a secluded road. Depending on what you hunt, you can rent a cabin and hunt on your own, without a guide; rent a cabin, and hunt with a guide; or stay in the main lodge, which can accommodate 40 hunters, and hunt with a guide. Just be careful of Debbie's homemade meals when you wander into the spacious dining room at the lodge. With turkey, pork roast, stews, veggies and more baked goods (the cornbread is to die for) than you can eat, you'll find yourself taking on more calories than you can work off.

Conklin Lodge and Camps

P a t t e n ,   M a i n e

Bear, moose and deer are hunted on timber company land in northern Maine.

VITAL STATISTICS:

Game/Arm/Seasons:
BEAR:
Sept. through Nov.
DEER:
Bow: Oct.
Firearms: Nov.
MOOSE:
Early Oct.

Rates:
BEAR $900/6 days
DEER from $425/5 days
MOOSE $1,500/6 days

Accommodations:
WOOD LODGE AND CABINS
NUMBER OF ROOMS 5 CABINS
MAXIMUM NUMBER OF HUNTERS: 28

Meals: Roasts, steak, pork

Conference Groups: No

Guides: Included

Gratuity: Hunter's discretion

Preferred Payment:
Check

Other Activities:
Bird hunting, fishing, waterfowling, golf, canoeing, swimming, boating, hiking, biking, antiquing, wildlife photography, bird watching, skiing

Getting There:
Fly to Bangor, rent a car and drive to the camp, or take the camp shuttle for $75 round-trip.

Contact:
Lester Conklin
Conklin Lodge & Camp
Box 21
Patten, ME 04920
207/528-2901

"HILL AND A SWAMP, hill and a swamp, hill and a swamp." That's how Lester Conklin describes the 350,000 acres he hunts north of Baxter State Park. The park is the northern terminus of the Appalachian Trail and Mt. Katahdin, at 5,267 feet, is the park's and the state's highest point. The land's mixture of scrub growth, high ridges and streams and bogs may account for the larger-than-normal deer that come out of Les' camps and the better-than-average hunter success rates.

Over the last few years, about 40 percent of the deer hunters using these camps have taken bucks. Clients on guided hunts are successful about 50 percent of the time. The rate drops to 30 percent for unguided hunts. Guided hunts are not the same as you'd expect in the West. In the Maine woods, four hunters share a single guide who designs a strategy based on weather, the capabilities of the hunters and the movements of the deer. He's kind of like a squad leader setting up an ambush. His job is to put you in a position to intercept moving deer. Tree stands over trails, still-hunting and stalking in light snow are all effective. Typical deer are 4- to 6-pointers that average about 170 pounds dressed. Older and bigger deer are nocturnal and incredibly sensitive to odors. That's why, despite their charm, you'll find no woodstoves in Les' cabins. "You can't go out and successfully hunt deer if you smell like smoke!" he says.

Conklin also offers bear hunting, with a 100 percent record over five years. From 14-foot tree stands, hunters are placed 20 to 30 yards downwind from the baits. At first you may see and hear nothing, or maybe just a stick snap or perhaps a little bleat. Suddenly the bear is on the bait. You're apt to rush the shot, but don't: good bullet placement is a must. The number-one handgun bear in the state of Maine, which was a massive creature with a 20-inch skull, was taken from Conklin's camps. Typical bears run between 150 and 200 pounds.

For those fortunate few hunters who draw a moose tag, the track record is 100 percent on bulls with spreads of 40 inches or better. Les likes to call them in. For one hunter, he called in 28 bulls before finding just the right one. And, if you're of a mind, grouse are plentiful and hunted without dogs in the Maine tradition. Guests stay in five modern log cabins tucked in the trees behind the main lodge where traditional meals such as Yankee pot roast and stuffed game hens are served family-style.

Foggy Mountain Guide Service

Dover-Foxcroft, Maine

An historic lumberjack camp is home base for this northern Maine outfitter.

VITAL STATISTICS:

Game/Arm/Seasons:
WHITETAILS:
Bow: Oct.
Gun: Nov.
BEAR:
Maine: Sept.

Rates:
WHITETAILS unguided from $250/6 days
BEAR from $995/6 days

Accommodations:
CABINS AND SUMMER VACATION HOMES
NUMBER OF ROOMS: FROM 2 TO 4
MAXIMUM NUMBER OF HUNTERS:
MAINE 12, CANADA 20

Meals: Varies by location

Conference Groups: Yes

Guides: Optional

Gratuity: Hunter's discretion

Preferred Payment:
Cash

Other Activities:
Bird hunting, boating, fishing, swimming

Getting There:
Fly to Bangor or Thunder Bay and rent a car.

Contact:
Wayne A. Boscowicz
Foggy Mountain Guide Service
RR2, Box 1140
Dover-Foxcroft, ME 04426
207/564-3404
Fax: 207/564-8209
e-mail: foggymtn@kynd.net,
Web: www.foggymountain.com

THE APPALACHIAN TRAIL winds through the 266,000 acres of low, rocky, forested mountains leased by Wayne Boscowicz between Moosehead Lake and Mt. Katahdin. The country is a vast patchwork of woodlots in various stages of succession, grassy bogs thick with stands of maple, popple, and beech ridges and abandoned farms. And a second parcel of 216,000 acres between Seboomook Lake and the Canadian border provides a deep wilderness served by a truly outstanding old Maine camp—Pittston Farm.

As is the case in Maine, deer are not many, but those that are there fall into the trophy category. A 200-pound buck is considered a "good" deer in these parts, but not uncommon. About 70 percent of Wayne's hunters see bucks and about 40 percent connect. One of the reasons for the relatively high success rate (the average for guided hunts in Maine is between 25 and 30 percent) may lie in the fact that the Seboomook Lake area has been closed to commercial hunting for a number of years. Bow season occupies the month of October and centerfire takes up November. Deer hunts may be guided or unguided.

Bear is something of a specialty of Wayne's, and the outfitter runs a fall hunt over bait that consistently produces bruins upwards of 150 pounds. Hunting, of course, is from stands and ground blinds. Typical shots for archers are 20 yards or less; handgunners about 30 yards; and riflemen shoot at 75 yards. Most hunters get their bear. Pittston Farm is one of the few remaining historic lumberjack camps; cabins are log and hearty meals are included, like Wayne's log lodge in the Moosehead/Katahdin area. For couples, there's also the option of staying in a posh summer home located on the lake.

Mike and Rhonda Brophy offer accommodations and great
north-country chow at their century-old Red River Camps
near Portage, Maine. One of three hunters takes a buck here, and all
agree that the price is down-right-reasonable.

Just what you'd expect from Allagash Guide Service
hard by the wilderness in Maine's great north woods: snug
log cabins with plenty of firewood stashed under the
front porch to ward off the damp and chill of late fall in
this land of birch and fir.

Gentle Ben's Hunting & Fishing Lodge

R o c k w o o d ,   M a i n e

Hunting from the main lodge or the satellite camp offers hunters a chance at big bucks and bears.

VITAL STATISTICS:

Game/Arm/Seasons:
BEAR:
Sept. through Nov.
DEER:
Bow: Oct.
Firearms: Nov.
MOOSE:
Early Oct.
Rates:
BEAR from $895/6 days
DEER from $695/6 days
MOOSE $1,500/6 days
Accommodations:
WOODEN LODGE
NUMBER OF ROOMS: 3
MAXIMUM NUMBER OF HUNTERS: 12
Meals: Family-style
Conference Groups: Yes
Guides: Included
Gratuity: $50
Preferred Payment:
Cash, MasterCard, Visa, check
Other Activities:
Bird hunting, fishing, canoeing, swimming, boating, hiking, biking, wildlife photography, bird watching, skiing
Getting There:
Fly to Bangor, rent a car and drive to the lodge.

Contact:
Bruce Pelletier
Gentle Ben's
Box 212
Rockwood, ME 04478
1-800-242-3799
207/534-2201
Fax: 207/534-2236
e-mail: gentleben@top.monad.net
Web:
www.maineguides.com/Gentle-Bens

YOU WON'T FIND MANY other hunters on Bruce Pelletier's new 10,000 acres 40 miles north of his main lodge in Rockwood. It's at the end of a gated paper-company road. Beyond the gate are ridges that stem down from three mountains, all in the 2,100-foot range, and a welter of low hills, streams and bogs. Deer here are not plentiful, but they are large. A 10-point buck will dress out at 200 pounds; the rack will generally have a 21-inch spread and score in the 140s. These are nice deer. In these big, dense woods, deer are moving all day. Still-hunting is the most effective way to bag these bucks, but sitting over scrapes also produces as does rattling and calling. Archers hunt from tree stands overlooking active trails. Firearms hunters track deer when there's been snow. Hunting is best in this area during the rut in November. About 35 percent of the hunters in this camp take home bucks.

Bear, of course, is another story. While nothing is certain but death and taxes, the odds are quite good for harvesting a bear. About 80 percent of hunters who hunt over baits are successful, and more than 90 percent who follow the hounds take a bruin. Bears harvested over baits are somewhat smaller, averaging about 200 pounds, than those taken with dogs. The reason? Older bears are wiser and approach bait sites only after dark. The later a big bear comes to the bait, the more likely it is that hounds will pick up his scent early the following morning and eventually tree or bring him to bay. Bruce has been running mainly bluetick hounds for the past 15 years. His dogs wear radio collars, and you can follow them electronically if you can't hear their calls. The trick is to convince the dogs to tree the bear somewhere other than the middle of a big bog. Bruce is working on that.

On the northern property, Gentle Ben's has opened a satellite camp, a comfortable wood cabin with all the amenities. The main lodge, which sees lots of anglers in summer, is located on Moosehead Lake and consists of a main dining room and three guest rooms with shared bath.

[E A S T]

Nelson L. Cole and Son

T h o r n d i k e ,   M a i n e

After hunting all day in the wilderness, modern lodging awaits you at the end of the day.

VITAL STATISTICS:

Game/Arm/Seasons:
WHITETAILS:
Bow: Oct.
Firearms: Nov.
BEAR:
Fall, mid-Sept. through Oct.; spring, May through June
BOBCAT:
Dec. through Jan.
Rates:
WHITETAIL $450/6 days
BEAR $900/6 days
BOBCAT $1,500/6 days
Accommodations:
FRAME AND LOG CABINS
NUMBER OF ROOMS: 6 WITH PRIVATE BATH
MAXIMUM NUMBER OF HUNTERS: 24
Meals: Cook for yourself
Conference Groups: No
Guides: Included
Gratuity: $25 to $100
Preferred Payment:
Cash, check
Other Activities:
Bird hunting, wildlife photography
Getting There:
Fly to Bangor or Ottawa and rent a car.

Contact:
Nelson Cole
Nelson L. Cole and Son
Rt. 2, Box 2750
Thorndike, ME 04986
207/948-3201
Fax: 207/942-5250

I F YOU'RE THINKING ABOUT HUNTING in Maine, that's just what you're thinking about. Hunting. It's a lovely state with thousands of miles of wilderness. Near towns, some of them all but abandoned, are old farmsteads marked by overgrown orchards and hay fields now slowly returning to forest. Beech ridges cross the landscape and in the lowlands are bogs and beaver swamps of cedar and spruce — the birthplace of the famed Maine guide boot with its rubber bottom and leather upper. The country is the stuff of hunters' dreams.

Deer hunting on the two square miles of woods that Nelson Cole uses can be quite good. Bucks run in the 180- to 200-pound class. Eight- to 10-pointers are not rare among harvested bucks. A typical hunt will find you taking a stand early in the morning over rub and scrape lines, and in the evening perhaps along a heavily traveled route from bed to feed. During the day, you and your partners will push patches of swamp to kick out a buck. You'll see grouse and maybe a bear, and the damp Maine cold will penetrate to your bones and you'll return to the rustically modern lodge and adjacent cabins that night as ready for dinner as you've ever been in your life. And, if you're lucky, you may have harvested a buck.

You'll be more likely, though, to harvest a black bear of 150 pounds or more hunting from Nelson Cole's cabins between Jackson Pond and Drake Lake up in Washington County near Brookton. This is boggy country, but the Walters hounds don't mind. They'll tree a bear or bring it to bay and it's up to you to follow even if it means wading through a swamp up to your navel. Hunting bears with hounds is exciting and success rates run close to 65 percent.

Northern Outdoors

The Forks, Maine

Stand hunting is the name of the game whether you hunt from the modern lodge or the Western-style tent camps.

VITAL STATISTICS:

Game/Arm/Seasons:
WHITETAILS:
Rifle: Nov.
Muzzleloader: Early Dec.
Rates:
Lodge from $510; wilderness $675/6 days
Accommodations:
VACATION RESORT OR TENT CAMPS
NUMBER OF ROOMS: 52, MOST WITH PRIVATE BATH
MAXIMUM NUMBER OF HUNTERS: 100
Meals: Waited tables in lodge; family-style in camp
Conference Groups: Yes
Guides: Included
Gratuity: Hunter's discretion
Preferred Payment:
Cash, Discover, MasterCard, Visa, check
Other Activities:
Biking, bird watching, canoeing/rafting, fishing, snowmobiling, swimming, wildlife photography
Getting There:
Fly to Bangor or Portland and rent a car.

Contact:
Jim Yearwood
Northern Outdoors
Rt. 201, Box 100
The Forks, ME 04985
800/765-7238
Fax: 207-663-2244
e-mail: jim@northernoutdoors
Web: www.northernoutdoors.com

IF YOU ASK WAYNE HOCKMEYER, he'll tell you the best way to bag one of Maine's big bucks is by sitting on a tree stand. In Maine! Ayuh. The best deer hunting in these huge woods occurs when fall begins to freeze into winter. Gentle rains, rains that would be snow in another week or two, chase the last leaves from beeches and oaks, and frost in the night turns them as brittle as Christmas ornaments. Not even James Fenimore Cooper's legendary Deerslayer could move through these woods with stealth enough to sneak up on a wary backwoods buck.

That's why Northern Outdoors almost exclusively places its hunters in stands. The chance of seeing deer is almost twice that of still-hunting. And hunting from a stand takes a discipline that's not apparent at first glance. Think just anyone can sit still for hours on end, concentrating on the woods in front of them? He who downs four cups of coffee with breakfast will be as fidgety as a colt waiting for his first race. Coughing is verboten as is scratching that itch. So what to you do? Watch the sun kiss the crown of that tall beech where deer have been feeding and stream down its gray trunk to warm the ground below. Hear the sighing of the deep forest, the chatter of red squirrels and their endless gathering, the wing beats of the cedar waxwing moving south through the woods. Most hunters quit their stands at 10 a.m., but hunters who sit all day are usually the ones who harvest big deer.

From his resort in The Forks, where the Dead River joins the Kennebec, Wayne hunts a 15-square-mile area of private paper-company land. Guests are accommodated in the lodge with its rustic yet thoroughly modern bedrooms with private baths, bar and restaurant. Before dawn, guides load hunters into four-wheel-drives to get them on their stands before dawn. You'll be collected at mid-morning, if you want, and returned to the lodge for lunch. Another session of hunting is slated for late afternoon. About 100 miles northwest of Baxter State Park, Wayne runs a pair of Western-style tent camps. Hunters here are aiming for trophies, those big bucks that carry curved racks of eight points or better. Wayne runs Mountain Camp for dedicated stand hunters. Eleven miles away is Pond Camp, where stands are the rule, but no one will mind if you get down once in a while to stretch. Hunter success in both camps is about twice the state average, but hunters pass on a lot of spike and forkhorn bucks.

Pine Grove Lodge

B i n g h a m ,   M a i n e

VITAL STATISTICS:

Game/Arm/Seasons:

DEER:
Muzzleloader: Dec.
Bow: Oct. through Nov.
Centerfire: Nov.

BEAR:
Bow: Sept.
Centerfire: Oct. through Nov.

MOOSE:
Any arm: Oct.

BOBCAT:
Any arm: Dec. through Jan.

Rates:
BEAR from $800/5 days
DEER $500/5 days
MOOSE $1,000/5 days
BOBCAT $1,000/5 days

Accommodations:
WOODEN LODGE AND CABINS
NUMBER OF ROOMS: 15
MAXIMUM NUMBER OF HUNTERS: 34

Meals: Roasts, stews and, of course, beans

Conference Groups: No

Guides: Included

Gratuity: Hunter's discretion

Preferred Payment:
Cash, MasterCard, Visa

Other Activities:
Bird hunting, fishing, waterfowling, canoeing, swimming, boating, hiking, biking, antiquing, wildlife photography, bird watching, skiing, snowshoeing

Getting There:
Fly to Bangor or Augusta and rent a car.

Contact:
Robert Howe
Pine Grove Lodge
HCR 65, Box 76
Pleasant Ridge
Bingham ME 04920
207/672-4011

Still-hunting through Maine's woods is the way to take large deer at this lodge.

PICTURE YOUR TYPICAL MAINE GUIDE: tough, taciturn and traditional. Now picture him briefing his hunters on the routes they'll follow through the trackless Maine woods using state-of-the-art GPS. There you have Robert Howe, Pine Grove owner and head guide. The most effective technique for finding the big deer here is to still-hunt through the cedar thickets and over the low ridges of beech from one woods road to another. In practice, a line of eight hunters works slowly through the endless countryside. The idea is to jump deer, but not panic them. With luck, and it takes a good bit of luck in these parts, once flushed, a buck will offer one of the hunters a shot.

Bob says it flatly: "If you want deer meat, don't come to Maine." You're better off in Alabama, where you can kill two deer per day. In some regions of the country where deer populations are booming, hunting is strictly from stands and you take your pick of deer that amble by. To some, that's more akin to shooting than hunting. On the other hand, if hunting with stealth and strategy through Maine's big woods for a 6- or 8-point buck that will dress out at 175 pounds whets your appetite, then hunting in Maine may be for you. It's tough hunting with some interesting wrinkles. Ever try float-hunting for deer from a handmade cedar canoe?

Bear is the other mainstay of Bob's portfolio. During the first two weeks of the season, he hunts over bait; the second two weeks overlap with dogs; the final two weeks are dog only. By dogs he means a pack of six hounds. On baited hunts, some of the stands are so accessible that handicapped hunters can do quite well. Hunting over baits demands patience. With dogs, perseverance is required. Hounds will bring a bear to bay or tree and hunters need to be close behind. Running through Maine woods is not for the faint of heart. But hunter success on bears averaging 175 pounds is nearly 100 percent.

When it comes to certainties there's always moose hunting. If you get drawn (now a very uncertain probability) you're virtually guaranteed to harvest a trophy bull. Bob will show you several and you'll pick the one you want. Another certainty is grouse. There are lots of them, and the certainty is that they'll fool you most of the time.

Pine Grove Lodge is a year-round operation. Rooms are in the lodge and a bunkhouse nearby. For breakfasts you'll find eggs, meats and baked beans, lunches of soups and pheasant stew and dinners of roasts and fowl that would founder an army.

Red River Camps

Portage, Maine

Guided group hunts out of rustic log cabins on Whitman Mountain.

VITAL STATISTICS:

Game/Arm/Seasons:
WHITETAILS:
Firearms: Nov.
BEAR:
Firearms: Sept.
Rates:
From $825/3-day hunt any species
Accommodations:
VINTAGE LOG LODGE AND CABINS
NUMBER OF ROOMS: 9
MAXIMUM NUMBER OF HUNTERS: 25
Meals: Downeast cooking
Conference Groups: Yes
Guides: Included
Gratuity: Hunter's discretion
Preferred Payment:
Cash, check
Other Activities:
Bird hunting, fishing, canoeing/rafting, wildlife photography
Getting There:
Fly to Presque Isle and the lodge will take you the rest of the way for $80 round-trip.

Contact:
Mike Brophy
Red River Camps
Box 320
Portage, ME 04768
207/435-6000
off-season: 207/528-2259

WHERE IN THE WORLD would you find a pond on top of a mountain? Maine, of course. In fact there are more than a dozen blackwater ponds around Red River Camps, which sits high on Whitman Mountain, about 20 miles due south of the Canadian border at St. Francis. Well worn by glaciation, the mountains here are not as steep as others in the southwestern part of the state. In fact, you wouldn't even know there were mountains if the maps didn't tell you so. You'll need maps and a compass if you hunt these woods of heavy spruce, pine, beech, maple and birch.

There's about 30 percent chance that you'll harvest a buck during the month-long rifle season as a Red River deer hunter. And better deer hunters do better (as if that's any surprise). But the emphasis at Red River Camp is on the hunt, not the harvest. Groups of four or five tend to book one of the log cabins at the camp. With two guides per hunter group, they'll spend a week as easy or as hard as they want to make it. Breakfast is at 5 a.m. or so and dinner a dozen hours later. In between, guides will take you to areas where sign is fresh and deer have been active. You may take a stand watching a rub or scrape, or a route from the thick black cover deep in a spruce swamp where deer bed in bad weather to that ridge where mast lies heavy in the beech grove. Stay out all day or come back for lunch — it's your call.

In September, bear hunting is on the docket. Thirty baits are maintained within 10 miles of the camps. After a morning's fishing for brook trout, hunters are taken to a rugged lumber stand within 20 yards of an active bait. Then the sitting and waiting begins. With luck, a boar will slip through the forest with no more noise than falling dusk and you'll have a shot. No more than 10 hunters are hosted during each of the two weeks that Red River runs bear hunts. The success rate runs about 70 percent.

At night, after the hunt, you'll groan under the load of fresh breads and ham and turkey and roasts that emerge from this camp's kitchen. And later, as you sit around the woodstove and tell lies to one another, you'll know why folks have been coming to this camp for more than 100 years to hunt.

[E A S T]

Stony Brook Outfitters

W i l t o n ,   M a i n e

Bears with hounds or from stands and good-sized deer are available out of this lodge in the north woods of Maine.

VITAL STATISTICS:

Game/Arm/Seasons:
WHITETAILS:
Bow: Oct.
Gun: Nov.
Muzzleloader: Nov. through mid-Dec.
BEAR:
Canada: Mid-May through mid-June
Maine:
Hounds: Sept. through Oct.; bait
Sept. thorough Nov.
BOBCAT:
Gun: Nov. through Dec.
Rates:
MAINE bear from $900/5 days
CANADA BEAR, $850/5 days
WHITETAILS $600/5 days
BOBCAT $1,000/5 days
Accommodations:
RUSTIC WOOD LODGE
NUMBER OF ROOMS: 6 (4 HANDICAPPED-ACCESSIBLE)
MAXIMUM NUMBER OF HUNTERS: 15
Meals: Pot roast, ham, fried chicken
Conference Groups: No
Guides: Included
Gratuity: 5 to 10%
Preferred Payment:
Cash, check
Other Activities:
Bird hunting, fishing, wildlife photography
Getting There:
Fly to Bangor or Portland and rent a car.

Contact:
Bob Parker
Stony Brook Outfitters
55 Morrison Hill Rd.
Wilton, ME 04294
800/322-2327

S O THE BEAR HUNTING QUESTION boils down to this: How well do you handle mosquitoes and blackflies? Think that insect repellents will help? Wrong! Bears can smell them, too. To fill your fall bear tag over bait in Maine's north woods, you'll need one-piece camo coveralls, an olive turtleneck, camo gloves, a wide-brimmed hat, a headnet and dark green or brown duct tape. Sealed inside your suit, you'll hear bugs, you'll see bugs, but the bugs won't bite you (except for that enterprising sucker who shouldered his way through the mesh and is preparing to dine on your proboscis).

Evidently, clients who hunt with Stony Brook have mastered the anti-bug business. Success rates over bait verge on 80 percent. Hunting is from 14-foot stands and baits are placed five feet or so off the ground. Why so high? Jaye-Ellen Parker, who with her husband Bob founded Stony Brook nearly 20 years ago, explains: "A little bear will slap the can, but a big bear will stand on its hind legs and eat. That gives hunters a better chance to examine the bear and archers a better shot at the bear's vitals." Spring bear hunting in Maine was outlawed a few years ago, but Stony Brook leases rights to 1,000 square miles of New Brunswick, just across the border.

If sittin' without scratchin' isn't your game, you can hunt bear with hounds. Blueticks, Plotts and Walkers are labors of love for Bob. Two clients will hunt over a pack of four hounds equipped with telemetry collars to facilitate tracking. Bob will check out prints and scat at bait sites, and if a bear is big enough he'll loose the dogs. Then begins the chase of a dozen miles or more through the rough mountains of Maine's north woods. Average bear size is 170 pounds and 95 percent of hunters get their trophy.

Stony Brook hunts some 1,200 square miles of Maine's northern mountains. Beech ridges and swampy drainages in between hold good-sized deer. A typical trophy carries eight points and weighs about 180 pounds. Normally, hunting is from stands over rubs, scrapes and trails in the early morning and late afternoon. During midday, still-hunting occasionally pays off. About one in four harvest trophy bucks here.

Bear and deer are Stony Brook's staples, but they also run hunts for bobcat and moose, if one is lucky enough to draw a moose permit. Hunters stay in the lodge in Weld, a functional affair with six bunkrooms varying in size to accommodate parties from two to eight. Baths are shared and meals are the kind that keep lumberjacks going. Cook Phil Rafter's bean soup draws raves and requests for the recipe.

Big Moore's Run Lodge Ltd.

Coudersport, Pennsylvania

Try for trophy whitetails in the heart of God's Country.

VITAL STATISTICS:

Game/Arm/Seasons:
WHITE-TAILED DEER:
Bow: Early Oct. through mid-Nov.
Centerfire: Late Nov. through mid-Dec.
TURKEY:
Centerfire: Spring, early through late May; fall, late Oct. through late Nov.
Rates:
WHITETAIL $595/3 days
TURKEY from $495/2 days
Accommodations:
MODERN LODGE
NUMBER OF ROOMS: 6
MAXIMUM NUMBER OF HUNTERS: 9
Meals: Steaks, game, seafood
Conference Groups: Yes
Guides: Included
Gratuity: Hunter's discretion
Preferred Payment:
Cash, American Express, Discover, MasterCard, Visa, check
Other Activities:
Biking, bird watching, flyfishing, golf, hiking, wildlife photography
Getting There:
Fly to Bradford Regional Airport, rent a car and drive to the lodge, or for $80 round-trip a van from the lodge will meet you at the airport.

Contact:
Bill or Barb Haldaman
Big Moore's Run Lodge Ltd.
RR #3, Box 204A
Coudersport, PA 16915
814/647-5300
Fax: 814/647-9928
e-mail: bigmoors@penn.com
Web: http://users.penn.com/~big-moors/html

WITH MORE THAN 1.1 million deer hunters, Pennsylvania is one of the top states in the country when it comes to whitetails. The state has more than 1.25 million whitetails, with an annual kill of 350,000 deer.

Potter County, known as God's Country to many Pennsylvania residents, is the state's best-known deer hunting county. Bordering New York in the heart of the Allegheny Mountains, Potter County has broad ridges and steep slopes, with elevations rising to more than 2,500 feet. Forests cover most of the county.

The hub of Potter County is Coudersport, which offers hunters easy access to the many state forests and game lands in the area. This is big buck country, offering classic Pennsylvania whitetail hunting. And in the heart of it all, in sprawling Susquehannock State Forest, is Big Moore's Run, a classy, well-run lodge. Bill and Barb Haldaman have been operating the lodge for 11 years now, catering to fall whitetail and turkey hunters, spring turkey hunters and fishermen. Bowhunters, who hunt in October, are placed in tree stands in the state forest and on game-rich land owned by the lodge. Once rifle season starts in late November, firearms hunters get their chances from tree stands on the first day of the hunt, and then participate in organized "pushes."

"These aren't drives," stresses Haldaman. "When we push, we first post our hunters in places that overlook natural escape routes. Our guides then move slowly through the woods, along game trails and through bedding areas, gently moving deer in the direction of our standers. The trick is to not alarm the deer into flight."

Big Moore books only a limited number of hunters each year, as the focus here is on quality hunting, not quantity. Last year, 65 percent of the hunters had shooting opportunities.

Once tagged out, hunters may shoot sporting clays or attend the new wing-shooting school at Big Moore's Run. Or they may choose to grab a book and relax in the lodge's comfortable living room. The log lodge is on the side of a wooded hill with a deck overlooking the lawn, lake and Susquehannock State Forest. Guests stay in simply furnished, comfortable rooms with private baths. Family-style dinners include game birds, trout and New York strip steaks.

111

SOUTH

ALABAMA, DELAWARE, FLORIDA, GEORGIA, KENTUCKY, LOUISIANA, MARYLAND, MISSISSIPPI, NORTH CAROLINA, SOUTH CAROLINA, TENNESSEE, TEXAS, VIRGINIA, WEST VIRGINIA

AH, THE SOUTH. Good ol' boys, laid-back hunting and great hunting lodges. You climb out of your warm bunk, stoke up on grits and eggs or biscuits and gravy with sausage, and drive out to your shooting-box stand. After a short walk, you'll climb up onto your stand and sit there, waiting for a heavy-beamed buck to step out into the clover patch. That's the picture in the deep South where deer populations are booming. With the exception of Texas, hunting becomes tougher and populations somewhat thinner as the elevation of the land increases. White-tailed deer in the fall, turkey in the spring. Black bear and wild boar round out the big game pool here. In areas not served by a lodge or outfitter, you can often find a guide by calling the local office of the state department of natural resources, or by checking with a gun shop in the area where you'd like to hunt.

Lodges:

ALABAMA
1 MASTER RACK LODGE
2 WATER VALLEY LODGES
3 WHITE OAK PLANTATION

FLORIDA
4 BIENVILLE PLANTATION
5 OSCEOLA OUTFITTERS

GEORGIA
6 BROUGHTON PLANTATION

KENTUCKY
7 BUCKS & BEARDS

MISSISSIPPPI
8 CIRCLE M PLANTATION
9 McKENNA RANCH
10 PEARL RIVER OUTFITTERS
11 ROSE HILL PLANTATION

NORTH CAROLINA
12 BUFFALO CREEK GUIDE SERVICE

SOUTH CAROLINA
13 BUCK RUN HUNTING LODGE
14 COWDEN PLANTATION
15 DEERFIELD PLANTATION
16 LITTLE RIVER PLANTATION

TEXAS
17 777 RANCH
18 ADOBE LODGE HUNTING CAMP
19 BLUE RIVER OUTFITTERS
20 CAPROCK OUTFITTERS, INC.
21 DAVE PARK OUTFITTING
22 DOLAN CREEK HUNTING, INC.

Resources:

ALABAMA DEPARTMENT OF CONSERVATION AND NATURAL RESOURCES,
DIV. OF GAME AND FISH
WILDLIFE SECTION
PO Box 301456, Montgomery, AL 36130-1456; 334/242-3469; Web www.dcnr.state.al.us/agfd

DELAWARE DIVISION OF FISH AND WILDLIFE, WILDLIFE SECTION
Dnrec Dover, DE 19901
302/739-3441
Web: www.dnrec.state.de.us

FLORIDA GAME AND FRESH WATER FISH COMMISSION
620 S. Meridian St.
Tallahassee, FL 32399-1600
850/488-1960
Web: www.state.fl.us/gfc/

GEORGIA WILDLIFE RESOURCES DIVISION
2070 U.S. Hwy. 278 SE
Social Circle, GA 30025; 770/918-6400
Web: www.dnr.state.ga.us/

KENTUCKY DEPARTMENT OF FISH AND WILDLIFE RESOURCES
#1 Game Farm Rd.
Frankfort, KY 40601; 502/564-3400
Web:
www.state.ky.us/agencies/fw/kdfwr.htm

LOUISIANA DEPARTMENT OF WILDLIFE AND FISHERIES
Box 98000
Baton Rouge, LA 70898-9000
504/765-2800
Web: www.wlf.state.la.us

MARYLAND DEPARTMENT OF NATURAL RESOURCES, WILDLIFE AND HERITAGE DIVISION
E-1 580 Taylor Ave., Annapolis, MD 21401; 410/260-8540
Web: www.dnr.state.md.us

MISSISSIPPI DEPARTMENT OF WILDLIFE, FISHERIES AND PARKS
Box 451, Jackson, MS 39205
601/362-9212
Web: www.mdwfp.com

NORTH CAROLINA WILDLIFE RESOURCES COMMISSION
Division of Wildlife Management
512 N. Salisbury St.
Raleigh, NC 27604-1188
919/733-7291
Web:
www.state.nc.us/wildlife/management

[S O U T H]

SOUTH CAROLINA DEPARTMENT OF
NATURAL RESOURCES
DIVISION OF WILDLIFE AND
FRESHWATER FISHERIES
Box 167, Columbia, SC 29202
803/734-3889
Web: www.dnr.state.sc.us

TENNESSEE WILDLIFE
RESOURCES AGENCY
Box 40747, Nashville, TN 37204
615/781-6500
Web: www.state.tn.us/twra

TEXAS PARKS AND WILDLIFE
DEPARTMENT
4200 Smith School Rd.
Austin, TX 78744; 512/389-4505
or 800/792-1112
Web: http://www.tpwd.state.tx.us

VIRGINIA DEPARTMENT OF GAME AND
INLAND FISHERIES
4010 W. Broad St., Box 11104
Richmond, VA 23230-1104
804/367-1000
Web: www.dgif.state.va.us

WEST VIRGINIA DIVISION OF
NATURAL RESOURCES
Building 3, Room 819
1900 Kanawah Blvd. E., Charleston
WV 25305; 304/558-2771
Web: www.dnr.state.wv.us

---

*A gentle haze envelops the timber lodge at
Broughton Plantation, an hour east of Atlanta.
Hunt deer early and late here, and fill in the midday
hours with quail or bass. Who says the livin's only
lazy in the summertime?*

Master Rack Lodge

Union Springs, Alabama

Trophy whitetails are there for the taking in the heart of Alabama's woodlands.

WANT TO KNOW THE SECRET behind the 130- to 140-point Boone & Crockett racks that consistently come off J.L. Pipkin's 3,500-acre trophy area? They feed on Super-Juiced honeysuckle! Here's the deal. Honeysuckle is high in protein. Super Juice is a fertilizer. Pipkin has designed a system that essentially soaks the roots of that sweet-smelling vine in the dietary supplement, producing up to three tons of feed for about $20! He doesn't allow hunting over the honeysuckle plots, but deer that feed there wander the trophy area where they'll pass into your sights.

Located 10 miles south of Union Springs near the headwaters of the Conecuh River, Master Rack offers hunting on some 7,500 acres of mixed woodland and fields. Swampy river bottoms thick with tangled vine offer heavy cover. Mornings and evenings, whitetails drift out of the woods and into fields of corn, peas and beans. More than 70 strategically placed shooting houses and three score portable steel shooting stands give hunters a wide view of the surrounding terrain. The shooting houses are roofed, reasonably weatherproof and, in some cases, heated.

The acreage is divided into two sections. On the trophy land, hunters are allowed one buck a day but each must carry an eight-point rack or better, with a 15-inch minimum spread. The remaining 4,000 acres carry a four-point minimum. Hunter success on the trophy area runs about 50 percent and climbs to 75 percent in the regular area. Does are available at no additional charge for those who want freezer meat.

As is traditional in these parts, hunters eat a light breakfast and are taken to their assigned stands by their guides before dawn. By 10 a.m. it's time to head back to the lodge for a hearty lunch and nap. Back on the stand by midafternoon, you'll watch deer begin to move as the day cools. Typical hunts span three days. The lodge offers a special early season for archers, beginning on Oct. 1. A month later, centerfire arms become legal. Deer hunting comes to a close at the end of January. Turkeys, averaging 19 pounds, are hunted here in spring.

The lodge is comfortable—10 bedrooms, all with private bath and five with handicapped access. In the main hall, dinners of fried chicken, turnip greens and cornbread are served family-style. Nobody goes hungry here.

115

Water Valley Lodges

B u t l e r ,   A l a b a m a

Hunt for trophy bucks on this carefully managed 10,000-acre spread in the famed Black Belt region.

FOR MORE THAN 20 YEARS, the Utsey family has managed some 10,000 acres of prime Black Belt countryside for deer. Terrain here, where Alabama rubs up against Mississippi, is long and low. Patches of swamp, connected (drained isn't quite the right word) by a nest of streams, provide heavy cover for big bucks, as do stands of oak and pine. But there's open land too, field after field of row crops augmented with feed plots where corn, soybeans, millet, sunflowers and hearty grasses are planted. Combine this with moderate temperatures and the long growing season and you have a honeyhole for whitetails, turkeys, wild boar and, given the wetlands, ducks.

Hunting here is semi-guided. Mornings find hunters placed on stands over scrapes, rubs and trails. Your guide will take you and your partner out long before sunup. You may ride in a four-wheeler or a boat, or maybe walk with the guide to your blind. There you'll wait and watch. About 10:30, you'll be collected and taken back to the lodge for "dinner." Afterwards only the most stalwart manage to avoid napping before taking the field for the afternoon session that begins about 2:30 and lasts until dark. Many afternoon hunts involve scanning broad fields, clear-cuts or food plots from elevated shooting boxes. Alabama's deer harvest is liberal indeed; no one goes home empty-handed, though as a management tool the lodge does require that antlers at least spread beyond the ears (a penalty is imposed if you shoot something smaller). Limited doe hunts are also available. Wild boar are a bonus, as are ducks as long as the season is open.

Water Valley isn't the kind of place that runs scores of hunters through their stands in the course of a week. Reservations are limited to eight hunters for each of the three-day hunts. They stay either in the main lodge or cabins, all built of wood. A group may book into a cabin and do their own cooking, otherwise Southern cuisine is served family-style at the main lodge. Special dietary requirements can be accommodated, although an additional fee may be charged. To hunt here you'll need to get an Alabama license before you come, and bring a couple of ice chests for the venison you'll want to take home.

Game/Arm/Seasons:
WHITETAIL:
Bow: Oct. through Jan.
Centerfire, muzzleloader: Nov.
through Jan.
TURKEY:
Centerfire: Mid-March through April
Rates:
WHITETAIL:
Bow from $900/3 days
Centerfire from $1,190/3 days
TURKEY:
Centerfire from $1800/4 days
Accommodations:
MODERN YET RUSTIC WOOD LODGE
NUMBER OF ROOMS: 10
MAXIMUM NUMBER OF HUNTERS: 16
Meals: Country cooking
Conference Groups: Yes
Guides: Included
Gratuity: Hunter's discretion
Preferred Payment:
Cash, MasterCard, Visa, personal
check
Other Activities:
Antiquing, bird hunting, bird watch-
ing, fishing, golf, tennis, wildlife
photography
Getting There:
Fly to Montgomery and be met by the
lodge-arranged van for an extra
charge.

Contact:
Robert Pitman
White Oak Plantation
5215 CR. 10
Tuskegee, AL 36083
334/727-9258
Fax: 3334/727-3411,
e-mail: whiteoakhunts@mind-
spring.com,
Web:
www.americaoutdoors.com/woak/inde
x.html

White Oak Plantation

Tuskegee, Alabama

Bo Pitman's place is famous throughout the South for trophy deer and first-rate accommodations.

DEEP, DARK AND FERTILE, the soil in the central swath of Alabama is rich in minerals and other nutrients. Deer grow big here—an eight-point rack with a 16-inch spread is the minimum. And they are plentiful: the limit is one buck per stay and one doe per day. And for a slight fee you can take an extra buck. Not only will a three-day hunt at White Oak or its nearby economical sibling put horns on your wall, but you'll stuff your freezer so full of venison that you'll never worry about "mad cow disease" again!

Bo Pitman started White Oak in 1983 with a modest spread of 550 acres. Today he manages 15,600 acres for trophy bucks. The initial tracts were gently rolling pastures and mixed forests of hardwoods and pine interspersed with swamp and languid creeks. Over the past dozen years, the Pitman clan has thinned the forest, creating timber plots, feed plots and roads shouldered with clover and grass. A perpetual state of harvest and propagation assures a wealth of cover and fodder ranging from new growth to mast from mature hardwoods.

Hunting here is best described as semi-guided, though you can have your own guide if you wish. You'll draw a stand—one of more than 500 towers, shooting houses or ladder stands on the property—based on your abilities, physical condition and whether you're hunting with bow or firearm. Before dawn you'll be taken to your stand where you'll sit and watch crossings or scrapes where bucks have been particularly active. Evening hunts are typically over fields. You will see deer and that, friends, leads to this dilemma. If you're a money-in-the-bank hunter, you'll nail the first big deer that comes your way. But if a drop of gamblin' blood flows through your veins, you'll wait for the next one. Sometimes, though, the first one's the biggest. Too bad. Life's tough. Combo hunts are popular here. Hunt ducks and preserve quail in the fall; they go nicely with deer. And in the spring, try a trophy tom.

That White Oak deserves to call itself a lodge there is no doubt. Long and low, the lodge trails along a lake (bass, if you're of a mind). Rooms have private baths; meals are exemplary and service is first-class. For those who prefer slightly less luxurious accommodations—four bunks to a room and shared baths—there's Red Oak, a couple of miles down the road.

[S O U T H]

Bienville Plantation

W h i t e   S p r i n g s ,   F l o r i d a

Southern hospitality and big bucks. Who could ask for more?

VITAL STATISTICS:

Game/Arm/Seasons:
WHITETAILS:
Bow: Mid-Sept. through mid-Oct.
Centerfire: Early Nov. through mid-Jan.
Muzzleloader: Late-Oct. through early Nov.

Rates:
From $475/day

Accommodations:
MODERN LOG PLANTATION HOUSE
NUMBER OF ROOMS: 25, ALL WITH PRIVATE BATH
MAXIMUM NUMBER OF HUNTERS: 50

Meals: Gourmet Southern cooking

Conference Groups: Yes

Guides: Included

Gratuity: $10 to $50 per day

Preferred Payment:
Cash, check, credit cards

Other Activities:
Bird hunting, bird watching, boating, canoeing, fishing, golf, waterfowling, wildlife photography

Getting There:
Fly to Jacksonville, rent a car and drive to the lodge or hire the lodge van for $150 per party.

Contact:
David Bethune
Bienville Plantation
111 Orange St., Suite 101
Macon, FL 31201
800/655-6661 or
912-755-9311
Fax: 912/744-9672

FLORIDA IS A STATE that's not known for big whitetails. But north, along the Georgia and Alabama borders, the situation is quite different. Here, in the piney woods with their cypress swamps and stands of oak, is habitat that produces some truly awesome bucks. Good deer are four or five-year-olds that carry 10 or 12 points with spreads of 16-inches-plus. Average bucks are eight-pointers. Nobody pays serious attention to anything smaller.

Most of the best land is so tied up in private leases that even those with the deepest pockets have trouble gaining access. Yet for less than the price of a typical Western hunt, you can find yourself smack dab in the lap of 20,000 acres of fine whitetail country with a healthy dose of ducks, quail and bass thrown in for good measure.

We're talking about Bienville Plantation, well known for its vast acerage of pines and hardwoods and fields and ponds that regularly produce lunker largemouths. It wasn't always so. About a decade ago, Bienville Forest Investments bought the plantation from Continental Can, with an eye toward managing it for timber. Managers soon realized that with a little coaxing, the tract could become a hunting and fishing paradise. Timber was selectively harvested, food plots planted, roads improved and a deer-management plan implemented. The result is the sine qua non of Florida hunting resorts.

Deer season begins with archery hunting in late September and continues through muzzleloading and then rifle season into mid-January. Hunting is exclusively from stands over feed plots, access trails, and rub and scrape lines. You'll find no still-hunting or drives. Some die-hard hunters stay in the stands all day, and they're the ones who harvest the best bucks. But most of Bienville's guests may see the sun come up over a duck pond, shoot a few quail in mid-morning, sleep off lunch and then sit in the stand through twilight. While archers have first shot at deer, cooler weather in November moves whitetails into the rut. The hunting is best during the first two weeks of rifle season. An average whitetail weighs about 180 pounds, and racks must be at least eight points with a 15-inch spread. You can harvest one buck and one doe at Bienville, and hunter success rate is very high. Guests stay in plush log cabins beneath the pines and feast on excellent regional cuisine in the main lodge.

Osceola Outfitters

St. Cloud, Florida

Handicapped hunters will delight in record-book bucks along with 'gators and turkey.

VITAL STATISTICS:

Game/Arm/Seasons:
ALLIGATOR:
Bow, centerfire, muzzleloader: May through July, Sept. through Oct.
BOAR:
Bow, centerfire, muzzleloader: All year
DEER:
Centerfire, muzzleloader: Nov. through Jan.
TURKEY:
Shotgun: Mid-March through April
Rates:
ALLIGATOR: $3,200/3 days
BOAR: $300/2 days plus $150 trophy fee
DEER: $300/2 day plus $500/buck trophy fee
TURKEY: $1,250/3 days
Accommodations:
MODERN LODGE
NUMBER OF ROOMS: 3
MAXIMUM NUMBER OF HUNTERS: 6
Meals: Southern regional cuisine
Conference Groups: Yes
Guides: Included
Gratuity: $50-$100 per hunter
Preferred Payment:
Cash, company check
Other Activities:
Waterfowling
Getting There:
Fly to Orlando, and rent a car.

Contact:
Hoppy Kempfer
Osceola Outfitters
13150 Center St.
St. Cloud, FL 34773
Ph: 407/957-3593

CAMPS THAT SPECIALIZE in hunts for the physically challenged are few and far between. Many outfitters can and do make do. Success depends on the outfitter's understanding of the hunter's handicap and ability to provide transportation to and cover at a good stand, as well as guides and extra hands needed to recover and dress downed game. Successful handicapped hunts are fulfilling in the extreme for client and outfitter.

Hoppy Kempfer, honcho of Osceola Outfitters, has made something of a specialty of this. For a couple of years he's hosted Buckmasters' Disabled Rifle Camps at his lodge on a 20,000-acre ranch south of Orlando. Undulating with little more than a gentle swell here and there, lots of ponds, stands of cypress and ubiquitous palmetto provide habitat for whitetails, turkey, and alligators. Deer here tend to be smaller than in the more northern parts of the state. A buck that scores 100 by Boone & Crockett standards will make the state record book for this zone. That means most eight- and ten pointers are shoe-ins.

Handicapped hunters scan rub lines and trails from ground blinds fashioned from palmetto by guides. Rolling their wheelchairs into the blinds in the pre-dawn chill, hunters play the waiting game. Does are legal game, but most hold out for bucks of six points or better. Wild boars roam the ranch, and the trick is to keep a curious hog from spooking a skittish buck.

Of course Osceola Outfitters serves hunters who are not physically challenged as well. Swamp buggies fashioned from ex-military four-bys haul them far into the ranch, into areas seldom visited by other hunters. Typically two hunters share a guide, but one-on-one hunts can be arranged in advance. For those whose bent is somewhat exotic, Hoppy offers rifle and bow hunts for 'gators in early summer and fall. Got room for an 11-footer on your wall?

Accommodations are modern and clean and meals often feature local delicacies such as smoked venison or boar and 'gator. The ranch is located about an hour southeast of Orlando, and a number of clients combine family vacations to Disney World and other theme parks with their hunts at Osceola.

Broughton Plantation

N e w b o r n ,   G e o r g i a

*Two hours from Atlanta you'll find good
deer hunting and one helluva Southern breakfast.*

VITAL STATISTICS:

Game/Arm/Seasons:
DEER:
Bow, mid-Sept. through mid-Oct.
Centerfire, muzzleloader: mid-Oct.
through Dec.

Rates:
From $350/day

Accommodations:
RUSTIC LOG LODGE
NUMBER OF ROOMS: 4 WITH PRIVATE BATH
MAXIMUM NUMBER OF HUNTERS: 10

Meals: Hearty (and we mean
hearty!) homestyle

Conference Groups: Yes

Guides: Included

Gratuity: $40/day

Preferred Payment:
Cash, credit cards, check

Other Activities:
Bird hunting

Getting There:
Fly to Atlanta, rent a car, or engage
the lodge van at no charge.

Contact:
Jim Babcock
Broughton Plantation
P.O. Box 172
Newborn, GA 30056
Ph: 706/342-2281
Fx: 706/342-9810

SAD FACT IS that the best deer hunting in the South lies in private hands. Sure, vast tracts of public land — the mountains of north Georgia and swamps in the southern part of the state — contribute to the annual buck harvest. But there, unless you work your way back in and deep, odds are you'll encounter other hunters.

So what are your options? Joining a club is the choice favored by most Peach Tree Staters. But for the traveling hunter, that's not an economically viable option unless the hunter plans to be in the area six to eight times each season. The other is to book a hunt at a private lodge. At Broughton Plantation you can have it both ways.

This old dairy farm lies just beyond the sleepy village of Newborn, a couple hours east of Atlanta via I-20. The country rolls beneath second-growth forests of pine and scrubby oak interspersed here and there with bean and corn fields and acreage that lies fallow. Broughton's manager runs hunts on four parcels of land totaling 2,000 acres. Hunters mount stands before dawn and dark and sit and wait and watch. Book a day's hunting or sign up for a three- or five-day package for which the days don't have to be consecutive. It's a little like joining a private club.

Owners Warren and Ken Howard live on the property along with their mother and dad. Thus this is a dandy place for families, and a number of hunters bring camo'd spouses and kids out for their first venison. Both bucks and does are legal here, though antlered deer must be at least eight points to be harvestable.

Some hunters just come for the day and beat it back down the interstate to Atlanta at night. Others avail themselves of one of four bed rooms complete with private bath. Those who spend the night will groan after all the fried chicken, pork chops and chicken-fried steak complete with corn, beans, greens and fatback. You'll founder on cornbread and butter and strawberry preserves, and when morning comes with grits, eggs, sausage and biscuits and gravy, you'll say what the hell and let your belt out one more notch.

Bucks & Beards

Crofton, Kentucky

With 40 deer per acre, you'll have a pretty good chance of taking a deer.

VITAL STATISTICS:

Game/Arm/Seasons:
WHITETAILS:
Bow: Mid-Sept. through mid-Jan.
Centerfire: Third week of Nov.
Muzzleloader: Mid-Dec.
TURKEY:
Bow and shotgun: Mid-April through early May

Rates:
WHITETAILS: from $795/3 days
TURKEY: $750/3 days

Accommodations:
MODERN RANCH HOUSE AND TRAILER
NUMBER OF ROOMS: 10
MAXIMUM NUMBER OF HUNTERS: 20

Meals: Chicken, fish, pork and country accompaniments

Conference Groups: Yes

Guides: Included

Gratuity: Not encouraged

Preferred Payment:
Cash, money order, check

Getting There:
Fly to Nashville, rent a car and drive to the lodge.

Contact:
Jerry Woolsey
Bucks & Beards
Box 218
Crofton, KY 42217
502/424-9848

ROUGHLY 30 MILES EAST of the Land Between the Lakes and 60 miles west of Bowling Green, Crofton is a small town that sits in the midst of some of the region's finest deer and turkey habitat. Gentle ridges wooded with oak and hickory provide mast and sloping hillsides thickly tufted with cedar and pines offer cover for whitetails that slip into fields of corn and soybeans to feed. The area supports what may be the best deer herd in the state.

This is not the hyperbolic boast of an outfitter. John Phillips, deer program manager from Kentucky's Department of Fish and Wildlife Resources, estimates that the density of deer in northern Christian County around Crofton is about 40 deer per square mile. He says that Christian is one of the state's leading producers of trophy deer.

Five-year-old bucks typically score 150 or better, but the chances of harvesting a 130 or better buck is admittedly slim, says Jerry Woolsey. For more than a dozen years, he's been operating Bucks and Beards, a guide service with 10,000 acres under lease in Christian County. Hunting is from tree stands, with the best opportunities coming during the rut in October and early November. Stands overlook scrape lines or trails between bedding and feed plots. Jerry and his guides take groups of four to seven hunters to their stands and then pick them up at pre-arranged times. Otherwise, hunters are on their own. The success rate for archers and rifle hunters is around 75 percent, and it increases slightly for muzzleloaders who hunt the last three weeks of the season. These woods and fields also produce turkeys averaging 20 pounds during the spring gobbler season.

Hunters here are housed either in the recently remodeled modern main lodge or a three-bedroom, two-bath house trailer. Meals, as you'd expect in this part of the country, are solid: chicken, barbecued pork, fish, corn, green beans, slaw. It's the food that sustains farmers for those long hours in the fields. The trick for deer hunters is to stay awake in the stands.

Circle M Plantation

M a c o n ,   M i s s i s s i p p i

Land where corporate magnates chase deer and quail.

VITAL STATISTICS:

Game/Arm/Seasons:

WHITETAILS:
Bow: Aug. through Jan.
Centerfire: Mid-Nov. through early Dec.; mid-Dec. through Jan.
Muzzleloader: Early through mid-Dec.
TURKEY:
Bow, Shotgun, Muzzleloader: March 15 through May 1

Rates:
DEER $600/2 days (bow and muzzleloader); $700/2 days (centerfire)
TURKEY $350/day (lodging and meals additional)
QUAIL $500/day

Accommodations
MODERN FRAME PLANTATION HOUSES
NUMBER OF ROOMS: 12; 10 WITH PRIVATE BATH
MAXIMUM NUMBER OF HUNTERS: 15
Meals: Fine Southern cooking
Conference Groups: Yes
Guides: Included
Gratuity: 8% service fee added to bill
Preferred Payment:
Cash, check, credit cards
Other Activities:
Biking, bird hunting, fishing, hiking
Getting There:
Fly to Columbus and take the lodge van for $35.

Contact:
Lanier Long
Circle M Plantation
Rt. 3, Box 710
Macon, MS 39341
601/726-5791
Fax: 601/726-9300

BEYOND A PAIR OF OLD IRON GATES between weathered brick posts sits a genteel frame country home of faintly Georgian style. Stately trees shade the white-columned front porch, and, were you not bent on a trophy whitetail, you'd be of a mind to tarry there, soaking up tranquillity. For more than three-quarters of a century folks have come here to hunt the 6,500 acres on the Noxubee River in east-central Mississippi. The first sportsman to own the Circle M was the governor of Oklahoma, who bought the place in the 1920s. Later, the presidents of Archer-Daniels, General Mills, and Weyerhaeuser pooled their pennies and purchased the plantation for its bird hunting. (By birds, we mean quail.)

Quail is the Circle M's mainstay, but from October through January, host Lanier Long and his guides serve about 120 deer hunters. From stands and blinds overlooking feed plots; rub and scrape lines; swamp and river bottom; and trails through piney woods, hunters wait for whitetails that average eight points with 14-inch or better spreads. Hunters are up at 4:30, fed a light breakfast and driven to their stands long before sun lightens the sky. The morning hunt wraps up about 9:30 or so. Back at the lodge, there's a light snack waiting. Then there's the choice of bird hunting, a round of five-stand sporting clays or bass fishing in one of the plantation's four ponds. Lunch and a nap refresh body and soul before the evening hunt begins around 3:30 p.m. Circle M charges by the day with a two-day minimum, and more than half of its guests harvest bucks. Guests are allowed one doe per day and everyone goes home with venison.

Circle M offers hunters private lodges that will accommodate up to five hunters. Each contains four bedrooms and most have private baths. They're tastefully furnished in a blend of traditional and modern style. Dinners of such Old South favorites as fried quail and venison are served in the wide-pine-board-floored dining room where, if a chill haunts the air, a fire will warm the hearth. Catering not only to individuals, Circle M hosts many corporate groups.

Hard to believe that this tranquil setting of a lake-front cabin, one of five at Bienville Plantation close to Lake City, Florida, was once a booming phosphate mine. Today, you'll find more than 15,000 acres of prime whitetail, waterfowl and quail habitat.

Autumn can be balmy in Pachuta, Mississippi. On the 5,000-acre McKenna Ranch, you can relax in rockers on the main lodge's front porch and tell lies about the 10-pointer that got away—all this after a hearty Southern dinner that featured chicken-fried steak.

McKenna Ranch

P a c h u t a ,   M i s s i s s i p p i

You can take two trophy-class bucks from this 5,000-acre spread.

VITAL STATISTICS:

Game/Arm/Seasons:
WHITETAILS:
Bow: Oct. through late Nov.
Centerfire: Late Nov. through late Jan.
Muzzleloader: Early through mid-Dec.
TURKEY:
Bow, centerfire: March through April
Rates:
Bow from $500/2 days; centerfire, muzzleloader $750/2 days
Accommodations:
LOG PLANTATION HOUSE AND CABINS
NUMBER OF ROOMS: 12
MAXIMUM NUMBER OF HUNTERS: 10
Meals: Family-style Southern cooking
Conference Groups: Yes
Guides: Included
Gratuity: Hunter's discretion
Preferred Payment:
Cash, check
Other Activities:
Bird hunting, bird watching, canoeing/rafting, fishing, wildlife photography
Getting There:
Fly to Meridian, rent a car and drive to the lodge, or the lodge van will pick you up for $50 per person.

Contact:
Steve McKenna
McKenna Ranch
741 County Rd. 313
Patter, MS 39347
601/727-4926 or
601/727-3085
Fax: 601/727-4926
e-mail: SBMcKenna@aol.com

ALABAMA GETS ALL THE PRESS these days about its black belt bucks. But look out, Mississippi's on the rise, thanks to folks like Steve and Betty McKenna. Six years ago, Steve opened his 5,000-acre spread to private hunters. What they can find is a mixture of feed plots, forests, creek bottoms and a little swamp with a seven-mile pipeline down the middle. The pipeline and the feed plots have been planted in corn yielding 12 percent protein. Normal corn contains about 7 percent. All told, come fall, he expects a crop of 6 million ears, all for whitetails.

That bodes well for racks on the bucks that wander the ranch. Hunters are allowed to take two bucks. All must be at least six-pointers, although eight-pointers are preferred. One can have a spread of less than 15 inches and the other must be larger. And if that isn't enough to fill your freezer, your tag permits you one doe. About half of his hunters get their bucks. Those who work the hardest, naturally, are most successful.

As is typical of Southern-style plantations, hunters down heavy breakfasts and then are taken to their stands by guides, one for every two guests. Depending on your preference and how the deer are moving, you will be taken to a tripod, tree, tower or natural stand. From there, you'll watch travel routes, rubs and scrapes and feed plots until midmorning. The same scenario is followed for the late afternoon/evening hunt. Normally everyone comes in for lunch and a snooze, except those dedicated deer hunters who know that bucks also move at midday. With a can of soda, a couple sandwiches, a few cookies and a jug of water stashed in their daypacks, these guys sit on stand all day. They see a lot of small bucks and does. Patience pays. Invariably a bigger buck will come along to chase the smaller ones away. Intelligence also contributes to success. Hunters and guides write down the location, sex and size of each deer they see in notebooks provided for the purpose. At night, guides study the information and lay individual plans for each hunter.

Hunting here is strictly a Monday-through-Friday affair. The ranch is closed on the weekends when the surrounding woods see what pressure there is from local hunters. They tend to push deer back on the ranch where they'll be for the next batch of McKenna's guests. The two guest cabins of four rooms with some private baths are rustic and comfortable. Meals are served in the main log lodge, and then there are rocking chairs to work off the fried chicken, gravy and biscuits.

Pearl River Outfitters

Hunt real deer down in the hell holes of Mississippi.

VITAL STATISTICS:

Game/Arm/Seasons:
WHITETAIL:
Centerfire: Oct. through Feb.
Rates:
$2,750/3 days
Accommodations:
VINTAGE FRAME PLANTATION HOUSE
NUMBER OF ROOMS: 4 WITH SHARED BATH
MAXIMUM NUMBER OF HUNTERS: 6
Meals: Fine dining from trained chef
Conference Groups: No
Guides: Included
Gratuity: 5 to 10% of hunt cost
Preferred Payment:
Cash, check
Getting There:
Fly to Jackson, rent a car and drive to the lodge.

Contact:
Andy Dyess
Pearl River Outfitters
355 Long Cove Dr.
Madison, MS 39110
601/856-0933
Fax: 601/362-3599
e-mail:
pearlriveroutfitters@mailcity.com
Web: PearlRiverOutfitters.com

THEY'RE CALLED "HELL HOLES," ravines so thick with oak that nothing goes down in them except bucks and those who hunt them. A phenomenon associated with the wanderings of the rivers in the southwestern part of the state, hell holes may drop 400 or 500 feet from the piedmont plain down to the level of river bottoms. On the prairie-like plain are those endless stands of piney forest and some hardwoods, broken here and there by a row-crop farm. In the main, the country is managed for timber.

Bucks grow big here on the 3,400 acres Andy Dyess leases. A trophy would top 150 and 130s to 140s are not so uncommon. The minimum is an eight-pointer scoring 130 or better. Chances for a 10-pointer are good. The reason: Outfitter Andy Dyess, who runs a law office in his spare time, is protective of his bucks. No 4WDs approach the areas where his tree stands and ground blinds are located. You'll walk in alone, scented down and wearing rubber boots, following directions provided by your guide. Hunting is strictly from stands; there's no wandering around. Hunting with a north wind is best because then wind direction is dependable. The acreage you're hunting today has not been hunted this season and it won't be hunted tomorrow unless there's a very good reason to do so. To hunt here is like having opening day every morning. You won't find many archers hunting here, and if any show up, they'll be carrying rifles. Bowhunting isn't allowed. And the best part is that only one or two hunters are in camp at any given time. A line-them-up, move-them-in, get-them-a-deer-and-send-them-home operation this ain't. It's like hunting with a personal mentor. The best time to be here is at the peak of the rut with the new moon in January.

Detail counts in this game and Andy has his hunting plan honed to a keen edge. And accommodations at his 1840s house with the wrap-around veranda on the Pearl River is tailor-made for a night of unwinding. You won't be able to do much else after a dinner of roast pork stuffed with rosemary and sun-dried tomatoes. For a rate of $2,750, the fare here, you get every bit of what you pay for.

Rose Hill Plantation

Bentonia, Mississippi

Bucks or bass? Here you don't have to choose.

VITAL STATISTICS:

Game/Arm/Seasons:
WHITETAIL:
Bow only: Oct. through Jan.

Rates:
From $1,200/4 days

Accommodations:
MODERN LODGE
NUMBER OF ROOMS: 3, WITH SHARED BATH
MAXIMUM NUMBER OF HUNTERS: 6

Meals: Shrimp scampi, char-grilled fish, Southern fried chicken

Conference Groups: Yes

Guides: Included

Gratuity: $100

Preferred Payment:
Cash, credit card, check

Other Activities:
Antiquing, biking, bird hunting, bird watching, fishing, riding, wildlife photography

Getting There:
Fly to Jackson and you'll be picked up.

Contact:
Tom Shipp
Rose Hill Plantation
1079 Passons Rd.
Bentonia, MS 39040
601/755-8383
Fax: 601/755-2020
Web: www.hunting.net/rosehill

SO YOU'VE SPENT THE MORNING on stand and passed up on that eight-pointer with the 14-inch spread. It'd be a nice deer anywhere else in the country, but here in central Mississippi there are bigger. Now you're sitting on the back porch of Tom Shipp's house, a glass of iced tea close at hand, and a big splash catches your attention. It's that bass by the weeds near the dock. Maybe you can seduce him with Tom's rod. It's either that, or a nap. What the heck, there's time to do both before your afternoon hunt.

Soon after the second war for independence, as that 1860s unpleasantness is called down here, Tom's relatives bought Rose Hill, near Bentonia, 30 miles north of Jackson. Like most plantations, it grew and shrank depending on the economy. Today it contains about 2,000 acres, devoted to growing corn, soybeans, milo and cotton. Now deer eat the first three crops, but they bed down in high cotton. Why? Insecticides used to control weevils also drive away flies and other stinging bugs. Deer evidently find bedding down in a cotton field as comfortable as we would find sleeping on a screened porch.

At dusk, deer slip out of the cotton heading for green fields, and invariably some of the bigger bucks will pass by stands that Tom and his guides have placed along game trails. You'll catch them moving to food throughout the season, but during the rut, rattling and grunting works best.

A typical deer taken on Rose Hill and the 3,000 acres of adjacent property Shipp leases is an eight-pointer with a 15-inch spread. Deer with racks bigger than 16 points have been seen and their sheds found after the season. And the doe-to-buck ratio is better than 2:1. During a three-day hunt, clients see more than a dozen deer that would earn bragging rights anywhere else. The size of the deer so amazes Eastern hunters, that they sometimes lose their cool and blow reasonably easy shots. Adds new meaning to "luck of the draw." Of 30 archers who hunted last year, five took good bucks. Firearms are not permitted; if they were, the harvest would have been much higher. In any event, the hunts must have been successful; 60 percent of those hunters are coming back next year. And you can bet they enjoyed Tom's new three-bedroom, two-bath lodge of Western red cedar and the fine home-cooked meals.

Buffalo Creek Guide Service

Selma, North Carolina

Some of the biggest bucks in North Carolina are found in the Selma area.

OPEN TO BOW, muzzleloader, rifle or shotgun hunts, Buffalo Creek Lodge has almost 5,000 acres of prime hunting country: flat land with slight ridges of hardwood and pine thickets surrounded by vast tracts of cypress swamps. The land is also laced with peanut fields, which deer and other game consider a prime food source. The high protein in peanuts helps to grow some of the biggest racks found in North Carolina.

Most hunting here is done from tree stands (there are 80 on the property) and shooting houses overlooking peanut fields, hardwood ridges or corn feeders. The prime time to get a big buck here is during the rut, which occurs roughly from the last week of October to Nov. 20. Two deer may be taken per day, with a limit of five per season, and there are no antler restrictions on bucks (although there is a modest fine if you shoot a button buck). Bobcats can also be taken from the mid-October to mid-February.

The lodge itself is clean and comfortable, with four bedrooms, two baths and a lounge with a television set and VCR. Three meals a day are provided—a gut-breaking breakfast with coffee, juice and milk, sandwiches and soup for lunch, and a hearty supper featuring steak, chicken, pork with sides, and venison. Bag lunches are made for those who prefer to stay out and hunt all day.

For hunters after trophy whitetails, Buffalo Creek recently opened a new lodge on more than 1,000 acres of prime deer habitat in Sampson County. Featuring food plots, automatic feeders and mineral feed stations that help ensure quality bucks, this farm is similar to a Texas ranch, with tower blinds and shooting houses. You'll see a lot of six-point-plus bucks on this property; just don't shoot the first one, as his bigger brother might be coming down the trail right behind him!

[S O U T H]

Buck Run Hunting Lodge

E s t i l l ,   S o u t h   C a r o l i n a

With a long season and a huge whitetail population, this low-country lodge caters to families and small groups.

VITAL STATISTICS:

Game/Arm/Seasons:
WHITETAIL:
Bow, centerfire, muzzleloader: Mid-Aug. through early Jan.
TURKEY:
Centerfire: Mid-March through early May
Rates:
WHITETAIL or TURKEY from $870/3 days
Accommodations:
MODERN LODGE
NUMBER OF ROOMS: 6
MAXIMUM NUMBER OF HUNTERS: 12
Meals: Steak, pork, chicken, seafood
Conference Groups: No
Guides: Included
Gratuity: Hunter's discretion
Preferred Payment:
Deposit: cash or check; balance is cash only
Other Activities:
Bird hunting, bird watching, wildlife photography
Getting There:
Fly to Savannah, Georgia, rent a car and drive to the lodge, or be met by a van from the lodge.

Contact:
Pete Simmons
Buck Run Hunting Lodge
Rt. 1, Box 14-B
Estill, SC 29918
803/625-3791
Fax: 803/625-0525
e-mail: buckrhc@aol.com
Web: www.buckrun.com

LOCATED IN HAMPTON COUNTY, where white-tailed deer populations and annual harvests are traditionally No. 1 or 2 statewide, Buck Run Hunting Lodge offers the serious whitetail hunter an experience he or she will never forget. Open August 15 through January 1 each year, the lodge, in the South Carolina low country, offers the longest and most liberal deer season in the country.

With more than 30 years of whitetail experience, owner Pete Simmons makes sure that every one of his guests gets a quality hunt tailored to his or her specific needs. Careful pre-hunt planning and preparation on 6,000 acres of hunting properties are all part of his daily routine.

To ensure the personal touch, all hunts at Buck Run are personally guided and are limited to 10 to 12 people each hunting session, which makes it ideal for husband/wife or father/son/daughter teams. Church groups, small businesses and civic groups all book time at the lodge each year. "Families and small groups are our specialty," says Pete's better half, Sandra.

Most hunting, according to Simmons, is done from elevated stands or tower blinds from heights of 12 to 24 feet. Stands are strategically located over natural food plots and agricultural fields of soybean/peas, wheat/rye and corn, or in prime hardwood flats and bottoms, where deer frequently go to feed and make scrapes and rubs. Shots generally range from 30 to 75 yards in wooded areas, and to more than 150 in the fields. No calibers smaller than .243, and no shotguns, please!

The lodge itself is not fancy, but modern and comfortable. It's smoke-free, and has private bed and bathrooms, central air and heat, TVs, VCRs, stereo and pool tables. All meals are home-cooked by co-owner Sandra Simmons, who guarantees that you'll gain at least five pounds during your stay. Steaks, pork chops, chicken and seafood are her specialties.

Cowden Plantation

Jackson, South Carolina

VITAL STATISTICS:

Game/Arm/Seasons:
WHITETAIL:
Bow, centerfire, muzzleloader: Mid-Aug. through Nov.
HOGS:
Bow, centerfire, muzzleloader: Mid-Aug. through Feb.
TURKEY:
Bow, shotgun: Spring and fall
Rates:
DEER, HOGS and TURKEY from $250 per day
Accommodations:
FARMHOUSE
NUMBER OF ROOMS: 3
MAXIMUM NUMBER OF HUNTERS: 12
Meals: Southern cooking for groups of three or more
Conference Groups: Yes
Guides: Included
Gratuity: $25
Preferred Payment:
Cash, MasterCard, Visa, check
Other Activities:
Bird hunting, bird watching, fishing, waterfowling, wildlife photography
Getting There:
Fly to Augusta, Georgia and you'll be picked up.

Contact:
James K. Jarrett
Cowden Plantation
383 Brown Rd.
Jackson, SC 29831
803/471-3616
Fax: 803/471-9246
e-mail: jarrett@groupz.net
Web: www.jarrettrifles.com

Want a poke at a long-range deer?
Come to Kenny's bean field.

WELCOME TO THE HOME of the ultimate bean-field rifle. A bean-field rifle gives everyday hunters the capability of making clean one-shot kills out to 500 yards. Good ol' boys knew that big bucks don't come out to feed until last light, if then. And these wise old deer were just as apt to come into the south end of a field of soybeans while you're a third of a mile away watching the north end. In such situations, you've got two choices. You can cuss the fates that put you on the wrong end of the field. Or you can try and stretch your current cannon, hoping that you've guessed the wind and trajectory correctly.

Well Kenny Jarrett, a tractor-riding bean-field farmer, got to thinking about it during those interminable days tilling his uncle's land near Cowden. He figured that by applying the tricks the benchrest crowd worked on their one-holers, truing the action, pillar bedding and precision chambering, in the main, he could get a hunting rifle to do the same thing. So long story short, he did it. Now making about 100 custom rifles a year, none leaves his shop unless it shoots well indeed. And his private proving ground is now open for trophy deer and hog hunting.

On 10,000 acres along the Savannah River just about 16 miles southeast of Augusta, Georgia, Jarrett and his crew have erected 114 stands overlooking feed plots, some of which will give you a chance for a long bean-field shot. Roofed and equipped with shooting rail and chair, these stands are something you'll like. And even hunters like your humble scribe who are older, overweight and out of shape, will find them safe and secure. They're also ideal for younger hunters. Special areas of the property are managed for trophy bucks, and on others there's no restriction on size. The plantation contains 11.5 square miles laced with 145 miles of roads. They run past the fields and through oaks draped with moss and across creeks that lead to a thick cypress swamp. Wild boar roam these parts, and they're hunted from stands over baits. And, as you'd guess, this is turkey heaven come spring.

Clean and comfortable accommodations are found in an old farmhouse. When it comes to food, you've got three options. Do your own cooking, eat at the Buckhead Diner in town or make sure there's at least three in your party. Then Kenny will lay on a cook who'll fatten you with her first platter of buttery biscuits. Hunting rates here are by the day.

129

Deerfield Plantation

S t .   G e o r g e ,   S o u t h   C a r o l i n a

Hunt trophy whitetails in Southern style from this 110-year-old plantation.

VITAL STATISTICS:

Game/Arm/Seasons:
WHITETAILS:
Bow, centerfire, muzzleloader: Aug. 15 through Jan. 1
TURKEY:
Bow, centerfire, muzzleloader: March 15 through May 1
WILD BOAR:
Bow, centerfire, muzzleloader: Year-round
Rates:
From $825/3 days (any species)
Accommodations:
VINTAGE FRAME PLANTATION HOUSE AND CABIN
NUMBER OF ROOMS: 8; 6 WITH PRIVATE BATH
MAXIMUM NUMBER OF HUNTERS: 24
Meals: Southern cooking, family-style
Conference Groups: Yes
Guides: Included
Gratuity: $50 to $100
Preferred Payment:
Cash, MasterCard, Visa
Other Activities:
Antiquing, biking, bird hunting, bird watching, canoeing/rafting, fishing, golf, waterfowling, wildlife photography
Getting There:
Fly to Charleston, rent a car and drive to the plantation.

Contact:
Hugh Walters
Deerfield Plantation
709 Gum Branch Rd.
St. George, SC, 29477
803/563-7927

FIELDS OF SOUTH CAROLINA'S low country grow prodigious harvests of peas, beans and corn. But that's not all they produce. At dusk healthy whitetails emerge from thick swamps and stands of scrubby oak to take their suppers among the freshly tilled row crops. These are heavy deer, often eight-pointers weighing around 180 pounds.

The exceptional whitetail populations of Dorchester County led Hugh Walters to open Deerfield Plantation to hunters a decade ago. With 10,000 acres of private hunting, 3,000 reserved for trophy deer with racks of at least a 15-inch spread and eight points or better, Walters' hunters seldom go home empty-handed. During the first six weeks of the season from mid-August through September, the limit is one deer per day. Then things get going good and throughout the balance of the season—it's open until Jan. 1—you can shoot two deer per day. Best times to hunt are the pre-rut in the first weeks of September and then during the rut proper in early November. More than a few hunters aim for late August and the chance to take a six-pointer still in velvet.

Hunting here is semi-guided. You're roused about an hour and a half before sun-up, fed a continental breakfast and driven to your stand for the morning. Everyone hunts from stands; yours may be an enclosed shooting house overlooking a field of oats or rye, or a perch atop a railed tripod stand 12 feet above a patch of cutover pine lands. Average shots are generally about 100 yards. With no more than 24 hunters on the spread at any given time, you'll seldom see another soul in the field. What you will see is deer, plenty of them, and the trick is to wait for a buck with a rack of bragging quality. In late morning, after the deer have stopped moving, the driver will collect you and bring you back to the plantation house for dinner (only a Yankee would dare call it lunch). After a nap, you'll return to the field to catch deer moving as night begins to fall.

While the name of the game is deer, spring turkey hunting from March 15 to May 1 is also very good. Typical gobblers sport 10-inch beards and 1 1/4-inch spurs. Twenty-pounders aren't rare. Neither are wild hogs in the 200- to 300-pound class.

Built in the late 1880s, the old frame plantation house is as comfortable as a favorite pair of boots. There are six guest rooms in the main lodge and another two with private baths in a cabin nearby. The menu here is definitely Southern, featuring venison, seafood and chicken as well as pork and beef.

Little River Plantation

Abbeville, South Carolina

Hunt for trophy bucks.

VITAL STATISTICS:

Game/Arm/Seasons:
WHITETAIL:
Bow: Mid-Sept. through early Oct.
Centerfire: Early Oct. through early Jan.
Muzzleloader: Early Oct.
TURKEY:
Centerfire: Early April through early May
Rates:
WHITETAIL DEER and TURKEYS from $950/3 days
Accommodations:
RUSTIC LODGE
NUMBER OF ROOMS: 8
MAXIMUM NUMBER OF HUNTERS: 18
Meals: Southern fare: beef, potatoes, vegetables, dessert
Conference Groups: Yes
Guides: Included
Gratuity: Hunter's discretion
Preferred Payment:
Cash, American Express, MasterCard, Visa, check
Other Activities:
Bird hunting, bird watching, canoeing, fishing, golf, hiking, waterfowling, wildlife photography
Getting There:
Fly to Augusta, Georgia, rent a car and drive to the lodge or be picked up by a lodge vehicle for $50.

Contact:
Jim Edens
Little River Plantation
Box 1129
Abbeville, SC 29620
864/391-2300
Fax: 864/391-2304

IF YOU'RE LOOKING FOR a down-home Southern deer camp, look no further than Little River Plantation in the South Carolina Piedmont, in Abbeville and McCormick counties, about five miles from the Georgia border. This is the area where most of the state's trophy bucks come from, and the folks at Little River—having been in the business for 15 years—know how to hunt them.

Rack bucks abound in this region, which has been famous for quality deer hunting since colonial days, when hides were shipped to England via Charleston, where Englishmen couldn't get enough buckskin. Between 1699 and 1715, in fact, an average of some 53,000 skins per year were sent across the Atlantic. By the end of the colonial period, the total was likely more than 7 million.

Such heavy trade hurt the deer herd, and cotton-farming practices didn't help. But since then the herds have come back in force. Today, there are so many deer that hunters can take 10 deer (no more than two a day) in a season that runs from early archery in September into late rifle in January. Hunters at the plantation take a number of trophy-class bucks each year, while just about everyone fills his tag (the annual success rate is more than 85 percent). Owner Jim Edens and his sons manage several thousand acres of prime deer habitat, so pressure is kept low and hunters can look forward to a variety of stand sites. Hunters are encouraged to hold their fire until they see a buck that's at least six points, which pretty much guarantees that most hunters are going to get a good wallhanger. Little River prides itself on catering not only to handicapped hunters, but to family groups as well. Perhaps that's one reason why Edens gets an 85 percent repeat business.

The lodge itself, a 1930s-era barn that's been refurbished, overlooks a yard dominated by old oaks and sycamores, with an understory of dogwoods, redbud and honeysuckle. To complete the classic Southern setting, dining is pure South: beef, potatoes and veggies, to be sure, but also barbecued offerings, fried chicken and peas, not to mention biscuits and gravy with grits for breakfast.

777 Ranch

Hondo, Texas

Take a whitetail or African safari right in the heart of Texas.

VITAL STATISTICS:

Game/Arm/Seasons:
ELK:
Centerfire: Sept. through March
WHITE-TAILED DEER:
Centerfire: Mid-Nov. through mid-Jan.
BOAR, EXOTICS:
Centerfire: Year-round
Rates:
$250 per day single occupancy; kill fee for each animal taken is extra and fees vary by animal from $600 to $7,500
Accommodations:
MODERN LODGE
NUMBER OF ROOMS: 24, ALL WITH PRIVATE BATH
MAXIMUM NUMBER OF HUNTERS: 24
Meals: Steaks, pork chops, chicken
Conference Groups: Yes
Guides: Included
Gratuity: $30 per day per person
Preferred Payment:
Cash, Discover, MasterCard, Visa, check
Other Activities:
Bird hunting, bird watching, boating, fishing, golf, hiking, swimming, tennis, waterfowling, wildlife photography
Getting There:
Fly to San Antonio International, rent a car and drive to the ranch, or take the free shuttle to the ranch at noon and from the ranch at the end of your trip. If you require transportation but cannot meet the noon shuttle, there is an additional fee of $50.

Contact:
V.K. Christiansen
777 Ranch Inc.
Private Road 5327
Richter Lane South
Hondo, TX 78861-5445
830/426-3476
Fax: 830/426-4821
e-mail: 777ranch@777ranch.com
Web: www.777ranch.com

THE WORLD FAMOUS 777 RANCH has been in existence for more than 30 years, offering hunts for everything from trophy white-tailed deer to wild boar to exotics. Whatever you want to hunt, the 777 can arrange it for you.

It all started with whitetails, which grow huge racks in this part of Texas (west of San Antonio). Biologists tell Kevin Christiansen, owner of the 15,000-acre ranch, how many deer need to be culled from the herd each year to keep it healthy, and he obliges, guiding hunters to stands in areas where big bucks are known to be. A large number of does must also be removed from the herd each year, which hunters are urged to do. Wild boar are also taken in the same general areas where hunters go for whitetails, which is a bonus, as the feral pigs usually top the 200-pound mark.

The 777 also offers more than 50 exotic species from which to choose. In fact, three decades ago the 777 Ranch imported and released dozens of species from four continents. Many of the species are now more populous at places such as the 777 than in their native lands. To help ensure a healthy herd and finance the conservation projects, guests are allowed to hunt over-the-hill bucks and rams. Much of the meat from these trophies is donated to the Salvation Army to help feed the needy.

It doesn't matter whether you're a seasoned expert or a first-timer; you needn't worry about anything except enjoying yourself at the 777. Many who have traveled to the resort rate the staff as the operation's finest attribute. The Ranch is also easy to reach, being only 45 minutes from the San Antonio airport.

Hearty meals of steak, pork chops, or chicken are served at the ranch, either on the poolside veranda or in the huge sporting room of the main lodge. Accommodations range from double-occupancy suites to secluded complexes where corporate meetings or family reunions can be held in private.

Adobe Lodge Hunting Camp

San Angelo, Texas

Deep in the heart of Texas is a ranch where hunters take whitetails that average 16 inches and 8 points!

VITAL STATISTICS:

Game/Arm/Seasons:
WHITE-TAILED DEER:
Bow: Oct.
Centerfire: Nov. through Dec.
Muzzleloader: Nov. through Dec.
TURKEY:
Bow, centerfire, muzzleloader: Early April through mid-May
Rates:
WHITETAIL $2,850/4 days
TURKEY $950/3 days
Accommodations:
MODERN LODGE
NUMBER OF ROOMS: 4
MAXIMUM NUMBER OF HUNTERS: 8
Meals: Barbecue brisket, stir-fry venison, ribeye steaks
Conference Groups: No
Guides: Included
Gratuity: $150
Preferred Payment:
Cash, check
Other Activities:
Wildlife photography
Getting There:
Fly to San Angelo and be met by a van from the lodge.

Contact:
Skipper Duncan
Adobe Lodge Hunting Camp
Box 60127
San Angelo, TX 76906
915/942-8040

I N THE BUSINESS SINCE 1985, Skipper Duncan has one of the finest deer hunting operations in the Lone Star State—and that's really saying something, when you consider how many first-rate whitetail operations there are in Texas. But let some of Duncan's clients tell it.

"Great hunting, guides, food and accommodations equal a great experience." Ken Austad, La Mesa, California.

"This was my fourth hunt. It always keeps getting better." Dr. Vic Hamilton, Alexander City, Alabama.

"I have been booking professional guided hunts for over 20 years. Never before have I checked off 100 percent "excellent" rating in all categories." Bill Knapp, Wethersfield, Connecticut.

"Excellent hunting, excellent food, excellent atmosphere. The chances of shooting an above-average buck are excellent." Robert Scipioni, Myerstown, Pennsylvania.

The list of accolades goes on and on. But for good reason. With a repeat business of almost 75 percent, Duncan's Adobe Lodge has an almost 100 percent success ratio for gun hunters. And these are big bucks, too, with many carrying 10-point racks that place in the Boone & Crockett record book. In 1997, the top deer taken on the ranch was a 16 1/2-inch 11-pointer that gross scored 150.625. Bucks in the 130- and 140-class are almost commonplace.

Most hunting is done from Chevy Suburbans, driving back roads on private ranches. If a good deer is spotted, then you get out and walk, stalking and rattling to pull your deer into range. Blind hunting is also available, and hunters may shoot three does free of charge.

Duncan has two camps. The main Adobe Lodge, which can accommodate eight hunters at a time, 80 for the season, is on the ranch itself; hunters who stay there hunt its 2,500 acres of mesquite savannah with low, rolling hills and river bottoms filled with pecan trees, plus 40,000 acres on other private ranches in the area. The McManus Camp, which can hunt four clients at one time, 24 per season, is about 20 miles away and hunts a number of private ranches as well. Both camps are in the middle of prime whitetail country. And when you return from a long day afield, be prepared for some fine Texas tablefare, including barbecued brisket, stir-fried venison and ribeye steaks.

Blue River Outfitters

T h r o c k m o r t o n ,   T e x a s

An overlooked part of the country is producing its share of Boone & Crockett-class bucks.

VITAL STATISTICS:

Game/Arm/Seasons:
WHITETAIL:
Bow: Early Oct. through late Dec.
Centerfire: Mid through late Nov.
Muzzleloader: Late Oct. through early Nov.
BOAR:
Bow, centerfire, muzzleloader: Year-round
TURKEY:
Bow, centerfire: Early Apr. through early May
Rates:
WHITETAIL $2,000/3 days (centerfire and muzzleloader); $1,800/5 days (bow)
BOAR $100 per day
TURKEY $600/3 days
Accommodations:
RUSTIC LODGE
NUMBER OF ROOMS: 4
MAXIMUM NUMBER OF HUNTERS: 12
Meals: Steaks, pork loin, home-made breads
Conference Groups: Yes
Guides: Included
Gratuity: $100
Preferred Payment:
Cash, check
Other Activities:
Bird watching, fishing, hiking, swimming, wildlife photography
Getting There:
Fly to Oklahoma City, rent a car and drive to the lodge.

Contact:
Joe Moberley
Blue River Outfitters
Box 250
Throckmorton, TX 76483
940/849-0053
Fax: 940/849-005
e-mail:
sales@blueriveroutfitters.com
Web: www.blueriveroutfitters.com

WHEN IT COMES TO white-tailed deer hunting in the South, most hunters think of Alabama, Mississippi and Texas. But Oklahoma? It's not exactly the first state that comes to mind. Hunt the 15,000-acre Blue River Ranch, however, and your opinion of deer hunting in the Sooner State will change in a hurry.

Just a three-hour drive from the Dallas-Fort Worth area, the ranch is located in the cross timbers region in the southeastern part of the state. It's a working cattle ranch, consisting of rolling pasture interspersed with hardwood bottoms and fingers of brush that make excellent travel corridors for the deer, and predictable hunting spots. The scenic Blue River, nine miles of which runs through the middle of the ranch, resembles a clear Texas Hill Country stream, gurgling over a limestone bottom. It's about as pretty a setting as you'll find to go hunting.

With so much cover, and food sources that include acorn, pecan, persimmon, sumac and plenty of browse and forbs, the ranch supports a large deer herd. Small scattered fields of wheat and fescue are maintained along the river's edge to provide extra forage, not only for the deer, but for the many wild turkeys, feral hogs and bobwhite quail that also call this region home. But whitetails are why people come here, and for good reason: there are true monsters roaming the ranch. The herd, carefully managed for quality bucks, and with a buck-to-doe ratio of 1:3, contains its share of Boone & Crockett-class bucks, a couple of which are shot each year, by bow as well as gun hunters. Most hunting is done from tree stands, and more than a few hunters have been known to rattle their bucks into range. A doe or buck decoy might be just the thing to entice that long-tined 10-pointer the final few yards into bow range.

The lodge itself is modern and comfortable, accommodating up to 12 people. It has all the conveniences of home, including telephone, fax, TV, fireplace, pool table and library—perfect for relaxing after an arduous day afield.

Caprock Outfitters, Inc.

Pampa, Texas

Try for mulies and whitetails in the heart of west Texas.

VITAL STATISTICS:

Game/Arm/Seasons:
MULE DEER and WHITETAIL:
Bow: Late Sept. through Oct.
Centerfire: Mid-Nov. through early Dec.
ANTELOPE:
Bow and centerfire: Early to mid-Oct.
RIO GRANDE TURKEY:
Centerfire: Nov. through Dec.
Rates:
MULE DEER $2,500/5 days
WHITETAIL $1,500/3 days
ANTELOPE $1,500/2 days
RIO GRANDE TURKEY $750/3 days (2 turkeys)
Accommodations:
FARMHOUSE
NUMBER OF ROOMS: 4
MAXIMUM NUMBER OF HUNTERS: 8
Meals: Steak, chicken, quail, pork
Conference Groups: Yes
Guides: Included
Gratuity: $100
Preferred Payment:
Cash, MasterCard, Visa, check
Other Activities:
Bird hunting, bird watching, fishing, hiking, waterfowling, wildlife photography
Getting There:
Fly to Amarillo, Texas and the lodge van will meet you.

Contact:
Wayne Bruce
Caprock Outfitters, Inc.
Box 799
Pampa, TX 79066-0799
800/692-4659
806/665-1336
Fax: 806/665-0893
e-mail: caprock@pan-tex.net
Web: www.pan-tex.net/usr/c/caprock/index.html

CAPROCK OUTFITTERS is a full-service guide company founded by Wayne Bruce 13 years ago. Caprock provides quality hunts for several types of west Texas game. All hunts are fair chase (no high fence) on terrain that varies from plains, where hunters hunt out of stands, to rugged canyons that can only be hunted on foot or horseback.

Two types of mule deer hunts are offered. The first, fully guided for five days, is out of a base camp. This hunt is on 52 sections of private property, with a ranch house serving as the center of operations. The second, called the Western hunt, is fully guided on 10 sections of private property in the breaks of the Palo Duro Canyon. Hunters stay in bunkhouses, and all hunting is on foot or horseback.

Whitetail hunts are also available in combination with mule deer hunts. Caprock is also issued a limited number of antelope permits per year, and offers fully guided hunts for them on a first-come, first-served basis.

Turkeys and aoudad sheep are available in November and December, with turkeys huntable in April as well.

[**S O U T H**]

Dave Park Outfitting

F o w l e r t o n ,   T e x a s

Quality hunts in three game-rich states.

VITAL STATISTICS:

Game/Arm/Seasons:
COLORADO
ELK AND MULE DEER:
Bow: Late Aug. through late Sept.
Centerfire: Mid-Oct. through early Nov.
Muzzleloader: Mid-Sept.
NEW MEXICO
MULE DEER:
Centerfire: Early through mid-Nov.
ANTELOPE:
Centerfire: Late Aug. and late Sept.
TEXAS
WHITETAIL:
Centerfire: Early Nov. through mid-Jan.
TURKEY:
Centerfire: Late March through early May

Rates:
Colorado MULE DEER and ELK
$1,500/ 5 days (drop camp)
Colorado ELK from $2,950/5 days (rifle)
New Mexico MULE DEER from $2,750/5 days
ANTELOPE from $1,500/2 days
Texas WHITETAIL DEER from $3,500/3 days
TURKEY $450 per day

Accommodations:
LODGE, PRIVATE RANCH HOUSES AND WALLED-TENTS
NUMBER OF ROOMS: 3; 1 WITH PRIVATE BATH
MAXIMUM NUMBER OF HUNTERS: 8

Meals: Home cooking
Conference Groups: Yes
Guides: Depends on type of hunt
Gratuity: 10%
Preferred Payment: Cash, check
Other Activities:
Bird hunting, fishing, waterfowling, wildlife photography
Getting There:
Fly to the appropriate airport, rent a car and drive to the meeting point.

Contact:
Dave Park
Dave Park Outfitting
Box 493, Fowlerton, TX 78021
830/373-4478
Fax: 830/373-4478

HUNTING PARTS OF COLORADO, New Mexico and Texas, Dave Park Outfitting devotes itself to giving each hunter a quality hunt, no matter what you're after.

In Texas, the primary focus is on trophy whitetails. Hunts are conducted on several private ranches totaling nearly 15,000 acres in LaSalle and McMullen counties in south Texas. These are three- and five-day package hunts, which include meals, lodging and 4WD transportation. Hunters can successfully rattle in bucks, especially at the end of December, when the rut is in progress. Only mature bucks may be taken, as Park Outfitting manages these ranches for quality bucks. Bonus game includes javelina, hogs and predators.

Park offers guided elk, drop-camp elk and mule deer, and ranch house elk and mule deer hunts in Colorado. The drop camps in particular are a true wilderness experience; Park will ride you into camp on horses, then come back and check on you periodically. Otherwise, you're on your own—in a game-rich area. You can use rifle, bow or muzzleloader here, depending on the season. Same for the ranch-house hunts, which aren't nearly as rough as the drop camps (although you're still hunting on your own, without a guide). The guided hunts, out of Gunnison, are out of a deluxe wall-tent camp. Using a combination of horses, 4WD vehicles and foot, depending on the weather and location of game, Park's guides can get you into some real trophies. Only six to eight hunters a year are taken on this hunt.

In New Mexico, Park Outfitting concentrates on mule deer, antelope and trophy elk. These hunts take place on private ranches, with hunters staying in a comfortable ranch house for the week. Chances for success are high, especially if you can shoot accurately. Stand hunting, stalking and organized drives are all used, depending on where the game is located.

Dolan Creek Hunting, Inc.

D e l   R i o ,   T e x a s

Take your pick of trophy whitetails in the south Texas brush country.

VITAL STATISTICS:

Game/Arm/Seasons:
WHITETAIL:
Centerfire: Mid-Nov. through early Jan.
Rates:
From $1,500/5-day stand hunt
Accommodations:
RAMADA INN IN DEL RIO, TEXAS
MAXIMUM NUMBER OF HUNTERS: 20
Meals: Catered buffet at Ramada Inn
Conference Groups: Yes
Guides: Included
Gratuity: Hunter's discretion
Preferred Payment:
Cash, check
Other Activities:
Bird hunting
Getting There:
Fly to San Antonio, Texas, and rent a car.

Contact:
John Finegan
Dolan Creek Hunting, Inc.
Drawer 420069
Del Rio, TX 78842-0069
830/775-3129
Fax: 830/775-6163 #99
e-mail: dcreek@drtx.com
Web: www.dolancreekhunting.com

IF YOU WANT A CHANCE at a trophy whitetail buck, the south Texas brush country is where you ought to go. And if you're headed in that direction, look no farther than Dolan Creek Ranches. Oriented toward families, Dolan Creek leases ranches throughout the region, which is mostly rolling hills covered with vegetation typical for the Rio Grande area.

Current deer populations are excellent here, with prime buck-to-doe and deer-per-acre ratios. Hunters can be assured of seeing many 8- to 12-point bucks in the 16- to 20-inch-spread class. The age structure of the herd here is so remarkable that renowned deer researcher Dr. James Kroll has heartily endorsed the Dolan Ranches, stating that "It is a pleasure to fully endorse Dolan Creek; and recommend your operation to any serious whitetail hunter." Dolan is one of only three operations ever endorsed by Kroll.

Your guide will pick you up each morning before sunrise at your motel (in most cases the Ramada Inn), in order to be in the field at legal shooting time. Vehicles are used extensively on the safari-style hunts, giving a hunter a chance to look at several good bucks per day. Hunting areas are exclusive to you (and a partner, if you wish) and your guide, so you'll have no pressure from other hunters in the area. Blind or stand hunts are also available for those who prefer the challenge and solitude of waiting for prime game movement times.

Along with whitetails and turkeys (huntable in spring), you may also see and have a shot at bobcats, coyotes and an occasional mountain lion. Black bears, while sometimes seen in the region, are protected.

Meals are hotel fare, depending upon where you stay. And that can be just fine, especially considering how good these hunts are.

Dynamic Hunting & Fishing Service

S o n o r a ,   T e x a s

What is a guaranteed hunt?

VITAL STATISTICS:

Game/Arm/Seasons:
WHITETAIL:
Bow: Oct. through Nov.
Centerfire: Nov. through Jan.

Rates:
From $1,750/3 days plus room and board

Accommodations:
MOTELS
NUMBER OF ROOMS: 10 WITH PRIVATE BATH
MAXIMUM NUMBER OF HUNTERS: 20

Meals: Restaurants or buffets

Conference Groups: Yes

Guides: Included

Gratuity: 5 to 10%

Preferred Payment:
Cash, MasterCard, Visa, check

Other Activities:
Antiquing, biking, bird hunting, bird watching, boating, fishing, swimming, waterfowling, wildlife photography

Getting There:
Fly to San Angelo, San Antonio or Corpus Christi and rent a car.

Contact:
Doug Borries
Dynamic Hunting &
Fishing Service
14812 Glendale Rd.
Ocean Springs, MS 39564
800/843-4868

DO YOU CRINGE when someone offers a "guaranteed" hunt, you know, one of those "no kill, no pay" deals? Well you're not alone. It's the kind of language usually associated with hunting on a fenced preserve, or with a hyper outfitter who encourages his clients to shoot the first deer that happens to wander by. Both such operations violate the spirit of fair chase. On the other hand, scores of outfitters offer their hunters a trip the following year if this year's fails to deliver as promised. That's a pretty good guarantee. Sometimes, as they say, stuff happens.

The best way to check out an outfitter is to talk to those who know him and his operation. And the references panned out in spades for Doug Borries, who runs Dynamic Hunting. Doug is one part booking agent and two parts outfitter, and the hunts he directs in Texas live up to expectations. On his nine leased ranches west of Sonora, hunters scope at least 20 bucks a day. An average buck scores 120 or so. Success rate is 100 percent. Why? Hunting deer over bait is legal in Texas. On the ranches, electronic feeders open at the same hours every day, and deer, who are creatures of habit if not disturbed, hear the chow call. You'll shoot from ground blinds positioned on routes to and from the feeders.

This system allows very precise management of deer herds. Shoot a four- or five-year-old deer of eight points with a score of 115 or less, and you'll pay a $1,000 trophy fee. If a buck scores more than 115, your tab is $1,500. These rolling hills with their pasture, brush and oak motts, which are two- to three-acre stands of scrubby oak, also teem with exotics gone native. You're liable to see axis, sitka, black buck and fallow deer as well as whitetails. Shoot an exotic and you've added $1,250 to your bill. Accommodations — hotels and restaurants of Sonora — are at your expense. On his ranches in the sandy lands of cactus and mesquite in south Texas, whitetails run a little larger. A 130 eight-pointer is average. The price jumps another $500, and accommodations are in a fine ranch where all motel-style guest rooms have private baths. Room and board adds $150 per day to the base price of your hunt.

Doug caters to a lot of corporate groups, to first-time hunters and to youngsters hunting with parents. And here you know just what you pay for and you get what you pay for. That's pretty straight shooting.

*Keys to a successful hunt in the mesquite
country of Texas include good optics and a good Jeep, like
Krooked River guide Terry Burden's "Wild Thing" which
carries youover rutted roads with the sure footedness of
a mule, but none of its stubbornness.*

*Sitting on 7,600 acres of mixed pine and hardwoods
on the Dan River in southern Virginia, Falkland Farms has been
a hunting retreat since the Roaring 20s. You'll find
big whitetails, turkey and quail.*

[S O U T H]

Krooked River Ranch

H a s k e l l ,   T e x a s

*Big bucks roam these 43,000 acres
of rolling mesquite.*

VITAL STATISTICS:

Game/Arm/Seasons:
DEER:
Bow: Oct.
Centerfire: Nov. - early Jan.
Rates:
DEER: from $1,850/4 day plus $1,000 kill fee
Accommodations:
CABINS
NUMBER OF ROOMS: 7
MAXIMUM NUMBER OF HUNTERS: 30
Meals: Family-style steak, tacos, fish
Conference Groups: Yes
Guides: Included
Gratuity: 10%
Preferred Payment:
Cash, check, credit cards
Other Activities:
Bird hunting, fishing, waterfowling
Getting There:
Fly to Abilene and the lodge will pick you up at no charge.

Contact:
Roy & Becky Wilson
Krooked River Ranch
PO Box 85
Haskell, TX 79521
Ph: 915/773-2457
Fx: 915/773-2541
e-mail: krro@westex.net

DRIVING SOUTHWEST from Lubbock, west Texas seems as flat as a billiard table. But within 30 miles, the land begins to fall away into the valleys of the Brazos River tributaries. Gone are the vast irrigated farms where cotton and peanuts are grown. In their place are gently rolling hills studded with mesquite and scrubby oaks and pine. This is ranch land, big ranch land, and Krooked River encompasses some 43,000 acres of it.

Deer are plentiful. Roy Wilson, who runs Krooked River, manages the herd for trophy bucks. Eight-pointers or better are the rule here. Nice 10-pointers are fairly common, and once in a while somebody bags a 12-point beauty. Leaving the lodges in a four-wheel-drive pickup long before dawn, you'll jounce over rutted oil-field roads as you head to the meadow you plan to hunt. That's what Roy and his crew call the parcels of land assigned to each guide and his pair of hunters. But don't be fooled. This isn't your standard 25 acres where Bossy grazes on lush green grass. It's more like 2,000 acres — a mix of river bottom, a wheat field or two, and mile after mile of open mesquite woods that roll and climb to table-rock plateaus.

Good glass is essential. With 10X binoculars, you can estimate the mass of the rack on that buck working through the brush half a mile away. A spotting scope comes in handy, too. You'll spend a good bit of time scanning hillsides trying to determine where the deer are moving. Once you're satisfied that they're working an area, you'll move in, throw up a ground blind and wait. Dawn and dusk are the most effective times. If you can will yourself to sit truly still, a buck may get curious enough to walk right up to your blind. Don't count on it, though. Bring at least a .270 with a 3x10 power scope sighted in at 200 yards. Practice your shooting at that distance before you come, so you'll know where your rifle really shoots.

While the breakfast bell rings about 5 — and there's plenty of sausage and gravy and biscuits as well as cold cereal and fruit — you can count on coming in for a substantial hot lunch and nap before heading out for the evening. Dinners are family affairs — in fact this lodge caters to parents who like to take their teenagers hunting. Roy and Becky, his wife, and their kids all pitch in to provide a comfortable and well-run lodge. And if you fill you're deer tag early, stick around for quail, ducks and geese or hogs. There's plenty of game at Krooked River.

Rafter W Ranches

Sonora, Texas

Trophy whitetail management at its finest in southwest Texas.

VITAL STATISTICS:

Game/Arm/Seasons:
WHITETAIL and RIO GRANDE TURKEY:
Centerfire: Early Nov. through late Dec.

Rates:
Whitetail and turkey combo $2,600/4 days

Accommodations:
RUSTIC LODGE
NUMBER OF ROOMS: 9; 6 WITH PRIVATE BATH
MAXIMUM NUMBER OF HUNTERS: 12

Meals: Steaks, turkey breast, pork

Conference Groups: No

Guides: Included

Gratuity: Hunter's discretion

Preferred Payment:
Cash, check

Other Activities:
Wildlife photography

Getting There:
Fly to San Angelo, Texas, and be met by a representative of the lodge.

Contact:
Jack Wardlaw
Rafter W Ranches
Box 944
Sonora, TX 76950
915/387-3377
Fax: 915/387-3173

TROPHY WHITETAILS are what draw hunters to the Rafter W. Ranches, and for good reason. With more than 32,000 acres on a working ranch, and with a rule that allows only one buck to be taken per 1,000 acres per year, Rafter consistently produces bucks that score 130 Boone & Crockett points and better.

Hunter success on the Rafter W Ranches is 100 percent for deer and turkey, but the hunt is not guaranteed. Rather, the success rate is a reflection of a management system that the Wardlaw family, who own this spread, has had in place for 14 years.

Early in the season, the most successful approach is to hunt from blinds that overlook feeders. Later in the season, during the rut (late November/early December), it's best to get into a stand that lets you watch bucks looking for hot does and rival bucks fighting back in the mesquite and cedar breaks, then try to rattle and call them into range.

Hunters can also hunt Rio Grande turkeys at Rafter; plus, hunts can be arranged for javelina and exotic deer such as sitka, fallow and axis. Recommended firearms would include flat-shooting rifles (such as .270s) topped with variable scopes. Good binoculars also come in handy for antler evaluation.

Accommodations at the Rafter W Ranches are comfortable at a modern main lodge that features 12 beds in nine guest rooms, a dining room, plus a backyard with fireplace. Meals include breakfasts of eggs, pancakes and cereal; lunches of soup, sandwiches and chili; and dinners highlighted by steak, brisket, pork loin, ribs and turkey breast. Special diets can be taken care of as well.

[S O U T H]

Sycamore Creek Ranch

D e l   R i o ,   T e x a s

A Badlands ranch offers up some good hunting for whitetails and free-roaming exotics.

VITAL STATISTICS:

Game/Arm/Seasons:
WHITETAIL:
Centerfire, muzzleloader: Early Nov. through mid-Jan.
AXIS DEER, SITKA DEER, AOUDAD SHEEP:
Centerfire, muzzleloader: Early Oct through mid-Jan.

Rates:
$2,500/3 days. Included in the rate is 1 WHITETAIL BUCK, 2 WHITETAIL DOES, 1 AOUDAD EWE. An AOUDAD RAM is $1,500 extra. Additional fees are charged for any exotics taken.

Accommodations:
MOTEL AND LODGE (BY SPECIAL ARRANGEMENT)
NUMBER OF ROOMS: 3 IN LODGE
MAXIMUM NUMBER OF HUNTERS: 6

Meals: Eat at local restaurants unless special arrangements have been made to stay at the lodge.

Conference Groups: No
Guides: Included
Gratuity: 10 to 15%
Preferred Payment:
Cash, check

Other Activities:
Bird hunting, bird watching, fishing, waterfowling, wildlife photography

Getting There:
Fly to San Antonio, Texas, rent a car and drive to the ranch.

Contact:
Dave Terk
Sycamore Creek Ranch
12015 San Pedro Ave.
Suite 200
San Antonio, TX 78216-2836
210/495-4545
Fax: 210/494-7770

THE SOUTHWEST TEXAS BADLANDS is a country that has been tamed, at least to some extent. Cowboys still roam the land and ride their horses across the western terrain. Only now they aren't chasing rustlers or outlaws, they're chasing cattle, sheep and goats.

This is a land where the sage blooms, the cactus grows and crystal-clear water flows. It's a land of blue skies with incredible southwest Texas sunsets.

It's also a land where Dave Terk, an internationally recognized big game hunter, has set up his Sycamore Creek Ranch. With some 15 square miles of rough hills, brushy flats and sycamore and oak bottoms, the ranch offers diverse and challenging hunts for exotics such as aoudad sheep and axis deer—most of which have been on the ranch, roaming wild, for more than 20 years—as well as for native, trophy-class white-tailed deer.

"Because I've hunted the world over, I know the types of problems that can occur," states Terk, referring to the logistics and personal service that's required to keep clients satisfied. This is one reason why Terk keeps things relatively simple and limits the number of hunters on his operation to six at a time.

"This is a family ranch hunted only to keep the game in balance," he says. "Harvests are determined yearly, and only the number of animals in excess are taken. No more."

Good management is key. To ensure a healthy herd of good whitetails, for example, Terk requires guests to take bucks of eight points or better, and he encourages hunters to shoot up to two does to keep the buck/doe ratio in balance.

Don't forget to bring along a fishing rod and shotgun, as bass fishing in nearby Lonesome Dove Lake and duck and quail hunting on the ranch itself are available, if you finish your big game hunts early. The Mexican border is only 30 minutes to the south, so a shopping trip might also be in order

The ranch house itself is relatively small, so hunters stay at the La Quinta Inn, which is a first-class motel only 15 minutes from the ranch. There are many restaurants in the area, and in Acuna.

Garry Wright Texas Adventures

Ingram, Texas

Hunt for exotics or white-tailed deer in Texas and Michigan.

VITAL STATISTICS:

Game/Arm/Seasons:
WHITETAIL DEER, EXOTIC DEER, SHEEP, GOAT, IBEX, ANTELOPE, GAZELLE, ORYX:
Centerfire, muzzleloader: Year-round

Rates:
All species $200 per day; $125 per day no lodging or meals

Accommodations:
MODERN LOG LODGE
NUMBER OF ROOMS: 2
MAXIMUM NUMBER OF HUNTERS: 4

Meals: Steaks, chicken, vegetables, wine

Conference Groups: No

Guides: Included

Gratuity: Hunter's discretion

Preferred Payment:
Cash, check

Other Activities:
Antiquing, bird hunting, bird watching, fishing, golf, hiking, swimming, tennis, wildlife photography

Getting There:
Fly to San Antonio, Texas, and the lodge will provide round-trip transportation for $100.

Contact:
Garry Wright
Garry Wright Texas Adventures
102 Hwy. 27 East, Suite 181
Ingram, TX 70825-3323;
803/367-3209
Fax: 803/367-3309
Web: www.garrywright.com

BASED JUST AN HOUR out of San Antonio, Garry Wright runs a first-class operation for exotic game and free-roaming nilgai and whitetails. With hunting concessions on 34 ranches in Texas and Michigan, and more than 30 exotic species available, Wright will guide you to the animal you want. He can also arrange African hunting trips and fishing excursions to Costa Rica. In a nutshell, he does it all.

According to Wright, "Your dream hunt may take you to a 5,500-acre ranch in the heart of the Texas Hill Country, home to unlimited free-roaming Axis deer and aoudad sheep. Or, you may venture into the brush county of south Texas in pursuit of some of the biggest and wildest exotic sheep that can be found." And if it's whitetail you want, Wright or one of his guides can put you onto a Texas trophy. Or if you want to book at his Michigan spread, he'll take you on a deep-woods still-hunt for big-racked bucks that may go 300 pounds.

To service all of his concessions, Wright runs eight lodges ranging from log rustic to a two-story lodge in Limestone Rock, Texas. The main lodge in Ingram can accommodate four guests at a time, has a deck overlooking the hill country and has meals that range from ribeye steaks to rock cornish game hens, served with wild rice, squash and red wine.

[S O U T H]

Falkland Farms Hunting Plantation

S c o t t s b u r g ,   V i r g i n i a

For a change of pace, try hunting whitetails in the traditional way of the South: with dogs.

VITAL STATISTICS:

Game/Arm/Seasons:
WHITETAILS:
Bow: Oct. through Jan.
Muzzleloader: Early Nov.
Shotgun: Mid-Nov. through Jan.
TURKEY:
Bow, shotgun: Mid-April through mid-May
Rates:
From $230/day
Accommodations:
VINTAGE FRAME PLANTATION HOUSE
NUMBER OF ROOMS: 7
MAXIMUM NUMBER OF HUNTERS: 14
Meals: Country cooking
Conference Groups: Yes
Guides: Included
Gratuity: 15%
Preferred Payment:
Cash, MasterCard, Visa, checks
Other Activities:
Antiquing, biking, bird hunting, bird watching, boating, canoeing/rafting, fishing, golf, waterfowling, wildlife photography
Getting There:
Fly to Danville or Raleigh, rent a car and drive to the plantation.

Contact:
Tom Rowland
Falkland Farms
Hunting Plantation
1003 Falkland Landing
Scottsburg, VA 24589
804/575-1400

VIRGINIA'S SOUTH-SIDE COUNTRY, that swath of pine and oak that stretches along the commonwealth's border with North Carolina, is a haven for deer and turkey. You'll find other game there, too — mainly bobwhite quail and ducks. Some would call this land rolling, but hills are less than 100 feet above languid creeks and the local mountain is only 50 feet higher.

From one of several dozen tripods topped with shooting boxes, deer hunters overlook feed plots, trails to and from bedding areas, and rub and scrape lines. From before dawn and then later in the afternoon, you'll hunt from the stand with a bow, shotgun or muzzleloader (rifles and handguns are not permitted) and the odds favor you instead of the deer.

There is good hunting from the stands, and deer are often six- to eight-pointers. But the real fun is hunting deer over dogs, the old Southern tradition. Falkland Farms maintains a kennel of beagles just for this purpose. Baying through the woods, beagles drive deer toward a line of hunters spaced 600 to 1,000 yards apart in a two-square-mile area. Armed with shotguns loaded with buckshot, hunters wait for deer coming along the routes out of the dense cover where they've bedded down. You can hear the dogs moving the deer, and before you know it, a buck will be passing your stand. Hunter success on these hunts is very good.

The plantation is one of the largest private land holdings in Virginia and contains about 7,600 acres. It fronts on the upper reaches of Buggs Island Lake. Long, low islands, faintly swampy in spots, offer outstanding habitat for deer. Duck hunting is good here too, especially for wood ducks early in the season and mallards later on. In spring, the plantation opens its acreage to turkey hunters. These hunts are one-on-one, and success rate on gobblers of about 20 pounds is roughly 75 percent.

The core of the plantation dates from the 18th century, but it wasn't until the 1920s that the old farmhouse was rebuilt in the style of a classic Southern hunting lodge. Porches on the first and second floors offer vantage points to view the tranquil countryside. Inside, the decor, a simple blend of varnished wood and plain fabric, is distinctly 1920s. The walls are full of mounts taken on the property and pictures of old men and old double guns from the days when a coat, collar and tie were required dress for gentlemen hunters. The food is modest but ample.

Fort Lewis Lodge

Millboro, Virginia

A stone's throw from Washington, this luxurious lodge offers top-notch whitetail and turkey hunting.

VITAL STATISTICS:

Game/Arm/Seasons:
WHITETAILS:
Bow: Mid-Oct. through early Nov.
Centerfire: Third week of Nov.
Muzzleloader: Second week of Nov.
TURKEY:
Bow, shotgun: Mid-April through mid-May

Rates:
WHITETAIL from $600/3 days
TURKEY from $450/3 days

Accommodations:
MODERN TIMBER AND GLASS LODGE AND LOG CABINS
NUMBER OF ROOMS: 13 WITH PRIVATE BATHS
MAXIMUM NUMBER OF HUNTERS: 18 GUN SEASON; 5 TURKEY SEASON

Meals: Country cooking with a continental flare

Conference Groups: Yes

Guides: Included

Gratuity: $40

Preferred Payment:
Cash, check

Other Activities:
Antiquing, biking, bird hunting, bird watching, boating, canoeing/rafting, fishing, golf, swimming, wildlife photography

Getting There:
Fly to Roanoke, rent a car and drive to the lodge.

Contact:
John Cowden
Fort Lewis Lodge
HCR 03, Box 21A
Millboro, VA 24460
540/925-2314

WITH ABOUT 3,600 ACRES of river bottom hardwood ridges, and reasonable populations of both deer and turkey, Fort Lewis Lodge is a convenient destination for hunters who want good Virginia whitetails and luxury. Tucked in the remote Cowpasture River Valley an hour north of Hot Springs, the lodge is within an easy day's drive of Washington, DC. It's one of those places where the hunting member of a couple stands at least a 50-50 chance of filling the tag, and a nonhunting spouse can find plenty to enjoy.

The lodge is a working farm. Corn and soybeans are grown commercially. While they turn a little profit, owner John Cowden doesn't mind if deer eat their share. That may be why nice deer are harvested in the willow-choked channels between the fields and the river. Tower Hill, the high point on the serrated ridge northwest of the lodge, tops out at 3,245 feet. But like most of the folded and faulted mountains in the Southeast, these get steeper toward their crests, and climbing can take your breath away almost as quickly as one of Colorado's 10,000-footers. On the other hand, thickets of laurel and pine, and stands of oak, hickory and beech provide cover and mast on the slopes. And across the ridge are the public hunting lands of the Washington and Jefferson National Forests.

Cowden and his crew maintain roughly 100 stands and hunters are welcome to bring their own. The six-week season is relatively short but limits are generous: two bucks and one doe on a three-day gun hunt. Archers are permitted three deer of either sex. During the opening three days of gun season, which usually runs in mid-November, it's bucks only. An average six- to eight-point buck will dress out in the 125-pound range. Normally, one guide serves four hunters.

The action does not stop with winter at Fort Lewis. Come mid-April, spring gobbler season cranks into full blast. The lodge only takes five clients per three-day hunt and you may hunt with or without your own guide.

Accommodations in the main lodge and two cabins are strictly first-class, with color-coordinated drapes and spreads, private baths and a sitting room with overstuffed furniture fronting a rock hearth where a log fire burns. Opt for one of the cabins if you can, and you'll go to sleep at night, lulled by the embers of your dying fire. Meals are served in a remodeled mill and you'll dine on heavenly roasts, grilled steaks, veggies and homemade pastries and pies.

145

Oak Ridge Estate

A r r i n g t o n ,   V i r g i n i a

Five thousand acres of mountain hardwoods, thick cedar ridges, feed plots and deer less than three hours from Washington, D.C.

VITAL STATISTICS:

Game/Arms/Season:
WHITETAIL:
Bow: Oct. through mid-Nov.
Centerfire, muzzleloader: Late-Nov. through early Jan.
Rates:
$750/3-day hunt
Accommodations:
BRICK INN
NUMBER OF ROOMS: 6 WITH SHARED BATH
MAXIMUM NUMBER OF HUNTERS: 8
Meals: Breakfast and sack lunch, dinners by advance arrangement
Conference Groups: Yes
Guides: Included
Gratuity: Hunter's discretion
Preferred Payment:
Cash, check
Other Activities:
Antiquing, biking, bird hunting, bird watching, fishing, swimming, wildlife photography
Getting There:
Fly to Charlottesville, rent a car and drive to the lodge.

Contact:
Fred Clarkson
Hunt Manager
Oak Ridge Estate
2300 Oak Ridge Rd.
Arrington, VA 22922
804/263-8676

BELOW CHARLOTTESVILLE, Virginia's landscape takes on a jumbled look. Hills, ridges and low mountains run kind of helter-skelter. They're the eastern foothills of the Blue Ridge, a country scored by the James River Valley and its numerous tributaries. When Thomas Jefferson was president, plantations rooted first in tobacco and later row crops, then livestock covered all but the mountains in these rolling uplands. Oak Ridge was assembled in the early 1800s and its fine mansion built in 1802. Save a few Union cavalry raids to tear up railroad tracks, the region was spared the ravages of the Civil War. It simply lacked strategic importance, and that isolation has accrued to its benefit as prime hunting real estate today.

Owned by financier Thomas Fortune Ryan and his heirs from 1851 to 1991, Oak Ridge was the epitome of a wealthy country estate. More than 80 outbuildings including a greenhouse with a rotunda and the only remaining stone railroad station in Virginia are found on its grounds. Today, they stand silent, awaiting restoration at the hands of owner John Holland. Surrounding the mansion are acres and acres of prime whitetail and turkey country, a region where the deer population is so heavy that hunters are encouraged to take a doe or two for the freezer along with a trophy buck.

Hunt manager Fred Clarkson, who grew up in this county and has hunted on the estate for more than 40 years, has imposed an eight-point-or-better limit on bucks. To augment natural feed, he's added a dozen feed plots and plans to increase that number by three or four per year. On the edges are tree stands and shooting boxes. Though the season in Virginia runs about 90 days, only 30 hunters will work the property for deer, and never will there be more than eight at a time. Hunting is from stands. Clarkson will take you out in the morning, collect you for lunch and return you for the late-afternoon hunt. Still-hunting is discouraged. Along with deer, Oak Ridge offers preserve hunts for pheasants and quail, plus hunting for spring gobblers.

Guests stay in the estate manager's house—Brick House Inn—a bed-and-breakfast with six rooms, some with shared bath, and a wide screened porch. A full commercial kitchen caters banquets at the mansion and can provide gourmet dinners by special arrangement with groups of hunters. Otherwise, restaurants are available in either Lynchburg or Charlottesville, about 30 miles away in opposite directions.

Primland Meadows

Dan, Virginia

Hunt whitetails morning and evening and pheasants at midday.

VITAL STATISTICS:

Game/Arm/Seasons:
DEER:
Bow: Oct. - mid-Nov.
Muzzleloading: early Nov. and late Dec.
Centerfire: late Nov.

Rates:
$175/day plus $350 trophy fee

Accommodations:
PRIVATE GUEST HOUSES
NUMBER OF ROOMS: FROM 2 TO 4 PER HOUSE
MAXIMUM NUMBER OF HUNTERS: 12

Meals: Full-service restaurant

Conference Groups: Yes

Guides: Optional

Gratuity: Hunter's discretion

Preferred Payment:
Cash, check

Other Activities:
Bird hunting, fishing

Getting There:
Fly to Martinsville and rent a car.

Contact:
Reservations
Primland
4621 Busted Rock Rd.
Meadows of Dan, VA 24120
Ph: 540/251-8012
Fx: 540/251-8244
e-mail: primland@swva.net

THE BLUE RIDGE PARKWAY snakes down Virginia's backbone. To the west is the Shenandoah Valley and below that Roanoke and a high plateau which melts into the headwaters of the Tennessee Valley north of Bristol. The western valley is well known because Interstate 81 races through it. But east of the parkway is a different story. Here the foothills are steep and forested with oak, hickory, maple and sweet gum. For three centuries, settlers tried to wrest a living from corn, hogs and cattle on little farms tight by cold creeks that turned slow and warm where the land flattens. Timber companies bought up vast tracts, stripped the forest and moved on. Developers followed, but their success was limited. The hills east of the Blue Ridge are remote, yet not enough to draw the East Coast equivalent of Montana's California crowd.

All that bodes well for deer on Primland, a 14,000-acre estate that's managed mainly for upland birds. The deer don't mind. They thrive on cover plots of milo and sorghum planted every spring for pheasants, chuckar and quail. Streams and ponds — the latter are stocked with trout and bass — provide water, and laurel thickets high on the slopes of the foothills offer virtually impenetrable cover. Hunting is from stands here. You'll find them overlooking scrape lines, trails between bedding and feeding areas and near food plots. Typical bucks run 160 pounds dressed. An eight-point-or-better rule applies to bucks, but hunters may also harvest does. Overall, hunter success rate exceeds 80 percent.

Primland is one of a network of international resorts; its sibling lodges include Luttrellstown Castle on the East Coast of Ireland and Domaine des Etangs near the Cognac region of France. As you'd expect, accommodations at Primland are first-class. Guests reside in cottages, many of which were built as vacation homes. Meals are served in a restaurant or you may prepare your own steak au poivre. Guides are available for deer hunting, and personal chefs are available on request.

147

THE MIDWEST

ARKANSAS, ILLINOIS, INDIANA, IOWA, KANSAS, MICHIGAN
MINNESOTA, MISSOURI, NEBRASKA, NORTH DAKOTA,
OHIO, OKLAHOMA, SOUTH DAKOTA, WISCONSIN

I N KEEPING WITH THE pragmatism that spreads like morning sun across the great prairies, most who travel the Midwest to hunt abundant public and private lands do so without the services of a lodge or outfitter. But every sporting-goods store knows at least one local guide, and state game agencies can also be a huge help. Whitetails abound here. They may be the big grainfield deer, those from blackwater swamps of northern woods, or trophy bucks from rolling hardwood plateaus. Bowhunters have long and generous seasons, though rifle hunters get their share, too. Bear hunting is limited, and those lodges and outfitters that serve deer hunters in the fall also run bird hunts, not to mention turkey hunts in the spring.

Lodges:

ILLINOIS

1 CARTER'S HUNTING LODGE

2 PRAIRIE HILLS HUNT CLUB

IOWA

3 MIDWEST USA

KANSAS

4 VERDIGRIS RIVER OUTFITTERS

5 WOLF RIVER OUTFITTERS

MISSOURI

6 DOUBLETREE FARMS

SOUTH DAKOTA

7 STUEKEL'S BIRDS & BUCKS

8 TROPHIES PLUS OUTFITTERS

References:

HUNTING MICHIGAN WHITETAILS
by David Richey
Sportsman's Outdoor Enterprises
Box 192, Grawn, MI 49637

WISCONSIN HUNTING
by Brian Lovett. Krause Publications
700 E. State St.
Iola, WI 54990-0001

MICHIGAN BIG-GAME RECORDS
(4 editions)
GREAT MICHIGAN DEER TALES
and
UNDERSTANDING MICHIGAN
BLACK BEAR
by Richard P. Smith, Smith Publications
814 Clark St., Marquette, MI 49855

OHIO'S TROPHY WHITETAILS
by Mark Hicks
Big River Press
Box 130, Millfield, OH 45761
800-447-8238.

Resources:

ARKANSAS GAME AND FISH
COMMISSION
Information Section, 2 Natural
Resources Dr., Little Rock, AR 72205
501/223-6300
or 800/364-4263 ext. 6351
Web: www.agfc.state.ar.us

Illinois Department of Natural
Resources, Lincoln Tower Plaza, 524 S.
Second St., Springfield, IL 62701-1787
217/785-0067
Web: dnr.state.il.us

INDIANA DIVISION OF
FISH AND WILDLIFE
402 W. Washington St., Room W-273
Indianapolis, IN 46204
317/232-4080; Web:
www.dnr.state.in.us/fishwild/index.htm

IOWA DEPARTMENT OF
NATURAL RESOURCES
Wallace State Office Building, East
Ninth and Grand Ave., Des Moines, IA
50319; 515/281-5145
Web: www.state.ia.us/wildlife

KANSAS DEPARTMENT OF
WILDLIFE AND PARKS
900 SW Jackson St., Suite 502
Topeka, KS 66612-1233
785/296-2281
Web: www.kdwp.state.ks.us

MICHIGAN DEPARTMENT OF
NATURAL RESOURCES
Wildlife Division, Box 30444, Lansing
MI 48909-7944; 517/373-1263
Web: www.dnr.state.mi.us

MINNESOTA DEPARTMENT OF
NATURAL RESOURCES, DIVISION OF
FISH AND WILDLIFE
500 Lafayette Rd., St. Paul, MN
55155-4007; 651/297-1308
Web: www.dnr.state.mn.us

MISSOURI DEPARTMENT OF
CONSERVATION
2901 W. Truman Blvd., Box 180
Jefferson City, MO 65102-0180
573/751-4115
Web: www.conservation.state.mo.us

R e s o u r c e s

NEBRASKA GAME AND PARKS
COMMISSION
2200 N. 33rd St., Box 30370
Lincoln, NE 68503; 402/471-0641
Web: www.npgc.state.ne.us

NORTH DAKOTA STATE
GAME AND FISH DEPARTMENT
100 North Bismarck Expy.
Bismarck, ND 58501; 701/328-6300
Web: www.state.nd.us/gnf

OHIO DIVISION OF WILDLIFE,
1840 Belcher Dr., Columbus, OH
43224-1329; 614/265-6300
Web: www.dnr.state.oh.us/odnr/wildlif

OKLAHOMA DEPARTMENT OF
WILDLIFE CONSERVATION
1801 N. Lincoln,
Box 53465, Oklahoma City, OK
73152; 405/521-3851
Web: www.state.ok.us/~odwc

SOUTH DAKOTA DEPARTMENT
OF GAME, FISH AND PARKS
523 E. Capitol, Pierre, SD
57501-3182; 605/773-3387
Web:
www.state.sd.us/state/gfp/index.htm

Carter's Hunting Lodge

Milton, Illinois

Thanks to the Conservation Reserve Program, you can take trophy-class deer from this lodge.

VITAL STATISTICS:

Game/Arm/Seasons:
WHITETAILS:
Bow: Mid-Oct. through Jan. 15
Shotgun: Late Nov. through early Dec.
Muzzleloader: Mid-Dec.
TURKEY:
Bow, shotgun: Mid-Apr. through mid-May

Rates:
Bow from $1,500/5 days
Shotgun $3,000/3 or 4 days
Muzzleloader $3,000/3 days

Accommodations:
VINTAGE FRAME FARMHOUSE
NUMBER OF ROOMS: 3
MAXIMUM NUMBER OF HUNTERS: 12

Meals: Family-style lunch and dinner

Conference Groups: No

Guides: Included

Gratuity: $100

Preferred Payment:
Cash, check

Getting There:
Fly to St. Louis, rent a car or take the shuttle to the lodge at your expense.

Contact:
Dale Carter
Carter's Hunting Lodge
Box 259
Milton, IL 62352
217/723-4522

FROM ITS JUNCTION with the LaMoine, the Illinois River turns south and begins cutting through the plains. It forms the border between Pike County to the west and Scott County to the east, and scores of steep ravines lead from the high cropland to the river below. Creeks wind through the coulees, the sides of which are heavily timbered in oak and beech with occasional stands of cedar. Up on the plains, you'll find woodlots that are too wet or too rocky to plow. The rest of the country is planted in corn and soybeans with an occasional pasture for cows. Farmers in this neck of the woods have been pretty good about setting aside Conservation Reserve Program (CRP) acreage. This land has everything needed to grow record-book buck — and it does!

Dale and Nathan Carter, who operate a classic old farmhouse as a hunting lodge, lease about 5,000 acres of CRP and cropland for archery, shotgun and muzzleloading hunts. In the morning you'll hunt from stands strategically placed over scrape and rub lines. In the evening you may find yourself watching a route from a bedding to feeding area. Your chances for a good buck are excellent here; the area has produced a number of Pope & Young deer. Archers score about 30 percent on bucks of 130 or better, and more than half of the shotgun hunters take bucks of 140 or better. And, while there's one guide for every two hunters, the guide's job is to see that his hunter is safely situated in a tree or portable stand well before daylight. Should a hunter fire at a deer, the guide will track it. Though Dale encourages the taking of mature bucks of three years and older, he adds teeth to his suggestion by charging hunters an additional $500 for taking any buck of less than seven points. The knife cuts both ways: harvest a buck that scores 150 or better and he pays you $250! Now, how's that for a trophy fee. You can also take advantage of the excellent turkey hunting in April and May.

[M I D W E S T]

Prairie Hills Hunt Club

Macomb, Illinois

Is the state of the Illinois a trophy deer state? You bet.

OT MUCH MORE than a couple hours' drive from Chicago and St. Louis is more than 2,000 acres managed intensively for big whitetails. Centered in McDonough and Hancock counties, Prairie Hills has pulled together a number of parcels of prime habitat: heavily wooded ravines through which flow little creeks, big tracts of forest bordering fields of bean and corn, and patches of Conservation Reserve Program (CRP) land so thick with brambles and brush that only a whitetail buck could love it. You'll find some food plots and stands of newly planted oak and hickory nut-bearing trees. It'll be years before these trees produce, but you have to admire the commitment of the guy who planted them.

That's Jeff Judgens, who founded Prairie Hills four years ago. He grew up in this part of the world and knows almost everybody around. That's why he's been able to amass such good acreage for his hunts. There's no lodge or tent camp here; everybody stays at motels in town and dines at local restaurants like the Red Ox Supper Club. Your guide will pick you up at your motel at 4:30 in the morning and drive you out to the farm where you'll hunt that day. Quietly you'll get out of the Suburban and you'll close the door gently lest you spook every deer in five miles. Hunters who harvest the best bucks ride their stands all day. But others just have to walk. That's okay too. You can walk, sit, scan treeline and walk some more — to your heart's content.

A harvestable buck is an 8-pointer with enough spread to his rack to get the curve of the antlers out past the ears. Most hunters see three or four deer of this size in a day. Some will edge into the 12-point range. If you bag a doe, Jeff will give you $50 for thinning his herd. Shoot an undersize buck, and you'll have to ante up. This section of the state is shotgun only; buck shot or slugs, and nobody is using buckshot. The shotgun success rate is about 60 percent. Archers who hunt the early season do better than the 40 percent score for the lodge. Come spring, Prairie Hills will treat you to some fine gobbler hunting.

VITAL STATISTICS:

Game/Arm/Seasons:
WHITE-TAILED DEER:
Bow: Early Oct. through mid-Nov.
Shotgun: Early Dec. through mid-Jan.
Muzzleloader: Late Nov. through early Dec.
TURKEY:
Bow, shotgun: Mid-Apr. through mid-May

Rates:
From $950/3 days

Accommodations:
MOTELS AND RESTAURANTS IN TOWN

Meals: Restaurants in town

Conference Groups: No

Guides: Included

Gratuity: $50

Preferred Payment:
Cash, check

Other Activities:
None

Getting There:
Fly to Quincy or Peoria and you'll be picked up.

Contact:
Jeff Hudgens
Prairie Hills Hunt Club
321 University Dr.
Macomb, IL 61455
309/833-4747
Fax: 309/833-4019
e-mail: Prairie@Macomb.com

Midwest USA

Cantril, Iowa

*More than 7,000 private acres await
the budget-minded deer hunter.*

VITAL STATISTICS:

Game/Arm/Seasons:
WHITETAILS:
Bow: Oct. through early Dec.
Shotgun: Early through mid-Dec.
Muzzleloader: Late Dec. through
early Jan.
TURKEY:
Bow and shotgun: Mid-Apr. through
mid-May
Rates:
From $1,600/5 days
Accommodations:
MOTEL
NUMBER OF ROOMS: 8 WITH PRIVATE BATHS
MAXIMUM NUMBER OF HUNTERS: 24
Meals: Café style
Conference Groups: No
Guides: Included
Gratuity: $50
Preferred Payment:
Cash, check
Other Activities:
Bird hunting, fishing
Getting There:
Fly to Des Moines, and rent a car.

Contact:
Rodney or Todd Hughes
Midwest USA
Stockport, IA 52651
319/796-2262
off-season:
214 5th St.
Rt 1, Box 184
Mayfield, PA 18433
717/876-4086
e-mail: rhughes@aol

"THE NEXT WORLD RECORD buck will come from here!" local hunters say. How many times have you heard that said? There's always a chance, and in some places, the chances are better than others. In southeastern Iowa, hunters who are really dedicated are taking some very nice bucks. Will the next world record come from here? Well, the odds don't favor it, but there's always a chance.

Don't let that cast a wet blanket on your plans. If you're looking for a place to harvest that trophy of your dreams, and you want to do it on a budget, considering the hunts offered by Midwest USA is well worthwhile. Owner/manager Rodney Hughes was born and raised in Stockport, about three miles from Cantril, the outfitter's base of operations. His nephew Todd has lived in the area all his life. He knows the farmers, those who are having trouble with deer, and those who may be willing to lease woodlots and a little cropland for hunting. Over the past three years, Midwest has pulled together more than 7,000 acres. Most is in the undulating hills within 25 miles of Cantril, but there's a small patch across the border in Missouri. Rodney rotates parties so that no farm is hunted for two consecutive weeks, and generally any farm is seldom hunted more than once a season.

Hunting is mainly from tree stands along routes to and from feeding and bedding areas and over rub and scrape lines. Shotgun and muzzleloader hunters use the stands during the first weekend of their hunts. That's when local hunters are moving through the woods, putting the odds in favor of the hunter who stays put. Later in the season, hunters take part in quiet drives. Rodney's strategy is as simple as it is effective. Hunters are placed on escape routes and the drivers go upwind of the patch of cover to be pushed. Often, just the scent of the drivers is enough to get the deer going. Drivers slowly work their way through the woods trying to ease the deer down the routes toward the hunters. In a typical year, slightly more than half of the hunters will put an 8-point or better rack on the wall; a 125-scoring buck is typical. Hunters who wait for the next buck stand a pretty good chance of seeing something bigger.

To house and feed hunters, the Hughes bought the Starlight Motel and Café in Cantril. Rooms with private baths are available for groups of hunters from two to eight. Meals take the form of a continental breakfast, sack lunch and a hearty dinner.

Verdigris River Outfitters

N e o d e s h a ,   K a n s a s

Trophy deer are the norm at this relatively new outfitting service.

VITAL STATISTICS:

Game/Arm/Seasons:
DEER:
Bow: Oct. through Dec.
Centerfire: Early Dec.
Muzzleloader: Late Sept.
TURKEY:
Bow or shotgun: Early Apr. through mid-May
Rates:
DEER:
Bow: $2,000/5 days
Centerfire: $3,000/6 days
TURKEY:
Bow or shotgun: $995/3 days
Accommodations:
FARMHOUSE
NUMBER OF ROOMS: 3
MAXIMUM NUMBER OF HUNTERS: 8
Meals: Country cooking
Conference Groups: Yes
Guides: Included
Gratuity: $50 to $100
Preferred Payment:
Cash, check
Other Activities:
Quail hunting, bird watching, golf, wildlife photography
Getting There:
Fly to Tulsa, Oklahoma and meet the lodge van.

Contact:
Doug Arnold
Verdigris River Outfitters
RR2 Box 324
Neodesha, KS 66757
316/325-2708
Fax: 316/325-2585

THE VERDIGRIS RIVER rises in the fields about a dozen miles south of Emporia and flows south-southwest toward the Oklahoma border. As it nears Neodesha, the river begins to wind through a rich bottom. Cottonwoods crowd the channel and oxbow cut-offs in the bottoms. On higher, drier land, row crops of mainly corn and soybeans grow among intermittent rolling hills. Patches of oak and swaths of pasture cover some of the hillsides. And occasionally a tributary to the Verdigris cuts a shallow canyon. A drive through this country on any morning or evening will show you deer.

Abundant fodder with high mineral content generates good racks on these bucks. Eight out of 10 of those taken by archers on 1997 hunts guided by Verdigris River Outfitters qualified for Pope and Young. The biggest was a dandy that scored just shy of 170. Hunting from portable tree stands, ladder stands, 16-foot tripods and ground blinds, 30 archers harvested 30 bucks that scored an average of 139. In most cases, shots were taken at 25 yards or less. During rifle season, the size average increased to the neighborhood of 160. One rifleman nailed his buck, a nice 8-pointer, at 45 steps after watching the whitetail walk toward him from 400 yards away. Sometimes you can't wait them out. Shooting across a pasture at a distance later measured at 700 yards, another hunter filled his tag by connecting with a big buck that scored 169 points. That marksman knew his .30-06, knew the ballistics of his load and had spent lots of time on the range. The cover provides a wide range of shooting conditions, and come spring, you'll find turkey here as well.

Doug Arnold, owner of this outfit, has been guiding for the past five years and has more than 8,000 acres, mostly small farms under lease. During archery season, one guide serves three hunters; in rifle season, the ratio drops to 1:2. Guests stay in a comfortable farmhouse that sleeps eight. One guest room is handicapped-accessible. All share baths and good country cooked meals featuring the likes of steak and roast chicken. While this operation is relatively new, it has a growing reputation. Best to book a year in advance.

Wolf River Outfitters

Hiawatha, Kansas

Self-guided archery and guided rifle hunts produce good-scoring whitetail bucks.

THE MISSOURI RIVER, downstream from St. Jo, flows through lovely bluff and bottom country. East of the river, in Missouri, is a broad floodplain and wetlands that draw waterfowl. To the west rise the bluffs, capped by stands of red and white oak and broken by steep wooded defiles. Behind the bluffs stretch the row-croplands that nourish big Kansas whitetails. This is marvelous deer country that consistently produces bucks scoring between 130 and 170, and it's where Jim Aller, head of Wolf River Outfitters, holds a lease on a 4,000-acre bluff-country farm.

Archers do reasonably well here. More than 80 percent had good shots at bucks and three out of 10 harvested bucks of eight points or better on Jim's "semi-guided" hunts. Muzzleloaders and rifle hunters were more efficient, with a 67 percent average. On the farm, Jim has erected a number of semi-permanent shooting towers and API Grandstands and will set up ladder stands as needed. Big bucks are nocturnal feeders in this area, and it's best to waylay them going to and from the fields. Each stand overlooks a corridor deer use to move from the heavy cover where they bed during the day. One is located on a pond, and there are a couple on pastures for dawn and dusk shooting. Hunters stay in a milk barn that's been remodeled into a comfortable two bedroom, three bath lodge. During self-guided archery and muzzleloading hunts, clients have the run of the place and do their own cooking. During rifle season, the home team comes in and prepares the likes of smothered buffalo steaks, sweet potatoes and hot apple pie for hunters and their guides.

Along with his holdings on the bluffs above the river, Jim also hunts 6,000 acres that include several farms in neighboring Brown County. Here the terrain is rolling farmland of fields and woodlots. Farther north in Nebraska, he leases an additional 7,000 acres for bowhunting. "The land is the same, the hunting is the same, the deer don't know about state lines," says Jim. And hunter success rates are the same as well. What's different is that in Nebraska, archery permits are available over the counter. For all hunts in Kansas (archery, muzzleloader and rifle), hunters must file applications by May 30. While deer hunting is Wolf River's meat and potatoes, the same lands produce nice gobblers averaging 20 pounds in the spring. The limit is two birds per hunter. About 40 percent take both birds and 70 percent get at least one.

VITAL STATISTICS:

Game/Arm/Seasons:
DEER:
Bow: Oct. through Dec.
Centerfire: Early Dec.
Muzzleloader: Late Sept.
TURKEY:
Bow or shotgun: Early Apr. through mid-May
Rates:
DEER:
Archery: $1,500 /6 days
Centerfire: $2,750/5 days
TURKEY:
Bow or shotgun: $450/3 days
Accommodations:
REMODELED BARN
NUMBER OF ROOMS: 2
MAXIMUM NUMBER OF HUNTERS: 10
Meals: Hearty home cooking on guided hunts
Conference Groups: No
Guides: Included
Gratuity: $100
Preferred Payment:
Cash, credit card, check
Other Activities:
Well, eating.
Getting There:
Fly to Kansas City or St. Joseph, Missouri, and rent a car.

Contact:
Jim Aller
Wolf River Outfitters
RR5, Box 10
Hiawatha, KS 66434
785/742-3277
e-mail: wro@kcds.com
Web: www.kcds.com/wro

[M I D W E S T]

Double Tree Farms

L i c k i n g , M i s s o u r i

We're talking deer,
but, oh! those turkeys.

VITAL STATISTICS:

Game/Arm/Seasons:
WHITE-TAILED DEER:
Bow: Early Oct. through mid-Jan.
Centerfire: Mid-Nov.
Muzzleloader: Early Dec.
Rates:
WHITE-TAILED DEER $1,350/4 days
TURKEY $800/3 days
Accommodations:
MODERN FARM AND GUEST HOUSE
NUMBER OF ROOMS: 3
MAXIMUM NUMBER OF HUNTERS: 6
Meals: Continental yet country,
family-style
Conference Groups: Yes
Guides: Included
Gratuity: Hunter's discretion
Preferred Payment:
Cash, check
Other Activities:
Antiquing, biking, bird hunting, bird
watching, boating, canoeing/rafting,
fishing, swimming, wildlife
photography
Getting There:
Fly to St. Louis or Springfield and
rent a car.

Contact:
Jim Ludan
Double Tree Farms
18463 Dixon Rd.
Licking, MO 65542
573/674-4142
Fax: 573/674-4018
e-mail: sclmofarm@aol.com

IF YOU'RE LOOKING for a perfect landscape for whitetails and turkeys, check out south-central Missouri, a couple hours north of Branson. Hundreds of little creeks well up from icy springs and flow gently through bottoms forested in oak and hickory. Higher, atop the limestone bluffs, are stands of pine. Fields are few and far between, which is why Jim Ludan, owner of Double Tree Farms, has carved out 20 or so in his 1,200 acres of forest. The food plots are planted in clovers, alfalfa and grains in a mixture designed to nourish whitetails and turkeys.

Stands overlook food plots, scrape lines and trails. You know the drill. Hunt the stands early and late and maybe slow hunt in between, if lunch and a nap don't command your midday. Archers will be completely at home here as will rifle hunters, though the season for centerfire folks is only 11 days in mid-November. There's really no best time to hunt, though the rut coincides with the last week of archery season and the opening of the rifle season. So far, the best deer to come off the property scored 163, and it's totally realistic to expect to harvest a 14-inch 8-pointer dressing out at 165 pounds. Hunter success runs in the high 90s.

Not to be overlooked is the large population of turkeys. During the 21-day spring season, gobblers in the 20-pound-plus range are the norm. If taking a tom with a bow turns you on, get a license for fall and plan to hunt the last two weeks in October. Spring turkey hunts stop at 1 p.m. by state law. That means you can either cool your heels or float the Big Piney for trout and smallmouths, another cool thing to do.

Double Tree is one of those places that is utterly noncommercial. You stay in a private guest house where meals may be served if you wish. Or you can dine in the main lodge if you want. If you do, though, you're asking for "Trouble," a little red fox who moved in with Jim and Shari a year or so ago. Trouble only lives up to his moniker once in a while, and you'll forget him when you dine on Shari's superb cuisine prepared with a French flair.

Stukel's Birds & Bucks

Gregory, South Dakota

The focus is on pheasants, but there are some big bucks around, too.

VITAL STATISTICS:

Game/Arm/Seasons:
PHEASANT:
Mid-Oct. through mid-Dec.
MULE DEER:
Centerfire: Nov.
Rates:
PHEASANT from $900/2 days
MULE DEER $2,500/4 days
Accommodations:
MODERN LODGE
NUMBER OF ROOMS: 16
MAXIMUM NUMBER OF HUNTERS: 30
Meals: Buffalo steak, pheasant, prime rib, blackened salmon, wine with all dinners
Conference Groups: Yes
Guides: Included
Gratuity: Upland game $75 per hunter, big game $200 to $300
Preferred Payment:
Cash, check
Other Activities:
Bird hunting, fishing, sporting clays, waterfowling
Getting There:
Fly to Sioux Falls or Pierre, rent a car and drive to the lodge. Shuttle can be arranged at an additional cost.

Contact:
Frank Stukel
Stukel's Birds & Bucks
Rt. 1, Box 112
Gregory, SD 57533
605/835-8941
Fax: 605/835-9218
e-mail: fstukel@gwtc.net
Web: www.up-north.com/stukels

THE PRIMARY FOCUS of Stukel's is pheasants, and with more than 12,000 acres in the heart of ringneck country, brothers Ray, Frank and Cal can put clients into good hunting for wild birds on a consistent basis. The Stukels handle up to 200 bird hunters a season and can accommodate as many as 20 hunters at a time. This is a hands-on operation, however, so the three brothers (and their staff) try to book smaller groups so that everyone gets the attention they deserve.

Pheasant hunts are run on a preserve basis before the regular season opens on the third weekend of October; after that, it's mostly wild bird hunting. Hunts can also be arranged for sharp-tailed grouse, prairie chickens, Canada geese (this hunt takes place about an hour north of Gregory, along the Missouri River) and turkeys (both spring and fall).

Mule deer hunters also have a chance at a good corn-fed buck in this area. Hunters stay at a secluded cabin along the Missouri. Deer season opens the first Saturday in November, which overlaps with the pheasant season, so most people book combo hunts, concentrating first on getting a buck, then heading out after birds. The Stukels only book four to six hunters a year to ensure that the quality of the bucks stays high.

"There's not much that we can't offer for this part of the world," notes Ray.

Accommodations are first-rate. With 9,000 square feet of living space, the main lodge comfortably houses two to 30 guests. There are 16 bedrooms, nine bathrooms, two fireplaces, three phone and fax lines, two "office" work areas, plus living and dining rooms, a spa, pool table and television. The food is equally first-rate, with meals centered around buffalo steaks (you can hunt them on the property as well), roast pheasant, prime rib, blackened salmon and fine South African wines.

[M I D W E S T]

Trophies Plus Outfitters, Inc.

B e l l e   F o u r c h e s ,   S o u t h   D a k o t a

Hunt parts of three states for deer and antelope.

VITAL STATISTICS:

Game/Arm/Seasons:
WHITETAIL and MULE DEER:
Bow: Sept. and Oct.
Centerfire: Nov.
ANTELOPE:
Bow: Sept. and Oct.
Centerfire: Early Oct. through early Nov.
MERRIAM'S TURKEY:
Bow and centerfire: April
Rates:
WHITETAIL and MULE DEER from $1,750/3 days
ANTELOPE $1,200/3 days
TURKEY from $850/3 days
Accommodations:
MODERN LODGE
NUMBER OF ROOMS: 9
MAXIMUM NUMBER OF HUNTERS: 15
Meals: Roast beef, chicken, lasagna served family-style
Conference Groups: No
Guides: Included
Gratuity: $50 per day or 5%
Preferred Payment:
Cash, check
Other Activities:
Wildlife photography
Getting There:
Fly to Rapid City, South Dakota, and rent a car, or transportation can be provided by the lodge for $100 round-trip.

Contact:
R. Mike Watkins
Trophies Plus Outfitters
Box 623
Belle Fourches, SD 57717;
605/892-4894
605/645-2169
800/248-6899
off-season:
1872 E. Cardinal
Springfield, MO 65810
417/883-0808

THE OUTFITTING BUSINESS can be a tough one. If you don't have access to prime national forest land, you're pretty much relegated to hunting private land. And make no mistake about it, hunting on private leases can be extremely good.

Trophies Plus, Mike Watkins' operation, has the private lease business down to a science. With tracts of prime game country in Montana, Wyoming and South Dakota, they hunt where the game goes.

"We operate where South Dakota, Montana and Wyoming come together, to provide us the opportunity to hunt all three states," states Watkins. "We specialize in deer, antelope and turkeys, and only hunt private ranches to assure quality hunts."

Watkins explains his philosophy this way: "We believe each hunt should be a quality hunting experience. It should be remembered long after the trophy mounts have faded and lost their luster. To this end, we strive to make each hunt a totally satisfying experience, so much so that the only easing of the pain as the hunt ends is the knowledge that next year's hunt has already started counting down."

Trophies Plus runs antelope hunts from three to seven days and combines them with deer hunts. Hunters stay either in motels or tent camps on private ranches. In Wyoming, they hunt 11 different management areas in three general regions: the Shirley Basin, north of Laramie, east central, northwest of Lusk, and the northeastern corner near the town of Colony. In Montana, TP hunts the 700 region in the southeastern corner of the state, near Alzada. Success rates run between 95 and 100 percent, with bucks averaging more than 14 inches.

For mule and white-tailed deer, hunters again hunt out of motels, ranch houses and tent camps on private ranches, in east-central Wyoming, northeastern Wyoming, southeastern Montana and western South Dakota. Big bucks of both subspecies are plentiful in these regions. And if you can shoot out to 200 yards with accuracy, your chances of getting a trophy-class animal are good. A .270 or 7mm are calibers of choice out here.

Trophies Plus can put you where the game is. You just tell them what you're looking for, and they'll make it happen. Archery seasons generally open in September and run into October for deer and antelope, with rifle season running the month of November for deer, mid-October into mid-November for antelope. And if you're in the area in April, don't forget to bring a shotgun, as Merriam's turkey are legal then.

ROCKY MOUNTAINS

COLORADO, IDAHO, MONTANA, UTAH, WYOMING

W INDING UP the long valley, your horse is third in the pack train, and you're headed for an alpine glen below the highest of the dark timber. Wilderness, some of it closed to vehicles and chainsaws, is the rule rather than the exception. Most hunters catch their vittles and shut-eye in tent camps. Elsewhere, ranches host hunters with varying degrees of luxury. Outfitters abound but are vastly outnumbered by elk, mule and white-tailed deer, antelope, sheep, goats, bears and cougar. Opportunities for solo hunting on public land exist, but the best chances for success — free from interference from other hunters — comes when you hunt with an outfitter. Big game populations are sensitive to harsh winters, and state game agencies are working hard to improve quality and quantity. Seasons are reasonably predictable, but the numbers of permits and regulations change with some frequency. Keep in touch with the state game people for the latest word.

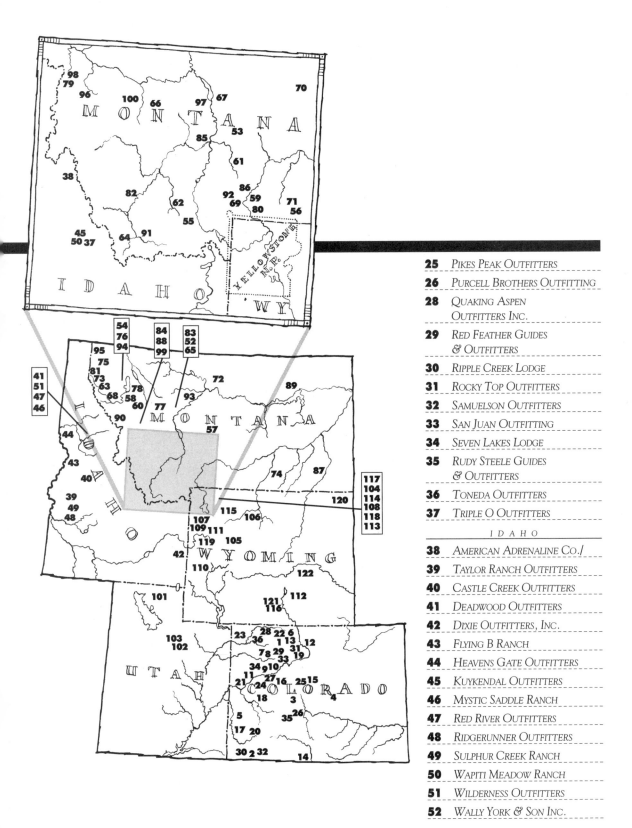

North America's GREATEST Big Game Lodges & Outfitters

[R O C K Y   M O U N T A I N S]

Lodges & Resources

References:

FISHING & HUNTING GUIDE
TO UTAH
by Hartt Wixom
Plaza Publishing Co.
801/972-6180

HOW TO HUNT MONTANA
by Ron Spomer
Wilderness Adventures Press
800/925-3339

Resources:

COLORADO DIVISION OF WILDLIFE
6060 Broadway
Denver, CO 80216
303/297-1192
Web: www.dnr.state.co.us/wildlife

IDAHO FISH AND GAME DEPARTMENT
Box 25, 600 S. Walnut St.
Boise, ID 83707
208/334-3700
Web: www.state.id.us/fishgame

MONTANA DEPARTMENT OF FISH,
WILDLIFE AND PARKS
1420 E. 6th Ave.
Helena, MT 59620
406/444-2535, Web: fwp.state.mt.us

UTAH DIVISION OF
WILDLIFE RESOURCES
1594 W. North Temple, Suite 2110
Box 146301
Salt Lake City, UT 84114-6301
801-538-4700
Web:
www.nr.state.ut.us/dwr/!homeytg.htm

WYOMING GAME AND FISH
DEPARTMENT
5400 Bishop Blvd.
Cheyenne, WY 82006
307/777-4600
Web: www.gf.state.wy.us

4+2T Ranch

H a y d e n ,   C o l o r a d o

Hunt from horseback for mule deer and elk.

SOUTH OF HAYDEN, in the Yampa Valley, the land rises through brushy foothills, climbing toward the 10,000-foot Flat Tops. Capped with deep forests of fir and spruce and cut by sharp canyons, the Flat Tops are prime summer range for elk. Come fall, the herds begin to filter down from the high woodlands, heading south. They linger awhile on Horse Mountain and in the surrounding Bureau of Land Management (BLM) and national forest land before moving south to their winter range in the valleys.

At the end of a gravel road with two locked gates, 4+2T Ranch encompasses the crest of Horse Mountain (9,200 feet). Enveloped on three sides by public land (the nearest access is four miles away) and protected on the fourth by a private ranch, 4+2T is true wilderness. Located in Elk Area Number 12, a territory managed over the past dozen years for trophy bulls, the ranch consistently produces 5x5s and better.

From his frame lodge set in the aspens 1,400 feet below the mountain peak, owner/outfitter Craig Tomke runs four five-day elk hunts. You'll rise early, eat a huge breakfast (okay, there's yogurt and fruit for those who are sane), then ride horseback to a saddle or canyon rim regularly traveled by elk and mule deer. There, you'll dismount and begin your hunt. During the course of the season, almost all of Tomke's hunters will get a chance at a good-sized animal. Tomke can put you in front of the game; then it's up to you.

Licenses can be purchased over the counter during the first two hunts, but for the final two—typically the last week in October and the first week in November— licenses must be bought in advance. Mule deer permits are readily available except for the first week in November, when they're drawn by lottery. While there's a good chance of taking a bull or buck during the first two hunts, the end of October is really the prime time to go, as snow starts to cover the Flat Tops and the big boys finally begin to move down from the high country. This may be best time for a trophy.

Craig also offers archery and blackpowder hunts for elk and deer. He runs hunts for antelope on private lands in September and early October, and a freezer-filling hunt for cow elk in December. You also might want to pack some fishing tackle into your duffel, as 4+2T Ranch has a number of ponds stocked with fat rainbows. You can even fish them through the ice.

VITAL STATISTICS:

Game/Arm/Seasons:
ANTELOPE:
Bow: Aug.
Centerfire, muzzleloader:
Sept. through Oct.
ELK and MULE DEER:
Bow: Late Aug. through late Sept.
Centerfire: Mid-Oct. through mid-Nov.
Muzzleloader: Mid-Sept.

Rates:
$3,000/5 days

Accommodations:
TIMBER LODGE
NUMBER OF ROOMS: 4
MAXIMUM NUMBER OF HUNTERS: 8

Meals: Steaks, chops, shrimp

Conference Groups: No

Guides: Included

Gratuity: Hunter's discretion

Preferred Payment:
Cash, personal check

Other Activities:
Fishing, hiking, bird watching, horseback trips, wildlife photography

Getting There:
Fly to Hayden/Yampa Valley Regional Airport where a van from the lodge will meet you.

Contact:
Craig T. Tomke
4+2T Ranch
Box 896
Hayden, CO 81639
970/276-4283

7M Guide Service

Durango, Colorado

Try for elk, mule deer and bighorn sheep in the rugged San Juans.

VITAL STATISTICS:

Game/Arm/Seasons:
ELK and DEER:
Bow: Sept.
Muzzleloader: Mid-Sept.
Centerfire: Mid-Oct. through mid-Nov.
SHEEP:
Bow: Mid-Aug. through early Sept.
Centerfire and muzzleloader: Early Sept. through early Oct.

Rates:
ELK and DEER from $2,500/5 days
SHEEP $4,500

Accommodations:
WALL TENTS
MAXIMUM NUMBER OF HUNTERS: 6

Meals: Chef's choice with homemade pies

Conference Groups: No

Guides: Included

Gratuity: Hunter's discretion

Preferred Payment:
Cash, check

Other Activities:
Fishing

Getting There:
Fly to Durango and Mazzone will meet you.

Contact:
Seven Mazzone
7M Guide Service
Box 1933
Durango, CO 81301
970/259-2170

THE WEMINUCHE WILDERNESS is a vast primitive area that sprawls across the tops of the San Juan Mountains north and east of Durango. Dominated by the Needles—Eolus, Sunlight and Windom peaks, all above 14,000 feet—the terrain is a welter of rocky alpine peaks and cirques with tarns that issue thin streams that widen and twist through grassy basins.

From its base tent camp in a basin at 10,000 feet, 7M hunts this raggedly beautiful country of broad parks studded with islands of pine and fir. Depending on game movement, spike camps are sometimes down at the 9,000-foot level in the "quakies"—aspens whose leaves shimmer in the slightest breeze. Other spike camps might be up in the timber above 11,000 feet. "It's not," as outfitter Seven Mazzone says, "for the faint of heart."

Elk in these parts run in the 4x5 range, and deer 4x4 or better. Hunter success ranges upwards from 35 percent, with the rate for bow and muzzleloader hunts better than that. During rifle season in mid-October through mid-November, there may be some bugling the first few days, but after that things get pretty quiet. Occasional cow calling may work, but in the main it's walk and spot and stalk, then walk some more. Mazzone will also place hunters in stands and put on drives for them.

The base camp is a classic affair of wall tents with woodstoves, cots and sleeping pads, and a cook-tent-cum-dining- room. What's special is the cook, whose chicken cacciatore and homemade pies are provender unexpected in this rugged wilderness. The drop camps are similar, without cook.

Mazzone also offers hunts for bighorn sheep. The success rate on these hunts is close to 100 percent and rams are generally in the three-quarter to full-curl range. Tags are drawn by lottery, however, and you have to apply for quite a few years before you build up enough preference points to have a chance at a permit.

VITAL STATISTICS:

Game/Arm/Seasons:
ELK AND DEER
Bow: Late Aug. through Sept.
Centerfire: Mid-Oct.
Muzzleloader: Mid-Sept.

Rates:
RIFLE deer from $1,875/5 days
RIFLE elk from $1,975/5 days
BOW DEER from $1,175/5 days
BOW ELK from $1,675/5 days
Unguided $985/5 days

Accommodations:
LOG CABINS
NUMBER OF ROOMS: 9
MAXIMUM NUMBER OF HUNTERS: 22

Meals: Game, pasta, fish

Conference Groups: Yes

Guides: Included

Gratuity: $100

Preferred Payment:
Cash, check

Other Activities:
Fishing, hiking

Getting There:
Fly to Gunnison and be met by a van from the lodge.

Contact:
Phillip Steiner
Adventure Enterprises
#2 Illinois County Rd. 742
Almont, CO 81210
970/641-4708
Fax: 970/641-1690
e-mail: ae@youngmind.com

Adventure Experience, Inc.

A l m o n t ,   C o l o r a d o

Big bulls and bucks await those willing to work for them.

THE GUNNISON NATIONAL FOREST covers much of central Colorado. It climbs steadily from the west, gaining almost a mile of elevation from the town of Gunnison to Cottonwood Pass on the Continental Divide. Adventure Outfitters runs hunts three miles west of the pass, near Taylor Park.

The head of the hunting operation is Phillip Steiner, who has guided in this area for more than 14 years. This terrain is steep and timbered, a combination favored by big bulls. Elk average 5x5, while 4x4 mule deer are fairly common. The best elk hunting occurs in bow season—late August to late September—and the first week of rifle season, which usually falls around the second week of October. That's also when mule deer hunting reaches its peak.

You won't get saddle sore at this camp, but you may walk a bit. Hunters arrive in camp—four cabins and a main lodge—by four-wheel-drive. Early the next morning, you and your hunting partner will hike or ride ATVs farther into the wilderness to areas where game has been moving. There, you may set up on stand, or you may do some glassing and stalking. Archers hunt the willow and aspen bottoms around the base camp, and the fingers of a dozen draws that lead from the main basins up toward the ridges. The success rate for archers is close to 100 percent; rifle hunters are successful 50 percent of the time. Adventure Experience also offers non-guided hunts for less than half the price of guided hunts.

Hunters stay in cozy log cabins with plenty of room and dine on game and pasta in the main lodge. There you'll also find a sauna, a hot tub—blessed relief after a hot day on a cold mountain—and showers.

What a hunt! You left Geneva Park Outfitter's camp
high in Colorado's Rockies long before daylight; settled into
a ground blind an hour later; bugled up a majestic 6 x 6 that you
took with one shot; and by 10:00 a.m. he was quartered and packed in
meat bags for the ride into camp. Not a bad morning's work.

Investor Henry Kravis knows a good thing when he sees it. That's
why he bought Seven Lakes Lodge at the foot of the Flat Tops
near Meeker, Colorado, and turned it into a first-class hunting
and fishing resort. The quality of the hunting is
matched only by the fine tablefare.

[R O C K Y   M O U N T A I N S]

All Seasons Ranch

C o l o r a d o   S p r i n g s ,   C o l o r a d o

Take a fully guided or do-it-yourself hunt through the same outfit.

ESTLED IN THE MOUNTAINS outside of Steamboat Springs, All Seasons Ranch has been running wilderness hunting trips for more than 30 years. Purchased 10 years ago by "Doc" Bruce Cottrell, the ranch offers quality elk and mule deer hunting trips, both full-service and drop camp, for bow, muzzleloader and rifle hunters. All hunts take place in the Beaver Flattops area of the Routt National Forest, beautiful, rugged, game-rich country northeast of Steamboat.

Cottrell offers hunters three options. The first, a full-service guided camp, is a full tent-camp operation. Everything is provided. You'll have your own cot and foam pad ("Sorry, we don't put mints on the pillow," jokes Cottrell.), the firewood is split and stacked in your tent, and a well-balanced menu is planned and prepared for you. The horses are tended and saddled, the guides are dedicated to helping you find the animal you want and they'll dress and pack out your game. "We hunt on horseback, on foot, on stands — whatever it takes," states Cottrell.

Hunters who don't want to be so pampered can stay in one of the ranch's equipped drop camps, which are fully set up and equipped prior to your arrival. Cottrell and his crew provide sleeping and mess tents, complete with woodstoves and precut wood, cooking and eating utensils, water buckets, lanterns and fuel, ground cover and cots. He'll pack you and all your food and gear into camp, point out the best hunting areas, then leave you on your own, returning to check on you every day. You guide yourself, dress your own game and cook your own meals, although a camp cook/camp jack can be provided for an extra $135 a day. He'll basically run the camp for you, preparing meals and cutting firewood.

The non-equipped drop camp, for the true do-it-yourselfer, is basically a packing service. Cottrell and his crew will pack you and all of your gear and supplies into a predetermined site, check on you daily and pack out your game and gear at the end of the hunt. This one is only available during archery and blackpowder seasons. But what a fun way to get away from it all!

VITAL STATISTICS:

Game/Arm/Seasons:
MULE DEER AND ELK:
Bow: Late Aug. through late Sept.
Centerfire: Early Oct. through early Nov.
Muzzleloader: Mid-Sept.

Rates:
All hunts are mule deer/elk combos for 7 days with 5 days of hunting
Guided $1,900
Equipped drop camp $700
Non-equipped drop camp $500

Accommodations:
TENTS
MAXIMUM NUMBER OF HUNTERS: 8 ON GUIDED HUNTS; 6 IN DROP CAMPS

Meals: Steaks, chicken, turkey, chili, trout

Conference Groups: No

Guides: Included on guided hunts

Gratuity: $50 to $100

Preferred Payment:
Cash, check

Other Activities:
Fishing

Getting There:
Fly to Yampa Valley Regional Airport in Hayden and be met by a representative of the outfitter, or fly to Denver and rent a car.

Contact:
"Doc" Bruce Cottrell
All Seasons Ranch
6135 Templeton Gap Rd.
Colorado Springs, CO 80918
719/596-2047
Fax: 719/596-2047

Blue Creek Outfitters

Naturita, Colorado

*Hunt the forests for elk and canyon rims
for mule deer in the Uncompahgre region.*

VITAL STATISTICS:

Game/Arm/Seasons:
ELK and DEER:
Bow: Late Aug. – Sept.
Centerfire: Mid-Oct. through mid-Nov.
Muzzleloader: Mid-Sept.
BEAR:
Bow, centerfire, muzzleloader: Sept.
MOUNTAIN LION:
Bow, centerfire, muzzleloader: Jan.
Rates:
ELK and LION: $2,500/6 days
DEER and BEAR: $1,500/6 days
Accommodations:
CABINS AND TENTS
MAXIMUM NUMBER OF HUNTERS: 6
Meals: Family-style
Conference Groups: No
Guides: Included
Gratuity: $50 to $100
Preferred Payment:
Cash or check
Other Activities:
None
Getting There:
Fly to Grand Junction and be met by lodge van.

Contact:
Scott Dillon
Blue Creek Outfitters
Box 65
Naturita, CO 81422
970/864-2250
Fax: 970/864-7309
e-mail: dillon@GJ.net
Web: www.gj.net/~dillon

THE UNCOMPAHGRE PLATEAU swings northwest from Red Mountain Pass, separating the San Miguel and Dolores rivers from the lower Gunnison. Much of the plateau is in a national forest that rises to mesas topping out between 6,600 and 7,700 feet. Heavily forested and cut by numerous canyons, the country holds elk, mule deer, black bear and mountain lions.

Scott Dillon has been operating Blue Creek Outfitters in this area for 15 years. One guide generally works with two hunters, though one-on-one hunts are available. Bowhunting season kicks things off toward the end of August, when archers work out of tent camps in the Uncompahgre National Forest. Guides bugle in bulls—4x4s and some bigger—as close as 15 yards. Bugling is also the most effective technique during the 10-day blackpowder season in mid-September (a special license is required). Later, in rifle season, tactics change to riding and spotting, then stalking 5x5s in the scrub oaks and aspen.

Deer in the Uncompahgre are also known for their size, and they're hunted from the Blue Creek Ranch in the Dolores River Valley. Tree stands and spot-and-stalk hunting tactics are favored by experienced hands. Rifle hunters also get their bucks in the meadows or up along the canyon rims. No horses on these hunts; it's all on foot. Blue Creek Outfitters also offers spot-and-stalk hunting for bears averaging about 200 pounds around berry patches, plus mountain lion hunting in winter (January is the best month).

Whether you hunt from the tent camps or from the ranch with its rustic cabins, everything except personal gear, sleeping bags and firearms or bows is provided. Generally there'll be no more than six hunters in camp.

A.J. Brink Outfitters

G l e n d e v e y   R o u t e ,   C o l o r a d o

Try a drop-camp hunt to really get into prime elk country.

VITAL STATISTICS:

Game/Arm/Seasons:
ELK:
Bow: Late Aug. through late Sept.
Centerfire: Mid-Oct. through mid-Nov.
Muzzleloader: Mid-Sept.
BIGHORN:
Centerfire: Early Sept. through early Oct.

Rates:
ELK: From $1,350/5 days
BIGHORN: From $2,800/5 days

Accommodations:
TENTS
MAXIMUM NUMBER OF HUNTERS: 6 TO 8

Meals: Steaks, pork chops, casseroles, vegetables

Conference Groups: No

Guides: Included

Gratuity: Hunter's discretion

Preferred Payment:
Cash, check

Other Activities:
Trail rides, fishing, wildlife photography

Getting There:
Fly to Laramie and rent a car.

Contact:
Jim Brink
A.J. Brink Outfitters
Glendevey Rt., CO
via Jelm, WY 82063
970/435-5707
Fax: 970/435-5707
Web: www.miraclemile.com/ajbrink

CATERING TO SMALL GROUPS of hunters (from eight to 10), and specializing in individual attention, A.J. Brink Outfitters has a well-run pack-in camp in the Rawah Wilderness Area in north-central Colorado. The pack-in rides into camp are awe-inspiring, with views stretching all the way into Wyoming.

The hunting in this area isn't so bad either, with elk averaging 5x5, and bighorn sheep and trophy mule deer possible. Hunting seasons start as early as August, with archery deer and elk; and stretch to mid-November for rifle hunters. Bighorn sheep weighing up to 170 pounds may also be hunted (you have to draw a permit first) from early September to early October.

Brink Outfitter's hunters need only bring personal gear, such as a sleeping bag, clothing (pack both light and heavy clothing, as the temperatures can really vary in this region, especially in the early part of the season), and firearms (a .30-06 is fine for deer and sheep, though you may want something bigger, such as a .300 or .338 Win. Mag., for elk). The guide/hunter ratio is usually one guide to two or three hunters; horses are used to get to hunting areas and are kept at the main camp.

For those wishing to go it on their own, Brink also offers drop-camp options in prime game country. Drop-camp hunters provide all of their own gear, with Brink packing everything in and out and checking on the hunters every other day. Drop camps will soon be available in Unit 25, a prime game area in the Flat Tops Wilderness area of the White River National Forest.

Those staying at the main tent camp can expect excellent table fare, ranging from rib eye steaks/baked potatoes/salads to pork chops/stuffing/applesauce/green beans to roast beef or Mexican casserole—just what the doctor ordered after a tough day chasing elk in the mountains. Special diets can also be accommodated.

Buffalo Horn Ranch

Meeker, Colorado

The Ranching for Wildlife program is a big success in this part of the state.

VITAL STATISTICS:

Game/Arm/Seasons:
ELK and DEER:
Ranch for Wildlife: Sept. through Dec.
ELK and DEER:
Bow: Sept.
Muzzleloader: Mid-Sept.
Centerfire: Mid-Oct. through mid-Nov.
Rates:
ELK: $5,000/5 days
Combo: $7,000/5 days
Drop camp: $1,000/5 days
Accommodations:
MODERN LOG LODGE
NUMBER OF ROOMS: 12
MAXIMUM NUMBER OF HUNTERS: 20
Meals: Buffet and fine dining
Conference Groups: Yes
Guides: Included
Gratuity: 10 to 15%
Preferred Payment:
MasterCard, Visa, check
Other Activities:
Fishing, bird hunting, waterfowling, swimming, hiking, bird-watching, wildlife photography
Getting There:
Fly to Grand Junction, rent a car and drive to the ranch.

Contact:
Jim Walman
Buffalo Horn Ranch
13825 CR 7
Meeker, CO 81641
970/878-5450
Fax: 970/878-4088
Web: incwine.com/3242

COLORADO'S RANCHING for Wildlife program looks like it may open up more and better elk hunting for guided and unguided hunters alike. Ranches that participate in the program get a 90-day season to run guided hunts, with the public allowed access for a set number of days. These ranches are also required to manage their properties in ways that encourage big game populations.

The 20,000-acre Buffalo Horn Ranch, near Meeker on the White River, is one such ranch. There's not a lot of elevation differential among these rolling hills and sharp ridges well northwest of the Flat Tops. Cover is mostly pinion pine, scrub oak, serviceberry and cedar. Grasses climb the flanks of the ridges before merging with stunted trees. It's good cover, and there's plenty of water.

The season opens early in September and continues to December. The three-month season offers a number of advantages. Here, rifle hunters can hunt elk in September, a time normally reserved for archers and muzzleloaders. And later, after the seasons have closed in most other areas, they can hunt elk that have moved down from the highlands into this lower winter range. Hunting with your guide, you'll do a lot of spotting from horseback and stalking to get into range. Pickup trucks are available for those who prefer four wheels. Other sections of the ranch are better suited to stand hunting. It's your choice. Hunter success on bulls exceeded 90 percent last year, with typical racks scoring 260.

The ranch also has a drop camp about six miles from the main lodge for do-it-yourselfers. Regular seasons apply, and hunter success is about 50 percent.

The main lodge is a modern two-story of taffy-colored pine. There's little roughing it here. About half of the rooms have private baths and the others share. Rooms are made up daily, and meals verge on fine dining. The fields surrounding the lodge are loaded with pheasants, chukars and huns, and the kennel holds bird dogs ready to go to work. If those distractions aren't enough, there's always that mile on the White River. Bring your fishing rod.

Buford Guide Service

Buford,   Colorado

Hunt in the heart of elk and deer country, out of a newly refurbished lodge.

VITAL STATISTICS:

Game/Arm/Seasons:
ELK and DEER:
Bow: Late-Aug. through Sept.
Muzzleloader: Mid-Sept.
Centerfire: Mid-Oct. through mid-Nov.

Rates:
From $1,100/5 days

Accommodations:
BUNKHOUSE
NUMBER OF ROOMS: 2
MAXIMUM NUMBER OF HUNTERS: 6

Meals: Turkey, pork chops

Conference Groups: No

Guides: Included

Gratuity: $100

Preferred Payment:
Cash, personal check

Other Activities:
Fishing, hiking, bird watching, wildlife photography

Getting There:
Fly to Grand Junction, rent a car and drive to the lodge.

Contact:
Tom Tucker
Buford Guide Service
24284 CR 8
Meeker, CO 81641
970/878-4596

FORTY YEARS AGO, Tom Tucker's dad started a guide service out of a little store in Buford. He hunted the Flat Tops—a high, broad wilderness area known for its many parks verdant with thick summer grasses and dense stands of loden fir. Sharp valleys separate the tops of these mountains. It's the kind of cover that holds game and requires more than a little stamina to hunt. When the herds begin moving down from this high, isolated range, the woods are literally flowing with elk.

Starting as his dad's chief assistant—"unpaid," is how Tucker summarizes the job—he learned game and the guide business from the bottom up. Today, Tucker hunts the areas between Sleepy Cat and Burrow mountains. This is about as far off the paved road as you can get, and the region contains a number of high alpine parks—Salt, Lost, Long, Pattison—as well as mature timber and scrub aspen and oak. You'll hunt on foot, spotting and stalking, or out of a stand, as conditions dictate.

Bow and muzzleloading hunts for elk are available by lottery permit. Applications generally need to be submitted by the end of March. While the season opens in late August, it's really too warm then and the elk have yet to move. Bugling starts toward the middle of September—the opening of muzzleloading season—and that's when hunting begins to get good. Muzzleloading permits are not easily obtained, however, and require a number of preference points.

Licenses for hunting elk with rifles is another story. They're available over the counter for the region's three seasons, and your chances of taking a trophy may be slightly better during the first. You can hunt deer while hunting bull elk during the first two seasons, but not during the third unless you've been successful in the draw. Bulls and bucks in this area are generally 4x4s or better.

The typical hunt with Buford Guide Service matches four clients with a guide for five days. You can hire your own guide for an additional $1,500 if you prefer. In 4WD vehicles, you'll leave the comfortable, newly remodeled bunkhouse at dawn and return well past dark. If you can stay awake, you'll find meals are hearty affairs of turkey or chops served family-style in the main lodge.

Capitol Peak Outfitters

Carbondale, Colorado

Big bulls and bucks out of guided and drop camps.

VITAL STATISTICS:

Game/Arm/Seasons:
ELK and DEER:
Bow: Late Aug. through Sept.
Muzzleloader: Mid-Sept.
Centerfire: Mid-Oct. through mid-Nov.
Rates:
ELK and DEER from $1,600/5 days
Accommodations:
WALL TENTS
MAXIMUM NUMBER OF HUNTERS: 8
Meals: Fresh meat, produce
Conference Groups: Yes
Guides: Included
Gratuity: 10%
Preferred Payment:
Cash, personal check
Other Activities:
Fishing, hiking, wildlife photography
Getting There:
Fly to Aspen and take a shuttle van for $60.

Contact:
Steve Rieser
Capitol Peak Outfitters
0554 Valley Rd.
Carbondale, CO 81623
970/963-0211
Fax: 970/963-0497
off-season:
35035 N. 3rd. Ave.
Box 13
Phoenix, AZ 85027
602/516-1157

HERE'S AN OPERATION that's straight-forward, and if the hunters are straight shooters, everyone will get a bull. A number of 6-point bulls and 5-point bucks are taken each year under guide/owner Steve Rieser's tutelage from the areas he hunts north and a little west of Aspen.

Capitol Peak holds permits for Game Management Units 43, 47 and 444. It operates guided and drop camps in Maroon Bells and Hunter Frying Pan wilderness areas, both in the White River National Forest. Maroon Bells is a rugged area, even by Colorado standards. The outfitter's namesake mountain stretches to 14,000 feet and is surrounded by others in the 13,000-foot class. Below timberline are a number of rounded ridges of grass and trees. The second area, Hunter Frying Pan, lies between the Roaring Fork River to the south and the Frying Pan drainage on the north. This area is a little less rugged than Maroon Bells. Both, along with a 600-tract of private land abutting the national forest, provide good habitat for elk and deer.

Guided bow and muzzleloader hunts are run from a tent camp deep in the Hunter Frying Pan wilderness. This camp is a good half-day's ride from the trailhead, but the elk hunting makes it worth it. Bugling brings bulls in close, with many shots taken at less than 30 yards. There are seldom more than six hunters and three guides in camp (one-on-one hunts are available). A different camp is used for rifle hunting. You'll ride to this one in a vehicle, then hunt horseback during your stay. Hunter success rates on both deer and elk have averaged 50 percent for the past dozen years, and eight out of 10 hunters get reasonable shots. Sometimes, depending on how the game is moving, Rieser will set up a spike camp farther back in the wilderness.

Accommodations on seven-day guided hunts are big, wood-heated wall tents where meals include plenty of fresh produce and meat prepared by the camp cook. Capitol also offers drop-camp hunting in the Maroon Bells and on private land west of Hunter Frying Pan. Drop camps are similar to the base camp, except the tents are smaller and you do your own cooking.

Challenge Outfitters

E a g l e ,   C o l o r a d o

Location, location, location—that's the foundation for good elk hunting.

VITAL STATISTICS:

Game/Arm/Seasons:
ELK, DEER:
Bow: Sept.
Centerfire: Mid-Oct. through early Nov.
Muzzleloader: Mid-Sept.
Rates:
$2,200/6 days (bow and muzzleloader); $2,700/5 days (rifle)
Accommodations:
TENT CAMPS
MAXIMUM NUMBER OF HUNTERS: 6
Meals: Home-style steaks, chicken, chops
Conference Groups: No
Guides: Included
Gratuity: $250
Preferred Payment:
Cash, check
Other Activities:
Bird watching, fishing, wildlife photography
Getting There:
Fly to Eagle County Regional Airport and you'll be picked up.

Contact:
Steve Dahmer
Challenge Outfitters
PO Box 640
Vail, CO 81658
970/653-4515
Fax: 970/845-9135
e-mail: bcbuck174@sprynet.com:

IN COLORADO, AS ELSEWHERE, most hunting is done on national forest, Bureau of Land Management or other state or federal lands. Outfitters are granted exclusive licenses to operate in specific areas. Yet, while their licenses mean no other outfitter can bring paying clients into an area covered by a permit, there's nothing to stop an individual or group from riding in and setting up camp. While rigorous terrain makes it unlikely that anyone other than an outfitter's clients will be hunting his patch of wilderness, it can happen. When it does, your hard-earned hunt can become a shambles.

Controlling access is the name of the game. Challenge Outfitters leases the 30,000-acre Piney Valley Ranch and holds Forest Service permits to operate two camps farther up the Piney River. The only way into this country is through the ranch. Thus the odds of other hunters bumping your elk are pretty long. During your hunt, you and five other hunters will have a considerable chunk of Game Management Unit 36 all to yourselves. A blend of flat-bottomed valley, rolling hills of aspen and brush, steep timber and alpine basins makes this a nearly ideal environment for elk and mule deer. Depending on the weather and movement of game, you'll either hunt from a base camp near Marma Lake below Rock Creek Park or over on the North Fork of the Piney, which drains the land between Piney Peak and Slate Mountain, both 11,000-footers. Challenge Outfitter's camps are well organized and have heated wall tents with wooden floors and bunk beds. At times elk are harvested less than a mile from camp, but normally you'll ride sure-footed mountain horses up into the wilderness to reach a meadow before daylight.

Because of the management program at the ranch, you will likely see several branch-antlered bulls every day. Only 4x4 or better bulls can be taken in Unit 36, but there's no antler restriction on mule deer bucks. Average bulls tend to score 250 to 300 Boone & Crockett points, and bucks range between 120 and 180. Hunter success is very good for an outfitter in this price range, and 70 percent of rifle hunters take bulls. Virtually every archer gets good shooting, and generally half connect.

Colorado Hunting Adventures

Parachute, Colorado

A little weirdness in the wilderness conjures up some bull.

WHO ELSE BUT JOHN MYER, a custom gunsmith from Boyce, Virginia, would bring to elk camp a big magnum stocked with an exciting piece of French walnut with a semi-schnable of mastodon tusk radio carbon dating back to 53,000 B.C. Eccentricity often is the parent of pure weirdness. With one shot, John took a bull with four points of finger length bunched at the top of one antler. It was the strangest bull to come out of the five camps Brad Knot runs in the Kannah Creek region of Grand Mesa National Forest.

The camps are situated at 8,400 feet in moderate to rugged terrain. Four of the camps, Service, East Two, West Two and the base Camp on Cheever, are situated on tributaries to Kannah Creek. From Indian Point to Point Peninsula is a height of land that separates these four camps from his fifth in Alkali Basin, accessible via 4WD, where he runs semi-guided hunts. You know the drill at the base camp: saddled up and on the trail before dawn to reach the locale of the day's hunt before daybreak. You'll hunt back to camp on horseback or on foot, depending on terrain and the vagaries of elk. In the other camps, you set your own agenda, but the cook at Alkali Basin may have some ideas about dinner.

Elk are primarily hunted in the Kannah Creek drainage. In archery season, bugling and cow calling can be very effective, and sometimes calling works in the first rifle season. As the season progresses, spotting and stalking becomes the more effective strategy. Across the ridge on Alkali Creek, an area that tends to be quite steep, rocky and isolated, mule deer predominate. A typical mulie is a 4x4, while across the ridge elk are in the 5x5 class. You'll also find some black bear in this neck of the woods, and if your fireplace needs to be graced by a rug of the same, arrange for a permit so you'll be ready if opportunity strikes. Overall success rates on elk here top 60 percent.

Comanche Wilderness Outfitters

Ft.   Collins,   Colorado

Have patience, gain those preference points, then go hunt.

VITAL STATISTICS:

Game/Arm/Seasons:
ELK:
Bow: Late Sept. through late Oct.
Centerfire: Mid-Oct. through mid-Jan.
Muzzleloader: Mid-Sept.
DEER:
Centerfire: Late Oct. through early Nov.; early to mid-Dec.
ANTELOPE:
Centerfire: Late Sept. through early Oct.
Rates:
ELK from $3,250/6 days
DEER from $3,000/6 days
ANTELOPE $1,000/3 days
Accommodations:
MOTELS OR TENT CAMPS
MAXIMUM NUMBER OF HUNTERS: 6
Meals: Restaurants and family-style in camp
Conference Groups: No
Guides: Included
Gratuity: 10 to 15%
Preferred Payment:
Cash, check
Other Activities:
Bird hunting, fishing, waterfowling, wildlife photography
Getting There:
Fly to Denver, and the lodge will collect you for $14 per person.

Contact:
Scott A. Limmer
Comanche Wilderness Outfitters
Box 1965
Ft. Collins, CO 80522-1965
970/223-5330

FOR THE PAST DECADE, Scott Limmer and his Comanche Wilderness Outfitters have been building an enviable inventory of elk, deer and sheep hunts, some of which are as tough to be drawn for as they are highly successful.

Working out of a ranch that borders the 265,000-acre Rocky Mountain National Park, hunters who are lucky enough to draw permits for Unit 20 can hunt elk migrating out of the park in November, December and January. Snow is limited in the relatively low mountains and valleys of the ranch, even during these, the opening months of serious winter. Success rates on big 5x5 or better bulls runs 90 percent plus. And the fee is about what you'd pay for a two-on-one guided elk hunt anywhere else. The catch? First, one needs to accumulate three preference points. To do this you need to have applied for and not been drawn for other limited hunts during each of the last three years just to get into the lottery. Second, meals and accommodations, which will cost about another $1,000 for a week at a motel in the nearby ski resort town of Estes Park, are not included. Still, if you're drawn, the odds are stacked in your favor, and the sticker price is about half that charged by other high-percentage private-land hunts. This same ranch can be hunted earlier in the season: archers need no preference points to be drawn, but muzzleloader and centerfire shooters need at least two points for each of Colorado's remaining four seasons.

Staging out of Ft. Collins on the eastern edge of Unit 19, Scott operates a string of tent camps in the Roosevelt National Forest. Scott outfits a maximum of six hunters during each week of the season, and he's loath to operate guided hunts and drop-camps at the same time. If six hunters book guided hunts, he'll forego renting the drop camps, which consist of a heated 12x8 wall tent plus stove, table and sleeping pads, for unguided hunts and use them as spike camps for two hunters and their guide. Bulls of 300 Boone & Crockett or Pope and Young are not all that unusual, but mostly 4x4s and 5x5s are the rule. About two out of three hunters bag an elk. Primarily elk terrain, some nice mule deer are occasionally harvested here. Along with elk, Scott runs mule deer hunts on private ranches in eastern Colorado, and hunts for bighorn sheep, Shiras moose and antelope for which permits need to be drawn.

Eagle Spirit Outfitters

Steamboat Springs, Colorado

If a hot shower, a martini, a crisp salad and a 6x6 bull would make your day, you've found the right spot.

VITAL STATISTICS:

Game/Arm/Seasons:
ELK, DEER:
Bow: Sept.
Centerfire: Mid-Oct. through early Nov.
Muzzleloader: Mid-Sept.
BEAR:
Bow: Sept.
Centerfire: Mid-Oct. through early Nov.
MOUNTAIN LION:
Bow, centerfire: Mid-Nov. through March

Rates:
ELK, DEER, BEAR $3,000/7 days (bow and muzzleloader); $3,850/7 days (rifle)
MOUNTAIN LION $3,500/7 days

Accommodations:
SKI LODGE
NUMBER OF ROOMS: 5, ALL WITH PRIVATE BATH
MAXIMUM NUMBER OF HUNTERS: 12

Meals: Near gourmet
Conference Groups: No
Guides: Included
Gratuity: $100
Preferred Payment:
Cash, check
Other Activities:
Fishing, wildlife photography
Getting there:
Fly to Hayden and the lodge van will meet you at no charge.

Contact:
Miles Hogan
Eagle Spirit Outfitters
Box 775792
Steamboat Springs, CO 80477
888/416-8102

ELK HUNTS are arduous, comprised as they are of terrain that would challenge a seasoned Sherpa; wall-tent camps that, outfitter boasts to the contrary, are seldom really warm or ever dry; and food that's as good as if you'd opened the cans yourself. So after a day chasing wapiti, what would you say to hanging your hunting duds in a closet, showering with all the hot water you want then slipping into fresh jeans and a sweater before joining the others for a libation and then dinner accompanied by good wines. Sound like your kind of elk hunting? Read on.

The lodge is three miles south of Steamboat, surrounded by aspens and overlooking the resort. Eagle Spirit owner Miles Hogan leases it annually during the hunting season. Using it as his base, he and his guide drive hunters to nearby private ranches with resident herds of elk. Miles leases some 20,000 acres, and he manages hunting on them to ensure continuing populations of elk and mule deer. On each of his ranches some areas are strictly off-limits to hunters. These areas have been set aside as sanctuaries for elk. In them elk are never pressured. Consequently they're less likely to wander off the ranches.

Terrain varies from high-mountain meadows to stands of dark timber, patches of oak brush and rolling sage. It can be as difficult and demanding as you want, or as easy. Well, maybe not that easy. This outfitter specializes in archery hunting, and that means lots of cow calling and bugling, and shots as close as 10 yards. Tree stands have been placed at wallows. Hunters are also posted at access routes to meadows and likely crossing points on ridges separating drainages. You probably won't see a horse because you'll ride in 4WDs to the area you'll hunt and then walk to your hunting spot. An amazingly high — nearly 70 percent — of hunters harvest bulls which must be 4x4s or better. Mule deer bucks generally sport 4x4 racks with spreads of about 24 inches. Elk harvests are consistent throughout the season, with the second week of October traditionally providing the best deer hunting. Miles also guides for bear in the fall, but it's purely incidental to his elk and deer hunts.

Echo Canyon Guest Ranch

L a   V e t a ,   C o l o r a d o

Trophy bucks and bulls, one-on-one hunts, 20,000 private acres—sound good?

VITAL STATISTICS:

Game/Arm/Seasons:

ELK, MULE DEER:
Bow: Late Aug. through late Sept.
Centerfire: Mid-Oct. through mid-Nov.
Muzzleloader: Mid-Sept.
LION:
Bow, centerfire: Mid-Nov. through March
TURKEY:
Bow, shotgun: Mid-April through mid-May

Rates:
Single species $3,500/7 days;
two species $4,500/7 days
TURKEY $500/2 days

Accommodations:
LOG LODGE AND CABIN
NUMBER OF ROOMS: 15 WITH PRIVATE BATH
MAXIMUM NUMBER OF HUNTERS: 6
Meals: Excellent, family-style
Conference Groups: Yes
Guides: Included
Gratuity: Hunter's discretion
Preferred Payment:
Cash, Discover, MasterCard, Visa, check

Other Activities:
Biking, canoeing/rafting, fishing, golf, riding, wildlife photography

Getting There:
Fly to Colorado Springs, rent a car and drive to the ranch.

Contact:
Dave Hampton
Echo Canyon Guest Ranch
Box 328
La Veta, CO 81055
800/341-6603
Fax: 719/742-5525
e-mail: echo@rmi.net
Web: www.guestecho.com

HUNTING ONE-ON-ONE with a guide adds significantly to your chances of bagging a good bull or buck. So does hunting on private land. In Colorado, one of the spots where you get both is on this guest ranch tucked beneath 13,684-foot West Spanish Peak in the Sangre de Cristo Mountains. The ranch lies about 5,000 feet below the crest of the mountains, and the country is not as rugged as a glance at a topo suggests. Rather, the country here is big and open, with lots of chaparral and ponderosa pine. Still, valleys narrow as they gain elevation and their flanks steepen. Climbing northern slopes, the forest thickens and provides heavy cover.

It is here that very good mule deer are found. And Echo Canyon harvests no buck with less than a 26-inch spread. Hunting these deer is particularly challenging; patience and perseverance pays big-time. If you take this hunt you won't see many bucks, most likely only two or three in a week. But the ones you see will be well worthwhile. Then, it's up to you. About three out of four hunters are successful in filling their mule deer tags. Elk are hunted lower on the ranch and a typical bull scores 300 plus. In south-central Colorado, the rut begins in mid-September and continues into November. Here rifle hunters, as well as archers and muzzleloaders, hunt bugling bulls. Snow generally comes by the final week of rifle season, the first week of November, and while the hunting is tougher, some very good bulls are taken. And while Echo Canyon does not run bear hunts per se, the season coincides with elk and deer rifle season. If you think you might want a bear, buy a tag.

Lions are really owner Dave Hampton's first love. As soon as the last elk hunter leaves the lodge, he's out running his Blue Ticks, Plotts and Walkers. While he guarantees that his clients will get their cat (if not they come back next year free) Dave isn't in the business of shooting just any lion. Only toms of 150 pounds or so, and an occasional "troublesome" female, are harvested. Come spring, Merriam's turkeys are on the agenda.

There are seldom more than four clients per hunt and they all hang their duds at the guest ranch, a 13,000 square-foot lodge of log and glass with six rooms with private baths. Near the lodge are four guest cabins. You'll find all the hallmarks of a great, laid-back Western resort here, along with some of the best cooking east of the Continental Divide.

Geneva Park Outfitters

C o n i f e r ,   C o l o r a d o

No walk in the park this, first you've got to survive the draw.

VITAL STATISTICS:

Game/Arm/Seasons:
ELK, DEER:
Bow: :ate Aug. through late Sept.
Centerfire: Mid-Oct. through early Nov.
Muzzleloader: Mid-Sept.
BIGHORN SHEEP:
Bow, centerfire: Early Aug. through early Oct.
MOUNTAIN GOAT:
Bow, centerfire: Early Sept. through early Oct.
Rates:
ELK $2,200/7 days
DEER $1,700/7 days
BIGHORN SHEEP $4,200/9 days
MOUNTAIN GOAT $2,100/5 days
Accommodations:
TENT CAMPS
MAXIMUM NUMBER OF HUNTERS: 6
Meals: Grilled steaks, spiced rice, salads
Conference Groups: No
Guides: Included
Gratuity: $75
Preferred Payment:
Cash, check, money order
Other Activities:
Fishing, wildlife photography
Getting There:
Fly to Denver International and rent a car, or be picked up for $50 per person.

Contact:
Terry Sandmeier
Geneva Park Outfitters
Box 771
Conifer, CO 80433-0771
303/838-6311

SOME GUYS JUST LOVE THEIR WORK, and Terry Sandmeier is one of those. He pays the bills by guiding elk and deer and sheep hunters in the awesomely steep Mount Evans Wilderness Area east of County Road 381 south of Georgetown. Here, elk average 5x5 and 250 on the Boone & Crockett scale, and mulies are typically 4x4s with 27-inch spreads. Taking only six hunters per week, Terry gives his clients lots of personal attention. Almost everyone has at least one good shot, but not everyone connects. Such are the vagaries of hunting.

His elk and deer hunts are better than most, but if you ask Terry what really turns him on, he'll tell you in a flash: "Sheep." To hunt them in Colorado isn't easy from the get-go. First you must survive the Colorado license lottery and be drawn to receive a non-resident permit to hunt bighorn sheep. Generally success comes after two or three years. Next is physical conditioning. After notification in May that you've been drawn, you'll have four months to get yourself in shape to hunt two miles or more above sea level. Putting in hours on stair-steppers pays off on those mornings when you leave the base camp at 4:30 knowing you have to climb 2,000 feet or more to reach that little bowl where you spotted that herd of rams yesterday. It'll pay off once more when that full-curl ram that looks like a sure 180 B&C slips around to the right and you must clamor quickly and quietly over a rocky knob to get to the other side before he does. And it pays off big when you sit there, holding your bow at full draw waiting for the ram to take those two more steps that'll give you a clear shot. If you're gasping for breath, you'll miss for certain.

Aside from that, hunting sheep with Terry is a piece of cake. His horses are sure-footed, his tent camps are warm and clean, the food's always good and the coffee hot. Terry would rather be hunting sheep than anything else, and his reputation as one of the best in Colorado stretches back a decade or more. Sheep hunts are one-on-one and what could be better than that. P.S. Terry will also do his best to get your goat!

179

Gunnison Country Guide Service

G u n n i s o n ,   C o l o r a d o

Hunt big elk and mulies in some of Colorado's wildest country.

VITAL STATISTICS:

Game/Arm/Seasons:
ELK, DEER and BEAR:
Bow: Late Aug. through Sept.
Muzzleloader: Mid-Sept.
Centerfire: Mid-Oct. through mid-Nov.
Rates:
Unguided from $990/5 days
Guided bow or rifle from
$2,800/5 days
Accommodations:
WALL TENTS WITH HEATERS
MAXIMUM NUMBER OF HUNTERS: 6 OR 8
PER CAMP
Meals: Steak, chicken, spaghetti
Conference Groups: No
Guides: Included
Gratuity: $100
Preferred Payment:
Cash, check
Other Activities:
Fishing, hiking, bird watching,
summer pack trips, wildlife
photography
Getting There:
Fly to Gunnison and the lodge van
will meet you.

Contact:
John Nelson
Gunnison Country
Guide Service
Box 1443
Gunnison, CO 81230
970/641-2830

THE GUNNISON RIVER in north-central Colorado is one of the best trout streams in the U.S. The river originates in the highlands of the Gunnison National Forest, prime country for elk and, to lesser degree, mule deer. It's been John Nelson's favorite haunt for the 20 years that he's been guiding hunters.

Nelson offers guided hunts from his fully staffed base camp three miles from the end of an old jeep trail. With all the comforts that heated wall tents can provide, you and another hunter will share a guide in your quest for North America's second-largest member of the deer family.

For experienced clients who know about hunting in the rugged highlands, Nelson will set up drop camps complete with tents, stoves and other requisite gear. Bring your own sleeping bags and food. From there, you're on your own. For seven days or more, you have the run of the mountains. One of Nelson's four guides will check on you every few days to make sure things are going smoothly.

Guided or unguided, you'll hunt the slopes and draws in the mountains and high meadows of the national forest. This is public land, but other hunters generally don't make it this far into the backcountry. Archery in this part of the state begins in late August, with base camp farther up in the mountains because the elk have not started moving by then.

Muzzleloading, which comes in two weeks later, is usually conducted high up as well, unless the animals have begun to move. You'll ride out from base camp each morning, headed to areas where game has been sighted. Bugling brings the most success early in the season, while standing or stalking bring best results later on.

Typical elk taken here are 4-pointers or better, though big 6-pointers are always possible. Mule deer are normally three or four points (a side). Along with elk and deer, Nelson also runs hunts for bighorn sheep, mountain goats, black bear, antelope and lions.

Licenses for deer and elk are available at sporting goods, hardware and related stores up to midnight before opening day. The exception is the third week of the season, for which licenses are drawn in advance. You must apply for these in April. Nelson can handle all of the licensing for you if you book far enough in advance.

Hoza Guide and Outfitting

Norwood, Colorado

Tony Hoza can put you onto good elk or mule deer, but his specialty is mountain lions.

VITAL STATISTICS:

Game/Arm/Seasons:
ELK and DEER:
Bow: Sept.
Centerfire: Mid-Oct. through mid-Nov.
Muzzleloader: Mid-Sept.
MOUNTAIN LION:
Dec. through Jan.

Rates:
ELK and DEER:
Bow: $2,500/5 days
Centerfire: $2,750/5 days
MOUNTAIN LION
Bow, centerfire, muzzleloader:
$3,000

Accommodations:
LOG CABINS
MAXIMUM NUMBER OF HUNTERS: 5

Meals: Hearty family-style

Conference Groups: No

Guides: Included

Gratuity: $50

Preferred Payment:
Cash, check

Other Activities:
None

Getting There:
Fly to Montrose and you'll be met.

Contact:
Tony Hoza
Hoza Guide & Outfitting
Box 285
Norwood, CO 81423
970/327-4305

WITH A 6,000-ACRE RANCH right between the San Juan and Uncompaghre ranges, Tony Hoza sits in the catbird's seat. From the windows of his ranch house he can see elk moving on the mountains. He knows what they're doing because he's been there for more than a decade. The country surrounding the ranch is easy to moderately difficult, a network of plateaus and small canyons that range in elevation from 7,500 feet to 8,900 feet. Most of it is in scrub oak, pinion pine, juniper and aspen. Grassy parks dot the landscape.

The ranch supports 700 elk that are completely undisturbed for most of the year. To promote unpressured, natural hunting opportunities, Hoza takes only two bow and two blackpowder hunters a week during their respective seasons. The maximum number of hunters in camp is limited to five during the regular rifle season.

Some people might think that finding elk on a 6,000-acre ranch should be easy. Sometimes it is. When the summer has been relatively dry, for example, the elk tend to cluster in tight draws or canyons where there's enough water to produce food. Then, of course, they're hard to get to even though you know where they are. On the other side of the coin, a wet summer means lots of browse, which disperses the herd even as the rut begins. Tactics vary according to hunter skill, stamina, interest and, of course, on what the elk may be doing. But in the main you'll do a lot of sitting or spotting/stalking during rifle hunts. Bow and blackpowder hunters often shoot from stands or ground blinds. Success is about 80 percent for each.

While elk and mule deer hunting is Hoza's bread and butter, his passion is hunting mountain lions. He stresses "mature" when talking about these big cougars, for although the state allows hunting of cats as soon as they lose their spots and stop lactating, Hoza won't hunt them that young. He's looking for toms with skulls in the 14- to 15-inch range. A dozen of his cats have made Boone & Crockett. Naturally, he hunts with dogs—a handful of Plotts—and does it mainly on foot, with a little help from a pickup.

Hubbard Creek Outfitters & Pack Stations

H o t c h k i s s ,   C o l o r a d o

*This outfitter knows how
the other half lives.*

**VITAL
STATISTICS:**

Game/Arm/Seasons:
ELK, DEER:
Bow: Sept.
Centerfire: Mid-Oct. through mid-Nov.
Muzzleloader: Mid-Sept.
BEAR:
Centerfire: Sept.
Rates:
Call for rates
Accommodations:
RUSTIC BUNKHOUSE AND TENT CAMPS
NUMBER OF ROOMS: 2
MAXIMUM NUMBER OF HUNTERS: 8
Meals: Whatever the cook wants,
within reason
Conference Groups: No
Guides: Included
Gratuity: $50 to $100
Preferred Payment:
Cash, check
Other Activities:
Bird hunting, bird watching, fishing,
waterfowling, wildlife photography
Getting There:
Fly to Grand Junction and you'll
be met.

Contact:
Larry Allen
**Hubbard Creek Outfitters
& Pack Stations**
Box 25
Hotchkiss, CO 81419
970-872-3818
Web: ww.recwould.com

IF IT'S GOOD FOR LIVESTOCK, it's good for elk and deer. That's one facet of the philosophy of Larry Allen's Hubbard Creek operation. His 500-acre ranch is surrounded by forest service and Bureau of Land Management land about 60 miles east-southeast of Grand Junction. This is not excessively steep country, though when you get up on 10,304-foot Electric Mountain some of the slopes are fairly precipitous. It's country that elk stay in all year long, though snows will move them down a bit in winter.

Elk and deer inhabit pretty much the same terrain here, and their hunting seasons coincide. During the archery season in September, elk are bugling and they respond well to cow calls. That can continue into the first or even second week of rifle season in mid-October, but by then they've become smarter. They know that there's liable to be somebody with a gun waiting for them at the end of that plaintive call. You'll hunt from the main cabin on the ranch or from a tent camp, depending on where elk and deer are moving. Four-wheel-drives are used to get about on the ranch; from the tent camp you'll ride into the area chosen for the day's hunt. Then you're on foot. Hunting on the ranch generally picks up a little way into rifle season. Folks hunting public land push elk and deer onto the private property. This is Unit 521 and only 4x4 or better bulls are legal with over-the-counter non-resident licenses. An average bull is last year's spike that now carries a 5x5 rack. Archery success rates run about 40 percent and rifle is closer to 60 percent.

A fair number of mule deer also run these mountains, but hunting them can be tricky. Your best chance comes later in the season when snows have pushed them down into the sandstone and shale gulches below the ranch. Hunting the gulches is as rugged as anywhere in the West. You'll crab along the wall of one canyon glassing the other side for mulies. Seeing deer is the least of your worries. Getting into position for a reasonable shot is the challenge. Rather than climbing down to the streambed and fighting through thick stands of cedar and pinion pine, sometimes hunters will attempt a 400- or 500-yard shot across the canyon.

Larry is one of those low-key and solid outfitters who knows what it's like to save up $10,000 to buy a bighorn sheep hunt and to never get a shot. So he works hard to ensure, as best he can, that all of his hunters at least have an opportunity to harvest the trophy they seek.

K&K Outfitters

Early hunters get the trophy.

VITAL STATISTICS:

Game/Arm/Seasons:
ELK, DEER:
Bow: Late Aug. through late Sept.
Centerfire: Mid-Oct. through early Nov.
Muzzleloader: Mid-Sept. (draw only)
Rates:
$2,500/7 days fully guided
Accommodations:
TENT CAMPS
MAXIMUM NUMBER OF HUNTERS: 10
Meals: Family-style, meat and potatoes
Conference Groups: No
Guides: Included
Gratuity: $100 plus
Preferred Payment:
Cash, check
Other Activities:
Fishing, riding
Getting There:
Fly to Denver and rent a car, or pay for a shuttle.

Contact:
Marion Bricker
K&K Outfitters
Box 1002
Granby, CO 80446
907/887-2301
Fax: 970/726-0121

TRACING A STAGGERING LINE as it wanders from peak to peak, the Continental Divide bounds the north end of the Troublesome Creek Basin west of Willow Creek Pass. At 12,296 feet, Parkview Mountain is the highest peak in the area, and it gives you a clue to the lay of the land. Glaciation 10,000 years ago carved alpine basins and flattened their floors. Now, thin streams meander through these ancient, tiny plains and on them grow grasses and aspen. Mountainsides that face southeast are tufted with low brush and sage; those that face north are covered in heavy timber.

To be harvested in this region, elk must be at least a 4x4 and most hunters take bulls slightly larger. The owner of this outfit is Marion Bricker, and he's developed a style of hunting that produces the best opportunities for good bulls in the 126-square-mile area where he operates. From one of three tent camps, hunters ride out early and are posted along the fringe of a meadow where elk have been active. They'll wait for dawn to see if any elk are feeding. If not, Marion and his fellow guides will saddle up and slowly cruise the ridges above the meadows, pushing elk down to the hunters. During midday, hunters ride and spot, occasionally jumping elk, but mainly looking for sign and good places to sit and see what may come up the trail. Evenings find hunters watching meadow crossings.

Weather doesn't change things much up here. The herd is not really migratory. Snows in the second or third rifle season, mid- to late October, push elk down a bit and tend to bring them together as a herd. The very best time to hunt this country is during the third rifle season, normally the first week of November. Unless you survive the draw, you can't hunt buck mule deer in that final week. But the week before is nearly as good, and the mulies will be found in the noses of high aspen-covered ridges. A good buck is a 4x4 with a spread better than 24 inches. And, as you'd suspect, Marion's tent camps are warm and comfortable, and his cooks turn out plenty of pies as well as meals based on meat, potatoes, salads and fruit. Along with fully guided hunts, you'll also find semi-guided (one guide/cook/wrangler per camp) and drop-camp hunting. Bear hunting is also available during fall elk and deer hunts.

Lakeview Resort and Outfitters

L a k e   C i t y ,   C o l o r a d o

Hunt two states from one centrally located lodge.

VITAL STATISTICS:

Game/Arm/Seasons:
ELK and DEER:
Bow: Late Aug. through early Sept.
Centerfire: Mid through late Oct.
Muzzleloader: Mid-Sept.
MONTANA MULE DEER:
Centerfire: Mid through late Nov.
Rates:
ELK and DEER from $2,450/5 days
Montana MULE DEER $3,050/5 days
Accommodations:
WALL TENTS
MAXIMUM NUMBER OF HUNTERS: 6
Meals: Fresh meat, produce
Conference Groups: Yes
Guides: Included
Gratuity: 10%
Preferred Payment:
Cash, MasterCard, Visa, check
Other Activities:
Fishing, hiking, canoeing, boating,
bird watching, antiquing, biking, trail
rides, wildlife photography
Getting There:
Fly to Gunnison County and take a
shuttle van for $15 each way.

Contact:
Dan Murphy
Lakeview Resort & Outfitters
Box 1000
Lake City, CO 81235
970/944-2401
Fax: 970/944-2925
off-season: 970/941-5952

IT'S TOO BAD, REALLY. Lakeview has this wonderful lodge, snuggled in the Rockies on Lake San Cristobal. The lodge, its cabins and its cuisine are all first class. But do hunters get to stay there? Sure, but not while they're hunting. Then it's tents in the Uncompaghre, Grand Mesa, Powderhorn or Gunnison national forests of the rugged San Juan Mountains. That's where Lakeview's chief guide and owner Dan Murphy has been hunting Colorado's elk and mule deer for more than 20 years. Murphy also hunts 43,000 private acres in Montana for trophy mule deer during the rut.

Physical conditioning is the key to success for archery and blackpowder hunts in Colorado's San Juans. At this time—late August and September—elk herds are still very high, up in the thin timber just below the treeline. From a base camp at 9,000 to 10,000 feet, you'll climb another thousand or two before dawn just to get up to where the elk are. Then you'll begin to hunt. Glass, stalk, glass. You pull out your rangefinder and check the distance to a bull. Too far. Now it's more climbing, quietly, as dislodged rocks will clatter down the mountain and spook the herd. There's no horizontal land up here; just a bench or two that peters out in another wash of talus. The bulls, naturally, are on the other side. But sometimes they're down in the trees, where it's a bit easier to hunt. There's cover and, if it's early in the season, you can bugle in a bull.

Murphy's operation has a reputation for being first class. Each guide works with two hunters. You'll ride horseback into the base camp of wall tents and use the horses again to get closer to the game, if necessary. Bulls run better than 4x4 and, while most hunters have opportunities, about every other hunter brings a trophy off the mountains.

Murphy's Montana operation is similar, but the terrain is nowhere near as high or steep. Here, in the southeastern part of the state, elevations average an easy-breathing 2,300 feet. Still, you'll do a lot of spotting and stalking. Big 5-pointers are the rule, though some smaller ones are taken each year. The success ratio of this operation is near 90 percent.

Lamicq Guides and Outfitters

Grand Junction, Colorado

Hunt out of two ranches for trophy bulls, plus elk and deer.

VITAL STATISTICS:

Game/Arm/Seasons:
ELK, DEER, BEAR:
Bow: Late Aug. through Sept.
Centerfire: Mid-Oct. through mid-Nov.
Muzzleloader: Mid-Sept.

Rates:
Unguided from $400/5 days
Guided rifle from $2,900/5 days
Guided bow from $1,680/5 days

Accommodations:
LOG LODGE AND CABINS
NUMBER OF ROOMS 4
MAXIMUM NUMBER OF HUNTERS: 12

Meals: Meat and potatoes

Conference Groups: No

Guides: Included

Gratuity: 15%

Preferred Payment:
Cash

Other Activities:
Fishing, hiking, upland bird and
waterfowl hunting

Getting There:
Fly to Grand Junction and rent a car.

Contact:
John Lamicq Jr.
Lamicq Guides and Outfitters
635 19 1/2 Rd. SW
Grand Junction, CO 81503
970/243-1082

ROAN CREEK FLOWS THROUGH a series of canyons and flats northwest of Grand Junction, then tumbles down between two low mountain ranges anchored by 8,300-foot Kimball Mountain to the south. In the valley itself are more than 11,000 acres of Roan Creek and West Roan Creek ranches, all prime elk, deer and bear habitat. The ranches straddle natural migration paths for elk herds, and some excellent bulls—the ranch has about a 70 percent success rate on 6x6s—have been taken by rifle hunters during October and the first week of November. Outfitter John Lamicq, who's been guiding for 35 years in this area, specializes in archery hunts, though he takes rifle shooters as well. He's held Pope and Young records for mule deer and is a senior member of that organization.

Bow hunters get first shot at game on the ranch. Elk are in the rut in September, and their shrill whistles echo through the timber. Maddened by the notion that a rival wants the cows in his harem, a bull will abandon all caution to run off the challenger. The challenger in this case is your guide, using his call. At times bulls come charging as close as five yards from the hunter. Hard to miss at that range, if your nerves don't get you. Success rates come very close to 100 percent on these guided hunts; two out of three unguided hunters also get bulls.

Deer on these ranches also run large, with a typical trophy mulie carrying a 4x4 or 5x5 rack that may have a 35-inch spread. Field-dressed, the really big bucks here can tip the scales at more than 200 pounds. Most deer hunting here is done from tree stands, where the average shot is 20 yards. Hunters may also glass and stalk if they wish.

Unguided hunts—essentially rental of a cabin and permission to hunt the ranch—are available for about half the price of guided hunts. Normally a guide serves two or three hunters, but one-on-one hunts are available for an additional $600. For $500 per person, groups of six can rent a whole ranch for a week or so on Upper Roan Creek. Bring your own gear and grub. Otherwise, most hunters stay in cabins on the main ranch which, while not luxurious, are clean, comfortable and have running water and baths. Hunters can also enjoy good trout fishing, plus goose and pheasant hunting.

Little Grizzly Creek Ranch

W a l d e n ,   C o l o r a d o

For a most civilized hunt, look no further than this first class lodge.

VITAL STATISTICS:

Game/Arm/Seasons:
ELK:
Bow, centerfire, muzzleloader:
Mid-Oct. through early Nov.
Rates:
$6,000/5 days
Accommodations:
LOG LODGE
NUMBER OF ROOMS: 8, WITH PRIVATE BATH
MAXIMUM NUMBER OF HUNTERS: 8
Meals: Gourmet with vintage wines
Conference Groups: Yes
Guides: Included
Gratuity: $250
Preferred Payment:
Cash, check, credit cards
Other Activities:
Biking, bird watching, fishing, wildlife photography
Getting There:
Fly to Laramie, rent a car and drive to the lodge.

Contact:
Doug Sysel
Little Grizzly Creek Ranch
777 Co. Rd. #1
Walden, CO 80480
970/723-4209
off-season:
7113 N. Tatum
Paradise Valley, AZ 85253
602/952-9732
Fax: 602/840-7497
e-mail: lilgriz@paloverde.com
Web: www.little-grizzly-creek.com

W HO SAYS ELK HUNTING has to be a bust-your-buns business? Not Doug Sysel, impresario of Little Grizzly, a first-class ranch tucked behind the Rabbit Ear Range on the headwaters of the North Platte not far from Steamboat Springs. A step inside reveals plush black leather couches and chairs grouped before the massive stone hearth where a small fire chases October's chill. You meet the other hunters—a surgeon from Atlanta, a broker from Spokane, a couple of doctors from St. Louis and a Hall of Famer who pitched for the Cubs.

Doug shows you your room, the one in the loft at the top of the stairs and you work at stowing your gear until your nose pulls you toward dinner. First there are drinks and hors d'oeuvres. Then dinner opens with grilled asparagus with prosciutto and horseradish aioli. You move on to sweetbreads with pancetta ravioli with a sauce of wild mushrooms and Madeira. A salad of endive, smoked salmon and chive blossoms clean the palate, raising the curtains on oysters in scallop mousse and shredded potatoes. Sated yet? No? Good. There's rare tenderloin of beef with duck foie gras and fried leeks and turnips in a roasted shallot sauce. Dessert is a simple apricot baked in phyllo. All, of course, accompanied by appropriate vintages.

Over cigars and brandy, Doug lays out the plans for the morning hunt. On a big aerial photo, you can see the location of the stands from which you'll hunt. That's right. On this 1,000-private acres, Doug has erected shooting boxes over wallows and trail crossings regularly used by elk. No lung-searing climbs up bouldery ridges to get above elk here. Just a gentle walk over a hill to your stand. You're given the option of staying in your stand from dawn until noon, or still-hunting the cleared trail to the next stand where your guide will collect you when it's time for lunch. After lunch, the hearty head right back out. Wiser hunters catch a nap. Better to do so with your boots off in bed than to snooze in the shooting box. Most of Doug's hunters harvest good 5x5s, with many more than 320 Boone & Crockett. What's his trick? Easy. He allows no more than a handful of hunters, his acreage is private and he knows it like the back of his hand. There's only one thing strenuous about this hunt: hauling your well-fed bones out of bed in the wee hours before dawn.

Peters Hunting Service

Rangely, Colorado

Hunting elk from tree stands gives you the edge.

VITAL STATISTICS:

Game/Arm/Seasons:
MULE DEER, ELK:
Bow: Late Aug.-Sept.
Centerfire: Early Oct.-early Nov.
Muzzleloader: Mid-Sept.
Rates:
ELK, DEER $1,600/6 days (bow);
$1,900/5 days (rifle); $1,800/6 days
(muzzleloader)
Accommodations:
BUNKHOUSE AND TENTS
NUMBER OF ROOMS: 6
MAXIMUM NUMBER OF HUNTERS: 10
Meals: Family-style
Conference Groups: No
Guides: Included
Gratuity: Hunter's discretion
Preferred Payment:
Cash, check
Getting There:
Fly to Grand Junction and the lodge
van will meet you.

Contact:
Harley Peters
Peters Hunting Service
Box 268
Wrangle, CO 81648-0268
970/675-2574

ARCHERS HUNTING ELK with Harley Peters have an advantage. They hunt from tree stands, Eastern-style. If you're hunting bugling bulls from a ground blind, a typical shot will be between 25 and 50 yards. But Harley figured out that if you're hunting from a tree stand, elk will be less likely to see or scent you. Thus, they'll come closer, often 20 yards or less. Call it a competitive advantage. On 4x4s success runs around 50 percent, and hunting during the rut, which hits its stride in mid-September, is best. Stands overlook wallows and springs, game trails and ponds.

You'll still find bulls responding to calls in early October, and sometimes hunting from stands will pay off. But in the main, bulls are quieting down and concentrating on building up a reservoir of fat to get them through winter. Now's the time for walking and spotting and then moving into a position for a shot. The terrain on the western slopes of the Book Cliff Mountains is not as rugged as most. Southern slopes are covered with scrubby oak brush, pinions and cedar. Northern slopes are lodgepole pine, fir and spruce. Numerous logging roads weave through Harley's sections of Bureau of Land Management land. Needless to say, this real estate contains mule deer as well, but to hunt them you must pull a tag from the draw. Of the hunters that did, all harvested mule deer. Bear are also legal game during deer and elk seasons, and each year one or two hunters connect.

Harley operates a pair of camps. The first is a tent camp high up in the Book Cliffs and the second, a rustic frame bunkhouse, is on his ranch. Each accept a maximum of 10 hunters, though during big game season the number is more often six. And the food as you'd expect is basic, hearty and plentiful.

Phil's Bowhunting Adventures

M o n t r o s e ,   C o l o r a d o

Bowhunt for elk and pronghorn in the heart of the Rockies.

I F YOU'RE A BOWHUNTER, you've probably hunted deer, maybe bear. Now you're deep in the Rockies and there's a huge bull elk up ahead, blowing and snorting and tearing up brush. Your guide's playing "Hey, I'm the new hot stud and I want your harem," on his call, and the old boy who's ripping up the real estate wants you off his turf. Your blood's pumping. You've nocked your arrow. Suddenly, there he is — 25 yards away, broadside, looking curious and sort of foolish. You try to settle the sight behind and below his shoulder, but your heart's pounding and your mind's screaming "6x6". You finally let it fly. If you're lucky, very lucky...

"I don't know what it is," says Phil Phillips with a wry chuckle. "Hunters hear something that big crashing around out there and they get nervous." Buck fever, in Phillip's area of southeast Colorado near Trinidad, is not unusual. Surrounded by a pair of spreads that are in Colorado's Ranches for Wildlife program and abutting Vermejo Park at the New Mexican border, his 6,000 acres of undulating mountains is not difficult terrain. It's broken here and there by stands of pine and aspen and lots of open meadows. Typical bulls score in the 300 range. There are some that are bigger, but for an archer to pass up a heavy 5x5 is hard to do. Especially when you can smell its breath. Everyone gets a shot, but only 50 percent nail a trophy bull.

On the other hand, almost everyone has a successful hunt on the 40,000 acres of antelope habitat. In this country of rolling sage and grasslands near Maybell in northwest Colorado, Phillips's clients generally get their pronghorn in the first few of the hunt's seven days. From camouflaged stands at waterholes and crossings, bowhunters get chances at bucks known for thick—six inches at the base—if not long (a good one runs 13 inches plus) horns. Not only is the hunting hot, but so is the temperature. Because the property is enrolled in the Ranches for Wildlife program, the season here runs from July 10 to September 1. To manage sections of the ranch that are impossible for archers to hunt, Phillips books a few rifle hunters. Generally they fill their tag in an afternoon, then lounge around the ranch house and fish the nearby Little Snake River for smallmouth bass.

Pronghorn hunters stay in an old remodeled ranch house and feast on Mexican and American fare prepared by Leslie Phillips. The menu for elk hunters could not be any better, but it is more varied. They stay in a motel in Trinidad and dine at the town's restaurants.

Pikes Peak Outfitters

W o o d l a n d   P a r k ,   C o l o r a d o

Hunters have access to more than half a million acres with this outfit.

VITAL STATISTICS:

Game/Arm/Seasons:
ELK:
Bow: Late Aug. through Sept.
Muzzleloader: Mid-Sept.
Centerfire: Mid-Oct. through mid-Nov.
MULE DEER:
Bow: Mid-Nov. through mid-Dec.
Muzzleloader: Mid-Sept.

Rates:
Bow: ELK and DEER from
$2,500/7 days
Centerfire: ELK and DEER
$3,250/7 days
Muzzleloader: ELK and DEER
$3,000/7 days

Accommodations:
CABINS
NUMBER OF ROOMS: 6
MAXIMUM NUMBER OF HUNTERS: 16

Meals: Grilled steak, turkey

Conference Groups: Yes

Guides: Included

Gratuity: $50 to $100

Preferred Payment:
Cash, Discover, MasterCard, Visa, check

Other Activities:
Fishing, hiking, bird hunting, waterfowling, bird watching, wildlife photography

Getting There:
Fly to Colorado Springs and take the van to the lodge.

Contact:
Gary R. Jordan
Pikes Peak Outfitters
Box 9053
Woodland Park, CO 80866
800/748-2885
Fax: 719/686-0463
Web: www.pikespeakhunt.com

SOME OUTFITTERS have operations that are small and personal. Others can be huge. But Gary Jordan of Pikes Peak manages to be both huge and personal at the same time. First the huge part. Pikes Peak Outfitters hunt half a million acres of restricted access and private land. Diligence in securing good land pays off. Elk generally score 275 points, and mule deer run around 160. Combo hunts for elk and mule deer are held on the west and south flanks of Pikes Peak. Aspens and grassy meadows flow over the lower slopes that merge into dark timber as elevations close in on 10,000 feet. The weather, vagaries of elk herds, and whether you're using bow, muzzleloader or rifle will determine your hunting strategies. If elk are in the rut, your guide may employ bugling or cow calling. Later in the season, you'll do more still-hunting, spotting and stalking, and hunting from stands.

Trophy mule deer come from private ranches that Jordan leases in the eastern part of the state. Here, stands of cottonwood line the river bottoms and rolling prairies are broken by tight canyons thick with cedar and pinion pine. During the early season, in the first week of October, you'll ambush bucks as they move to and from feeding areas. Later, when bucks are in rut, you'll do more calling and stalking. Whether on the slopes of the mountains or on the plains, typical hunts join two hunters with one guide, although one-on-one hunts can be arranged.

When it comes to big game hunting, Colorado is, in effect, two states. West of Interstate 25, in the mountains, mule deer and elk tags can be bought over the counter at many sporting goods and other stores. Hunters still have to draw for prime units, particularly in the mid-September muzzleloading season and the late-October hunt for mulies. (In 1999, all deer licenses will be limited to those drawn.) However, east of the I-25, it's generally necessary to apply for a license. Applications must be filed by April 7 of the year in which you plan to hunt.

At Pikes Peak, hunters stay in snug cabins with shared baths. Meals are better than average and then some—eggs Benedict for breakfast and grilled steak for dinner. Special diets—heart healthy, vegetarian, salt/MSG-free—can be arranged.

Purcell Brothers Outfitting

P u e b l o ,   C o l o r a d o

In the business for more than 50 years, the Purcells can put you onto elk, deer, lions, bear, sheep, goats and elk.

VITAL STATISTICS:

Game/Arm/Seasons:
ANTELOPE:
Bow, centerfire, muzzleloader: Late Aug.
BEAR, DEER, ELK:
Bow: Aug. through Sept.
Centerfire: Mid-Oct. through mid-Nov.
Muzzleloader: Mid-Sept.
MOUNTAIN LION:
Bow, centerfire, muzzleloader: Mid-Nov. through March
SHEEP and GOATS:
Bow: Mid-Aug. through early Sept.
Centerfire, muzzleloader: Early Sept. through early Oct.

Rates:
ANTELOPE from $695/3 days
BEAR from $1,395/5 days
BIGHORN SHEEP $3,500/7 days
ELK and DEER from $1,350/5 days
MOUNTAIN GOATS from $2,500/7 days
MOUNTAIN LION $2,000/5 days
WHITETAILS from $1,800/5 days
ANTELOPE from $1,950/7 days

Accommodations:
VARIES BY SPECIES
MAXIMUM NUMBER OF HUNTERS: 12

Meals: Steak, chicken, vegetables

Conference Groups: No

Guides: Included

Gratuity: $100

Preferred Payment:
Cash

Other Activities:
Hiking, wildlife photography

Getting There:
Fly to Grand Junction (or other airport) and the lodge van will meet you.

Contact:
Dale Purcell
Purcell Brothers Outfitting
44 Sovereign Circle
Pueblo, CO 81005
719/561-1878

WANT TO HUNT MOOSE in Colorado? Well, you'll have to do it with someone other than Dale and Duane Purcell. They don't hunt moose, but this family operation, started by their granddad in 1942, runs guided hunts for everything else—elk, mule deer, bighorn sheep, mountain goats, mountain lions and black bears. Here's the rundown:

ANTELOPE: Hunted in the high plains in pinion-hill country southeast of Pueblo on a 36,000-acre ranch, antelope with 14- to 16-inch horns tempt hunters with shots from 150 to 400 yards. You need to be drawn for this hunt. But not for the 54,000-acre ranch among the broken lava buttes and canyons in northern New Mexico. Hunter success rate nears 100 percent at both.

BIGHORN SHEEP: Vehicular access is very poor in the Collegiate Peaks and Sangre De Cristo areas, and terrain is as rocky as it is vertical. Hunters who survive the draw—it generally takes four years to get a permit, but the success rate is around 100 percent—sleep in Eureka tents at about 11,000 feet and may hunt as high as 14,000.

BLACK BEAR: Since Colorado stopped the hunting of bears with bait and dogs, there's been little hunter interest in them. However, up in game management units 61 and 62 on the Uncompaghre Plateau, black bears are prime and in very good supply. They range between 250 and 400 pounds, though one weighing 626 pounds was taken recently.

ELK and MULE DEER: Same area as for black bear, units 61 and 62 generate their share of trophy bulls and bucks. Only 100 or so tags are sold each year for unit 61 (5 preference points are needed unless you spring for an extra $500 to purchase landowner points from Dale, then you'll need only two). Is it worth it? Hunts in unit 61 have been 100 percent successful on bulls in the 5-point class. The other area, Unit 62, has no restrictions. Success rate on Dale's spread in Unit 62 varies from 60 to 80 percent. You'll hunt out of the base camp (cabins with hot showers) and dine on whatever the cook dreams up.

WHITETAILS: The 36,000-acre eastern plains ranch, which is 22 miles east of Springfield, yields nice bucks in the 10-point and better class. But you need to be drawn (2 preference points). Success rate is 100 percent.

MOUNTAIN LION: With skulls measuring 14 to 15 inches, these are nice cougars. A pack of five hounds will run the cat and bring it to bay. Your job is to keep up with the dogs and dispatch the cat. But relax, you're on horseback. Canyon City provides accommodations and a choice of restaurants.

Quaking Aspen Outfitters Inc.

Gunnison, Colorado

Dave Mapes' outfit concentrates on the spiritual side of elk hunting.

VITAL STATISTICS:

Game/Arm/Seasons:
MULE DEER, ELK, BIGHORN SHEEP:
Bow: Sept.
Centerfire: Early Oct. through mid-Nov.
Muzzleloader: Mid through late Sept.
BIGHORN SHEEP:
Bow, centerfire: Early Sept. through early Oct.
Rates: $2,700/7 days
Accommodations:
TENT CAMPS
MAXIMUM NUMBER OF HUNTERS: 8
Meals: Steaks, roasts (lamb, beef, pork), soup, pasta
Conference Groups: No
Guides: Included
Gratuity: 10 to 15%
Preferred Payment:
Cash, check
Other Activities:
Fishing, riding
Getting There:
Fly to Gunnison and a representative of the outfitter will pick you up.

Contact:
Dave Mapes
Quaking Aspen Outfitters Inc.
Box 485
Gunnison, CO 81230
970/641-0529
Web: www.youngminds.com\qa

THE HUT, framed of limber willow poles, is covered with woolen blankets. Inside, in the pitch dark, sit a handful of hunters. Water from a ladle is splashed onto hot rocks; in a flash, steam fills the hut. "May the hunt go well," prays one hunter. "May an elk that is ready come before me. May his death be quick and painless, so he may pass to his next place." There is singing. A pipe is passed. More water is dashed on the rocks, more steam. Sweat oozes from your pores.

Before their hunts, Native Americans would pray to the spirits. To them, and to a small but growing number of hunters, the taking of game was not that at all. They believe in the circle of life that everything is a point on the circle of life. That, when it is time, everything gives way to another. The cougar eats the calf; man eats the elk; the grasses and shrubs that nourish the elk grow from the body of man. When one of his hunters takes an elk, Dave Mapes of Quaking Aspen Outfitters will offer a prayer for the elk, thanking him for his life and wishing him speed and safe progress for his journey on.

There is no mumbo-jumbo in this. Mapes and others believe that the spiritual world controls the cycle of things. The more closely you connect with the cycle, the more harmonious your life and the better your chances of achieving your goals. If you want, he'll take you into camp a day early so that you can take part in a sweat. He charges nothing extra for the ceremony, which he calls a "sacred hunt."

Hunting units 55 and 67 north and south, respectively, of the Gunnison National Forest in the LaGarita Wilderness, Mapes is more successful than many other outfitters who hunt public land. Most hunters have shots at elk of at least four points, and about 50 percent connect. His belief in spirituality carries with it an implicit fatalism: an animal that was missed by a rifle hunter while standing broadside at 50 yards was simply not ready to be taken that day. You'll ride into his camps on horseback. In his northern area, he runs a pair of tent camps for six to eight hunters each. To the south, a pair of four-person camps up near the Continental Divide are strictly for bow and muzzleloader hunts available only by draw. In addition to elk, Mapes hunts mule deer and bighorn sheep. Two hunters are served by a single guide, though for $100 per day, you can hire a private guide.

[R O C K Y   M O U N T A I N S]

Red Feather Guides & Outfitters

W a l d e n ,   C o l o r a d o

One of the state's top moose outfits also hunts elk and deer.

VITAL STATISTICS:

Game/Arm/Seasons:
ELK, DEER, MOOSE
Bow: Late Aug. through late Sept.
Muzzleloader: Mid-Sept.
Centerfire: Mid-Oct. through early Nov.
Rates:
Any species: $2,300/7 day
Accommodations:
ARCHERY: TENTS; RIFLE: HEATED CABINS
MAXIMUM NUMBER OF HUNTERS: 6
Meals: Hunter's choice (within reason)
Conference Groups: No
Guides: Included
Gratuity: $100 to $200
Preferred Payment:
Cash, MasterCard, Visa, check
Other Activities:
Fishing
Getting There:
Fly to Laramie or Denver, rent a car and drive to the lodge.

Contact:
Arnie Schlottman
Red Feather Guides
& Outfitters
Box 16
Walden, CO 80480
970/723-4204
off-season:
Box 935
Gypsum, CO 81637
970/524-5054

IN NORTH-CENTRAL COLORADO above Walden the snows come early and chase not only the elk, but also hunters, from the forests. It's good country, but different from elsewhere in the state. The land is not steep like the mountains to the south. It climbs from about 8,200 feet to the timberline at 10,000 feet. There's more heavy timber, dense stands of lodgepole pine that have been harvested only by nature. You won't find large, grassy parks here, but there are scores of small glades, and those are where the elk hang out.

Arnie Schlottman has been guiding hunters in this country for the past 15 years or so. He specializes in archery and early-season hunts. By the time the snows come at the end of October, he's out of there. "The elk are largely gone then, migrated out. I don't want to take a guy's money just for a walk in the woods," says Schlottman. That's admirable, but Schlottman's motives aren't totally altruistic. He's one of the few outfitters that offers good moose hunts.

First the elk. From his wall-tent base camp, Schlottman hunts up to six clients (the camp will serve a group of eight) with one guide for every two hunters. Generally, hunters will be riding well before daylight into areas where elk are likely to be found. Once off the horses, bulls are located by bugling and the stalk begins. During the day you'll work your way back to camp. During archery and muzzleloading seasons, everyone gets shots that are within their range. About one in three hunters bags a bull. For deer, operations shift to the Never Summer Wilderness Area along the Continental Divide north of Lake John in the North Park area. Mule deer are typically 4x4s in the mid-20s.

Moose hunting is centered on Gould, 18 miles south of Walden. This was one of the areas where moose were reintroduced to Colorado in the early 1980s. An average moose will carry a 44-inch rack. Early in the season they're found in the willows along river bottoms; later, as hunting pressure mounts, they move up into the timber. This is one popular area for moose, and getting a license—in 1997 there were 3,800 applicants for 112 tags—is just the luck of the draw.

Moose and deer hunters have it easy, at least in one regard. They're accommodated at Red Feather's main lodge. That means electrically heated cabins, hot showers, sauna, the works. And then there's the menu, which you get it in advance and cross off any items that don't whet your appetite and add any that do. Now how's that for service?

Ripple Creek Lodge

M e e k e r ,   C o l o r a d o

Elk filter in and out of high parks
and timber on steep slopes.

VITAL STATISTICS:

Game/Arm/Seasons:
ELK, DEER:
Bow: Late Aug. through late Sept.
Centerfire: Mid-Oct. through early Nov.
Muzzleloader: Mid-Sept.

Rates:
Lodge from $1,995/5 days;
camp $990/5 days

Accommodations:
LOG CABINS OR TENT CAMP
NUMBER OF ROOMS: 8
MAXIMUM NUMBER OF HUNTERS: 20

Meals: Barbecues, chicken,
family-style

Conference Groups: Yes

Guides: Included

Gratuity: Hunter's discretion

Preferred Payment:
Cash, Discover, Visa, check

Other Activities:
Bird hunting, bird watching, fishing,
wildlife photography

Getting There:
Fly to Hayden, rent a car and drive to
the lodge, or hire the lodge van at
$150 round-trip.

Contact:
Ken Jett
Ripple Creek Lodge
39020 County Rd. 8
Meeker, CO 81641
970/878-4725;
off-season:
3495 S. Pierce St.
Lakewood, CO 80227
202/989-4950

FORTY MILES EAST of Meeker lies the vast Flat Tops Wilderness of the White River National Forest. A broad highlands with elevations between 9,000 and 12,000 feet, the Flat Tops are dominated by heavy stands of dark timber broken by a maze of park-like meadows. Deep valleys cut by tributaries of the White River and broadened by glaciation are choked with blowdowns. These valleys offer some of the most challenging hunting in Colorado, and together with the meadows and mountains, hold one of the state's larger herds of elk.

Ripple Creek Lodge, comprised of eight log cabins each complete with kitchens and bathrooms, sits on the edge of the wilderness. Hunters either work out of the lodge itself, taking full advantage of hot meals, horses and one guide for every two hunters, or a permanent drop camp set up on Bear Creek, the next major drainage to the southeast. There hunters avail themselves of all the comforts of a fully-furnished tent camp, including food, but sans horses, cook or guide. Maps and practical advice are provided, then you're on your own. Unlike some outfitters with iron-clad schedules, it's possible to book into the lodge or the drop camp for periods of five, nine or 12 days. And at the camp on Bear Creek, hunters who book for 12 days see a considerable savings in the price per day, as the rate drops from roughly $200 per day to $125. They also have an increased opportunity to harvest a very good elk.

Why? Most week-long hunts are too short, unless you're hunting with an experienced guide. The guide knows, or should know, the landscape and where game is likely to be found. Drop-camp hunters have to learn the real estate and find the game themselves, all in less than a week. If you can stretch your stay, you'll spend the first few days learning the lay of the land and the remainder of your time doing what you came for: hunting. Bulls of 4x4 or better are the rule here; mule deer must be at least a spike unless the luck of the draw is with you. Hunter success on elk runs about 50 percent.

Rocky Top Outfitters

D o l o r e s ,   C o l o r a d o

High success on elk and deer make this outfit worth a look.

VITAL STATISTICS:

Game/Arm/Seasons:
ELK:
Bow: Sept.
Centerfire: Late Sept. through Oct.
WHITE-TAILED DEER:
Bow: Nov.
Centerfire: Nov. through Dec.
MOUNTAIN LION:
Bow, centerfire: Jan. through Feb.
TURKEY:
Bow, shotgun: April through May
Rates:
ELK from $4,250/7 days
DEER from $1,950/5 days
LION $2,950/7 days
Accommodations:
FRAME RANCH OR CABINS
NUMBER OF ROOMS: VARIES WITH LOCATION
MAXIMUM NUMBER OF HUNTERS: 10
Meals: First night is steak night
Conference Groups: Yes
Guides: Included
Gratuity: $100 to $400
Preferred Payment:
Cash, MasterCard, Visa, check
Other Activities:
Bird hunting, fishing
Getting There:
Fly to Alamosa or Cortez, Colorado, or to San Angelo, Texas, and you'll be met.

Contact:
Colorado Buck
Rocky Top Outfitters
Box 384
Dolores, CO 81323
970/882-2106
Fax: 970/882-2106

JUST NORTH of the famed Vermejo Ranch in New Mexico is a another huge spread of 80,000 acres that includes 14,000-foot Culebra Peak, the highest privately owned mountain in the world. Culebra and its siblings, Vermejo, Red and Purgatoire, form the backbone of the Sangre de Cristo Mountains, known as much in these parts for their timbered ruggedness as for high meadows and sagebrush flats. Some of the ranch is being logged and regenerating forest provides good browse for elk as well as mule deer. Logging roads provide easy access to the high country. Normally, hunters and guides are driven in 4WDs to the top of the ridges in the day's hunting area. When you hunt elk here, you'll have your own guide. He'll match the hunt to your abilities and preferences. Early in the season he'll call in bulls; later you'll spot and stalk. A normal bull runs in the 6x6 class and typically scores 300 or better. Hunter success rates are quite high for a fair-chase outfit, averaging better than 85 percent. Hunters stay in modern modular homes on the ranch. Rocky Top also offers a less expensive elk hunt on other private ranches in southern Colorado.

For deer, operations shift to two areas in Texas. In the Possum King area near the Rio Grande, Rocky Top hunts 28,000 acres of private ranch land. This is sage and big-canyon country with patches of live oaks, river bottoms and mesquite. Hunting is either from stands or safari-style from high-rack trucks. You'll ride on a comfortable bench mounted above the cab, glassing the plain for whitetails. When you spot one, you'll dismount and plan your stalk. Or, if the spirit moves, you can walk and try to rattle up a deer. No matter how you do it, the odds are better than 85 percent that you'll take a nice buck. The average for this ranch is about 10 points scoring 140 or so. You'll feel right at home when you return each night to the ranch house that Rocky Top uses as a lodge. Rocky Top provides hunts for smaller whitetails on a 30,000-acre ranch near San Angelo. An abundance of deer makes this a good choice for novice hunters or parents with children. With a limit of one buck and two does, everyone generally leaves with venison. And the new lodge with cabins for as many as 18 hunters is proving popular with corporate clients.

When elk and deer seasons are over, Rocky Top focuses on mountain lion, running hunts on the Ute Mountain Indian Reservation. Toms typically weigh 150 pounds or more and you'll hunt them over a pack of three or four hounds. Come spring, you'll hunt toms again; this time, long-bearded gobblers.

Samuelson Outfitters

F r a s e r ,   C o l o r a d o

Whether you do it yourself or hunt with a guide, you've got an excellent chance for a bull in the Arapaho Forest.

VITAL STATISTICS:

Game/Arm/Seasons:
ELK and DEER:
Bow: Sept.
Muzzleloader: Mid-Sept.
Centerfire: Mid-Oct. through Nov.
Rates:
ELK and DEER from $2,200/5 days
Accommodations:
WALL TENTS
MAXIMUM NUMBER OF HUNTERS: 8
Meals: Elk steaks, Mexican and Italian dishes
Conference Groups: No
Guides: Included
Gratuity: 10%
Preferred Payment:
Cash
Other Activities:
Fishing
Getting There:
Fly to Denver, rent a car and drive to Granby.

Contact:
Richard Samuelson
Samuelson Outfitters
Box 686
Fraser, CO 80442
970/726-8221

HUNTING IN THE 80,000 ACRES of Troublesome Basin in the Arapaho National Forest east of Kremmling is not as bad as it sounds. With pine and spruce on the northern slopes and aspen on the southern faces, you'll find few really steep spots and very little that's not accessible by horse. And an abundance of creek bottoms with their willows along the water and sage and grass on the benches provide ample feed. Habitat keeps these elk—a good bull is a 5x5—here most of the year. During mild winters, they don't migrate. And when winters are tough, they only move 10 to 15 miles.

During archery and muzzleloading seasons (you have to be drawn for the latter) calling does the trick. Your guide will set you in a place where bulls have been feeding. Then the talking begins. Some calling is used in the first days of rifle season, but after that Dick Samuelson, head of this outfit, relies heavily on drives. Hunters sit over crossings, low saddles or wallows, and then Samuelson and his guides move elk to them. The advantage, he explains, is that hunters are off their horses and ready for a shot. In other cases, clients will ride to the top of the ridge, about three hours from base camp, and then hunt back down afoot while the wrangler brings the horses. Hunter success runs about 65 percent.

High on the upper reaches of East Troublesome Creek, base camp is set in an aspen glade. Centered on the large 20x24-foot cooking and dining tent, and scattered under the trees are a handful of sleeping tents complete with woodstoves and with rugs on the floor. The menu is varied: chicken burritos and other Mexican fare along with elk steaks and spaghetti. For those who prefer to do it themselves, drop camps are also available. And if you've got your own gear, Samuelson will pack your entire outfit in wherever you can go.

San Juan Outfitting

D u r a n g o ,   C o l o r a d o

Southwest Colorado is the place to go for big bulls.

VITAL STATISTICS:

Game/Arm/Seasons:
ELK and DEER:
Bow: Sept.
Muzzleloader: Mid-Sept.
Centerfire: Mid-Oct. through mid-Nov.

Rates:
ELK and DEER:
Archery from $3,100/7 days
Muzzleloader $3,500/9 days
Centerfire from $2,800/7 days
Semi-guided from $2,150/7 days
Drop camps $985/7 days

Accommodations:
TENTS
MAXIMUM NUMBER OF HUNTERS: 6 TO 8

Meals:
Fresh meats, vegetables, homemade desserts

Conference Groups: No

Guides: Included

Gratuity: $100

Preferred Payment:
Cash, MasterCard, Visa, check

Other Activities:
Fishing, hiking, pack trips, wildlife photography

Getting There:
Fly to Durango and spend the night before the hunt in a motel.

Contact:
Tom Van Soelen
San Juan Outfitting
186 CR 228
Durango. CO 81301
970/259-6259
Fax: 970/259-2652
e-mail: sjo@frontier.net
Web: subee.com/sjo/sjohome.html

WANT TO HEAR A STORY that ain't no bull? Tom Van Soelen had hiked his hunter up into a draw where a bull had been bugling. The hunter, a guy with plenty of whitetail experience and who moved quietly, like a wraith, in the woods, was comfortably on his stand. Van Soelen bugled, the elk whistled and grunted and thrashed the brush. He was coming. He stepped through the brush, magnificent as only a rutting 6-point bull can be. The hunter gasped aloud. Tom moaned inwardly. Spooked by the hunter's reaction, the bull made for Utah in a single bound. "We've shot over 'em and under 'em and pulled nocks off arrows," says Van Soelen, laughing. That's the way it is. The only thing worse than buck fever is bull fever.

A 15-mile pack in carries Van Soelen's archers and muzzleloaders into the Weminuche Wilderness northeast of Durango. Base camp is in the Los Pinos drainage, terrain filled with classic, grassy bowls and rounded valleys. The camp is a bit above 10,000 feet and timberline is around 11,500. Rifle hunters hunt just out of the wilderness in the Pieda River area of the San Juans.

At first the country appears terribly steep, but after a sharp descent the trail levels off into a broad area of spruce and fir with a few parks ranging from a quarter acre to a recovering 800-acre burn. The biggest bull out of this camp scored 320 and it was taken near camp. Spotting and stalking on foot is the ticket here. During the first season, there's still a chance that bugling will produce. In the second season cow-calling can pay off. In the third season it's all stalking and still-hunting unless high snows have elk on the move. Most hunters have reasonable shots at legal elk. About 50 percent connect.

Van Soelen offers his clients three options, with a variation on the first. Guided hunts are the norm out of this tent camp, where dinners feature the likes of stuffed pork chops and homemade apple pie. Most times two hunters share a guide, but some opt for one-on-one hunts. You can still enjoy all the goodies of the full-service camp but without a guide, a savings of $650 for a week-long hunt. And Van Soelen has four drop camps where you're on your own.

Seven Lakes Lodge

Meeker, Colorado

Where the elk hunting is just as good as the roast rack of lamb with tapenade crust.

VITAL STATISTICS:

Game/Arm/Seasons:
ELK
Centerfire: Early Oct. through early Nov.

Rates:
ELK $5,500/6 days

Accommodations:
LOVELY MODERN LOG LODGE
NUMBER OF ROOMS: 8, PLUS 3 IN THE CABIN
MAXIMUM NUMBER OF HUNTERS: 10

Meals: Exquisite cuisine with wines to match

Conference Groups: Yes

Guides: Included

Gratuity: 15 to 20%

Preferred Payment:
Cash, check, credit card

Other Activities:
Hiking, fishing, riding, wildlife photography

Getting There:
Fly to Grand Junction and the lodge vehicle will pick you up.

Contact:
Steve Herter
Seven Lakes Lodge
738 County Road 59
Meeker, CO 81641
970/878-3249
Fax: 970/878-3635
off-season:
953 S. Frontage Road #106
Vail, CO 81675
970/878-4772
Fax: 970/476-5740
e-mail: 7lakes@cmn.net
Web: www.sevenlakeslodge.com

THE DRIVE into Seven Lakes Lodge is not overly inspiring unless you're thinking of the Flat Tops Wilderness, 235,035 acres of rugged volcanic cliffs, plunging valleys and a high subalpine plateau spread with strands of spruce and fir. Scores of streams feed the North Fork of the White River, draining countless lakes and ponds, some of which have yet to be named. More than 20,000 elk summer on the plateau. September's first chill winds herald the pre-rut period and by the end of the month the bulls are whistling hard, gathering harems. By the mid-October, the rut is in full swing. There is no better time to hunt this glorious country than the second week of October.

Under the tutelage of Steve Herter, manager of the lodge and one of the most respected guides in the West, you and your guide will map out a strategy that will have you both out on a ridge well before dawn. You'll listen, maybe call, listen some more and move down, then up, through heavy blowdown and boulders wedged by frosts from the cliffs above. You'll seek a new venue, ever closer to the action. The key is to be ready when it comes. While the terrain is steep on the flanks of the plateau, the cap is a gentle park-like area where walking is easy. Steve matches the physical abilities of hunters to variations in the countryside. As a result, most who hunt here fill their tags with 5x5 or bigger bulls.

The terrain and hunting are perfect complements to the lodge. Owner Henry Kravis has invested more than $6 million in renovating the one-time den for bootleggers. Mark Hampton's interior design is at once Western, but not of the trite cowboy school. Private guest rooms offer views of the White River valley and trout lakes surrounding the lodge. The menu is continental with a regional flare; dinner might open, say, with sweet corncakes layered with hickory-smoked trout, crème fraiche and roasted corn sauce. The wine cellar matches the meals. If time permits during your stay, have a go at the sporting clays course that also overlooks the valley, or play with lunker rainbows in the ponds. This is one place worth coming back to again and again and again.

[R O C K Y   M O U N T A I N S]

Rudy Steele Guides & Outfitters

Glenwood Springs, Colorado

A 13,000-acre ranch is your base camp for elk and deer. But Steele will guide you to antelope, as well.

VITAL STATISTICS:

Game/Arm/Seasons:
ANTELOPE:
Bow, centerfire, muzzleloader: Sept.
ELK and DEER:
Bow: Late Aug. through Sept.
Muzzleloader: Mid-Sept.
Centerfire: Mid-Oct. through mid-Nov.
Rates:
ELK and DEER from $3,250/5 days
ANTELOPE from $1,950/7 days
Accommodations:
HEATED TRAILERS
NUMBER OF ROOMS: 2
MAXIMUM NUMBER OF HUNTERS: 6
Meals: Hearty stews and roasts
Conference Groups: No
Guides: Included
Gratuity: $100
Preferred Payment:
Cash, check
Other Activities:
Fishing, bird hunting, wildlife photography
Getting There:
Fly to Grand Junction and the lodge van will meet you ($25 round-trip).

Contact:
Rudy Steele
Rudy Steele Guides
& Outfitters
Box 2503
Glenwood Springs, CO 81602
970/945-8100
Fax: 970/945-4949
e-mail: rsteele@sopris.net

A HIGH, ROLLING PLATEAU in the Book Cliff Mountains west of Rifle provides hunters, particularly those for whom a lot of walking is problematic, a good and easy place to hunt elk. Good, easy elk hunting is usually an oxymoron, but in this case you can have your cake and eat it too. The rifle hunter success rate runs in the 80-percent range on bulls and mule deer bucks of four points or better. For archers and muzzleloaders, the rate is higher.

Steele only takes about 18 rifle hunters per year, and that's one of the reasons why his hunter success rate is reasonably good. Only six hunters are permitted in camp during any period, unless a slightly larger group books the entire camp. Two hunters share a single guide. One-on-one hunts are generally not available.

Covering about 13,000 acres of sage and aspen, Steele's ranch is split by another parcel of 10,000 acres on which he holds exclusive rights. All of it is between 8,500 and 9,500 feet in elevation. You don't have to ride a horse here, because four-wheel-drives ferry hunters out to areas where bulls have been seen. From there you'll hunt on foot. In archery and muzzleloading seasons, calling is used to bring bulls into range. That may work in the first few days of rifle season, but generally spotting and stalking is the name of the game.

And there's no arduous day-long pack trip to get into the camp. You'll arrive by pickup. Not only does that make it easier for you, but also for the camp cook, who turns out hearty stews and succulent roasts from provisions too perishable and heavy for horsepacking. Hunters stay in remodeled office trailers and eat in a frame lodge equipped with hot showers.

Along with his guided deer and elk operation, Steele also runs drop camps where groups of four or six hunters can do their own thing. And if there isn't an antelope on your wall and you want one, Steele has a private ranch near Craig.

Toneda Outfitters

M o f f a t ,   C o l o r a d o

Mixed meadows, parks and peaks promise big elk.

VITAL STATISTICS:

Game/Arm/Seasons:
ELK, DEER:
Bow: Late Aug. through late Sept.
Centerfire: Mid-Oct. through early Nov.
BIGHORN SHEEP:
Bow, centerfire: Early Aug. through early Oct.
MOUNTAIN LION:
Bow, centerfire: Mid-Nov. through March
Rates:
ELK, DEER from $1,525/ 7 days (bow); $1,925/7 days (centerfire)
SHEEP $3,500/10 days
MOUNTAIN LION $2,300/10 days
Accommodations:
TENT CAMPS
MAXIMUM NUMBER OF HUNTERS: 6
Meals: Family cooking
Conference Groups: No
Guides: Included
Gratuity: Hunter's discretion
Preferred Payment:
Cash, check
Other Activities:
Bird watching, fishing, wildlife photography
Getting There:
Fly to Alamosa and Ed will meet you.

Contact:
Ed Wiseman
Toneda Outfitters
Box 336
Moffat, CO 81143
719/256-4866

ITH PANNIERS cinched tightly, the first string of three pack mules lopes dutifully behind Toneda's honcho, Ed Wiseman. Then comes a wrangler leading two more. You and your five hunting buddies and three guides (one for every two hunters) are next in line. In all, it's quite a parade. By now, an hour and a half into the ride, you're used to the rolling gait of your big bay mare. She's going to be your horse for the next few days, and you're glad. She's as docile, and the way she picked her way up the first rocky ravine told you that she's sure-footed, as well. This is good, because you're going to swing into the worn saddle every morning at 4:30 and ride her farther up into the San Juans for elk.

Ed's been guiding in this area for 35 years and he knows the countryside like the back of his hand. Your guides have, on average, worked for him for half-a-dozen years, and before the season opened they scouted the country thoroughly. The main base camp sits in the tall pines that fringe a meadow where elk have been shot. But most are found higher up, where you'll ride early each morning. The terrain is irregular. Steep slopes break and give way to benches crowned with clumps of aspen. These little plateaus, in turn, ascend again, turning into meadows that seem almost vertical before rounding into heavy timber. Above the timber is rocky talus. The camp and the areas you'll hunt are so remote that the odds of seeing hunters other than your party are infinitesimal. During the seven-day archery hunts from late August until the end of September, you'll challenge bulls with bugles or woo them with cow calls. The calls also work in the first of the two over-the-counter rifle seasons. Later, spotting and stalking is the order of the day. Bulls run in the 4x4 range and up. If a mule deer is high on your agenda, you may find yourself hunting out of one of Ed's camps in the Sangre de Cristo Mountains. The setup and terrain are similar, but the population of mule deer, particularly higher up, is greater. Bucks are generally 4x4s, as well.

For more than 20 years, Ed has been an official Pope and Young measurer, and he's become a specialist in hunting elk and mule deer with bows. Along with elk and mulies, Ed guides hunters for bighorn sheep in the mountains above the San Luis Valley and for mountain lions in the San Juans.

[R O C K Y   M O U N T A I N S]

Triple O Outfitters

H a m i l t o n ,   C o l o r a d o

Hike or ride from spike or permanent camps into prime elk terrain.

VITAL STATISTICS:

Game/Arm/Seasons:
ELK, DEER:
Bow: Late Aug. through late Sept.
Muzzleloader: Mid-Sept. through Sept.
Centerfire: Mid-Oct. through early Nov.
Rates: From $2,500/5 days
Accommodations:
LOG LODGE AND TENTS
NUMBER OF ROOMS: 3
MAXIMUM NUMBER OF HUNTERS: 6
Meals: Family-style
Conference Groups: No
Guides: Included
Gratuity: Hunter's discretion
Preferred Payment:
Cash, check
Other Activities:
Biking, bird watching, canoeing/rafting, fishing, golf, skiing, wildlife photography
Getting There:
Fly to Hayden, and rent a car.

Contact:
Larry Osborn
Triple O Outfitters
448 Co. Rd. 41, Box 99
Hamilton, CO 81638
970/824 6758
e-mail:
guides@coloradooutdoor.com
Web: www.coloradooutdoors.com

LARRY AND RETA OSBORN have deep roots in the Morapos Creek area of the White River National Forest. It's where they grew up, and they've hunted this land for more than 40 years. No wonder they love it. To the southeast are the Flat Tops, with their high peaks and black stands of lodgepole pine. To the west are the rolling, arid, high prairies of the Danforth Hills. South of Hamilton, Morapos Creek drains high foothills, few of which are steep enough to be called mountains, compared to those along the Continental Divide 100 miles west as the crow flies.

Their lodge on Morapos Creek between Wilson Mesa (8,763 feet) and Three Points Mountain (9,315 feet) is the primary base camp for elk hunting and summer activities, such as a wilderness outdoor school for women. Up the drainages, within a three- to five-mile ride from the lodge, Larry has a number of spike or drop camps complete with bunks, stoves, kitchen tents and the works. You and your party of four or so can rent a drop camp and hunt by yourselves. But increasingly, hunters are choosing the full-service option. This gives you one guide for two hunters, room and board in Triple O's lakefront lodge, horses to carry you into the backcountry if need be and care of your trophy.

Normally guides want to be up on the ridges well before daylight, either glassing meadows or posting hunters on those little gaps favored by bulls crossing from one drainage to another. Since much of the land around the Triple O is public, Larry wants his hunters as deep in the wilderness as practical. That way they're in position to intercept game pushed upwards by other hunters. Does the strategy work? You bet. In 1997, 70 percent of his hunters took bulls of 4x4 or better. It was a great year, but on average the success rate is closer to 50 percent. There are no guarantees in this camp, except for one. If a hunter hasn't had a reasonable shot during his five-day hunt and if there's space in camp, Larry will add another day to provide one more chance. You never know.

VITAL STATISTICS:

Game/Arm/Seasons:
BEAR:
Centerfire: Late Apr. through late May
ELK, DEER:
Centerfire: Mid-Sept. through mid-Nov.
BIGHORN SHEEP:
Centerfire: Aug. through Oct.
MOUNTAIN LION:
Centerfire: Late Nov.
Rates:
ELK/DEER combo $4,200
BEAR $1,700
BIGHORN SHEEP $6,200
MOUNTAIN LION $2,800
Accommodations:
WALL TENTS
MAXIMUM NUMBER OF HUNTERS: 3
Meals:
Western backcountry fare
Conference Groups: Yes
Guides: Included
Gratuity: Hunter's discretion
Preferred Payment:
Cash, MasterCard, Visa, check
Other Activities:
Bird watching, whitewater rafting,
fishing, hiking, swimming, wildlife
photography
Getting There:
Fly to Sun Valley, Boise or Idaho Falls
and take charter flight to airstrips
that access the camps at an additional
charge.

Contact:
Steve Zettel
**American Adrenaline
Co./Taylor Ranch Outfitters**
Box 795
Challis, ID 83226
208/879-4700
Fax: 208/879-4701
e-mail: zettel@cyberhighway.net

American Adrenaline Co./Taylor Ranch Outfitters

Challis, Idaho

*Hunt for trophy elk, deer, bighorn sheep and black bear
in The River of No Return Wilderness.*

THE AMERICAN ADRENALINE COMPANY of Challis, Idaho, specializes in wilderness rafting and fishing trips on the Middle Fork of the Salmon River. Nestled in the heart of the Rocky Mountains in central Idaho, the Middle Fork's headwaters begin near Sun Valley and follow the spectacular Sawtooth Mountain Range, in the largest wilderness area in the lower 48 states, the sprawling River of No Return Wilderness.

Owner Steve Zettel doesn't do only whitewater rafting trips, however. He offers fishing and horsepacking adventures and, through his Taylor Ranch Outfitters, a variety of hunts. Taylor Ranch, named for the homesteader who built a hunting-lodge business in the area more than 50 years ago, starts its operations in spring with six-day hunts for black bear, many of which run more than 250 pounds and some of which top 400. "We suggest groups of two hunters with two guides for this one," Zettel says. The hunts are conducted out of a wall-tent camp with horses and mules.

Elk and mule deer hunts are run the same way in the fall. Taylor Ranch's licensed fish and game units 26 and 20A are located on the last 15 miles of Big Creek, the largest tributary to the Middle Fork of the Salmon. The two wall-tent camps are in rugged, remote terrain that take eight hours to reach by horseback. Hunters fly to one of two airstrips in the area, then ride to the camps.

This is big country, with lots of elk and a respectable number of mule deer (not to mention bears). Each hunter is paired with one guide, with the first half of the season being best for bugle hunts for elk. During the second half, running into November, the mule deer rut has begun and your chances of taking a trophy buck are greatly improved.

Zettel also offers mountain lion hunts immediately after elk season in late November, running the big cats with hounds and trailing with horses and mules. And if you draw a tag, the bighorn sheep hunting in this area is tremendous August through October.

"Just make sure you pack a lot of different weight clothing," says Zettel, "because the temperatures can be anywhere from below freezing to shirt-sleeve weather.

"And don't forget your moleskin either," he concludes, "because you'll be doing a lot of walking, no matter what we're after."

Flying B Ranch near Kamiah, Idaho is well known for pheasants and chukars. Those who bring rifles soon learn of its elk and deer, however, and all experience plush accommodations and gourmet cuisine.

Castle Creek Outfitters

Salmon, Idaho

Get 80 miles from the nearest paved road, and you know you're into game country at its best.

VITAL STATISTICS:

Game/Arm/Seasons:
ELK and DEER:
Bow: Sept.
DEER:
Centerfire: Oct.
ELK:
Centerfire: Mid-Oct. through early Nov.
BEAR:
Centerfire: April through June
MOUNTAIN LION:
Centerfire: Nov. through Feb.
SHEEP and GOATS:
Centerfire: Aug. through Oct.

Rates:
WHITETAILS $2,500/5 days
ELK and DEER from $3,500/8 days
SHEEP and GOATS $6,000/10 days
LIONS $2,500/7 days
BLACK BEAR from $1,500/6 days

Accommodations:
WOODEN LODGE, CABINS
NUMBER OF ROOMS: 6
MAXIMUM NUMBER OF HUNTERS: 6
Meals: Hearty home cooking
Conference Groups: No
Guides: Included
Gratuity: 10 to 20%
Preferred Payment:
Cash, check
Other Activities:
Fishing, bird hunting, hiking, biking, wildlife photography
Getting There:
Fly to Missoula and rent a car, or take the lodge shuttle ($180 round-trip).

Contact:
Shane McAfee
Castle Creek Outfitters
Box 2008
Salmon, ID 83467
208/756-2548

WHEN SHANE MCAFEE says his ranch is isolated, he isn't kidding. It's 80 miles from the nearest paved road, deep in the southwest quadrant of Idaho's Unit 28. Peaks in this neck of the woods—Black Mountain, Woods, and Van Horn—don't quite scrape 10,000 feet, but they come very close. Valleys drop to 8,000 feet or so, and in between are miles and miles of steep, often rocky and sometimes timbered terrain.

Elk don't migrate out of this area. They're with the cows in the lower elevations during the September rut when archers hunt. Bugling can still bring in a bull when rifle opens in October, but by mid-month, bulls have headed up into the timber. Snow may push them down during the final week of the season. A good bull will go in the 280-300 range here, but most of five points or better score about 260.

None of this is easy hunting. Unless you're out in a spike or drop camp, you'll be roused from your slumbers at 3:30 a.m., fed a good breakfast and be riding out of the ranch no later than 4:30. That will get you into the areas where elk are feeding before dawn. Hunter success on elk runs 72 percent.

For hunters lucky enough to survive Idaho's draw, Castle Creek offers a bighorn sheep hunt in Unit 28, and Unit 27 to the west in the heart of the Frank Church River of No Return Wilderness. Horses will carry you, your guide and your gear into spike camps at the 8,000-foot level and for 10 days you'll hunt up as high as the sheep and goats wander. The drill is to ride until the sheep are spotted and backpack from there. You'll sleep in mountain tents and eat freeze-dried stew, but who cares? Success has been 100 percent on mature rams for the last 23 years.

Lion hunters in the Frank Church have met with similar success. Trophy toms run in the 160-pound class with skulls measuring 14 inches or better. You'll ride in 4WDs until cutting a track, then the hounds are loosed and the fun begins. Deep snow makes this an arduous hunt. Spring bear hunting, which entails riding and glassing as well as morning and evening hunts over bait, is also on the agenda at Castle Creek.

Headquarters for these operations is a 60-acre ranch on Castle Creek where Shane McAfee's dad started the outfitting business many years ago. The ranch is minuscule by Western standards, but how much land do you need for a few warm cabins (half with private baths), and a lodge that dishes up lasagna, chili and steaks?

Deadwood Outfitters

G a r d e n   V a l l e y ,   I d a h o

Elk populations are high, and Deadwood—in the business for 30 years—knows how to get the big bulls.

VITAL STATISTICS:

Game/Arm/Seasons:
ELK:
Bow: Sept.
Centerfire: Mid-Oct. through early Nov.
DEER:
Bow: Sept.
Centerfire: Last half of Oct.
Rates:
Guided from $3,000/6 days
Drop camps $1,250/6 days
Accommodations:
LOG CABINS
NUMBER OF ROOMS: 10
MAXIMUM NUMBER OF HUNTERS: 15
Meals: Roast beef, salmon, elk
Conference Groups: Yes
Guides: Included
Gratuity: $100
Preferred Payment:
Cash, MasterCard, Visa, check
Other Activities:
Fishing, rafting, swimming, boating, bird watching, trail rides, wildlife photography, skiing
Getting There:
Fly to Boise and be met by the lodge van ($100 round-trip).

Contact:
Tom Carter
Deadwood Outfitters
Box 412
Garden Valley, ID 97184
800/648-3675
Fax: 541/523-6399
off-season:
Rt. 1, Box 38
Baker City, OR 97814
541/523-6181

HEAVY SNOWS in recent years have not been kind to the elk populations of Idaho, but what a difference a couple degrees of temperature can make. When the Lolo area in the Selway-Bitterroots was struggling under a mantle of two or three feet of additional winter snows, 150 miles south and 2,000 feet lower, the precipitation was rain. That accounts for the good herd and excellent seasons chalked up by Deadwood Outfitters in the southern end of the Boise National Forest.

This terrain is not the rugged canyon-and-ridge country of the Frank Church River of No Return Wilderness, also to the north. Rather, here in the headwaters of the South Fork of the Salmon and Deadwood rivers you'll find alpine meadows dotted with stands of trees. North slopes are heavily timbered with firs and pine, but southern slopes are open with aspens. Clumps of willows fill river valleys. Elk is the primary trophy here, though it's a reasonable idea to purchase a deer tag in case you see a nice buck. Elk run in the 260 range, with the best bull of the 1997 season scoring 318. All of September is devoted to archery, with everyone having opportunities for one or two shots. About 50 percent take bulls. Rifle season for deer opens in the first week of October, and elk become legal the following week. There are two weeks of combo elk and deer, followed by a final week of elk-only in early November. Bulls tend to be 4x4s or 5x5s, and success among rifle hunters is better than for archers.

While Deadwood operates drop camps for hunters who want to be on their own, most opt to stay in the lodge on the river beneath Pilgrim Mountain. In the dark, two hunters ride with their guide deep into the wilderness, tether their horses and spot and stalk. During bow season when elk are in the rut, bugling is very effective. After working the meadows until dusk, there's the drowsy ride back to the lodge and log cabins, hot showers and good food cooked in a real kitchen. This family-run business has been operating for 30 years. Like many good outfitters, the mainstay of Deadwood's business is repeat clients. Several hunters have been coming to Deadwood for a decade or more. That says a lot for the hunting, the camp and the owners, Tom and Dawn Carter.

Dixie Outfitters, Inc.

Dixie, Idaho

Thar's gold in them thar hills. Also elk, mule and white-tailed deer, sheep and mountain goats.

VITAL STATISTICS:

Game/Arm/Seasons:

ELK, MULE DEER, WHITE-TAILED DEER:
Bow, centerfire, muzzleloader: Mid-Sept. through mid-Nov.

BLACK BEAR:
Bow, centerfire, muzzleloader: Spring, mid-April through mid-June; fall, mid-Sept. through mid-Nov.

MOUNTAIN LION:
Bow, centerfire, muzzleloader: Mid-Sept. through late March

BIGHORN SHEEP:
Bow, centerfire, muzzleloader: Late Aug. through mid-Sept.

MOUNTAIN GOAT:
Bow, centerfire, muzzleloader: Late Aug. through Nov.

Rates:
ELK, DEER, BEAR combo $2,200/7 days
BEAR $1,000/7 days (spring)
MOUNTAIN LION $3,000/10 days
BIGHORN SHEEP, MOUNTAIN GOAT $4,500/10 days

Accommodations:
RUSTIC LOG LODGE
NUMBER OF ROOMS: 5
MAXIMUM NUMBER OF HUNTERS: 7

Meals: Turkey, chicken, pork chops, Italian food

Conference Groups: No

Guides: Included

Gratuity: Hunter's discretion

Preferred Payment:
Cash, check

Other Activities:
Bird watching, fishing, hiking, wildlife photography

Getting There:
Fly to Lewiston, Idaho, rent a car and drive to the lodge, or take a shuttle flight at an additional charge.

Contact:
Ron, Pat or Brad West
Dixie Outfitters, Inc.
Box 33
Dixie, ID 83525
208/842-2417
Fax: 208/842-2417

DIXIE TOWN is an old gold-mining town, founded way back in 1862 when gold was discovered along Crooked Creek. Located almost 30 miles south of Elk City, Idaho, Dixie was inhabited by thousands of prospectors at the peak of the gold rush. Today, there are about a dozen year-round residents. The town consists of a small grocery store, post office and gas pump. There is also a combination cafe/salon. Dixie Outfitters, in operation for more than 40 years (but now run by new owners Ron, Pat and Brad West), headquarters out of the original livery stable that's been converted to a barn.

Dixie's tent camps in the high country are set up in the Gospel Hump Wilderness, the Salmon River (River of No Return) Wilderness Area and nearby national forest lands. The camps are five to 10 miles out of town and are reached by horseback only. Dixie's hunting area encompasses more than 100 square miles, with elevations from 5,600 feet at Dixie to more than 7,000 feet. The seasons for elk, mule deer and bear run from September into November.

"This is a family-run business," says Pat West. "We cater to a limited number of hunters and promise everyone a fair and honest hunt."

The deal is this: "We pack you into one of our regular tent camps, reached only by horse and mule," states West. "These camps are equipped with cots, stoves and firewood. We supply the food, cook and one guide for every two to three men. The hunter supplies his own sleeping bag and personal gear. Horses and mules are included in the seven-day hunt, and we'll pack out anything you shoot."

In this part of Idaho, your chances of taking a good-sized elk are excellent. But that's not all. Mule and white-tailed deer run large in this part of the state. Plus, there's good black bear hunting in both spring and fall. And if you draw the right tags, the Wests can take you for bighorn sheep or mountain goat. Cougar hunts go on from September into March, with January, February and March being the best times, as snow on the ground allows for easier tracking.

The main lodge in Dixie is headquarters for many of the hunts, and base camp for hunters headed to the tent camps in the high country. Meals at the lodge are worth the stay, including spaghetti, lasagna, chicken, turkey and pork chops. Special dietary needs are also catered to.

Flying B Ranch

K a m i a h ,   I d a h o

The hunting is tough, the trophies are there and the lodge will pamper you the moment you're back in camp.

VITAL STATISTICS:

Game/Arm/Seasons:

MULE DEER, WHITETAIL, ELK:
Bow: Late Aug. through late Sept.
Centerfire: Mid-Sept. through early Oct.
Muzzleloader: Late Nov. through early Dec.
BEAR:
Bow, centerfire, muzzleloader: Mid-April through mid-June
COUGAR:
Bow, centerfire, muzzleloader: Late Oct. through late March

Rates:
DEER from $2,500/5 days
ELK from $3,000/8 days
BEAR $3,000/5 days
COUGAR $4,500/7 days

Accommodations:
MODERN LOG LODGE AND BACKCOUNTRY TENTS
NUMBER OF ROOMS: 14 IN LODGE
MAXIMUM NUMBER OF HUNTERS: 20

Meals: Bacon and eggs, chicken and shrimp gumbo, lamb shanks

Conference Groups: Yes

Guides: Included

Gratuity: 15 to 20%

Preferred Payment:
Cash, American Express, MasterCard, Visa

Other Activities:
Bird hunting, bird watching, boating, canoeing/whitewater rafting, fishing, hiking, sporting clays, wildlife photography

Getting There:
Fly to Lewiston, Idaho, and be met by a representative of the lodge at no additional charge.

Contact:
Lisa Haight
Flying B Ranch
Route 2, Box 12C
Kamiah, ID 83536
208/935-0755
Fax: 208/935-0705

LEWIS AND CLARK passed through this slice of the Bitterroots in 1806 and described the territory with an awe they reserved for only the toughest country. Later, in the 1870s, Chief Joseph led his Nez Perce tribe north through these mountains, trying desperately to escape the pursuing U.S. Army. Gen. Howard, Joseph's pursuer wrote of the harsh and rugged terrain, the deadfalls and rushing creeks, and the treacherous slopes, all of which slowed his progress to a crawl, letting the Nez Perce escape. In the fall of 1893, the ill-fated Carlin hunting party ran into an early September snowstorm and eventually had to retreat, leaving some of their members to perish in the wilderness.

The Selway-Bitterroot wilderness doesn't care if you live or die. It's just there, waiting for you, holding more game than you could believe, if you're up to the challenge.

Idaho's Flying B Ranch, near Kamiah, makes that challenge a bit easier. The "B" has outfitting rights on 700,000 acres of the wilderness and maintains two elk camps high in the mountains. The Flying B also conducts whitetail, mulie, black bear and mountain lion hunts. Whitetails and mulies are both found on the outfit's 6,000-acre ranch. Bear hunts are run in the wilderness, and your chances of taking a trophy bear ranging in color from black to cinnamon to blond are excellent. To top it off, record tom cougars are regularly taken from this area. The cats are hunted with hounds during winter months when snow is on the ground. Hunters may use rifles, pistols or bows.

If you're lucky enough to get some time at the lodge instead of spending all your time in the mountains (that's not so bad either), plan for some major relaxing. It's palatial, 14,000 square feet with private rooms, baths, dining and living areas, plus a game room. And the menu is guaranteed to help you put on those extra pounds that you don't need. Breakfast features French toast, eggs Benedict, sausage and bacon; lunch is Louisiana chicken and shrimp gumbo with rolls; and dinner is smoked salmon appetizers and braised lamb shanks with roasted garlic, mashed potatoes and pearl onions.

If you need to work off some of those calories, and if your big game tags are filled, the ranch offers excellent bird hunting for pheasants, chukars, quail, and ruffed and blue grouse. Pack you 20 gauge side-by-side, and plan to use it!

Heavens Gate Outfitters

Riggins, Idaho

Try for an Idaho "grand slam" in Devil country.

VITAL STATISTICS:

Game/Arm/Seasons:
ELK and DEER:
Bow: Sept.
ELK:
Centerfire: Mid-Sept. through mid-Nov.
DEER:
Centerfire: Mid-Nov.
MOUNTAIN LION:
Centerfire: Dec. through Jan.
BEAR:
Bow and centerfire: Mid-April through May
Rates:
ELK from $2,800/8 days
DEER from $1,6505 days
LION $2,350/7 days
BLACK BEAR from $1,000/7 days
Accommodations:
RANCH HOUSE, TENTS
MAXIMUM NUMBER OF HUNTERS: 4 PER CAMP
Meals: Chicken, spaghetti, roast beef, salads, desserts
Conference Groups: Yes
Guides: Included
Gratuity: $50 to $200
Preferred Payment:
Cash, check
Other Activities:
Fishing, bird hunting, rafting, swimming, hiking, bird watching, wildlife photography, trail rides
Getting There:
Fly to Lewiston or Boise and you will be met.

Contact:
Darwin Vander Esch,
Heavens Gate Outfitters
Box 1403
Riggins, ID 83549
208/628-3062

WHERE IS THE GATE TO HEAVEN? In the Seven Devils Mountains, of course. There you'll find She Devil, He Devil, Devils Throne and Devils Tooth. You'll also find the Tower of Babel for good measure, as well as Heavens Gate, an 8,400-foot peak. If you want rugged terrain, it's here in the Nez Perce National Forest. Hell's Canyon of the Snake is just across the mountains. Deep and tight gorges and sharp ridges break up the heavy forest. Yet here and there are little level bowls where headwaters rise and glades of grass where elk will come to feed. Elk thrive here and it's the mother lode for Heavens Gate Outfitters.

From these parts, hunters guided by Darwin Vander Esch and his crew from Heavens Gate have put three bulls in the record books. In 1997, the outfitter took four that scored between 285 and 350. At 80 percent success, archers are more successful than firearms hunters. Still, 50 percent of rifle hunters fill their tags. Bulls tend to be larger during the early part of the season. Bugling brings them close. Later, spotting and stalking is the game and the hunting picks up a bit with the first snow, which makes for good tracking if it's not a blizzard. Hunts are conducted from a tent camp high up on an unnamed creek. If the weather is right, the same camp will be used for spring bear and lion.

For whitetails, operations shift to a private 4,000-acre ranch of grassy meadows and timber outside of Whitebird, a small town on U.S. 95 close to the state's border with Oregon. Deer run in the 8- to 10-point range with spreads of 20 inches plus. Success verges on 100 percent. If you hunt this ranch, you'll put up in Heavens Gate's rustic main lodge 30 miles south at Riggins.

For mule deer, the outfit heads up into the Frank Church River of No Return Wilderness: a four-hour drive and a three-and-one-half-hour horseback ride from the trailhead deep in units 20A and 23. The land is not as steep as Seven Devils, but easy it is not. Heavily timbered and cut by draws and bare rock, this is ideal country for spotting and stalking. Every morning of the hunt, you'll ride out from the tent camp anywhere from a half mile to 10 miles to areas where bucks are working. Four- and 5-point deer are the rule here; some are bigger. Elk and bear also inhabit the wilderness. Maybe you'll be the first to bag an Idaho "Grand Slam," all three species in a six-day hunt.

[R O C K Y   M O U N T A I N S]

Kuykendal Outfitters

P e c k ,   I d a h o

*The North Fork of the Clearwater is home
to this elk, bear and lion hunting operation.*

VITAL STATISTICS:

Game/Arm/Seasons:
ELK:
Bow: Last week in Sept.
Centerfire: Mid-Oct. through early Nov.
BEAR:
Centerfire: Late April through early June
MOUNTAIN LION:
Centerfire: Mid-Dec. through mid-Jan.

Rates:
Guided hunts
ELK from $1,800/7 days
BEAR $750/7 days
LION: $2,500/5 days

Accommodations:
WOOD-FLOORED WALL TENTS
MAXIMUM NUMBER OF HUNTERS: 6 PER CAMP

Meals: Steaks, chicken, meat loaf
Conference Groups: Yes
Guides: Included
Gratuity: $100
Preferred Payment:
Cash, personal check
Other Activities:
Fishing, hiking, wildlife photography
Getting There:
Fly to Lewiston and you will be met.

Contact:
Le Roy Kuykendall
Kuykendall Outfitters
1009 Old Melrose Road
Peck ID 83545
208/486-6033

I N 1918 A FOREST FIRE ripped through what would become the Clearwater National Forest, burning so intensely that the very soil was incinerated. When the fire was out, the landscape might have been lunar, for all that one could see of the rocky surface. Here, at the base of where Idaho narrows down into its panhandle, the growing season is very short. And it takes lodgepole pine and spruce a long time to grow even when the soil is abundant. Today, 80 years after the burn, the recovering forest is still far from mature, and that means more fodder than normal for elk.

In the midst of the old burn, along 23 miles of the North Fork of the Clearwater River, LeRoy and Chris Kuykendal hold the exclusive license to guide hunters and anglers. Elk are hunted from mountain camps located at roughly 5,200 feet. The highest peak (7,139 feet) in the neighborhood is Pot Mountain. In between is a troubled land of steep slopes cut here and there by open draws and a glacial lake or two. Camp is a collection of wall tents complete with wooden floors and stoves. There are six hunters (four if they're archers), one guide for every two hunters and a wrangler in each camp during the week-long hunts. Snow comes early to these parts. The rifle season closes in early November. The old rule of elk hunting—30 percent kill a bull, 30 percent see a quality bull but don't connect, and 30 percent may not see a bull—applies here, according to LeRoy Kuykendal. What happens to the other 10 percent is anybody's guess. LeRoy's a hunter, not a mathematician.

Winter doesn't close down this operation. It just shifts its focus to cats, mountain lions to be specific. Hunting with dogs, you'll work your way along the river until crossing their tracks and you'll scamper after the hounds on snowshoes through two to three feet of powder. Think running on snowshoes is cumbersome? Try it in snow this deep without them. Because the mountain lion population is booming, much to the detriment of deer, hunter success is very high.

LeRoy starts bear hunting in the end of April and continues through the first week of June. These hunts are extremely reasonable; $750 for a week-long, fully guided hunt. License, tag, and taxes (yes, Virginia, there is a tax on hunting) are extra. Bears are nice for this area; 200 pounds is the average. And if you opt for a spring bear hunt, by all means bring your fishing tackle. The North Fork of the Clearwater, a blue-ribbon trout river, flows past your door.

Mystic Saddle Ranch

C h a l l i s ,   I d a h o

Hunt elk in one of Idaho's best units.

VITAL STATISTICS:

Game/Arm/Seasons:
DEER:
Centerfire: Early through late Oct.
ELK:
Bow: Early through late Sept.
Centerfire: Mid-Oct. through early Nov.
Rates:
MULE DEER $2,926/8 days (guided)
ELK $3,996/8 days (guided);
$1,605/8 days (unguided)
Accommodations:
TENTS
MAXIMUM NUMBER OF HUNTERS: 8
Meals: Steaks, pork chops, pasta
Conference Groups: No
Guides: Included
Gratuity: $200
Preferred Payment:
Cash, MasterCard, Visa, check
Other Activities:
Canoeing/rafting, fishing, wildlife
photography
Getting There:
Fly to Boise and drive to Stanley the
night before your hunt begins.
Airport pickup is available for an
additional cost.

Contact:
Jeff Bitton
Mystic Saddle Ranch
Box 736
Challis, ID 83226
208/879-5071
Fax: 208/879-5069
e-mail: packid@cyberhighway.net
Web: www.mysticsaddleranch.com

SEPTEMBER IS A SPECIAL TIME of year. Elk combine courtship with violence, in a vast tournament where bulls compete for the right to breed. The young are weeded out almost immediately. Then it gets down and dirty, with the big 5x5s and 6x6s vying for control of the harem.

The winners have one aim: to gather as many cows as possible and then keep them for the entire rut. No matter how powerful or persistent the bull might be, it is not an easy task. Ousted bulls are always lurking, waiting to grab an estrous cow whenever the opportunity presents. Wolves and other predators, knowing the elk are herded up, follow the animals, looking for stragglers. And hunters are in the mountains— bowhunters in early September in most areas, rifle hunters as the season progresses.

Perhaps the most fun you can have on two feet is being afield, bow in hand, when the rut is in full swing. You'll be in your stand, perhaps overlooking a watering hole or a well-used trail. In the distance you'll hear the sounds of bugling elk echoing through the canyons. And the sound of an elk bugling is unlike any other sound you'll hear in the wild. It starts as a deep rasp, then rises quickly through several octaves to a ear-ringing, shrill scream before dropping off into a series of rough grunts. At close range, with a bull headed toward your stand, bugling, thrashing saplings, stomping his feet, your spine will tingle and you'll get that ohshit feeling in your bowels. If the bull comes your way, will you have the nerves to coolly draw your bow, then wait for the target to present itself? Among the best places to hunt rutting elk is along Idaho's Salmon River, where Mystic Saddle Ranch runs its bowhunts. Both guided and drop camp hunts are available. The area they hunt, Unit 36-A, boasts a bull-to-cow ratio of 4:10. Bulls in this area regularly score 280 to 290, with monsters more than 300 being taken each year. Annually, more than 50 percent of archers hunting with Mystic get a shot at a big bull.

This is rugged country, high-mountain terrain with camps located around 7,000 feet. Hunters and their gear are packed in by horseback. Then the walking and hunting is up to you.

Mystic also runs rifle hunts for elk after the rut is over at the end of September, plus rifle hunts for mule deer. Mulies are hunted in high, rolling terrain with sagebrush, open slopes and fingers of pines and aspens. The deer are plentiful, and 5x5 and better trophies are taken each year.

❖ *A Willow Creek Guide* ❖

───
North America's GREATEST *Big Game Lodges & Outfitters*
───
[R O C K Y   M O U N T A I N S]

Red River Outfitters

E l k   C i t y ,   I d a h o

Red River can put you in one of 11 drop camps located in prime elk country. They'll also guarantee you a lion.

VITAL STATISTICS:

Game/Arm/Seasons:
ELK and DEER:
Bow: Sept.
Centerfire: Mid-Sept. through mid–Nov.
BEAR:
Centerfire: Fall, mid-Sept. through Oct.; Spring, mid-April. through mid-June
MOUNTAIN LION:
Centerfire: Mid-Sept. through mid-March

Rates:
Guided hunts:
ELK and DEER from $2,600/7 days
BEAR or LION $2,500/7 days
Drop camps from $950/8 days

Accommodations:
WOODEN LODGE, CABINS AND TENTS
NUMBER OF ROOMS: 9
MAXIMUM NUMBER OF HUNTERS: 4 PER CAMP

Meals: Good solid food

Conference Groups: Yes

Guides: Included

Gratuity: Hunter's discretion

Preferred Payment:
Cash

Other Activities:
Fishing, swimming, hiking, bird watching, wildlife photography

Getting There:
Fly to Missoula, Spokane or Lewiston and rent a car.

Contact:
Lawrence Smith
Red River Outfitters
Box 138
Elk City, ID 83525
208/842-2633
e-mail: redriver@camasnet.com
Web: www.camasnet.com/~redriver

INDIANS AND GOLD MINERS used to take their ease, soaking away the ague in the somewhat sulfurous waters of the hot springs at the headwaters of the Red River. To get there, take the road east out of Elk City and turn north up the river to reach the springs. It's a trek of some 20 miles and the jumping-off point for the camps of Red River Outfitters. For the past few years, Red River has operated a string of 11 drop camps in the headwaters of Meadow and Baragin creeks just south of the Selway-Bitterroot Wilderness Area. It's a good area to hunt. The peak of Green Mountain, beneath which sits Red River's base camp, is only 7,227 feet high. It's surrounded by forest, not the heavy black forest of farther north, but thick timber all the same. Shots at elk will be in the 75- to 100-yard range. Success on bulls scoring between 260 and 280 from the drop camps has been running in the neighborhood of 30 to 40 percent. If the elk herd cooperates, that average should improve with fully-guided hunts. While whitetails (100- to 120-point scores) are reasonably abundant in this area, it's the elk that draw the hunters.

Lawrence Smith who with his wife Kathy, heads up this operation, also runs mountain lion hunts and he's one of the few outfitters who will guarantee hunters a cat. Hunting is very good. Two or three cats can be treed in a day. Much controversy surrounds guaranteeing game to clients. Obviously Red River Runs a "fair-chase" hunt. The problem is in the size of the cat that's taken. In Idaho, lions with spots or females with young are not considered legal game. That means, though, that yearling cats can be harvested, and some find that problematic. On the other hand, lions are the primary predators of deer and one of the reasons, along with heavy winters of late, that the deer population in western Idaho is down. Hunting cats of legal age provides a balance that can help improve deer numbers. That's the argument.

At Red River, lions average about 120 pounds. Hunting takes place in an utterly remote region nearly 90 miles by four-wheel drive vehicle and horse from the base camp. The season stretches from mid-September into March, but Red River focuses most of its activity from mid-November until the snow gets too deep, generally the end of December. Bear are also on this camp's game list; Red River runs both spring and fall hunts. Accommodations vary depending on location. The main lodge offers five rooms with private baths; tents in camps have canvas floors.

Ridgerunner Outfitters

K a m i a h ,   I d a h o

Located in one of Idaho's prime game units, this outfit can put you onto trophy elk, deer, black bears and cougars.

VITAL STATISTICS:

Game/Arm/Seasons:
ELK, DEER:
Bow: Early through late Sept.
Centerfire: Early Oct. through early Nov.
BEAR
Bow, centerfire, muzzleloader: Early May through late June
Bow, centerfire: Mid-Sept. through late Oct.
COUGAR:
Bow, centerfire, muzzleloader: Mid-Sept. through late Oct.

Rates:
Archery ELK or DEER $2,500/8 days
Rifle ELK or DEER $2,750/8 days
BEAR $1,750/7 days
COUGAR $3,200/10 days

Accommodations:
WALL TENTS
MAXIMUM NUMBER OF HUNTERS: 6

Meals: Steaks, chicken, roasts, chops

Conference Groups: No

Guides: Included

Gratuity: $100

Preferred Payment:
Cash, check

Other Activities:
Bird hunting, bird watching, canoeing/whitewater rafting, fishing, hiking, wildlife photography

Getting There:
Fly to Lewiston, Idaho, and be met by a representative of the outfitter.

Contact:
Ray Christopherson
Ridgerunner Outfitters
Box 1193
Kamiah, ID 83536
208/935-0757
Fax: 208/935-0398
e-mail: ridgerun@camasnet.com

HUNTERS IN THE KNOW get pretty excited about Idaho's Unit 10, North Fork and Copper Creek. And for good reason. According to Ray Christopherson, honcho of Ridgerunner Outfitters, Unit 10—where he keeps his camps in a 115-square-mile hunting area—has incredible numbers of game animals, because, he says, "of the terrain and availability of food. And when there are a lot of deer and elk in a particular location, you'll also have a lot of bears and cougars."

All of which explains why Christopherson's outfit has a great deal of success with visiting hunters. Unit 10 in particular is a rugged area—beautiful, but tough, with elevations running to 7,000 feet. But with so much game around, and with Christopherson and his guides tending to every detail people are bound to be pleased. As a client recently wrote, "The willingness of the Ridgerunner crew to assist us and make our hunt enjoyable was exceptional. The thing that impressed all of us was the hospitality."

Elk hunts involve everything from bugling bulls during the early archery season to riding the ridge tops and glassing open hillsides on the crisp mornings and evenings of rifle season. Guided bear hunts are conducted out of the base camp, with hunters either glassing hillsides for bears, then putting on a sneak or using bait or hounds. According to Christopherson, a number of large bears use this area, and the chance of taking a color-phase monster is pretty good. Lions are numerous in this area, too. Hunt them in November and December, following the hounds, by horse, snowmobile or on foot, depending on the snow conditions. And if you're lucky enough to draw a mountain goat tag in the state's lottery, Christopherson will take you to the Mallard-Larkin Pioneer Area, which has plenty of trophy-class goats. You better be in shape for this hunt, as it's a tough one.

Christopherson offers guided hunts with two hunters per guide out of one of his wall-tent camps; or he will set you up in a drop camp fully supplied with tents, stoves, lanterns, tools, cots and wood. He'll stay in touch with you by CB radio and have a packer visit your camp every few days to attend to your needs.

The camp accommodations are a good example of the outfit's hospitality. The base camp has a 24x30-foot, three-room, straight wall tent, with hot showers available daily. Christopherson's better half, Mary Dawn, sees to it that everything in camp is working smoothly while he's dealing with the animals and out guiding hunters. Her meals are great, including steaks, pork chops, roast beef and lamb, but her apple pie is to die for.

Sulphur Creek Ranch

B o i s e ,   I d a h o

Accessible by horse or plane, this ranch deep in the middle of the Frank Church has a lock on quality hunting.

VITAL STATISTICS:

Game/Arm/Seasons:

ELK:
Bow: Late Aug. through late Sept. Centerfire, muzzleloader: Mid-Sept. through mid-Nov.

MULE DEER:
Bow: Late Aug. through late Sept. Centerfire: Mid-Sept. through mid-Nov.

BEAR:
Centerfire, muzzleloader: Spring, Mid-April through mid-June; fall, Mid-Sept. through late Oct.

Rates:
FROM $2,400/8 DAYS

Accommodations:
FIVE MODERN LOG CABINS
NUMBER OF ROOMS: 12
MAXIMUM NUMBER OF HUNTERS: 8

Meals: Turkey, roast, chicken, potatoes, veggies, salad

Conference Groups: Yes

Guides: Included

Gratuity: 15%

Preferred Payment:
Check

Other Activities:
Bird hunting, fishing, hiking, horseback riding, wildlife photography

Getting There:
Fly to Boise and take a charter flight to the ranch for an additional charge.

Contact:
Tom T. Allegrezza
Sulphur Creek Ranch
7153 W. Emerald
Boise, ID 83704
208/377-1188
Fax: 208/377-1188

TOM ALLEGREZZA HAS a special spot, way back in the middle of nowhere, Idaho, and if you're interested in elk, mule deer and black bear in a remote, wild setting, listen up.

Sulphur Creek Ranch is a 160-acre guest ranch in the middle of the Frank Church Wilderness Area, one of the largest wilderness areas in the lower 48 states. The ranch itself is about three miles east of the Middle Fork of the Salmon River, 150 miles northeast of Boise. The only way to reach it is by air or horseback, which suits Allegrezza and his group just fine. There's less hunting pressure, because few people venture back this far on their own.

With massive mountains and thick pine woods, this is prime elk country, and the guides at Sulphur Creek know how to find them. Each morning they ride out well before daylight, heading to spots where they can glass large areas below— or, if it's September, where they can listen and try to pinpoint bugling bulls. Then it's a question of calling back and trying to get in a position where they can ambush a bull coming in to investigate the calls from a surrogate challenger.

Sometimes, if the bulls aren't within easy riding distance of the main lodge, Allegrezza has his guides and clients stay at one of the spike camps he has conveniently located in his 150-square-mile hunting territory. "They're equipped with quality equipment and supplies," he notes. "And the meals there are hearty and delicious, just like at the main lodge."

The main ranch itself is cozy and comfortable, with home cooking served family-style. The food is so good—turkey, Dijon chicken, roast beef, with all the fixings—that in summer, people fly in just for dinner or breakfast, then turn around and head back to Boise. The ranch itself has two modern cabins that sleep six, and three cabins that sleep three or four. Plenty of room for a large party of hunters, in other words. And plenty of country to hunt.

Archery elk and deer seasons open at the tail end of August and run into September, when rifle seasons start up. Bear also starts in mid-September, with bruins more than 200 pounds common in the area. They're also huntable from mid-April into June, which, when combined with some of the trophy cutthroat trout fishing in the area, might be just the thing you need.

Wapiti Meadow Ranch

Cascade, Idaho

Glassing with quality binocs is the foundation of a premier hunt with this Idaho outfit.

VITAL STATISTICS:

Game/Arm/Seasons:
ELK:
Bow: Early through late Sept.
Centerfire: Mid-Sept. through mid-Nov.
MULE DEER:
Bow: Early through late Sept.
Centerfire: Mid-Sept. through late Oct.
Rates:
From $2,500
Accommodations:
LOG LODGE AND CABINS AND WALL TENTS
NUMBER OF ROOMS: 7
MAXIMUM NUMBER OF HUNTERS: RANCH 7, CAMP 4
Meals: Prime rib, salmon, pork loin, flank steak, pasta
Conference Groups: Yes
Guides: Included
Gratuity: Hunter's discretion
Preferred Payment:
Cash, check
Other Activities:
Biking, bird hunting, bird watching, canoeing/rafting, fishing, hiking, horseback riding, skiing, snowmobiling, wildlife photography
Getting There:
Fly to Boise, rent a car and drive to the ranch or take a shuttle flight for $95 one way.

Contact:
Barry Bryant
Wapiti Meadow Ranch
H 72
Cascade, ID 83611
208/633-3217
Fax: 208/633-3219
e-mail: WapitiMR@aol.com
Web: www.guestranches.com/wapiti.htm

MOST SUCCESSFUL ELK HUNTERS will tell you that one of the keys to their success is their ability to carefully glass the open, rugged terrain of the West. For starters, realize that if you're hunting elk or mule deer, in the case of Wapiti Meadow Ranch, you're going to spend a lot of time with your face glued to a pair of binoculars. A cheap pair brings little but headaches and eye strain. And these lower-quality lenses won't help you pick out that mulie bedded down under some rimrock 1,000 yards away, or that elk slipping through a patch of lodgepole pines down in the canyon.

The key is to buy quality. Leupold, Swarovski, Zeiss, Steiner, Bausch and Lomb, Nikon—there are a lot of good names to choose from. And, unlike other products, here you generally get what you pay for.

What type of binocular? You'll be doing a lot of long-range glassing, so you really need high magnification and sufficient light-gathering ability. For all-round use, 8X to 10X binoculars are the way to go. A pair of 10x50 binoculars, for example, will allow you to see across that canyon and pull in enough light so you can really inspect the rack on that bedded buck. (Ten is the magnification power, 50 the size of the objective lens.)

Why stress the importance of binoculars? Because if you hunt a place such as Wapiti Meadow, in the River of No Return Wilderness, you'll be doing a lot of riding to high vantage points, where you'll get off your horse, hunker down behind some rocks or a downed tree and start glassing.

This is prime game country, with mature bull elk typically carrying 5x5 and 6x6 racks, and mule deer bucks carrying racks that average 24 to 30 inches. Wapiti's area encompasses every habitat from rutting zones to migratory areas to winter range. The ranch doesn't allow drop camps, so the game is unpressured and plentiful.

The wilderness camp, where many of the hunts take place, is complete with a full-time cook and packer. Comfortable heated wall tents, roomy cook and dining tents and excellent meals are guaranteed to rest, fill and fuel you. If you stay at the modern main log ranch, be prepared for excellent daily meals featuring prime rib, salmon, pork loin roasts, flank steaks, barbecued chicken breasts, pasta primavera and more. Then you can waddle out onto the porch, plop down in one of the rockers, pull out your 10x50s and glass the ridges that tower over Wapiti Meadow. You may even spot the elk you'll stalk tomorrow.

Wilderness Outfitters

C h a l l i s ,   I d a h o

If you want to get out in the middle of nowhere for your elk or mulie hunt, you can't get much farther out there than this.

VITAL STATISTICS:

Game/Arm/Seasons:

ELK, DEER:
Centerfire: Mid-Sept. through mid-Nov.

SHEEP, GOAT:
Centerfire: Late Aug. through mid-Oct.

BEAR:
Center fire: Spring, early May through mid-June; fall, mid-Sept. through early Nov.

COUGAR:
Centerfire: Mid-Nov. through late March

Rates:
ELK/DEER/BEAR combo $4,500/8 days
BEAR $4,500/8 days (spring)
SHEEP or GOAT $4,500/10 days
COUGAR $4,500/7 days

Accommodations:
RUSTIC RANCH HOUSE
NUMBER OF ROOMS: 3
MAXIMUM NUMBER OF HUNTERS: 6

Meals: Chicken, steaks, chops, Italian, Mexican served family-style

Conference Groups: No

Guides: Included

Gratuity: $50 to $100 plus

Preferred Payment:
Cash, check

Other Activities:
Bird hunting, fishing, hiking, wildlife photography

Getting There:
Fly to Boise and take a charter flight for $350 round-trip.

Contact:
Shelda Farr
Wilderness Outfitters
Box 64
Challis, ID 83226
208/879-2203
Fax: 208/879-2204

T HEY DIDN'T NAME THIS OUTFIT "Wilderness Outfitters" for nothing. Located on a private inholding deep inside the River of No Return Wilderness, Wilderness Outfitters' base camp can only be reached by bush plane. Flying over some of the narrow canyons and river bottoms of the Sawtooth Mountains on the way in is awe-inspiring. But then you land on the dirt strip, unload your gear and get ready for some awesome hunting.

Hunters out of Wilderness Outfitters hunt a large portion of the Middle Fork of the Salmon River within the Challis and Boise national forests. Wilderness Outfitters has exclusive rights to several hundred square miles of territory, and the only means of access to this remote area from base camp is by horse.

Owners Scott, Shelda, Justin and Jerrod Farr will take care of your every need while in camp or afield. You'll awaken each morning way before sunrise, have breakfast, then ride out into the hills. The horses are used mostly to get to the hunting area, as the actual hunting is done on foot only. If you get too far away from base camp, the Farr's have a number of spike camps where you can overnight.

As you ride through this rugged country, you'll be amazed at its beauty. Indian pictographs may be found on many of the rock walls, while along the rivers you'll come upon old trapper cabins, the first evidence of white settlers. Eventually, you'll climb up and up, overlooking vast country. If the elk are bugling, you'll stop and listen, trying to pin down the location of the bull before bugling back. If bugling season is over, you'll glass, looking for movement down below. If you spy a bull that you want to stalk, then the hunt is on. Five- to 6-pointers are the rule here, although some hunters get bulls even bigger. Use a rifle that's up to the task—.300 Win. Mag., .338, maybe a 7mm—and chances are you'll go home with a huge rack and a bunch of elk quarters and backstraps for the butcher.

The Farr's also run hunts for absolutely huge mule deer, bighorn sheep, mountain goats, black bears (spring and fall) and cougars.

At the lodge itself, you'll stay in one of three comfortable but rustic cabins, dining on chicken, ham, steaks, pork chops and lasagna, all served family-style. A bit of class, in the middle of nowhere!

Wally York & Son Inc.

Elk City, Idaho

This special corner of the Selway Bitterroot Wilderness is the place to go for a quality big-game hunt.

VITAL STATISTICS:

Game/Arm/Seasons:
DEER and ELK:
Bow, centerfire, muzzleloader:
Mid-Sept. through mid-Nov.
BEAR:
Bow, centerfire, muzzleloader:
Spring, mid-April through mid-June;
fall, mid-Sept. through Oct.
MOUNTAIN LION:
Handguns: Mid-Sept. through
mid-March

Rates:
DEER and ELK:
From $1,800/8 days
BEAR $2,600/8 days
MOUNTAIN LION $2,600/10 days

Accommodations:
WALL TENTS
MAXIMUM NUMBER OF HUNTERS: 8

Meals:
Solid, mountain fare

Conference Groups: Yes

Guides: Included

Gratuity: Hunter's discretion

Preferred Payment:
Cash

Other Activities:
Fishing, swimming, wildlife
photography

Getting There:
Fly to Lewiston and rent a car, or
catch an air shuttle for $350 per
person.

Contact:
W. Travis York
Wally York & Son Inc.
Box 319
Elk City, ID 83525
208/842-2367

LOOKING FOR A GUY who knows real estate? W. Travis York may be your man. In 1932, his dad established this outfitting company and began guiding hunters in the Selway Bitterroot Wilderness. From a camp on Warm Springs Bar in Running Creek's Unit 17, York and his hunters work slopes densely wooded with yew, pine and fir. On benches and in little valleys are patches of grass, interspersed with occasional wallows.

Elk are prime quarry here, big bulls with six points plus with spreads of 50 inches or more. It's not an easy hunt by any means. Early in the season, calling rustles up elk for bowhunters. Later, you'll do a lot of riding, climbing and stalking. Some of this country is pretty vertical and physical fitness is a key element in bringing down a bull. York isn't given to gilding the lily. While seven out of 10 hunters have realistic shots, only four out of 10 are successful. Next to physical conditioning, it pays to be able to shoot well.

Along with elk are mulies and whitetails. Hunted both during the October rut and in the snows of early November, mule deer bucks average a respectable four or five points with spreads between 28 and 34 inches. Hunter success runs about 75 percent. Whitetails are generally a little lighter than mule deer.

Black bears are also very good in this, the southern section of Game Management Unit 17. Averaging about 250 pounds, some of those taken each year will nudge 400 pounds. All color phases are possible.

Strictly fair-chance hunts, this is no walk in the park. That's especially true of the spring hunts during which a chopper may fly you into camp and you may have to hunt from snowmobile and snowshoe. Hunter success runs about 100 percent. Cougars are hunted during elk and deer season with handguns but without dogs. Later, after elk and deer close, it's legal to bring dogs into the woods. Again using his favorite .44 mag., York runs lion hunts over hounds. Hunting from snowshoe and snowmobile when the woods are filling with snow demands stamina like nothing else. But, on average, cats tip the scales at 140 pounds, with a really big tom going well over 200 pounds.

The base camp features wood-floored wall tents, cook tent and bath tent. Spike camps with wall tents and camp cook are also used, particularly on the popular and reasonably priced 10-day, one-on-one special trophy hunt. You may lose weight on York's hunts, not from any lack of good food, because you'll find meat and potatoes as well as fresh salads and scrumptious desserts on the menu, but from all that hiking.

[R O C K Y   M O U N T A I N S]

A Lazy H Outfitters

C h o t e a u ,   M o n t a n a

The scenic Bob Marshall Wilderness offers up elk (bugling or glassing) mule deer and bear.

VITAL STATISTICS:

Game/Arm/Seasons:
ELK and DEER:
Archery: Early to mid-Sept.
Rifle: Mid-Sept. through Nov.
BEAR:
Fall: Mid-Sept. through Nov., Spring: Mid-Apr. through May

Rates:
From $280/day

Accommodations:
TENT CAMPS AND LOG RANCH
MAXIMUM NUMBER OF HUNTERS: 6

Meals: Beef, chicken, fish served family-style

Conference Groups: Yes

Guides: Included

Gratuity: 15%

Preferred Payment:
Cash, check

Other Activities:
Fishing, riding

Getting There:
Fly to Great Falls and the lodge van will transport you for $75 round-trip.

Contact:
Al Haas
A Lazy H Outfitters
Box 729
Choteau, MT 59422
800/893-1155
e-mail: jahaas@3rivers.net
Web: www.recworld.com/alazyh

SINCE THE EARLY 1930S, A Lazy H Outfitters have been guiding hunters in the area known as the Bob Marshall Wilderness, 1.5 million acres of relatively roadless real estate that follows the Rockies southeastward from Glacier National Park. The Haas family—Allen, Sally and Joe—operate two camps, one for the bugling season and another for the general season. The first camp is located on Big River Meadows in Unit 151. The meadows itself is a long, open park in the midst of mountains that are reasonably walkable. Dense stands of lodgepole pine, Douglas fir and patches of blowdown provide cover for elk. Bugling and cow calling are the most effective tactics here. Bulls run in the 5x5 class and 40 percent of the hunters harvest trophies. Mule deer and black bear are found in this area as well. Mulies are nice bucks going 4x4 or so. Tags permit harvesting bucks, but not too many hunters are willing to divert their energies from elk hunting. To an even larger degree, the same is true with black bear.

After the bugling stops, the outfit moves up to a little strip of Flathead National Forest sandwiched between the Bob Marshall Wilderness, Great Bear Wilderness and Glacier National Park in Area 415, a few miles south of the town of East Glacier Park. Here, the game changes radically. Terrain consists of high, open hillsides that have been logged recently. Riding out before dawn to a height of land, hunters spend hours glassing the flanks of nearby ridges for elk movement. The region straddles the main migration route for elk leaving snowbound Glacier Park for their winter range. Physical stamina is a must; stalks involve as much climbing down as climbing up. Thirty percent of hunters bring out 5x5s from this area.

The final hunt of the calendar year is run from the A Lazy H Ranch on the South Fork of the Teton River, 25 miles west of Choteau. High mountains surround the ranch and late in the season it offers excellent hunting for mule deer. Spring brings bear hunting, and in both cases guests stay in the main ranch in a typical "bed and breakfast" arrangement—meaning private rooms and bath— except that dinner and lunch are also provided. Hunts vary in length from six to nine days and generally feature two hunters with one guide. A one-on-one hunt can be arranged for an extra $100 per day.

Avalanche Basin Outfitters

White Sulphur Springs, Montana

A variety of hunting techniques are available to elk hunters at this lodge in the Belt Mountains.

VITAL STATISTICS:

Game/Arm/Seasons:
DEER and ELK,
Bow: Early Sept. through mid-Oct.
Centerfire: Late Oct. through Nov.
MOUNTAIN LION:
Bow, centerfire: Dec. through mid-Feb.
Rates:
From $5,600/6 days
Accommodations:
WOOD CABINS
MAXIMUM NUMBER OF HUNTERS: 6
Meals: Family-style
Conference Groups: No
Guides: Included
Gratuity: $100
Preferred Payment:
Cash, check
Other Activities:
Fishing
Getting There:
Fly to Helena and the lodge van will meet you.

Contact:
Doug or Zita Caltrider
Avalanche Basin Outfitters
Box 17
White Sulphur Springs
MT 59645
406/547-3962
Fax: 406/547-3900
e-mail: avalanche4@juno.com
Web: www.avalancheoutfitters.com

THE BELT MOUNTAINS, about 60 miles south of Great Falls, might be a definite "also ran" when it comes to the scenic grandeur of the southwestern corner of the state. But this ancient range of mountains, none higher than 9,000 feet or so, have their steep and difficult places. Yet they're also known for long meadows and open woodlands interspersed with tight canyons and stands of dark lodgepole, fir and spruce. Not really migratory, elk here are old "residents" that change elevation with the seasons.

With 43,000 acres of private ranch on which to play, hunters can find countryside that meets different hunting techniques and styles. During the early season, calling is the most effective tactic used by archers. Elk are in the upper ends of the drainages then. The cover is difficult, and glassing, stalking and more glassing is the norm. It's not uncommon to look over more than 100 elk during a typical six-day hunt. Most archers, depending on the weather, get two or three shots at bulls—5x5s and 6x6s. About half can back up their stories with a set of antlers over the mantle.

Rifle hunters may have a bit of an advantage here—the success rate is high, at 70 percent. From camp, you'll ride via 4WD out into an area of active sign. Setting up first on the edge of a meadow to catch elk moving back toward deeper cover, you'll glass and glass. If the bull of your dreams is not to be found here, you'll climb up to the open flanks of the basin and glass some more. In a good week, hunters will have a choice of 20 bulls. Which one you pick and whether you nail him is up to you and the gods. Mule deer season coincides with elk, but the population here is not large and the chances of seeing a trophy buck are, admittedly, slim. Still some very nice 5-pointers are taken every year. And, along with the elk lease, there's another 11,000 acres of private river bottom where whitetails prowl. If you fill your elk tag early in the week, you'll just have to hunt these bucks of 4x4 and better. In addition, after elk and deer season closes, mountain lions become legal game. Hunted with dogs, a typical cat will run seven feet, and Doug Caltrider, headman of this outfit, has a no-kill, no-pay policy. That tells you about his success rate.

Accommodations are snug wood cabins for four hunters. Propane provides heat and light and the cook provides family-style fare.

[R O C K Y   M O U N T A I N S]

B&D Outfitters

K a l i s p e l l ,   M o n t a n a

Head deep into the Bob Marshall for trophy mule deer and elk.

VITAL STATISTICS:

Game/Arm/Seasons:
ELK and WHITETAIL DEER:
Bow: Early to mid-Sept.
Centerfire: Mid-Sept. through late Nov.
MULE DEER:
Bow: Early to mid-Sept.
Centerfire: Early Sept. through late Nov.
BLACK BEAR:
Bow: Early to late May
Centerfire: Spring, mid to late May; fall, mid-Sept. through late Nov.
Rates:
ELK/DEER combo from $2,200/7 days
BLACK BEAR from $1,500/5 days
Accommodations:
TENTS
MAXIMUM NUMBER OF HUNTERS: 8
Meals: Steak, chicken, turkey, pork chops, fish, pasta, vegetables
Conference Groups: Yes
Guides: Included
Gratuity: $50 to $200
Preferred Payment:
Cash, check
Other Activities:
Biking, bird hunting, bird watching, boating, canoeing/rafting, fishing, hiking, swimming, waterfowling, wildlife photography
Getting There:
Fly to Great Falls or Kalispell, Montana, and be met by the outfitter. There is a slight charge for fuel if flying into Great Falls.

Contact:
Bob Frisk
B&D Outfitters
Box 455
Kalispell, MT 59903
406/752-7842

THE BOB MARSHALL WILDERNESS AREA is where Bob Frisk's B&D Outfitters guides most clients. Base camp is 15 miles into the wilderness by horseback, and consists of wall tents for each party and a large cook tent.

With the coming of fall, the bugle season for elk provides bow and early rifle hunters with the unique opportunity to bugle in a trophy bull—surely one of the most exciting hunting experiences you can have! October is when mule deer generally go into the rut, which makes them more vulnerable to hunters. The snows also start the elk migrating down from the higher altitudes, through the area where B&D's hunters generally go.

Mountain lion season opens in the wilderness in early November, and hunters can combine that with elk and deer if they want. In December lion hunting is also available outside the wilderness from the lodge, and it runs until the quota is filled. Hunts for black bears and whitetails are offered from mid-September until mid-November (bears may also be hunted in spring). Most hunts are two hunters with one guide, although one-on-one hunts, along with drop camps, can be arranged. Hunts for bighorn sheep, shiras moose and mountain goats are available via a special permit drawing.

According to Frisk, "We operate as a small, personalized service, offering family-oriented discounts and hands-on service. We specialize in a true wilderness experience, with trips customized to the individual." Especially when his hunts take place in such a wild and beautiful part of the West, you can understand why that attitude has helped his outfit become a success.

On the flank of the Pioneer Mountains in central/southwest
Montana, Russ Kipp's Montana High Country Tours lodge
is the staging ground for elk, deer and bear hunts. You
can stay at the lodge with all of its amenities, or move to a
tent camp that's located where elk are active. The
choice is usually dictated by the bulls.

Beardsley Outfitting & Guide Service

E n n i s ,   M o n t a n a

*A tiny patch of heaven offers elk
in the 4x4 and 5x5 class.*

VITAL STATISTICS:

Game/Arm/Seasons:
ELK and DEER
Bow: Sept. through mid-Oct.
Centerfire: Late Oct. through Nov.
BEAR:
Centerfire: Fall: Sept. through mid-Nov.; spring: mid-Apr. through mid-May

Rates:
ELK and DEER from $3,000/6 days
BEAR from $1,300

Accommodations:
RUSTIC WOODEN LODGE AND CABINS
NUMBER OF ROOMS: 5; 3 WITH PRIVATE BATH
MAXIMUM NUMBER OF HUNTERS: 8

Meals: Healthy and hearty cuisine

Conference Groups: No

Guides: Included

Gratuity: 10 to 15%

Preferred Payment:
Cash, check

Other Activities:
Antiquing, biking, bird hunting, bird watching, boating, canoeing/rafting, fishing, golf, riding, skiing, swimming, waterfowling, wildlife photography

Getting There:
Fly to Bozeman, rent a car and drive to the lodge, or rely on the lodge van for $55.

Contact:
Tim Beardsley
Beardsley Outfitting
& Guide Service
Box 360
Ennis, MT 59729
406/682-7292
e-mail: tbbigsky@3rivers.com
Web: www.recworld.com/beardsley

TIM BEARDSLEY HAS FOUND himself a little bit of heaven at his 100-acre ranch up on Jack Creek Bench overlooking Ennis, the Madison River and the lake beyond. You wouldn't call this jewel of a ranch exactly tiny, not with its rustic main lodge and two guest cabins, but it's small compared to some of the 10,000-acre spreads in the neighborhood. Out the back door of the ranch is the entire Lee Metcalf Wilderness, which contains most of the western flanks of the Madison Mountains.

Hunters ride out every morning. "Doesn't make any difference whether they've know how to ride, they'll warm up to it pretty quick," Tim laughs. So how do you learn? "Hold on," he says. This is a great example of learning by doing—teachers call it experiential education. Horses carry hunters up into the high and open timber just below treeline. Then, if you're hunting during archery season when the elk rut is on, you can call them in. In mid-October when rifle season opens, spotting and stalking and stalking some more is how this game's played. Archers everywhere tend to be plagued by errant arrows. It's no different here. When the master of the harem comes crashing out of the woods hell-bent on fighting you for his lady friends, it seems quite reasonable to get a little fidgety. Maybe that's why only three out of 10 archers connect. Rifle hunters do better than twice as well as archers. Tim's hunters take their share of 4-pointers, but some walk away with 5x5s and 6x6s that are good bulls in anyone's book. Generally, two hunters share a guide.

Hunting here is not dictated as much by winter snows as in other locales. There's no waiting for bulls to begin their winter migrations. A resident herd of 300 to 400 head is in the area all year long. They may be augmented by some migratory elk, but in the main Tim's guests are hunting "residents." About 8 percent of the herd are mature bulls and another 15 percent are brush heads—young bulls with three and four points.

This is kind of a laid-back operation. Its fishing program has received Orvis' endorsement, and 80 percent of its hunters are repeat customers. The hunting is reasonably good for Montana's fair-chase operations, and the food—the likes of seafood and pasta, grilled chicken breasts and fresh green salads—stands head and shoulders over most.

Beartooth Plateau Outfitters

Cooke City, Montana

Ride horseback into the wilderness to spot and stalk for elk.

VITAL STATISTICS:

Game/Arm/Seasons:
ELK and DEER:
Bow: Mid-Sept. through early Oct.
Centerfire: Late Oct. through Nov.
SPRING BEAR:
Bow, centerfire: Mid-Apr. through May
Rates:
ELK and DEER from $2,800/7 days
BEAR: $1,500/5 days
Accommodations:
WALL-TENT CAMPS
MAXIMUM NUMBER OF HUNTERS: 8
Meals: Hearty chops, chicken and steak
Conference Groups: No
Guides: Included
Gratuity: $200 to $300
Preferred Payment:
Cash, check
Other Activities:
Fishing, riding
Getting There:
Fly to Billings or Butte, rent a car and drive to Wisdom.

Contact:
Ronnie Wright
Beartooth Plateau
Outfitters Inc.,
Box 1127
Cooke City, MT 59020
406/445-2293 or
800/253-8545
off-season:
Box 1028
Roberts, MT 59070

RONNIE WRIGHT RELIES ON WISDOM to get his big elk late in the season. We're not talking an excess of cerebral power here, though you'll see occasional flashes of that with this guy—who else carries a "horse phone?" Nope, we're talking Wisdom, Montana, that tiny town up in the Big Hole basin. Named by Lewis and Clark in honor of Thomas Jefferson, this bit of mecca is the jumping-off point for hunting the Pioneer Mountains of the Beaverhead National Forest. While the highest peak (Odell Mountain) tops 9,600 feet, the landscape is not overly rugged. But it is thick with pine, spruce, fir and heavy brush. Broken by reforesting clear-cuts and swaths of mountain grasses, habitat is good for elk in the 4- to 6-point range.

Hunters booked for Wisdom arrive in town on the day before and plan to overnight in the Nez Perce Motel. On the day of the hunt, the two-hour ride up into the West Pioneers begins. At the end of the trail you'll find a very comfortable camp, three tents for hunters, a cook tent and a shower tent. From the eight-hunter camp, you'll ride farther into the wilderness, tether the horses and then spot and stalk. The rut has pretty well run its course and bulls are leaving their harems. As the season progresses from late October toward its end on Thanksgiving weekend, the weather may push the elk and mule deer from the heights into draws and meadows. Count on snow.

To take advantage of bugling elk, Ronnie opens his operation in the Absaroka-Beartooth Wilderness of the Gallatin National Forest, which surrounds the northeast corner of Yellowstone National Park. From his base camp near Copeland Lake, less than half a mile from the state line, clients may hunt in Wyoming if they've successfully navigated the state's computer license lottery. There's a lot of up and down in this country, but like the Pioneers, it's not as rugged as some. Bugling elk respond to calling, and they're found in the high timber. At this camp, fishing is quite good, and in this part of the country, there's no better time to be on the water. Don't forget your pack rod, or plan a couple extra days after your hunt to fish the much-vaunted streams of Yellowstone. Spring bear hunts are also conducted in this region.

While Montana hunts are the foundation of Ronnie's business, he also runs elk, deer, bear, moose and sheep hunts in Wyoming.

[R O C K Y M O U N T A I N S]

Beaver Creek Outfitters

L e w i s t o w n ,   M o n t a n a

Trophy and meat hunters do well out of the tent camps of Beaver Creek Outfitters.

VITAL STATISTICS:

Game/Arm/Seasons:
ELK and DEER:
Bow: Sept. through mid-Oct.
Firearms: Late Oct. through Nov.
Rates:
Archery from $1,200/7 days
Firearms $2,000
Accommodations:
WALL TENTS WITH WOOD DOORS AND FLOORS
MAXIMUM NUMBER OF HUNTERS: 8
Meals: Roasts, potatoes and salads
Conference Groups: No
Guides: Included
Gratuity: $100
Preferred Payment:
Cash, check
Other Activities:
Riding, wildlife photography
Getting There:
Fly to Billings, Bozeman, or Missoula
and meet up with Clayton.

Contact:
Clayton Barkhoff
Beaver Creek Outfitters
RR 1, Box 1732
Lewistown, MT 59457
800/355-7557

A DECADE AGO, wildfire swept through 10,000 acres of the Little Belt Mountains searing the south slopes in the Lost Fork of the Judith River drainage. Regrowth comes slowly and it's not consistent. Like jackstraws, scorched blowdowns litter some hillsides, while others, untouched by the flames, are verdant. Pockets of new growth resemble jungle more than forest. It is these areas that hold elk.

Hunting this area is different. While bugling and calling works during bow season, after that success is predicated on finding bulls in the open when they move from one pocket of woods to another. Frequently, Clayton Barkhoff who runs Beaver Creek will post hunters on escape routes and then work slowly and quietly around stands of thick regrowth trying to push elk toward the hunters. Sometimes it works and sometimes it doesn't. The first rifle hunt occurs in mid-October before the herd has gathered and before cold weather has forced them to feed more frequently. Along with pushing pockets of timber, sneak hunting works well. Being able to fire a well-aimed shot has more to do with hunter success, which runs 40 percent for elk and 60 percent for mule deer, than anything else. As the season progresses, tactics turn more to glassing and stalking as elk concentrate and move lower down into the Lost Creek drainage.

And, while occasionally a client bags a 5x5 or bigger, most elk that are taken are spikes. During the last week of the season, elk of either sex are fair game. During firearm and rifle seasons, the rule is either-sex for mulies and whitetails. Hunters in these camps are looking for meat as well as trophies.

Just about a two-hour ride from the trailhead, Clayton's camps are clean and well managed. Wood framed and floored wall tents that are heated with wood-stoves contain full-sized built-in bunks. Two hunters have a tent to themselves. You'll also find a shower tent and, of course, a cook tent where roasts, spuds and salads are staples on the menu.

Big Salmon Outfitters

Ronan, Montana

Tent camps on Holland Lake are home to hunters going for early-season elk.

VITAL STATISTICS:

Game/Arm/Seasons:
ELK and DEER
Bow: Early Sept.
Firearms: Mid-Sept. through late Nov.

Rates:
From $2,800/8-day hunt any species

Accommodations:
WALL TENTS
MAXIMUM NUMBER OF HUNTERS: 8

Meals: Steaks, twice-baked potatoes, tossed salad, apple pie

Conference Groups: No

Guides: Included

Gratuity: $250 to $500

Preferred Payment:
Cash, MasterCard, Visa, check

Other Activities:
Bird watching, fishing, swimming

Getting There:
Fly to Missoula and rent a car, or arrange transportation with the outfitter for $50 per person one-way.

Contact:
Kehoe Wayman
Big Salmon Outfitters
Box 496
Ronan, MT 59864
406/676-3999
e-mail: Salmon@ronan.net
Web: www.bigsalmon.com

THE RIDE CARRIES YOU UP from Holland Lake, through the alders and cottonwoods, climbing through the gap between Tango Point and Gyp Mountain and down into Big Salmon Lake country. Narrow, lovely and teeming with cutthroat, the seven-mile-long lake lies in a deep valley among a series of low mountains in the headwaters of the South Fork of the Flathead. Elevations range from about 4,000 feet to 8,000 feet. Ridges are steep, in places reaching above treeline, and covered with talus. But there's a lot of open land too, and myriad streams and wallows favored by bulls in rut.

This is Unit 150 where rutting bulls can be hunted with rifles in mid-September after only a week of archery-only season. This gives gun hunters an advantage over other areas where rifle season typically doesn't begin until late October. Sure, winter comes early to this track deep in the heart of the Bob Marshall Wilderness, and heavy snows are always a possibility. Yet, snow moves and concentrates elk, which bodes well for hunters. Kehoe Wayman, head man of Big Salmon Outfitters, has guided in these parts for more than a dozen years. His focus is putting hunters on 6x6 bulls. From his tent camp (only two hunters per tent) on the lake, hunters are up at 4 a.m. and on the trail to get to the area they'll hunt at dawn. Hunting is afoot across ridges and meadows toward the prearranged landmark to which the wrangler has moved the horses. The best hunting is mid-September, during the peak of the rut. But there's another spike of bugling in mid-October as bulls seek cows that have yet to be bred.

You'll also find mule deer in the Big Salmon area. Harvested bucks are typically 4x4s, and they're taken above treeline. "I think they think they're goats!" quips Kehoe. And bear also are on the list. Here they tend to be the lighter phases of blonde and cinnamon and average 300 pounds. Mountain lions frequent these forests as well. If you cut the track of a big tom while elk hunting, the guide will radio the wrangler who will bring on the hounds. And, of course, should you be fortunate enough to book for the early part of the season, you'll want to bring a flyrod or spinning rod for cutthroats.

Black Mountain Outfitters

E m i g r a n t ,   M o n t a n a

Bugling elk make sweet music in the dawn.

VITAL STATISTICS:

Game/Arm/Seasons:

<u>ELK:</u>
Bow, centerfire: Mid-Sept. through mid-Oct.

<u>MULE DEER:</u>
Bow, centerfire: Late Oct. through late Nov.

<u>MOUNTAIN LION:</u>
Bow, centerfire: Dec. through Feb.

<u>BLACK BEAR:</u>
Centerfire: Mid-May through mid-June

<u>ANTELOPE:</u>
Bow, centerfire: Late Oct. through early Nov.

Rates:
ELK $3,500/8 days
MULE DEER, ANTELOPE from $2,000/5 days
MOUNTAIN LION $3,000/7 days
BLACK BEAR $1,500/5 day

Accommodations:
TENT CAMP AND RANCH HOUSE
NUMBER OF ROOMS: 3, SHARED
MAXIMUM NUMBER OF HUNTERS: 8

Meals: Chicken, marinated steak, roasts

Conference Groups: No
Guides: Included
Gratuity: $100
Preferred Payment:
Cash, check

Other Activities:
Fishing, wildlife photography

Getting There:
Fly to Bozeman (elk) or Billings (deer) and rent a car.

Contact:
Scott Sallee or Sandy Seaton
Black Mountain Outfitters
Box 117
Emigrant, MT 59027
406/222-7455
e-mail: BlackMtnZ@aol.com

SWINGING INTO THE SADDLE about 5 a.m., you wheel your horse to the right and follow outfitter Scott Sallee up the steep and narrow trail. Lodgepole pines as black as carbon filigree are silhouetted against a charcoal sky. Through gaps in the trees you catch glimpses of the stars that light your way, but you don't think of them. You're consumed with weary expectation on this, the morning of your first elk hunt.

Scott halts, dismounts, ties his horse to a tree, and you do likewise. Pulling your rifle from its scabbard, you follow quietly on foot. Up ahead the opening of the trail glows cool and gray in this world of black timber. And then you're there, on the plateau. Thick tufts of grass bow under hoary frost, yet each crystalline blade carries the light of a billion stars in the boundless sky.

As you settle into the ground blind, that old familiar whistle of elk that always ends in a wheeze drifts through the forest. Scott, with his calls, is a little to your left. Your eyes scan the meadow and the treeline opposite, and as the night sky purples into yellowish-blue, you hear Scott bugle. A bull challenges immediately. It is shooting light now, and you can see the bull crossing the meadow. You can take him if you wish, but it's too early, and from what you can tell he's only a spike. There will be better bulls, you tell yourself as the first sun begins to sweep the plateau.

Though you are on the Buffalo Plateau along the northern boundary of Yellowstone National Park, you can see the Tetons rising almost 100 miles due south. High and gently rolling, the plateau is a natural corridor for elk moving down out of the park into winter range. Typical bulls are 6x6, and success runs in the 70-percent range. From Scott's camp on Buffalo Fork of Slough Creek, you'll also hunt pockets of green timber that escaped the great Yellowstone blaze of '88.

For mule deer, Scott switches operations to a rustic abandoned frame ranch house ("Does it have a privy out back?" "No," says Scott, "It's not that abandoned."). You'll hunt mule deer in the 22- to 24-inch class over 90,000 private acres of sage and gumbo with deep breaks filled with tight clumps of junipers. Generally everyone gets a deer.

Mountain lion hunts are run from Scott and his wife Sallee's home in Emigrant. If there's snow, Scott will run up the valley on a snowmobile checking for tracks. When the ground is bare, Scott free-casts his Red Bones until one picks up a scent. Then begins the madness. As with mule deer, everyone is successful.

Bob Marshall Wilderness Ranch

St. Ignatius, Montana

This ranch is located smack in the middle of major elk and deer country.

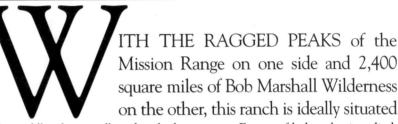

VITAL STATISTICS:

Game/Arm/Seasons:
WILDERNESS ELK and DEER:
Centerfire: Mid-Sept. through Oct.
LODGE DEER:
Centerfire: Nov.
BLACK BEAR:
Mid-Apr. through mid-May
Rates:
From $2,500/8-day hunt any species
Accommodations:
TENT CAMPS AND MODERN LODGE
NUMBER OF ROOMS: 4
MAXIMUM NUMBER OF HUNTERS:
LODGE: 8, CAMP: 6
Meals: Family-style
Conference Groups: Yes
Guides: Included
Gratuity: 5 to 10%
Preferred Payment:
Cash, check
Other Activities:
Biking, fishing, riding, skiing, wildlife photography
Getting There:
Fly to Missoula and the lodge van will pick you up.

Contact:
Virgil Burns
Bob Marshall Wilderness Ranch
St. Ignatius, MT 59865
406/745-4666
e-mail:
burns@wildernessranch.com
Web: www.wildernessranch.com

WITH THE RAGGED PEAKS of the Mission Range on one side and 2,400 square miles of Bob Marshall Wilderness on the other, this ranch is ideally situated in the middle of prime elk and mule deer country. Fingers of lodgepole pine climb the flanks of steeply rising mountains, to benches, opening here and there for parks and basins, and then climb again to the timberline. Above timber is talus and outcrop favored by mountain goats, but also by mule deer. To hunt goats here, you'll need to weather the lottery drawing, which is no mean feat. Mule deer tags come with your combo license for elk. For $100, you can add a ticket to tackle a black bear, and if you do score on a bear its color may be blonde or cinnamon. You may not want to take a black bear in the fall, though; pelts are better in spring.

Chief of this outfit is Virgil Burns, a mountain man who's guided the best for more than 20 years. He operates his main wilderness camp up on Shaw Creek, a headwater of the South Fork of the Flathead. Rising above the camp is 8,140-foot Shaw Mountain, and across the way is a 7,900-footer called Trio. Alpine lakes; basins with stream wallows; black timber thick with blowdowns; slick, steep, grassy meadows; slopes of talus and scree — you'll hunt it all from his tiny tent city. Your eight-day hunt may take you and your guide (one-on-one hunts are the most successful here) to mobile spike camps putting you closer to where the animals are moving. Bulls run in the 5x5-range, and mule deer, when you find them, are typically 4x4s. Best hunting is before and during the rut; rifles become legal in mid-September after a week of archery-only hunting. If there's a space, book as early as you can. Snow chases everyone out of the Shaw Creek Drainage by the end of October.

Around his rustic hilltop lodge, 21 miles north of Seeley in the Swan Valley off Route 83, Burns runs late-season hunts for whitetails and mule deer. You'll find some elk here as well, and more as the season progresses, but the population is not high enough to sustain commercial hunting. Deer, on the other hand, grow large. Mulies on the ridges have racks in the 24- to 30-inch range, and the whitetails, found lower down, are known for their heavy racks. You'll ride out in the early morning on horse or 4WD, returning at dark. Everyone who hunts out of the lodge sees deer. Accommodations at the lodge are first-class and the food is a notch above the rest.

Bridger Outfitters

B e l g r a d e ,   M o n t a n a

Outfitter Dave Warwood has been hunting off the northwestern corner of Yellowstone Park since 1973.

VITAL STATISTICS:

Game/Arm/Seasons:
ELK, MULE DEER:
Bow: Early Sept. through mid-Oct.
Centerfire, muzzleloader: Late Oct. through late Nov.
MOOSE:
Bow, centerfire: Mid-Sept. through late Nov.
ANTELOPE:
Centerfire: Early Oct. through early Nov.

Rates:
Rifle hunts from $2,650/6 days
Bow hunts from $2,400/6 days

Accommodations:
CABINS AND WALL TENTS (VARIES BY HUNT AND LOCATION)
NUMBER OF ROOMS: 6 IN CABINS
MAXIMUM NUMBER OF HUNTERS: 6

Meals: Meat, potatoes, veggies, salads served family-style

Conference Groups: No

Guides: Included

Gratuity: $50 to $100

Preferred Payment:
Cash, check

Other Activities:
Bird hunting, boating, canoeing/rafting, fishing, hiking, swimming, waterfowling, wildlife photography

Getting There:
Fly to Bozeman, rent a car and drive to the ranch, or be met at the airport by a representative of the outfitter.

Contact:
Dave Warwood
Bridger Outfitters
15100 Rocky Mountain Rd.
Belgrade, MT 59714
406/388-4463

MANY FIRST-TIME HUNTERS have no idea just how large an elk can be. Accustomed to whitetails, they may not be aware that, on average, an elk's head and body length is seven to 10 feet, with the shoulder height between four and five feet. (By comparison, a deer is four to six feet, with a shoulder height of about three feet.) So an elk is a huge target, one you can't miss, right? Wrong. When that wapiti is out at 300 yards and his tan hide and red/brown neck hair blends with his surroundings, finding a vital organ to hit with a 180-grain bullet suddenly isn't so easy.

What all that means, in a nutshell, is that it pays to have a good guide such as Dave Warwood, owner of Bridger Outfitters. Before your hunt, Warwood will make sure you're prepared—that you've gotten yourself in decent enough physical shape to withstand the rigors of hunting the high country off the northwestern corner of Yellowstone Park; that you've sighted your rifle in for (usually) two inches high at 100 yards; that you know how to shoot it accurately; that you've done some horseback riding ahead of time; and, of most importance, that you know what to expect on your hunt, that you have the right attitude.

Warwood runs three hunting camps. The first, a backcountry horse pack-in camp, is at the edge of the Lee Metcalf Wilderness outside of the park. This is a tent camp, with big bull elk the main quarry. Warwood is quick to point out that two recent bulls from this area scored 397 and 400-plus points B&C. This is a popular hunt with bowhunters and early-season rifle hunters.

Warwood's second hunt is from a ranch on the west side of the Bridger Mountains. This is big mule deer country, in particular, though there are plenty of elk to go around. "We found one buck, killed by a mountain lion, that had a 39-inch spread," Warwood notes. "And our guides have spotted one that looks to be over 40. He's still out there." Average spreads go 24 inches.

Warwood also leases private ranch lands for trophy hunts, with big whitetails, mulies, elk, antelope and turkeys available.

"I grew up hunting these same areas that I guide today," states Warwood. "I started guiding professionally in 1973, and know the habits and habitat of the wapiti and other big game in the area. We also know that hunting is more than just taking home a trophy. We work hard to give you memories and friendships that last a long time."

Broken Arrow Lodge

A l d e r ,   M o n t a n a

*Broken Arrow is a
do-it-yourselfer's dream.*

VITAL STATISTICS:

Game/Arm/Seasons:
ELK and DEER:
Bow: Early Sept. through mid-Oct.
Firearms: Late Oct. through Nov.
Rates:
From $695/7 days
Accommodations:
LOG LODGE
NUMBER OF ROOMS: 7
MAXIMUM NUMBER OF HUNTERS: 18
Meals: Family-style
Conference Groups: Yes
Guides: Not available
Gratuity: Hunter's discretion
Preferred Payment:
Cash, check
Other Activities:
Biking, bird hunting, bird watching,
boating, fishing, wildlife photography
Getting There:
Drive your own 4WD, or fly to
Bozeman and a representative of the
lodge will pick you up for $135
round-trip.

Contact:
Erwin Clark
Broken Arrow Lodge
Box 177
Alder, MT 59710
1-800/775-2928
Fax: 406-842-5437
e-mail: brokenai@mail.3rivers.net
Web: http:recworld.com

EVEN THOUGH YOU'RE HUNTING in the Scapegoats, if you're hunting out of Broken Arrow Lodge the only person you can blame for blowing that shot on an elk is the hunter. Broken Arrow is a do-it-yourselfer's dream: log lodge of honey pine, seven guest rooms accommodating groups from two to eight, and scrumptious meals timed to your schedule, not the cook's. But there are no guides, no full-service tent camp with wranglers and horses and no exclusive permits for sections deep in wilderness areas.

Erwin Clark figures it this way: lots of hunters would rather do it all themselves. And in so doing, save themselves a bundle of money. A seven-day hunt out of Broken Arrow costs about $100 per day. Or, if clients really seek a wilderness experience, Clark will set up a spike camp, provision it with grub and gear and pack hunters in on horseback, all for about $1,000 per week. You can save anywhere from $1,000 up through the program offered by Broken Arrow, yet there are some caveats.

As of this writing, Montana guarantees non-resident hunters booked with licensed outfitters a combination elk/deer license. The cost of an outfitter-sponsored license is $835. While hunters save about $350 if they apply for a regular non-resident elk/deer license, there's no guarantee that they'll be drawn. If you hunt at Broken Arrow, you'll have to apply for your own license (the deadline is mid-March) and the chances of being drawn are very good for areas 324 and 340 near the lodge. The second caveat is that transportation from the lodge to the area where you want to hunt is your responsibility. Most hunters bring their own vehicles.

Proof of the pudding is in the eating, or in this case, the hunter success rate. More than half of Clark's hunters take elk or deer. Terrain is broken, a quilt of lodgepole pines and firs and open parks. It's public land and pressure from resident hunters is heavy during the first three or four days of the season. But that soon falls off, and hunters who are willing to play the game the way the outfitters do, by planning the day's hunt the night before and then hiking into the hunting area in the dark before dawn, improve their odds dramatically. Clark continually scouts the area, at times via aircraft. With topo maps, and, increasingly, GPS units, each night he helps his hunters set up a five-point plan for the next day.

About half of Broken Arrow's hunters are experienced and half are novices, and the lodge is increasingly popular. If this hunt appeals to you, it's best to book two years in advance.

[R O C K Y   M O U N T A I N S]

Bullseye Outfitting

T r o u t   C r e e k ,   M o n t a n a

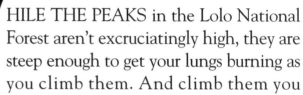

Hunt the Lolo for 6x6 elk and trophy mule deer.

VITAL STATISTICS:

Game/Arm/Seasons:
ELK and DEER:
Bow: Sept.
Centerfire, muzzleloader: Late Oct.
through Nov.
BEAR:
Bow, centerfire, muzzleloader: Fall:
Mid to late Sept.; Spring: Late April
through mid-May
MOUNTAIN LION:
Dec.
Rates:
ELK and DEER from $2,100/7 days
BEAR $1,500/7 days
MOUNTAIN LION $3,000/7 days
Accommodations:
LOG LODGE
NUMBER OF ROOMS: 2 WITH PRIVATE BATH
MAXIMUM NUMBER OF HUNTERS: 6
Meals: Steaks, spaghetti, chicken
Conference Groups: No
Guides: Included
Gratuity: $100
Preferred Payment:
Cash, check
Other Activities:
Biking, bird-watching, golf, wildlife
photography
Getting There:
Fly to Spokane or Missoula, rent a car
and drive to the lodge.

Contact:
Jeff Smith
Bullseye Outfitting
49 Vermilion Rd.
Trout Creek, MT 59874
406/827-4932
Web:
www.nwmontana.com/bullseye.html

WHILE THE PEAKS in the Lolo National Forest aren't excruciatingly high, they are steep enough to get your lungs burning as you climb them. And climb them you must if you're going to get a crack at bulls in the 6x6 class. These bulls, and mule deer bucks, stay high in the timber during the first weeks of the season. You'll find these big boys playing tag with the treeline and the tortuous scree and talus above it. Calling is the best way to pull in a bull, but when that fails, spotting and stalking may do the trick. As the first hunters in the woods, archers have a decided advantage. But there's an accompanying liability. Unless your nerves are as tough as titanium, it's hard not to lose your cool when a bull steps out not 20 yards away. Some pretty good mule deer bucks are also found at these elevations. And about 20 percent of Bullseye's hunters take both.

Bullseye uses tent camps to hunt the high country, but after the first week of rifle season in early October, snow chases hunters and bulls down the mountains. That's when Jeff Smith and his partner Ben Mummert say good-bye to canvas walls and hello to the hot showers of their two-guestroom lodge down on the road to the Vermilion River. From these quarters hunters are driven to jump-off points where they'll hike logging roads and forest trails as deep into the wilderness as they need to go—five to ten miles for a good bull, whichever comes first.

Some hunters come just for the deer hunting. Whitetails that score 130 points are fairly common, and a number of 140- to 150-class bucks are taken each year. Best hunting comes during the rut in November when rattling and grunting pays off and snow concentrates deer. For mule deer, it's best to find them early when they're still up in the high country. Horses will take you to within walking distance of clear-cuts and brush fields where browse is plentiful. About 90 percent of those who hunt only deer come home with venison and a rack.

Black bears (a five-footer is a keeper) are seldom the sole quarry during a fall hunt. But if you buy a license before you come to Montana, you'll be able to take one while hunting elk or deer. Spring is really the better time to hunt bear, though. Coats lack rubbed spots and elk and deer don't pose a distraction. Almost 80 percent of hunters bag bears averaging 250 pounds during spring hunts in May. The country also has lots of lions, and clients who hunt over dogs in December frequently take toms averaging 140 pounds.

Centennial Outfitters

L i m a ,   M o n t a n a

To get trophy elk, you have to follow their natural patterns.

VITAL STATISTICS:

Game/Arm/Seasons:
ELK and DEER:
Bow: Early Sept. through mid-Oct.
Centerfire: Late Oct. through Nov.
Rates:
Bow: $2,500/8 days
Centerfire: $2,700/8 days
Accommodations:
LOG LODGE, TENTS
NUMBER OF ROOMS: 3
MAXIMUM NUMBER OF HUNTERS: 8
Meals: Home-style cooking
Conference Groups: Yes
Guides: Included
Gratuity: Hunter's discretion
Preferred Payment:
Cash, money order
Other Activities:
Bird hunting, bird watching,
canoeing/rafting, fishing, riding,
waterfowling, wildlife photography
Getting There:
Fly to Idaho Falls or Butte, rent a car
and drive to the lodge.

Contact:
Mel Montgomery
Centennial Outfitters
Box 92
Lima, MT 59739
406/276-3463

THE CENTENNIAL MOUNTAINS snake east to west along the Continental Divide and the border between Montana and Idaho. To the east is Yellowstone; to the west are the Bitterroots. In this serrated land of sharp peaks and deep valleys rises the world's longest river, the Missouri. You can stand with a foot on each side of its headwater, and if fortune smiles, shoot that bull crossing 100 yards downstream. Elk move in a predictable pattern. In summer they prefer the cool seclusion of high, dense forests of lodgepole and fir on the north slope of the divide. It is a tangled country of blowdowns and hidden meadows just below treeline.

The rut occurs in the first week of the season when bulls leave their bachelor buddies and begin to collect their harems. Bugling, of course, is a very good strategy then. During the second week of rifle season, bulls begin splitting away from the cows, and by the third week it's rare to see bulls with cows. In the fourth week, most of the elk are down low, but the bulls are beginning to move back up the draws, heading for passes that will carry them across the divide and onto the warmer south-facing slopes in Idaho. The trick is to locate camps so hunters can take advantage of the natural cycle of these elk.

Depending on the weather, the first two hunts are conducted from tent camps in the headwaters area. No more than four hunters share these camps, which, by the way, offer hot showers. During the third week of the season, whether you hunt from a tent camp or the main lodge is a coin toss. In the fourth week, you'll just have to settle for the old log lodge near Lakeview. The hunter success rate on 5x5 and better bulls runs between 35 and 40 percent. Mule deer, black bear, antelope and moose are also on the big game roster here, but most hunters focus on elk. You'll need to purchase separate licenses for deer and bear, and trust the luck of the draw for antelope (not too hard) and moose (like winning the Irish Sweepstakes).

[R O C K Y M O U N T A I N S]

Central Montana Outfitters

G r e a t   F a l l s ,   M o n t a n a

Hunt deer, antelope and elk with a world-champion caller.

VITAL STATISTICS:

Game/Arms/Season:
ANTELOPE:
Bow: Early Sept. through early Oct.
Centerfire, muzzleloader: Early Oct. through early Nov.
DEER, ELK:
Bow: Early Sept. through mid-Oct.
Centerfire, muzzleloader: Late Oct. through late Nov.

Rates:
ANTELOPE from $1,550/5 days (archery)
DEER, ELK from $2,250/6 days (archery); from $2,450/5 days (centerfire, muzzleloader)

Accommodations:
TENT CAMPS
MAXIMUM NUMBER OF HUNTERS: 8

Meals: Good basic chow

Conference Groups: Yes

Guides: Included

Gratuity: $100 to $300

Preferred Payment:
Cash, credit cards (no AMEX), check

Other Activities:
Bird hunting, bird watching, canoeing/rafting, fishing, waterfowling, wildlife photography

Getting There:
Fly to Great Falls and meet Chad's shuttle.

Contact:
Chad Schearer
Central Montana Outfitters
Box 6655
Great Falls, MT 59406
406/727-4478
Fax: 406/454-1156
e-mail: cschearer@worldnet.at.net

MONTANA'S MIDDLE REGIONS are a troubled land, terrain of mountains lower than the Rockies, but in places quite as steep. Rivers have incised deepening valleys and feeder streams have cut sharp coulees on their way to the main channel. Broad plains of grass and sage are rumpled against the mountains, creating foothills—some barren of pines and some not.

This is big ranch country, grazing lands that roll over the countryside. On some, those where elevations are more moderate and the grass better, are found herds of antelope—families of a dozen or two—which, as the season progresses, become spookier and more wary with each passing day. You can hunt them a number of ways: with a long-range flat-shooting round such as the .25-06 pushed out of a heavy-barreled varmint rifle; stalking—playing out-of-sight, out-of-mind games, where you'll use the wind and cover to your advantage, easing up for a shot only when the range is right; or from a stand or blind, usually overlooking a popular waterhole. A typical antelope carries 15-inch horns.

Deer, both whitetails and mulies, are the meat-and-potatoes of this operation. A typical whitetail will equal or better 130 on the Boone & Crockett scale. Mule deer normally carry racks of 24 inches plus. Rattling and grunting will prove effective during the rut, but later spotting and stalking is the game here. Successful guides and their hunters master the art of moving slowly in weather that ranges from shirt-sleeve to bone-chilling cold. Patience pays big dividends.

On some ranches, you'll find resident herds of elk—average bulls are 5x5s—and head outfitter Chad Schearer is very selective about the ones he hunts. Calling is his specialty. In 1996 he took top honors in the Rocky Mountain Elk Foundation's Eastern Regional Championship. That same year he placed second in the World Competition. In 1997, he won the whole enchilada. To win in competition, calls must be perfect, but in the field, he says, there's no such thing. "Elk don't make perfect sounds." His rule of thumb: If you're calling an elk and screw up a note, pause and end the call with a chuckle.

Hunters are responsible for obtaining their own licenses, but Schearer will help you through the process. Depending on the species and its location, hunters stay in tent camps—sheltered from the incessant winds. Should you fill your tag early, there's opportunity for pheasants or grouse or perhaps ducks and geese, depending on the season. The smart archer brings a pack rod—September fishing is the best in the West.

Copenhaver Outfitters

Ovando, Montana

The tougher the terrain, the better the bulls.

VITAL STATISTICS:

Game/Arm/Seasons:
DEER, ELK:
Bow: Early through mid-Sept.
Centerfire, muzzleloader: Mid-Sept.
through late Nov.
Rates:
From $3,000/7 days (bow); $1,700/5
days (non-wilderness); $3,200/10
days (wilderness)
Accommodations:
TENT CAMPS
MAXIMUM NUMBER OF HUNTERS: 4
Meals: Bacon, eggs, steaks, burgers
Conference Groups: No
Guides: Included
Gratuity: $100 to $300
Preferred Payment:
Cash, check
Other Activities:
Bird watching, fishing, riding,
swimming, waterfowling, wildlife
photography
Getting There:
Fly to Missoula, and you'll be met.

Contact:
Steve Copenhaver
Copenhaver Outfitters
45 Cooper Lake Rd.,
Ovando, MT 59854
406/793-5547
e-mail: hlm5803@montana.com
Web: www.copenhaveroutfitters.com

DEEP IN the northern Scapegoat Wilderness rise the headwaters of the Blackfoot River. Among the larger is the Dry Fork, so named because the two-and-a-quarter-mile section of the creek just above its junction with the North Fork sinks below ground level during arid seasons. Above, the river flows through plunge pools and riffles populated by native cutthroat, but that's another story. Surrounding the upper reaches, Dry Fork is a land that is not as brutally rugged as some might have you believe. Sure, the peaks of Canyon and Falls points, Danaher and Concord mountains that range from 7,000 to 8,000 feet, are steep, as are the ridges that lead to their crests. But you'll also encounter gentle creek bottoms and hills that are round and bald. Stands of thick timber cover much of the mountain flank, but it's broken by open glens and meadows. It's true, and outfitter Steve Copenhaver will be among the first to tell you, too, that the best elk and mule deer are found in the densest cover.

From the trailhead, you'll ride 12 miles up into the Dry Fork drainage to a comfortable tent camp for four hunters. From there, hunting is on foot, generally one-on-one with your guide, unless you've chosen to share a guide with your partner. His first hunt of the season is for archers. Elk are in pre-rut and bugling brings them in. Rifle hunters get in on the calling action during the next two weeks, but as October wears on, spotting and stalking becomes more the norm. Steve also offers an early-season bowhunt and late-season rifle hunts for elk and deer in the Flathead National Forest.

Since the 1930s Steve's family has been guiding hunters in the Scapegoats. For the past 25 years he and his wife Donna have been running the business and they've compiled a reasonable record of success. He'll tell you the unvarnished truth: Of 354 hunters, 212 or 60 percent had an opportunity to shoot an elk. Of those, 132 or 62 percent took elk. The elk were pretty evenly divided among those of 4x4 or less, 5x5s or 6x6s or bigger. Most hunters come to Copenhavers to hunt elk. But some also want whitetails or mule deer. Of those, 142 had an opportunity for a shot and 92 connected. That's about 65 percent. Do these figures suggest that one out of every three hunters can't hit what they shoot at? Not entirely, because some were waiting for bigger racks (or that's what they'll tell you!).

Crow Creek Outfitters

T o s t o n ,   M o n t a n a

This overlooked part of Montana produced bigger elk and deer than you might ever imagine.

VITAL STATISTICS:

Game/Arm/Seasons:
ELK, DEER, BEAR:
Bow: Early Sept. through mid-Oct.
ELK and DEER:
Firearms: Late Oct. through late Nov.
LION:
Firearms: Dec. through Jan.
Rates:
(Call for quotes)
Accommodations:
LOG CABINS, MOBILE HOME, TENTS
NUMBER OF ROOMS: 10
MAXIMUM NUMBER OF HUNTERS: 8
Meals: Roasts, chicken
Conference Groups: No
Guides: Included
Gratuity: Hunter's discretion
Preferred Payment:
Cash, check
Other Activities:
Fishing
Getting There:
Fly to Bozeman and Mike will meet
you at the airport.

Contact:
Mike Parsons
Crow Creek Outfitters
314 Hwy. 285
Toston, MT 59643
406/266-3742

I F YOU FOLLOW U.S. HIGHWAY 89 from Livingston north, the route will take you along the western flank of the Crazy and Castle mountains and then, north of White Sulphur Springs, into the heart of the Little Belts. As Montana's mountains go, these are neither the highest nor the most rugged, and that bodes well for hunters who don't fancy scrambling across talus slopes for shots at elk or mule deer. While peaks in this area do reach 9,000 feet, most of the terrain is much lower, a blend of undulating hills and wide draws covered with grasses and stands of lodgepole pine and Douglas fir. Numerous streams feeding the headwaters of the South Fork of the Musselshell River drain this area.

Early in the season bowhunters will hunt from stands and ground blinds near wallows, a tactic that Mike Parsons has found very effective. For archers, this country lends itself to ambushes on routes to and from alfalfa fields, and to cow calling. Later, after the rut, it's not uncommon for firearms hunters to glass elk a mile to two away and then execute a successful stalk. The ranch on which Parsons hunts has yielded 4x4s or better for 65 percent of his clients. The figure includes spikes, which are legal in this game management unit. Because the ground is less arduous than that farther west, this may be a good option for first-time hunters: They'll be able to think about the game and not whether they'll ever be able to catch their breath.

Mule deer and whitetails bring even better results. Hunts on private ground produce bucks averaging just shy of 130 inches, with good bucks scoring 145 or more. Mule deer typically have spreads in the 20- to 24-inch class, but several of 26 inches plus are taken each season. Hunter success runs between 80 and 100 percent.

Parsons has a pair of camps in the north end of the Crazies where he's guided for 18 years. Both are log camps. The first contains a large 16x34-foot, propane-heated and lit bunkhouse with a log cookhouse next door. Showers are available at Parsons' main ranch three miles away. His second camp is a modern three-bedroom log cabin four miles to the west. Son Shannon, who's been working with his dad for the past several years, operates in the 225 square miles of the Little Belt Mountains to the north. Terrain is much the same and hunters have their choice of staying in a 70-foot mobile home or a tent camp farther up in the mountains. All of the rooms are handicapped-accessible.

Flat Iron Outfitting

T h o m p s o n   F a l l s ,   M o n t a n a

Mobility is the key to this operation's continued success.

VITAL STATISTICS:

Game/Arm/Seasons:
ELK and WHITETAILS:
Bow: Early Sept. through mid-Oct.
Centerfire: Late Oct. through Nov.
BEAR:
Bow, centerfire: Spring, mid-Apr. through mid-May; fall, mid-Sept. through mid-Oct.
MOUNTAIN LION: DEC.
Rates:
ELK and WHITETAILS from $1,495/7 days
BEAR $1,495/7 days
MOUNTAIN LION $3,000/7 days
(room and board are additional)
Accommodations:
MOTELS IN TOWN
MAXIMUM NUMBER OF HUNTERS: 8
Meals: Local restaurants
Conference Groups: No
Guides: Included
Gratuity: Hunter's discretion
Preferred Payment:
Cash, check
Other Activities:
Antiquing, bird hunting, bird watching, fishing, wildlife photography
Getting There:
Fly to Missoula and rent a car.

Contact:
Jerry C. Shively
Flat Iron Outfitting
3 Golf Course Rd
Thompson Falls, MT 59873
406/827-3666

JERRY SHIVELY, FLAT IRON'S HEAD GUY, has a different philosophy than most outfitters who pack hunters into remote wilderness camps that are miles from the nearest gravel road. Shively's clients stay in local motels and dine in nearby restaurants. Each morning, well before dawn, they drive to permit areas 121, 122 and 123 of the Lolo National Forest or the 2,500-acre ranch that he leases.

Shively's system is like a rapid deployment force: hunters may move at a moment's notice into areas where elk and deer are concentrated. He can adjust hunting strategies to take advantage of daily changes in weather and fine-tune hunts to match the desires and abilities of his clients. And at the end of a day's traipsing over the steep slopes glassing and stalking big game, there's a hot shower and dry clothes at the motel. This is a personal operation. Shively is both outfitter and guide for parties of three or four hunters.

Sound like an easy hunt? Well, it is and it isn't. For elk in the Lolo, you'll hike five to 10 miles a day over terrain that's closer to vertical than flat. Heavy timber and blowdowns give way to rocky slides, but here and there are those grassy alpine meadows where elk feed. If you harvest an elk, you and Shively will pack it out because the areas where he takes his clients are generally too rugged for horses. Hunter success on legal bulls, which must have brow tines longer than four inches, is about 25 percent.

The odds improve considerably when you're hunting whitetails on the private ranch where Shively has had exclusive access for the past decade. The ranch is flat and cut here and there by a few deep gullies. Only 300 acres are tillable, and they're usually in hay. Depredation by deer and elk makes growing row crops impossible. The ranch abuts the national forest and no hunting is allowed on the two other adjacent properties. In 1995, the largest whitetail taken on a guided hunt in Montana, a 151 buck, came from this ranch. While mule deer are also hunted on the ranch and in the national forest, don't count on filling your tag here. "For better mule deer, go to eastern Montana on the prairie," says Shively with typical bluntness.

Flat Iron Outfitting offers both spring and fall bear hunting, with the spring hunting along the grassy shoulders of logging roads, greening alpine meadows and scars of avalanche chutes being better. Pelts are also in much better condition in the spring. Mountain lion hunts over hounds are available in December when snow provides great tracking. Toms taken over Shively's hounds typically average 150 pounds.

Flying D Ranch

G a l l a t i n   G a t e w a y ,   M o n t a n a

So bring a shotgun. After taking your elk,
try your hand at a few pheasants.

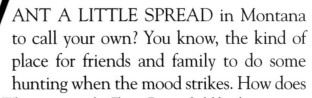

VITAL STATISTICS:

Game/Arm/Seasons:
ELK, DEER:
Bow: Early Sept. through early Oct.
Centerfire: Late Oct. through late Nov.
BISON:
Bow, blackpowder, single-shot:
Oct. through Jan.
Rates:
ELK $9,500/4 days
DEER $3,500 additional
BISON $3,500
Accommodations:
NUMBER OF ROOMS: 6; 3 WITH PRIVATE BATH
MAXIMUM NUMBER OF HUNTERS:6
Meals: French cuisine served family-style
Conference Groups: No
Guides: Included
Gratuity: 3 to 5% of package price
Preferred Payment:
Cash, check
Getting There:
Fly to Bozeman and the lodge van will meet you.

Contact:
Rob Arnaud
Flying D Ranch
Box 190
Gallatin Gateway, MT 59730
406/763-4419
Fax: 406/763-4801

WANT A LITTLE SPREAD in Montana to call your own? You know, the kind of place for friends and family to do some hunting when the mood strikes. How does 107,514 acres sound? When you visit the Flying D, you feel like the owner, so attentive and pampering is the staff. You, of course, have a personal guide and a horse that is more than tolerant. Rooms are private, as you'd expect, but the place hasn't been tricked up by some New York decorator. Nope, this place has the feel of an old-money ranch, with quality furnishings that are well and lovingly used.

So cut to the chase, right. In this case the chase is elk, minimum of 6x6 with a typical bull scoring 325. The ranch maintains a herd of 2,500 elk managed to sustain a cow/bull ratio of 2:1. Located 25 miles southwest of Bozeman, the low sage-covered hills that give way to grassy south-facing slopes and climb up toward the Spanish Peaks is not overly difficult terrain. Each morning you'll ride out from the lodge to a height of land. There, you'll dismount and begin to hunt on foot, spotting and stalking and spotting some more. In archery season, your guide will do his best to sound like a lonely cow, sometimes bringing bull elk in to 15 yards or less. Rifle shots during the last month of the season are generally less than 200 yards. Better than 90 percent of the Flying D's hunters harvest truly trophy bulls each year.

Elk are the big draw at the Flying D, and you can add mule deer or white-tails with a trophy fee. And if you've ever had the hankering to take a bison with bow, blackpowder or single-shot, here's your chance. The ranch also holds a wild herd of buffalo and hunts are available from October through January.

Golden Bear Outfitters

Judith Gap, Montana

Spring or fall, Walt Una's outfit offers a variety of options.

VITAL STATISTICS:

Game/Arm/Seasons:
ELK and DEER
Bow: Early Sept. through mid-Oct.
Firearms: Late Oct. through late Nov.
BEAR:
Mid-April through May
TURKEY:
Bow and shotgun: Spring, mid-April through early May; fall, early Sept. through early Oct.
MOUNTAIN LION:
Firearms: Early Dec. through mid-Feb.

Rates:
DEER and ELK from $2,100/7 days
BEAR $1,500/5 days
TURKEY from $900/3 days
MOUNTAIN LION $3,000/7 days

Accommodations:
LOG LODGE WITH CABINS AND TENT CAMP
NUMBER OF ROOMS: 3
MAXIMUM NUMBER OF HUNTERS: 10

Meals: Home cooking, family-style

Conference Groups: No

Guides: Included

Gratuity: $100

Preferred Payment:
Cash, check

Other Activities:
Bird hunting, bird watching, fishing, skiing, wildlife photography

Getting There:
Fly to Billings and the outfitter will provide round-trip transportation for $150 per group.

Contact:
Walt and Una Earl
Golden Bear Outfitters
Box 268
Judith Gap, MT 59453
406/473-2312

WITH SOME MONTANA outfitters, you get a limited bill of fare: deer or elk. But with Golden Bear, the menu's more varied. While the state's big game animals are the staples, here you'll also find a combo hunt for spring gobblers and bear, which is a neat and reasonable combination if there ever was one. And handicapped hunters find a warm welcome at Golden Bear as well.

That said, elk and deer are still the mainstays of this operation. The outfitter in charge of this outfit is Walt Una, who for more than 20 years has been hunting units 411 and 540 in the Big Snowy and Little Belt mountains of central Montana below Lewistown. Terrain is semi-rugged, with ridges topping out at 8,000 feet. Four-wheel-drives carry hunters to trailheads along the crests. From there the hunt is almost all downhill for the 3,000-foot trek to the base tent camp. Along the way are numerous basins forested with open stands of yellow pine and Douglas fir. Much of the landscape is in regrowth after logging or fires, and here and there are grassy meadows. An average bull is a 4x4 and one out of every two hunters brings one home. Better hunting is generally found later in the season after winter's first snows have brought the herd together.

Una also hunts 350,000 private acres out of his lodge of log cabins near Judith Pass. This is prime deer country. Two of his three cabins are handicapped-accessible and wheelchair-bound hunters do well on deer from ground blinds on travel routes to hay and alfalfa fields. And if wheelchair-bound hunters are willing, they can be in the thick of things for black bear as well. Montana's resident turkey is the Merriam's, much sought by hunters wanting to complete their grand slams. Spring black bear and turkey seasons overlap: hunt turkey in the morning and spot and stalk bear in the afternoon. Success rate on both has been 100 percent.

[R O C K Y   M O U N T A I N S]

Hawley Mountain Guest Ranch

M c L e o d ,   M o n t a n a

A relatively new operation that offers good prices and good hunting.

VITAL STATISTICS:

Game/Arm/Seasons:
ELK:
Bow: Sept. through mid-Oct.
Firearms: Late Oct. through mid-Nov.
Rates:
From $2,100/6 days
Accommodations:
MODERN LOG LODGE, TENT CAMP
NUMBER OF ROOMS: 4 WITH PRIVATE BATH
MAXIMUM NUMBER OF HUNTERS: 12 IN LODGE, 4 IN CAMP
Meals: Home-style buffets
Conference Groups: No
Guides: Included
Gratuity: 10 to 15%
Preferred Payment:
Cash, check
Other Activities:
Fishing, hiking
Getting There:
Fly to Bozeman or Billings and rent a car, or call for the lodge van at $175 round-trip.

Contact:
Ellen Marshall
Hawley Mountain
Guest Ranch
Box 4, McLeod, MT 59052
406-932-5791
Fax: 406-932-5715
off-season:
1335 Crown Dr.
Alameda, CA 94501
510-523-4053
Fax: 510 523-5188
e-mail: Bblewett@aol.com
Web: www.duderanch.org/hawley

PARADISE VALLEY, that wide swath cut by the Yellowstone, is probably the most famous valley in Montana. Millions of tourists travel along the river on U.S. 89, one of the main routes leading to the national park. But lying across the Absaroka Range to the east is another valley, as empty of travelers as the other is jammed. Odds are you've seen the river that drains it. The river is the Boulder and parts of *A River Runs Through It* were filmed near the Hawley Mountain Guest Ranch.

Hawley Mountain, a 10,000-footer that takes its name from a guy with the first name of Tom who carved out the 155-acre ranch in the 1880s, is home to the mid-Boulder elk herd. With only 500 elk, the herd is not large. It traverses the valley with the seasons, and in the spring cow elk calve in the pastures of the lodge. They summer high in the Absaroka-Beartooth Wilderness and when the snows come in mid-October, they move down into the winter range and are frequently joined by elk coming out of Yellowstone's high caldera.

If you're looking for an elk hunting operation based on a long history of good success rates, you'd better look elsewhere. New co-owners Bryant Blewett with wife Ellen Marshall took over management of the ranch just five years ago and recently reopened hunting operations. Eight miles from their log lodge is their base tent camp high on Meatrack Creek, where the Crow dried strips of elk in the relatively insect-free summers. The drainage is heavily timbered and broken by meadows. For archers, calling brings bulls in during the rut. During the first two weeks of firearms season, the camp offers opportunities to ambush elk as they come out of the high country. Then snow closes the camp and operations shift to the lodge. Here the drill is pretty straightforward: using 4WDs, hunters ride the pre-dawn darkness over forest service roads through 500,000 acres of high country to the jumping-off point for the day's hunt. Any antlered bull is legal during rifle season, and archers may take either sex.

Because Blewett and Marshall are working hard to reestablish their hunting business, rates here are very reasonable. A six-day one-on-one hunt in Meatrack camp runs $2,100 and from the lodge the fare's $2,400; licenses and personal items are extra. Is it worth it? There aren't many guarantees in big game, but at Hawley Mountain hunters are in the right place at the right time and the staff is dedicated, to say the least.

Chase Hill Outfitters

Big Sandy, Montana

More than 300,000 acres of public and private land are yours to hunt.

VITAL STATISTICS:

Game/Arm/Seasons:
ELK and DEER:
Bow: Early Sept through mid-Oct.
Centerfire: Late Oct. through late Nov.
ANTELOPE:
Bow: Early Sept through mid-Oct.
Centerfire: Early Oct. through early Nov.
Rates:
ELK and DEER from $2,950/7 days
Bow ANTELOPE/DEER combo from $1,950/7 days
Accommodations:
RUSTIC CEDAR RANCH HOUSE
NUMBER OF ROOMS: 3
MAXIMUM NUMBER OF HUNTERS: 8
Meals:
Five courses ending in killer desserts
Conference Groups: Yes
Guides: Included
Gratuity: $50 per day
Preferred Payment:
Cash, check
Other Activities:
Bird hunting, fishing, wildlife photography
Getting There:
Fly to Great Falls, rent a car and drive to the lodge, or the lodge van will pick you up.

Contact:
Bill Brown
Chase Hill Outfitters Inc.
HC 77 Box 851
Big Sandy, MT 59520
406/386-2447
Fax: 406/386-2435

AH, THE WIND, incessant, urgent, sweeping an armada of billowing clouds over the plains. You can hear the wind in the grass, and you know that for the hunt to be any good you've got to turn it to your advantage. That's tough. On the prairie the wind is constant and from one direction only. But you're sitting, hunched against a gnarled pine, still, waiting and watching and doing your best to pull that 6x6 bull down the draw past your stand. The arrow's already nocked and you tried out the shot, aiming at the two places where he's likely to show. Now the wind's worse. The puffs you felt on your face have become gusts. You're still downwind and that's good, but your scent is now swirling in the coulee.

Worrying about that makes your mind wander. You don't hear the twigs snap as the bull moves cautiously through the underbrush. If you had, you might have raised the bow. Now he's here, looking in your direction. The least movement will spook him. You know that. The waiting is exquisite torture. Make him turn his head, you ask your god. Your pulse throbs, you feel it on your wrist where the cuffs of your camo are tightly buttoned. His head moves to the left a little, and a little more, and still some more and you begin to raise your bow ever so slowly. He turns your way again and you freeze. Once more he swings his head to the left. You can see his terrific rack. You start to raise and draw and then he's gone.

He scented you or saw a bit of movement or whatever else makes bulls vanish in a second. But what a memory! And you've got five more days. Half of the bowhunters who hunt this little bit of heaven between Big Sandy and the Bear Paw Mountains take Pope and Young-class elk. Virtually all take mulies averaging 24 inches or better with those thick bases typical of racks coming out of the Missouri Breaks. And there are hunting spots on these 300,000 acres of private and permitted land that have not seen another hunter all season. It's just a matter of being out there. So you hunt from dawn until dark, driving and glassing and driving some more, bugling and cow calling if elk are ready to rut; rattling and grunting if deer are on the make. And after dark, when you pack it in, you'll find a piping-hot roast beef, all the trimmings and a slab of the cook's famed sour cream lemon pie for dessert. Pleasant dreams.

While it may not ensure a good hunt, a neat camp such as
Clay Barkhoff's of Beaver Creek Outfitters is one
measure of a well-run organization. Along with being located in
areas that have deer and elk, the best wilderness camps
should be clean and organized.

Some lodges, like Broken Arrow in Alder, Montana, provide
excellent accommodations and scrumptious meals, but the rest is up to you. You'll
navigate the lottery for your license, drive yourself up into the Scapegoats for
each morning's hunt, and pack out your own elk or deer as one out of every
two guests do. This is an ideal hunt for those who like to do things
on their own, and save some dollars in the process.

Wayne Hill Outfitting

N o x o n ,   M o n t a n a

*Hunt more than half a million acres in
two states out of one large, comfortable lodge.*

VITAL STATISTICS:

Game/Arm/Seasons:
ELK and DEER:
Bow: Sept.
Centerfire: Mid-Oct. through Nov.
BEAR:
Centerfire: Spring, mid-April through mid-May; fall, mid-Sept. through Nov.
MOUNTAIN LION:
Centerfire: Dec.

Rates:
ELK and DEER from $2,100/5 days
BEAR from $1,400/5 days
MOUNTAIN LION from $3,000/5 days

Accommodations:
MODERN LODGE
NUMBER OF ROOMS: 10
MAXIMUM NUMBER OF HUNTERS: 15

Meals: Wholesome home cooking

Conference Groups: No

Guides: Included

Gratuity: $50 and up

Preferred Payment:
Cash, check

Other Activities:
None

Getting There:
Fly to Spokane and a representative from the lodge will pick you up.

Contact:
Wayne Hill
Wayne Hill Outfitting
Box 1487
Noxon, MT 59853
406/847-5563
Fax: 406/847-8777
e-mail: nox8777@montana.com
Web: www.rosemart.com/wayne-hill/

WITH AN ENVIABLE REPUTATION for putting bowhunters on elk, Wayne Hill and his guides hunt about 450,000 acres in northwestern Montana and about 87,000 in eastern Idaho's panhandle. You won't find any tent camps in this operation. Each night you'll sleep warm and tight in a modern lodge outside of Noxon on Clark Fork. Why no tent camps? Hill believes that camps tend to tie hunters too closely to one area. If the game isn't there, he reasons, you lose. And he also argues that life in a cold, wet camp adds nothing to the quality or enjoyment of the hunt. He may have a point.

You'll find up to 15 hunters at the lodge at any given time, but don't let those numbers dissuade you. Each hunter is teamed with a guide, and that means one-on-one hunting. The two of you will leave the lodge in the dark of morning, headed in a 4WD into Idaho or Montana as season and license dictate. You'll be dropped off as far into the wilderness as it makes sense to go. Then you will hunt toward the pick-up point. The landscape on both sides of the border is steep, heavily forested in spots but broken with occasional patches of meadow. The best hunting is in September during the bugling season. As the season progresses hunts become tougher unless there's snow to move elk down. Then it can be very good. On average, success runs about 40 percent.

White-tailed deer are overrunning this area, particularly in the lower elevation, and hunter success in these areas runs about 85 percent. Eight-pointers are typical for whitetails, while 4x4 mulies are hunted high up, with similar kill rates. Black bears are strictly incidental to elk and deer hunting, but it probably makes sense to buy a tag. If you don't you'll just have to pass on that cinnamon boar that would have squared eight feet. December brings mountain lion hunting, with typical males running in the 140-pound class.

Last Stand Lodge

H a r d i n ,   M o n t a n a

Decisions, decisions! What'll it be today: deer, elk, huns or 'bows and browns as thick as your bicep?

VITAL STATISTICS:

Game/Arm/Seasons:
ANTELOPE, MULE DEER, ELK:
Bow: Sept.
Centerfire: Oct. - Nov.
Rates: from $1,100 for a 4-day ANTELOPE hunt to $4,000 for a 5-day rifle ELK hunt. Trophy fees apply.

Accommodations:
LOG LODGE AND CABINS
NUMBER OF ROOMS: 4
MAXIMUM NUMBER OF HUNTERS: 8

Meals: Fine family-style cooking

Conference Groups: Yes

Guides: Included

Gratuity: $100-$400

Preferred Payment:
Cash, check

Other Activities:
Bird hunting, bird watching, canoeing/rafting, fishing, waterfowling, wildlife photography

Getting There:
Fly to Billings and rent a car, or arrange for the lodge van to pick you up ($100 round-trip for a car full).

Contact:
Dave Egdorf
Last Stand Lodge
PO Box 434
Hardin, MT 59034
Ph: 406/665-3489
Fx: 406/665-3492
e-mail: egdorf@wtp.net
Web: uswestdex.com/iyp/laststand

I F EVER THERE WERE A LAND that deserved your best two weeks in autumn, it has to be the valley of the Bighorn in Montana. Along this sinuous tailwater are islands and fields that hold flocks of pheasants. Puddle ducks gabble in backwater sloughs and flights of Canada's trade overhead. Coveys of huns and sharptails hole up in tightly meandering stream courses that are almost impenetrably packed with choke cherries and buffalo berries. And here and there you'll find chuckar and big old cock pheasants — some pen-reared, some not.

But you didn't come here for the birds or the ducks or the trout. Bull elk bugled you in, or maybe it was the vision of a pair of mule deer bucks locking horns during the rut. You brought your bow or rifle, but if you're smart, a 20 gauge and a 6-weight fly rod found their way into your duffel as well. If you come in September, you'll call in elk and mule deer bucks. That strategy works into mid-to-late-October depending on the weather, but then the hunting strategy shifts to spotting and stalking and spotting some more. Generally speaking, each hunter is served by his or her own guide, but other arrangements can be made if you wish.

You'll work with lodge owner Dave Egdorf and his staff of guides to plan a hunt that suits you and your abilities. Dave hunts 300,000 private acres that back up to the Bighorn Mountains, and it includes terrain that matches every level of physical ability. You won't find horses at this lodge. You'll ride four-by-fours up into the bluff country and walk the ridges and glass for good bucks and bulls. A typical mulie grosses 180 points and elk average 350.

Located down a dirt road on a bend in the Big Horn, the lodge includes a large log house and an A-frame set in a copse of trees across the way. Meals, hearty and served with a flair and good wine, are family-style, and afterwards everyone sits back and shoots the bull even if you got one that morning. And if you did bag a buck, you'll just have to go fishing or chase waterfowl or upland birds. Ain't life grand!

Lazy JR Outfitters

Libby, Montana

Ain't nothing lazy about this elk hunt.

VITAL STATISTICS:

Game/Arm/Seasons:
ELK, DEER:
Bow: Early Sept. through early Oct.
Centerfire: Late Oct. through late Nov.
BEAR:
Centerfire: Mid-Apr. through mid-May
Rates:
ELK and DEER from $2,500/7 days
BEAR from $1,500/7 days
SPRING TURKEY from $1,000/7 days
Accommodations:
BUNKHOUSE OR TENT CAMPS
MAXIMUM NUMBER OF HUNTERS: 6
Meals: Family-style
Conference Groups: No
Guides: Included
Gratuity: Hunter's discretion
Preferred Payment:
Cash, Discover, MasterCard, Visa, check
Other Activities:
Bird hunting, bird watching, boating, fishing, waterfowling, wildlife photography
Getting There:
Fly to Kalispell and the lodge van will take you the rest of the way.

Contact:
JR or Mona Crismore
Lazy JR Outfitters
Box 1038
Libby, MT 59923
406/293-9494

HERE'S PROBABLY THE HARDEST WAY to hunt elk short of doing it on roller skates: tracking. You'll ride out with JR Crismore up into the timber and try to cut a track. Once you find one of ample size, you get off and walk — in the elk's footsteps. You go where he went, up, over, down, around, but mostly through thick brush. You don't have to be quick, in fact haste will bump him into the next county. Just persistent. Like one step after another for hours. You have an advantage over the bull, believe it or not. He's looking for a place to bed. You just got up. That's your advantage. You've got a second advantage too. Elk will follow a pattern. Once on the trail, JR knows pretty well where a bull's headed. So if you're careful, you second-guess him and maybe take a shortcut and get there first. Feel better now? Good, because there's never been a bull that will outwalk JR. And they call his outfit "Lazy." Tracking isn't a bunch of bull to JR; he's been doing it with good success for 25 years. And the tactic works best after the rut when bulls are moving back up to their high haunts to fatten up for the winter. Chances of bagging a bull run about 30 percent.

JR runs two types of hunts. During the first two weeks of the season, he works out of his ranch on Little Wolf Creek at the base of the Cabinet Mountains. This is deer country, with whitetails and some mulies higher up. Burned five years ago, the terrain is relatively open and lush with resurgent forest. A typical whitetail is a 140 and, with a little assistance from rattling and grunting, most hunters fill their tags. And, while mule deer are generally down in the western part of the state, numbers seem to be improving here. The persevering hunter can take a 4x4 with a spread of at least 24 inches.

Handicapped hunters are welcome at the Lazy JR. The forest service land where he hunts is closed to motorized vehicles, but there's nothing to keep a guy with wagon and team from traveling up to where deer and elk play. The physically challenged hunter who can ride in the back of a wagon can glass, spot and hunt with the best of them.

Lion Creek Outfitters

K a l i s p e l l ,   M o n t a n a

*A 10-mile horseback ride into camp puts you
in the middle of elk, whitetail and mule deer country.*

VITAL STATISTICS:

Game/Arm/Seasons:
ELK and DEER:
Bow: Second week in Sept.
Firearms: Mid-Sept. through late Nov.
BEAR:
Mid-Sept. through late Nov.
MOUNTAIN LION:
Late Nov. through mid-Feb.
Rates:
ELK and DEER from $2,350/7 days
MOUNTAIN LION $2,850/7 days
Accommodations:
TENT CAMPS
MAXIMUM NUMBER OF HUNTERS: 10
Meals: Family-style
Conference Groups: No
Guides: Included
Gratuity: $100
Preferred Payment:
Cash, check
Other Activities:
Bird hunting, bird watching, boating, fishing, riding, wildlife photography
Getting There:
Fly to Kalispell Glacier International, and rent a car.

Contact:
Cecil Noble
Lion Creek Outfitters
610 Patrick Creek Rd.
Kalispell, MT 59901
406/755-3723
e-mail:
horses@montanaadventres
Web: www.montanaadventures.com

PERSONAL SERVICE is the name of the game with this outfitter whose base camp is high on the creek of the same name in the Flathead National Forest. Unlike other outfitters who run several camps simultaneously, Cecil Noble runs only one. Along with Noble, you'll find a maximum of 10 hunters and five guides in camp during any given hunt. For an extra $400 you can have a guide to yourself.

The base camp on Lion Creek serves as the jumping-off point for early-season hunts that make use of a second camp on Palisades Lake just east of Lion Creek Pass. Both camps are in Game Management Unit 150, and the management plan allows rifles to be used on antlerless elk or brow-tined bulls during three weeks of September. From then on only antlered elk are legal. Deer season opens in mid-September as well and, along with elk, continues into the end of November. What does this mean for hunters. It means you can use a rifle or bow, your choice. Average elk are typical 5x5s, whitetails often have eight points or better, and mule deer are usually 4x4s. Hunter success rates on elk run 30 percent, and the rate for deer is somewhat higher.

The Bob, as it's called, typifies Montana's elk and deer wilderness. The area round the base camp is relatively flat. But on the 10-mile ride to the upper camp, you'll realize just how difficult that terrain can be. The trail carries you through mountains that are steeply flanked, broken occasionally by benches and avalanche scars. Dense timber is the rule but you'll also find occasional patches of grassy meadow. Hunting from either camp is from dark to dark. You'll leave camp before the sun lightens the sky and return well after it has set. Most of your hunt will be on foot, hiking down and hiking up, always climbing over a blowdown or boulder that's in your way.

Knowing that this kind of pace can wear a city slicker down, Noble suggests that you bring a pack rod and a handful of spinners or big nymphs. A day off from hunting spent catching and releasing native cutthroat and bull trout rejuvenates more than one's tired old legs.

Ron & Tucker Mills Outfitting

A u g u s t a ,   M o n t a n a

*Fit hunters find good bulls
on the Rockies' eastern slope.*

**VITAL
STATISTICS:**

Game/Arm/Seasons:
ELK, DEER:
Bow, centerfire: Mid-Sept. through
late Nov.
Rates:
ELK, DEER from $1,600/8 days
(unguided); $2,600/8 days (guided)
Accommodations:
TENT CAMPS AND CABIN
MAXIMUM NUMBER OF HUNTERS: 8
Meals: Family-style
Conference Groups: No
Guides: Included
Gratuity: $100
Preferred Payment:
Cash, check
Other Activities:
Bird watching, fishing, wildlife
photography
Getting There:
Fly to Great Falls and the lodge van
will meet you.

Contact:
Ron Mills
Ron & Tucker Mills Outfitting
Box 2
Augusta, MT 59410
406/562-3335
e-mail: bullsrus@3rivers.net

WHY WOULD YOU BOOK a hunt with a guy who tells you that only one of three hunters will get an elk? Veracity, mainly, but also good sense. Raising client expectations is a delicate business. It's great to whip up excitement about hunting elk and deer; everyone wants to live the dream. But if every rifle hunter thinks he's going to bag a bragging-sized bull during a week of hunting, somebody got his wires crossed. It doesn't happen that way. But when an outfitter tells you that 30 percent of his clients kill bulls, he's talking an average. You can boost your odds considerably by being in reasonable shape; being able to shoot your rifle offhand as well as from sitting or prone positions; learning how to move quietly and quickly through the woods; and continuing to hunt even when you're tired and it looks hopeless.

So runs advice from Ron Mills, who's been outfitting for a generation along the eastern front of the Rocky Mountains about 50 miles due west of Great Falls. Early in the season you'll find him up in the headwaters of the Blackfoot where Mineral Creek flows between Bugle Mountain and Mineral Hill. Sorry, folks, at 8,383 feet, "hill" is a misnomer. Terrain is steep and forested. The drill is to ride to the crest of a sharp ridge between drainages. Ron will post a couple of hunters to watch passes where elk cross. Others will hunt down through the slopes. Typically elk will move uphill when pushed, giving the guys atop the ridges a chance for a good shot. Rifles are legal in the early season here so bugling, spotting and stalking are good tactics. Early morning tends to be the best time to hunt elk in this drainage. Of the 15 hunters who hunt out of this camp during the first couple weeks of the season, five to seven will harvest bulls. About half will be "raghorns" in the 2-year-old class, the other half will be 4x4s with maybe a 5x5 or 6x6 thrown in.

In late October, hunting shifts to Lost Cabin Creek, 10 miles up into the eastern slope of the Rockies. Primarily mule deer country, hunting strategies are similar to Mineral Creek camp. By the time Ron moves into the camp on Lost Cabin, weather is moving game. Lower down and outside of the wilderness, which is winter range for elk, are a pair of private ranches where good hunters stand a much better than 50-50 chance of collecting a mulie in the 20- to 24-inch class. Some elk are taken here, as well. A tent camp and a wood camp are operated on opposite ends of the ranch.

Mission Mountain Outfitters

S w a n   V a l l e y ,   M o n t a n a

Owner Rick Bishop offers top hunting for elk and whitetails in the Bob Marshall, plus prime mulie hunting along the Missouri.

VITAL STATISTICS:

Game/Arm/Seasons:
ELK:
Centerfire, muzzleloader: Mid-Sept. through late Oct.
MULE DEER:
Centerfire, muzzleloader: First half of Nov.
WHITETAILS:
Centerfire, muzzleloader: Last half of Nov.
Rates:
ELK, DEER and BEAR $2,400/8 days
MULE DEER $1,500/5 days
Accommodations:
TENTS OR RANCH HOUSE
MAXIMUM NUMBER OF HUNTERS: 6
Meals: Home cooking, family-style
Conference Groups: No
Guides: Included
Gratuity: $100 to $200
Preferred Payment:
Cash, check
Other Activities:
Bird hunting, fishing
Getting There:
Fly to Missoula and the van from the lodge will meet you.

Contact:
Rick Bishop
Mission Mountain Outfitters
938 Rumble Creek Rd.
Swan Valley, MT 59826
406/754-2444

COME HUNTING SEASON, Mission Mountain's major domo, Rick Bishop, might seem a bit psycho. Half of his top-flight hunting operation for elk and whitetails lies deep in the Bob Marshall where the land is nicely mountainous. On the other hand, there's his permit on some 120,000 acres of prairie cut by those wonderfully tight cedar valleys that lead down to the Missouri River—prime mulie country.

First, elk and whitetails. Located at 5,600 feet on the headwaters of the Big Salmon River, Bishop's elk camp is as far into the backcountry as you can comfortably ride in a day. That means few other hunters. You and the other five hunters, along with three guides, will have more than 100,000 acres virtually to yourselves. The season starts in early September with an archer's bugle hunt for elk. Rifle hunters arrive with the certainty of snow in mid-October. Horses may take you a few miles from camp at the start of your day's hunt, but in the main you'll be hoofing it yourself. Along with elk in the 5x5 class, you'll also find good whitetails and, should the luck of the draw smile on you, there's the chance to take a goat from the mountain at the head of the valley. If, however, mountain hunting is not your forte but finding a trophy whitetail is, check out the hunting around Rick's ranch in the Swan River Valley. Almost everyone is successful here. The ranch is also headquarters for spring bear hunts.

If you haven't been to the Missouri River Breaks country to hunt mule deer, you have a treat in store. From dawn to sunset, the sun rolls over endless benches of rolling sage. Coulees that pinch and steepen at their heads and then broaden as they fill with cedars and willow cut the plateau and drop as much as 2,000 feet to the river below. Hunts, of course, start at the top of the coulees where you'll glass for trophy mule deer. Then you're out of the truck, scouting and stalking and working your way downhill. Accommodations are a farmhouse staffed with a cook who feeds the weary and weak when they return. About seven out of 10 bring back mule deer. And usually someone carries a shotgun, for you never know when the grouse will need thinning.

Bill Mitchell Outfitters

Hamilton, Montana

Hunt with an outfitter who mouth-calls for elk.

VITAL STATISTICS:

Game/Arm/Seasons:
ELK and DEER:
Bow, centerfire: Mid-Sept. through mid-Nov.
MOUNTAIN LION:
Bow, centerfire: Dec. through Jan.
BEAR:
Bow, centerfire: Late May through mid-June
Rates:
ELK and DEER: $2,850/8 days
MOUNTAIN LION: $2,850/8 days
BEAR, $1,500/7 days
Accommodations:
BUNKHOUSE, TENT CAMPS
MAXIMUM NUMBER OF HUNTERS: 8
Meals: Family-style
Conference Groups: No
Guides: Included
Gratuity: Hunter's discretion
Preferred Payment:
Cash, check
Other Activities:
Fishing, trail rides
Getting There:
Fly to Missoula and rent a car, or arrange for a ride from the outfitter at additional cost.

Contact:
Bill Mitchell
Bill Mitchell Outfitters, Inc.
364 McCarthy Loop
Hamilton, MT 59840
406/363-4129

WITH A SHARP INTAKE OF BREATH, Bill Mitchell emits the sound of an amorous bull. The bugle is more of a high-pitched whistle that trails into a guttural grunt. Bill taught himself to mouth-call elk like Native Americans once could long before diaphragm calls hit the market. He still sounds better. You might think that with nearly 30 years of hunting and calling in the Selway-Bitterroots elk would come to know his style. Not to worry. Those bulls that come close enough to find out just who's come calling normally get stuck with a broadhead or a little present from the folks at Nosler.

The beauty of hunting Idaho's Unit 17 is twofold because both rifle hunters and bowhunters can hear the bulls bugling at dawn, and the bulls lack caution during the late-August through early-October rut. But big bulls didn't get that way by being foolish or easy to find. Early in the season, Bill hunts from a pack camp in a little saddle forested with lodgepole pine. He stays in that camp until the snows force the outfit to move down to 5,000 feet and the camp on Deep Creek, which is accessible by 4WD. From there, depending on what the elk are up to, clients may hunt from spike camps or a tent for a few days. Along with the camps in Idaho, Bill also runs hunts in Montana from his ranch three miles south of Hamilton. With snow in the high mountains, elk begin to move into winter range in the low canyons along the Bitterroot River. A bunkhouse on the ranch provides accommodations. And every day hunters are driven up into the ridges to spot-and-stalk or track elk, deer and the occasional bear.

Speaking for operations on both sides of the state line, success on elk that usually go 5x5 runs 30 to 50 percent. Mule deer are also harvested here, but they pretty much take a back seat to elk. The same area during the depth of winter is excellent for hunting mountain lions. You'll ride snowmobiles up the frozen Selway River looking for a track. If it's a good set, the hounds are loosed and you're off! Bill's lion hunts are not for the physically unfit. Come spring, he heads back to Deep Creek, but this time for bear. Most hunts involve a good bit of spotting and stalking, but in Idaho some baits can be used.

Montana Guide Service

G a r d i n e r ,   M o n t a n a

Hunt for elk near the northern border of Yellowstone Park.

VITAL STATISTICS:

Game/Arm/Seasons:
ELK and DEER:
Bow: Early Sept. through mid-Oct.
Centerfire: Late Oct. through Nov.
Late season: Jan. through Feb.
MOUNTAIN LION:
Early Dec.
SPRING BEAR:
Mid-April through mid-May
Rates:
ELK and DEER:
Bow $2,950/6 days
Centerfire from $3,750/6 days
Late season $1,000/4 days
MOUNTAIN LION:
Centerfire $2,500/8 days
SPRING BEAR:
Centerfire $2,500/6 days
Accommodations:
MOTELS IN TOWN (OR A PRIMITIVE CABIN IF YOU INSIST)
MAXIMUM NUMBER OF HUNTERS: 8
Meals: Restaurants
Conference Groups: Yes
Guides: Included
Gratuity: 10%
Preferred Payment:
Cash, check
Other Activities:
Antiquing, biking, bird hunting, bird watching, canoeing/rafting, fishing, waterfowling, wildlife photography
Getting There:
Fly to Bozeman, and rent a car.

Contact:
Edwin Johnson
Montana Guide Service
Royal Teton Ranch
Gardiner, MT 59030
406/848-7265
e-mail: elk@gomontana.com
Web: www.montanaguide.com

WHEN HEAVY SNOWS COME to the high caldera that's Yellowstone National Park, the first elk to leave are bachelor bands of the old bulls. Like smoke, they drift over ridges and down draws following routes as old as the forest. For some, the trek carries them onto the Royal Teton Ranch, which shares eight miles of the park's northern border outside Gardiner. The northern Yellowstone herd of 25,000 elk is one of the largest in the country. Combine them with a few hundred more that live on the ranch year-round, and you're in fat city.

While the terrain here is as rugged as anywhere along the Continental Divide, the elk hunt here is perhaps the most civilized fair-chase hunt in the West. Unless insisting on staying in a traditional cabin where the sanitary facility is a two-holer out back, you'll opt for the Comfort Inn in Gardiner. Each morning you'll drive to the ranch, grab a bite of continental breakfast, sling your daypack and rifle into a warm and waiting 4WD and drive to the top of the ridge du jour. You want to be in position by first light; most elk are taken here in the first streaks of dawn. Early in the season, archers can call elk. Later during the rifle season, hunting is largely spot and stalk. And, if you don't mind the cold, the special Gardiner late-season draw hunt, which is four days of guided either-sex hunting for $1,000, might be for you. No matter which hunt you pick, you'll have worked your way back to the lodge by late morning. A cup of soup awaits, then you've got your choice of chasing mule deer in the jack pines or heading back to your motel for lunch and a nap. About 3 p.m. you'll rendezvous back at the ranch for the evening elk hunt. Makes no difference how late you get off the mountain, the restaurants in Gardiner stay open longer than you do. While late-season hunter success really depends on snowfall, hunters stand a better than 50-50 chance of taking elk.

The northern half of the Royal Teton Ranch is about 11 miles south of Livingston and the drill is much the same. So is the terrain, with the exception that hay fields and some row crops fill valleys instead of the sage and brush found at Gardiner. Montana Guide Service, which has exclusive rights to hunting on this ranch, also operates camps on Dry Creek and Rock Creek in the Gallatins. Hunts there can be guided or unguided as clients wish, and you can either stay in the camps and fend for yourselves or you can hang out in Livingston with all those creature comforts.

Montana High Country Outfitters

Noxon, Montana

For a 400-class bull, head to the western part of Montana.

VITAL STATISTICS:

Game/Arm/Seasons:
ELK and MULE DEER:
Bow: Early Sept. through mid-Oct.
Centerfire: Late Oct. through late Nov.
WHITETAILS:
Bow: Early through mid-Sept.
Centerfire: Mid-Nov. through late Nov.
BEAR:
Bow, centerfire: spring, early through mid-May; fall, mid-Sept. through late Sept.
MOUNTAIN LION:
Bow, centerfire: Dec.

Rates:
ELK and DEER: Bow $2,200; gun $2,600/6 days
BEAR from $1,600/6 days
LION and SHEEP $2,800/7 days

Accommodations:
LOG LODGE
NUMBER OF ROOMS: 3
MAXIMUM NUMBER OF HUNTERS: 10

Meals: Pork chops with mushroom sauce, stuffed steak

Conference Groups: No

Guides: Included

Gratuity: Hunter's discretion

Preferred Payment:
Cash, check

Other Activities:
Bird hunting, wildlife photography

Getting There:
Fly to Missoula and the lodge van will meet you.

Contact:
Tim Reishus
Montana High Country Outfitters
Box 1608
Noxon, MT 59853
406/847-2279
e-mail:nox2279@montana.com

I T'S AS NASTY AND GNARLY as it gets in the Lower 48. That's the way Tim Reishus describes areas 121 and 104 in the northern Bitterroot and Cabinet mountains where he guides clients for elk and deer. Vegetation is, in a word, dense. North slopes are heavy with larch and spruce. Cedars and pines choke brushy ravines. To the south, where there's more sun and warmth, heavy stands of fir give way to hardwoods and meadows of low shrub. These provide, evidently, a highly nutritious diet for elk. More 400-class bulls are harvested in this far-western section of the state than any other. Some hunters are lucky, like the archer who collected the 411 state record bull. But in the main these big bulls die of old age and they didn't get to be that big by being dumb.

From his log lodge near Noxon, a hamlet along the Clark Fork below Thompson Falls, hunters head out in 4WDs to the day's hunting areas. Finding good places to hunt isn't the problem. Deciding on which one is tough. Tim relies on more than a dozen years of guiding, scouting reports, the weather and hunches. It's become kind of intuitive when he's at his best. His bulls are better than average, though hunter success is steady at 40 percent. Not only does elk hunting in these parts demand stamina, but being able to move quietly and quickly, read sign, sense changes in wind and good marksmanship really count.

Those skills aren't so crucial when hunting whitetails. Three out of four hunters score on bucks that are typically 150 or better. Hunted in essentially the same areas (a combo license is guaranteed when the trip is booked through an outfitter), whitetails are found a little lower on the slopes. Hunting is largely a matter of glassing and stalking, standing near rub and scrape lines, or tracking. Mule deer are also a specialty of Tim's outfit, but there's nothing easy about them. Here they are found on high talus slopes above treeline, the same terrain as bighorn sheep. Hunters who brave heights are successful three out of four times. In the fall, bears are often encountered during elk and deer hunts, but the better time to hunt them is in the first two weeks of May, just after boars have left their dens. It's not unusual to see 10 or 15 on a hunt. The problem is choosing which one. And, for those with a yen to tree a cat, Tim runs mountain lion hunts over his Blueticks and Walkers during the first half of December.

Montana High Country Tours

D i l l o n ,   M o n t a n a

Bad weather in 1997 means good hunting for the next few years.

VITAL STATISTICS:

Game/Arm/Seasons:
ELK and DEER:
Bow: Early Sept. through mid-Oct.
Centerfire: Late Oct. through Nov.
BEAR:
Bow centerfire: Fall, Sept. through mid-Oct.; spring, mid-April through May
ANTELOPE:
Bow: Sept. through mid-Oct.
Centerfire: Mid-Oct. through mid-Nov.

Rates:
ELK and DEER:
Bow from $2,450; rifle from $2,750/7 days
BEAR from $1,750/ days
ANTELOPE from $1,750/7 days

Accommodations:
VINTAGE LOG CABIN AND TENTS
NUMBER OF ROOMS: 6 WITH PRIVATE BATH
MAXIMUM NUMBER OF HUNTERS: 12
Meals: Western family-style
Conference Groups: No
Guides: Included
Gratuity: $150
Preferred Payment:
Cash, MasterCard, Visa, check
Other Activities:
Bird hunting, canoeing/rafting, fishing, snowmobiling, waterfowling
Getting There:
Fly to Butte and rent a car, or take the lodge van ($50 additional).

Contact:
Russ Kipp
Montana High Country Tours Inc.
1036 E. Reeder St.
Dillon, MT 59725
406/683-4920
e-mail: montana@mhct.com
Web: http://www.mhct.com

THE WEATHER GOD rules elk hunting. Take the 1997 season. Unusually warm temperatures and an abnormal amount of rain kept the woods green into October. Browse was ample for elk in the high elevations of the Pioneer Mountains where Russ Kipp runs his hunts. Moderate temperatures meant that the elk didn't need to eat as much to provide sustaining calories. Consequently they were not forced to gather in areas where browse was concentrated, and that meant that they didn't move down out of the high elevations. So elk were harder to hunt. Instead of taking bulls in elevations around 7,500 feet, hunters had to climb another 1,500 to 2,000 feet just to reach the altitude where elk were hanging out. That's not as easy as it sounds. You must be able to scale the heights, have something left when you get there and not take all day doing it.

The upshot was that the harvest was off in Montana by more than 50 percent and down at Kipp's place by about 30 percent. Not a good year. But the future ought to be good. Since the winter kill and bull harvest was very limited, 1997's 3- and 4-year-olds should carry added weight and mass in 1999 and beyond. That's the good news.

Hunters who are fit stand a better chance of success on bull elk. Kipp estimates that hunters in their 40s and younger fill their tags most of the time. But those who are older and more likely to be in something less than great physical condition are less likely to be successful. To compensate, the outfitter locates his camps as close to feeding areas as practical, and he relies on extensive scouting to dope out locales where hunters need not walk more than a few miles to get into position for a shot. Overall success on elk runs an honest 70 percent for rifle hunters and about 85 percent for archers. About 80 percent of Kipp's archery hunts are based in alpine tent camps, while the same percentage of rifle hunts are headquartered in the lodge at the head of Grasshopper Valley. Built of log, the lodge features a huge stone fireplace, comfortable bedrooms for two and shared baths. And, as you'd suspect, the family-style meals have a distinctly Western flare. Bear, moose, deer and antelope are also hunted out of this lodge. Deer, bear and antelope can be added to an elk hunt. Moose is strictly by the luck of the draw.

Montana Safaris

C h o t e a u ,   M o n t a n a

Elk, mule deer and lion hunts are owner Rocky Heckman's specialty.

VITAL STATISTICS:

Game/Arm/Seasons:
ELK, MULE DEER, BEAR:
Bow: Early Sept.
Firearms: Mid-Sept. through Nov.
MOUNTAIN LION:
Firearms: Early Dec. through mid-Feb.

Rates:
Bugle season $3,200/9 days
General season $2,500/8 days

Accommodations:
WALL TENTS
MAXIMUM NUMBER OF HUNTERS: 10
Meals: Steak, roasts, stews with vegetables and salads
Conference Groups: Yes
Guides: Included
Gratuity: Hunter's discretion
Preferred Payment:
Cash, check
Getting There:
Fly to Great Falls and you will be met.

Contact:
Rocky or Lorell Heckman
Montana Safaris
21 Airport Rd.
Choteau, MT 58422
406/466-2004
e-mail: safaris@mail.3rivert.net
Web:
www.montanasafaris.simplenet.com

ROADS ARE INDEED FEW in the 2.3-million-acre Flathead National Forest. Nearly half of the forest is designated national wilderness where timber harvest and motorized vehicles are not permitted. Block faulting upended huge sheets of rock, creating peaks that scrape 9,000 feet. Glaciers sharpened the summits of the mountains and their connecting ridges, but they smoothed and rounded the slopes and intervening valleys, providing purchase for firs on the upper elevations and aspens down below. About 60 percent of the area is black, nearly impenetrable forest, and the remainder is open. Bands of tundra-like grasses run through the forests, creating parks and meadows where elk and deer feed. Among the northernmost of the national forests, winter comes early and it's said that it never really leaves the high peaks.

In mid-September when elk are bugling, Rocky Heckman, owner of this outfit, starts his rifle hunts on big, open, grassy slopes and heavy alpine jungle up in the Bob Marshall Wilderness and then later moves them south to the Scapegoat Wilderness southwest of Augusta. Hunting early for elk follows a regimen of calling, scrambling to get into position, and then working the bull in close enough for a good shot. Later in mid to late-October, as snows push hunters out of the Bob Marshall and into the Scapegoat, tactics switch to spotting and stalking. By early November, mule deer and elk are moving down the Dearborn River valley where Heckman sets up the season's final camps. Hunter success varies from year to year, but on average about 50 percent of his hunters take elk scoring between 250 and 300. Success on mule deer is somewhat higher, nudging 65 percent. He wraps up the season with mountain lion hunts over dogs. His toms run in the 150-pound class, and while there are no guarantees, hunters are successful virtually 100 percent of the time. Most hunts link two hunters with a guide, but one-on-one hunts are available.

There's an added advantage to hunting the early season, and it's kind of perverse. Camped on rivers the names of which Heckman won't divulge, hunters often wrap up their evenings with a little fishing for wild cutthroat and rainbow trout. Often, along with a flyrod, somebody brings along a rifle. And occasionally, the fishermen come laughing back to camp, calling for the packer, because some lucky so-and-so's dropped his bull less than a quarter of a mile from camp. Luck always counts.

[R O C K Y   M O U N T A I N S]

Monture Face Outfitters

G r e e n b a u g h ,   M o n t a n a

A small camp deep in the Bob, where Valerie whips up cuisine more suited to Park Avenue.

VITAL STATISTICS:

Game/Arm/Seasons:
ELK:
Bow: Sept. through mid-Oct.
Centerfire: Mid-Sept. through Oct.
Rates:
$2,800/7 days
Accommodations:
TENT CAMP
MAXIMUM NUMBER OF HUNTERS: 6
Meals: Fine wilderness cuisine
Conference Groups: No
Guides: Included
Gratuity: Hunter's discretion
Preferred Payment:
Cash, check
Other Activities:
Bird hunting, bird watching, fishing, riding, swimming, wildlife photography
Getting There:
Fly to Missoula and you will be met.

Contact:
Tom Ide, Sr.
Monture Face Outfitters
Box 27 Clearwater
Greenbaugh, MT 59836
1-888/420-5768 or
406/244-5763
e-mail:
info@montanaoutfitter.com
Web: www.montanaoutfitter.com

MONTURE CREEK rises between Young and Monahan mountains in the southern end of the Bob Marshall Wilderness. Both are 8,000-foot peaks, and between them is a wealth of rough ridges, steep draws and open rocky meadows tufted here and there with stands of dark pine and fir. There are only two ways into this country — on foot or on horseback. The latter is much preferred, and the one you ride will be seasoned and sure-footed. All you have to do is keep from falling off.

A few hours ride from the trailhead will bring you to Tom Ide's and Valerie Call's camp on the creek. Tom and Valerie run this operation, a small one by some standards. Seldom are there more than four hunters with Tom and Valerie in camp. Valerie cooks ("There's no reason I can't make hollandaise sauce in a wilderness camp," she says.) and Tom keeps things straight. During September's archery season and into the first week or so of rifle, bugling and cow calling are very effective for attracting bulls. And later, in October, cows not bred in September come into cycle again. That creates a kind of mini-rut. While 4x4 bulls are legal, Tom is very reluctant to harvest any smaller than 5x5. Hunters may see monster 7x7s or 8x8s, but getting a shot at one is a rarity. Over the eight years that Tom and Valerie have been running this hunting camp, hunter success has hovered around 40 percent.

While you may not be assured of shooting a bull, you'll likely taste the best elk tenderloin you've ever put a fork to. Valerie marinates it with a little soy, a little Worcestershire, some powdered garlic, coarse ground pepper and a touch of olive oil (not enough to alter the flavor of the meat). In a big cast iron skillet, she sears the meat quickly on each side and serves it medium rare. Try that one with rice pilaf, fresh vegetables and pineapple upside down cake for dessert. You won't find canned stews or creamed corn in this camp.

New West Outfitters

Helena, Montana

The challenge to hunting these camps, as with all others, is mental.

VITAL STATISTICS:

Game/Arm/Seasons:
ELK, DEER:
Bow: Early Sept. through early Oct.
Centerfire: Late Oct. through late Nov.
MOUNTAIN LION:
Dec.
Rates:
ELK, DEER:
Bow, centerfire from $3,450/8 days
(including license)
MOUNTAIN LION:
Bow, centerfire from $4,500/9 days
(including license)
Accommodations:
TENTS WITH WOOD WALLS AND FLOORS
MAXIMUM NUMBER OF HUNTERS: 10
Meals: Family-style
Conference Groups: No
Guides: Included
Gratuity: $100 to $200
Preferred Payment:
Cash, check, credit cards
Other Activities:
Fishing, riding
Getting There:
Fly to Butte and the lodge van will
pick you up.

Contact:
David Moore
New West Outfitters
Box 6052
Helena, MT 59604
406/475-3218
Fax: 406/475-3349
e-mail: nwobmw@in-tech.com

SITTING IN A MAKESHIFT ground blind, the hunter glasses the hillside. His view is perfect. A log provides a rest for his rifle. The wind is coming toward him. It is a flawless setup. Two days before, he'd taken his mule deer and now he is trying for an elk. Any elk. When you're restricted to a wheelchair, you may not be quite so choosy about which elk. With luck, he'll fill his combo tag; something few hunters, resident or not, achieve.

From the treeline, a lone cow steps forward; "Wait," cautions the guide. Another cow shows, bigger, this time. Still the guide urges restraint. Though antlerless elk are legal for this hunter, the guide wants all the elk in this little band to clear the timber before any shots are fired. You never know who's bringing up the rear. A third elk squeezes from the trees, and it was the biggest cloven-hooved animal the hunter had ever seen. As the guide was telling him to wait, the hunter squeezes off the round. The big cow wobbles and two 5x5 bulls run past her before she hits the ground.

Dave Moore is a bright guy who has a different take on the outfitting business. You won't find him married to a watershed or two in a specific game management unit. Nope, Dave has a host of tent camps with wood floors, walls and electricity scattered throughout the Beaverhead National Forest. He hunts primarily on public ground, and his forte is matching the hunting camp to the hunter. Tell him you're a 60-year-old desk jock whose idea of exercise is jumping to conclusions and that you want to take a 350-class bull, and he'll tell you your odds are...well, you get the idea. But let the same guy ask for a fun hunt with a chance for a spike or raghorn, and your chances skyrocket. If this same 60-something hunter works out on a regular basis and gives up smokes, he'll be able to hunt the rugged timber where the big bulls hide. Tell Dave what you want and what you can do, and he'll plan a hunt for you.

Elk and deer are his bread and butter, but his passion is big cats. Mountain lions. Hunt lions with him and you'll be driving the back roads at midnight scouting for a set of prints big enough and fresh enough to loose the hounds on in the morning. On any given night, you and Dave will put 400 some miles on the four-by-four. He covers a lot of miles through country that runs from Yellowstone up to Kalispell. That's why he harvests big cats in the 150-pound range.

Northstar Trophy Outfitters

L i v i n g s t o n ,   M o n t a n a

Bowhunters can find a little piece of mule deer heaven in the foothills of the Little Belt Mountains. Rifle hunters can get in on the action with whitetails and elk.

BOWHUNTERS, LISTEN UP! Ever wanted your own ranch, if only for a week? Well, Greg Fine, who's been a licensed outfitter for the past half dozen seasons, may have just the deal for you. On a private spread of 55,000 acres in the foothills of the Little Belt Mountains, you and a handful of pals will chase mulie bucks of Pope and Young class. Ponderosa pine rolls over some of the hills, while others are grassy. Shallow ravines drop quickly into deep valleys where cover is thick. You'll find the deer in the pines and have a fairly good shot at waylaying one as it moves out to feed. No rifle hunters are permitted on this property, so from one season to the next it's just you and the bucks, some of which score in the 300s. Hunter success is about 35 percent.

For whitetails, Fine moves down into the Mussellshell River bottom country near Harlowton. High and open, this is a land of prairies and breaks. You'll find whitetails concentrated in the willow and cottonwood scrub along the river and the creeks that join it. Here hunters use bows or, later in the season, rifles. While only one in three will shoot bucks scoring 130 or better, a number of hunters also settle for smaller racks. Twenty miles away in the high plains you'll find antelope, which are hunted out of the same log cabin. Bowhunters also may want to throw in a fishing rod. Rumor has it that the Mussellshell holds some very big browns.

Fine, of course, gets around. For elk, he guides clients on private ranches in the foothills of the Beaverhead Mountains southwest of Dillon. The terrain is not particularly rugged, but physical conditioning still plays a key part in hunter success. Your best shot at a bull in the 280-class will come during archery season, when calling can bring them in to 30 feet. Seventy percent of Fine's hunters get shots; 30 percent take home bragging-size bulls.

Powder River Outfitters

B r o a d u s ,   M o n t a n a

The overlooked southeastern corner of Montana has more to offer than most people realize.

U.S. ROUTE 212 CUTS OFF a huge chunk of Interstate 90 between Spearfish, South Dakota, and Crow Agency, Montana. By daylight, you can make time on this two-lane road through this land of few mountains, red rock buttes, cedar-choked canyons and high, almost arid plains. But you'll not do so well between dusk and dawn. The reason: deer, both whitetails and mulies. The grassy shoulders of the road, diligently mown by highway crews, provide scores of miles of tender new growth, the kind that deer love. Drive 212 at night and you have to avoid getting your deer with your front bumper instead of your rifle.

Ken Greslin and his partner Doug Gardner run Powder River Outfitters out of Broadus, a tiny hamlet halfway along 212 (it's the only place where you can buy gas and a hamburger and fries along the route). The Powder River cuts northeastward through town, and its bottoms hold whitetails of bragging size. A typical buck scores between 130 and 160 Boone & Crockett. You'll hunt these deer by taking up stand on deer trails between bedding and feeding areas, or by pushing through the cottonwoods and willows thickets along the Powder. Mule deer—24-inch 5x5s as a rule—frequent draws in the pine-covered ridges. Drive your 4WD along old wagon trails that follow the high ground as you glass the ravines below. Grunting and rattling can bring in bucks just before the rut in November, the best time for archers.

Physical stamina is not so in demand here, but patience and perseverance are. You'll see lots of racks on almost every hunt, as the buck-to-doe ratio here is one of the best in the state. If you're patient and hold off on the first big buck you see, the odds favor getting a bigger one. You'll also find some elk here, but they're really incidental to the deer. Licenses for archery elk hunting are readily available, but rifle hunting permits must be drawn. Antelope licenses, both bow and firearm, must also be drawn in a lottery.

Lacking the lung-bursting elevations of the Rockies, hunting Powder River country would seem to be a breeze. In one sense that's true. But what these plains lack in altitude, they make up for with persistent and bitter winds. Dressing for success is important, and you'll be glad to return to the ranch house, shed your gear, and slide a chair up to the table for a hot and wholesome family-style dinner.

[R O C K Y   M O U N T A I N S]

Rich's Double Arrow Ranch/Outfitters

S e e l e y   L a k e ,   M o n t a n a

Hunt the Bob Marshall for elk and deer, with excellent chances at both.

VITAL STATISTICS:

Game/Arm/Seasons:
ELK, DEER, BEAR:
Bow: Early through mid-Sept.
Firearms: Mid-Sept. through Nov.
LION:
Dec.

Rates:
ELK and DEER:
Bow from $1,750/5 days; firearms from $2,100/6 days

Accommodations:
LOG LODGE AND GUEST CABINS AND TENT CAMP
NUMBER OF ROOMS: 6 WITH PRIVATE BATH
MAXIMUM NUMBER OF HUNTERS: 8

Meals: Beef, chicken, fish and all the trimmings

Conference Groups: Yes
Guides: Included
Gratuity: 5 to 10%
Preferred Payment:
MasterCard, Visa

Other Activities:
Bird hunting, bird watching, fishing, riding, snowmobiling, wildlife photography

Getting There:
Fly to Missoula and rent a car, or have the lodge van pick you up at no charge.

Contact:
Jack Rich
Rich's Double Arrow Ranch/Outfitters
Box 495
Seeley Lake, MT 59868
406/677-2317
Fax: 406/677-3530
e-mail: richranch@montna.com
Web: www.richranch.com

IT'S IN THE BLOOD. Around the turn of the last century, old Hank Calhoun saddled up with Teddy Roosevelt and took him hunting down in Wyoming. Hank was C.B. Rich's granddad, and in 1948, C B. established the ranch and outfitting service that son Jack runs today. A lot of trail's been covered since then, and in the main the Bob Marshall Wilderness and the Blackfoot/Clearwater valley have been getting better. When the Rich family chose the Bob, the elk herd in Unit 150 numbered about 200. Now there's close to 900, and about 20 percent are mature bulls.

Otherwise, things have stayed pretty much the same. The trail to the wilderness camp, hunted early in the season, ambles up through heavy forest, crossing the ridge at Pyramid Pass before dropping down to Leota Park on Youngs Creek. The tent camp itself sits on a meadow fringed with lodgepole pine at 6,000 feet. Three mountains, Pyramid, Marshall and Leota, form a basin 10 miles in diameter around the camp. The basin contains a number of higher basins, the headwaters of little streams known for cutthroats, if you remembered to bring a rod. While terrain can be steep and good physical condition is a must, it is more open than most. Yet thick jumbles of blowdowns and brush provide cover for elk. Three out of four hunters have good shots at elk, and those hunters who are mentally prepared, meaning willing to work hard for each of the eight days in the hunt, usually bring out an elk.

In Leota Park, Rich runs one early-season archery hunt and three rifle hunts (elk will still be bugling during the first of these), but snow chases him back down to the ranch by mid-October. There, elk hunting is completely dependent on weather. If heavy snow gets elk moving, the migration will pass into the valley and on the mountainsides and hunting will be good. If not, elk will hole up in dark timber. Post-rut, pre-migration elk are most difficult to find. Yet even if conditions aren't right for elk, you can still harvest good whitetails of the 130 to 160 Boone & Crockett class. Riding by 4WD up into the highlands and then spotting and stalking or standing over scrapes and rub lines gives every hunter at least one good shot. How well hunters connect is up to them. If you hunt the late season dates of mid-October through November, you'll have to rough it in the lodge or guest cabins with their comfy beds and private baths. And after deer season, for those hearty souls, comes a month of mountain lion, with cats running between 130 and 150 pounds.

Rock Creek Lodge

Hinsdale, Montana

Whitetails and mule deer along with a few big bull elk for archers hearty enough to hunt them.

VITAL STATISTICS:

Game/Arm/Seasons:
DEER:
Bow: early Sept. through mid-Oct.
Centerfire: late Oct. through Nov.
ELK:
Bow: Sept. through Oct.
Rates:
$400/day
Accommodations:
MODERN LODGE
NUMBER OF ROOMS: 3 WITH PRIVATE BATH
MAXIMUM NUMBER OF HUNTERS: 6
Meals: Home cooking
Conference Groups: Yes
Guides: Included
Gratuity: $100 per trip
Preferred Payment:
Cash, check
Other Activities:
Bird hunting, bird watching, riding, waterfowling, wildlife photography
Getting There:
Fly to Glascow, and someone will pick you up.

Contact:
Dean & Patti Armbrister
Rock Creek Lodge
PO Box 152
Hinsdale, MT 59241
Ph: 406/648-5524
Fx: 406/648-5524
e-mail:
rock-creek-lodge1@juno.com
Web: finditlocal.com/rockcreek

AFTER THE BREAK ON THE TRAIL, you slip into the straps on your pack and leverage the load high on your shoulders. Bending carefully, you pick up your bow and head down the path to the campsite far into a wildness called the Missouri Breaks. Coulees choked with firs finger their way up out of the bottoms, reaching toward grassy prairie above. After half-day walk you reach the destination. Tents are pitched near the lake, where you'll bathe if you're of such a mind. Here in early October, you may not have to break the ice. Food on these hunt's comes from Uncle Sam's deli, a civilian version of that culinary masterpiece the MRE, of which Gulf War vets are so fond. Drinking water is carried in as well. Too bad nobody's figured out a dehydrated version. On this rugged hunt, your backpack and sleeping bag are your best buds. If you find a six-by bull, you may stuff your pack with grub and your sleep sack and spend a night out close to where he's rounding up his harem.

Not for everybody, this raw-boned hunt is loved by those who are physically and mentally fit enough to pull it off. For those of us with a greater fondness for creature comforts (rooms with private bath and good food), Rock Creek offers outstanding accommodations in a new lodge. You'll find mule deer and whitetails in manageable terrain. These hunts are quite different from each other. Whitetails are found in the alfalfa field bottoms of the Milk River, where you'll shoot from portable tree stands or ground blinds. Hunters whose camo is really good can get away with hiding in a ditch. For mulies, the drill is the old spot-and-stalk game. From the tops of bluffs hunters and guides glass the bottoms of coulees. Hunters who can cover lots of ground, and who can make 250-yard shots consistently from the prone position, are most successful.

Dean Armbrister, who with wife Patti, runs this show, is a stickler for marksmanship. Every hunter makes a trip to the range and demonstrates his proficiency before the hunt. Those seeking whitetails should be comfortable with making 100- to 200-yard shots. Mule deer hunters need to be accurate at longer ranges. It's not so much the caliber that makes a difference, but shot placement. A one-shot kill at 200 yards is a whole lot easier than that hail-mary round fired at your fleeing trophy. Both whitetails and mulies average five points western count.

Rugg's Outfitting

S u p e r i o r ,   M o n t a n a

Hunt two states with the same outfit, and you double your chances.

GEOLOGY makes all the difference. The Bitterroots are a big upthrust slab of sedimentary rock which tilt back toward Idaho. Their rugged slope, called the "cut face," looks into Montana. The St. Joe and Clearwater national forests, on the Idaho side, are cut by a number of roads. The Montana side, because of its steepness, is not. So what happens when elk and deer seasons are open in both states?

Yup! Road access and ease of obtaining a license encourage a lot of hunters to push up the Idaho side. Elk and deer slip through the notches and passes and filter down into the thick woods that envelop the steep flanks of ridges that fall away to valley floors hundreds of feet below. The terrain here is not as difficult as in Ray Rugg's second camp. But you'll work up a sweat while getting your deer or elk. While some massive bulls have been taken from this corner of Montana, any brow-tined bull is legal. This may be a good place to fill your freezer, and Rugg only hunts it in the third week of firearms season.

He opens the season farther north in the Great Burn Wilderness. Here, the grade is 100 percent, meaning that for every foot of horizontal distance, elevation changes by one foot as well. The ruggedness of this discourages most hunters, so pressure on this area is light. The heavily timbered north slope, long open meadows broken with patches of tag alder, and lots of creeks combine to make this ideal habitat for elk in the 280-inch range and mule deer with 5x5 racks or better. Hunter success is better than 50 percent.

From his modern guesthouse on the 800-acre ranch five miles west of Superior, Rugg runs whitetail hunts where everybody, even handicapped hunters, has a good chance of tagging a 8-pointer. Used only every other week during the season, the ranch is available to no more than four hunters per week. One-on-one hunts are quite reasonably priced here ($500 additional), making this a great place for those of limited hunting experience. Along with the Montana hunts, Ray and his troops also guide in Idaho.

VITAL STATISTICS:

Game/Arm/Seasons:
DEER and ELK:
MONTANA:
Bow: Early Sept. through mid-Oct.
Centerfire: Late Oct. through Nov.
IDAHO:
Bow: Late Aug. through late Sept.
Centerfire: Early through late Oct.
Rates:
ELK and DEER:
Bow from $2,500/7 days
Centerfire from $2,750/7 days
MOUNTAIN LION $2,500/3 days
Accommodations:
TENT CAMPS, RUSTIC LODGE AND CABINS
MAXIMUM NUMBER OF HUNTERS: 6
Meals: Hearty Western fare
Conference Groups: Yes
Guides: Included
Gratuity: 7%
Preferred Payment:
Cash, check
Other Activities:
Bird hunting, canoeing/rafting, fishing, skiing, snowmobiling, wildlife photography
Getting There:
Fly to Missoula and the lodge van will pick you up.

Contact:
Ray Rugg
Rugg's Outfitting
50 Dry Creek Rd.
Superior, MT 59872
406/822-4240
e-mail: spr4240@montana.com
Web: www.marsweb.com/rugg

Rush's Lakeview Guest Ranch

L i m a ,   M o n t a n a

Headquarter in the main ranch or a base camp, and hunt with or without a guide for elk, deer and bear.

VITAL STATISTICS:

Game/Arm/Seasons:
ELK and WHITETAILS:
Bow: Early Sept. through mid-Oct.
Centerfire: Late Oct. through Nov.
Rates:
Base camp from $350/day
Spike camps from $750/7 days
Accommodations:
RUSTIC CABINS OR TENTS
NUMBER OF ROOMS: 18
MAXIMUM NUMBER OF HUNTERS: 50
Meals: Home-style cooking
Conference Groups: Yes
Guides: Included
Gratuity: Hunter discretion
Preferred Payment:
Check
Other Activities:
Bird hunting, fishing, riding, snow-mobiling, swimming, waterfowling
Getting There:
Fly to West Yellowstone or Idaho Falls, rent a car and drive to the ranch.

Contact:
Keith Rush
Rush's Lakeview
Guest Ranch
Monida Star Rt.,
Lima, MT 59739
406/276-3300

AT ONE TIME Keith Rush had dozens of tent camps scattered in the area around Red Rock Lake Wilderness and National Wildlife Refuge, a favorite breeding ground of the trumpeter swan and habitat with a high population of elk. Now he operates eight while running most of his hunts from a base camp, a full-service, year-round resort. Hunters and horses load up each morning and head out to areas on the northern flanks of the Continental Divide. Terrain is rugged, with more ups and downs than most other locales in Montana. Draws filled with lodgepole pine, spruce and fir steepen as they climb toward the treeless crest of the Centennial Mountains. Yet interspersed on the slopes are scores of small, grassy parks and little valleys choked with aspen and willow. And it's here that you'll see elk, bear and deer.

Hunting is from horseback or afoot, depending on the dictates of terrain, weather and game. Early in the season, calling pays off for archers. As the season progresses, spotting and stalking becomes the more efficient strategy. Elk and deer are not particularly migratory here. They just move down from the highest elevations as winter's weather worsens. Hunting in this country is very dependent on weather. Rush has been in this business for nearly half a century, and he refuses to talk about hunter success rates. "Too many damn variables for them to mean anything," he says. Typical elk and deer are 5x5s.

Rush's hunters have the option of staying at the ranch or driving, with trailered horses in tow, to trailheads leading to the area selected for the day's hunt. The benefit of this is extreme mobility. You can go where the game is and other hunters aren't. In addition, hunters can select one of the eight camps. Depending on the fees paid, you can have the services of a wrangler, guide or cook. Or Rush will pack you in and leave you alone until he picks you up a week later. Hunters headquartering at the ranch enjoy rustic cabins (some with private baths), the sauna and all the home-style cooking a belly can hold.

S&W Outfitters

B i g   S k y ,   M o n t a n a

You can hunt for whitetails, mulies or elk out of two camps operated by S&W.

VITAL STATISTICS:

Game/Arm/Seasons:
ELK and DEER
Bow: Early Sept. through mid-Oct.
Firearms: Late Oct. through late Nov.
Rates:
Bow combo hunts from $2,150/6 days
Firearms combo hunts from $3,500/6 days
Accommodations:
FRAME BUNKHOUSE AND LOG CABIN
MAXIMUM NUMBER OF HUNTERS:
WOLF CREEK 4
EAST FORK 8
Meals: Salmon fillets, baby back ribs, chicken parmesan
Conference Groups: No
Guides: Included
Gratuity: $100 to $500
Preferred Payment:
Cash, check
Other Activities:
Fishing, wildlife photography
Getting There:
Fly to Billings or Bozeman and a representative of S&W will meet you.

Contact:
Brad Hunzel
S&W Outfitters
Box 160502
Big Sky, MT 59716
406/995-2658
Fax: 406/995-4494

WITH OPERATIONS IN TWO AREAS, the Madison Range 30 miles south of Ennis, and the Big Snowy Mountains a similar distance south of Lewistown, S&W puts hunters in areas with high populations of elk and deer respectively.

Ennis, of course, is headquarters for fishing the Madison River, one of Montana's premier trout streams. The river valley runs between the Gravely Mountains on the west and the peaks of the Madisons to the east. The valley itself is broad ranchland, faintly arid and rising from bench to bench into foothills rife with aspen-thicket draws. Ever steepening, the hills climb the flanks of the mountains and support stands of heavy black timber, predominantly lodgepole pine, before becoming treeless at the summit of 11,000-foot Imp Mountain and its only slightly shorter neighbor, Finger Mountain. Wolf Creek drains these crests, and it's here that S&W runs its firearms hunts for elk on 24,000 acres of private ranch and 10,000 acres of adjacent Forest Service land. The region supports a resident herd of about 700 animals, augmented by 2,500 or so that winter in ranch pastures. Success rate on bulls from S&W's log cabin camp on Wolf Creek is about 65 percent. Typical bulls score between 260 and 280.

Over 100 miles to the north is S&W's East Fork camp in the midst of 40,000 acres of private land and 2,100 acres of public land. Terrain here is not quite as vertical as in the Wolf Creek area, and the region teems with whitetails and mule deer. Elk averaging 320 or so are hunted here during the archery season only. Best hunting for mulies is during the peak of their rut from November 15 to about November 20. Whitetails peak the following week. Average bucks score 130 to 140 inches, and hunter success is better than 60 percent. A long, low wood camp, East Fork has all the comforts of home.

Scapegoat Wilderness Outfitters

Fort Benton, Montana

Regenerating burn areas are giving up more than a few trophy bulls.

VITAL STATISTICS:

Game/Arm/Seasons:
ELK, DEER:
Bow: Early through mid-Sept.
Centerfire: Mid-Sept. through late Nov.
Rates:
From $2,500/7 days
Accommodations:
Tents
Maximum Number of Hunters:
6
Meals: Well, the turkey is to rave about.
Conference Groups: No
Guides: Included
Gratuity: $100
Preferred Payment:
Cash, MasterCard, Visa, check
Other Activities:
Bird hunting, fishing, waterfowling, wildlife photography
Getting There:
Fly to Great Falls International Airport and you'll be met by a representative of the outfitter.

Contact:
Bill Plante
Scapegoat Wilderness Outfitters
Headquarters Box 824
Fort Benton, MT 59442
800/242-HUNT
or 406/662-3210

OKAY, HOW STEEP IS STEEP? Bill Plante of Scapegoat Outfitters puts it this way: Some of the meadows he hunts are so steep you can't see more than 150 yards up or down. He's talking about the flanks of the Continental Divide, which traces a wandering path through the Lolo National Forest. To the east, the land falls away to high prairie. To the west is a wilderness of mountains and rock slides, thick forest and high alpine basins in which scars of old burns and grassy parks are set like jade among the black timber.

Burns are a big thing here. While Yellowstone was all but engulfed in the famed fire of '88, a separate blaze scorched 32 straight miles of wilderness. Outfitters whose permit areas lay in the path of the flames lost everything. Plante's operation was just outside the burn, and now regenerating forest is providing habitat and fodder for herds of elk and deer. Early in the season, archers hunt high basins and the little streams that drain them. Elk will be found near wallows, and calls are effective in bringing 5- and 6-pointers into the open. Shots range from 15 to 40 yards. With rifle season included, the success rate runs around 70 percent.

Mule deer and whitetails are found in this neck of the woods, as well. Mule deer aren't threatened with winter kill here because, when heavy snows begin to bury their favorite haunts along the high divide, they merely drop down into winter range on the prairie, four miles to the east. Whitetail populations are good, but, says Plante, "Most of the guys who see mulies of 300 pounds forget about whitetails!" Eight out of 10 hunters kill mule deer with heavy racks in the 24- to 30-inch class. Bears are definitely an adjunct to deer and elk hunting. Each August, when the cook tent is being erected for a new season, the resident grizzly—Bruno—comes by to check it out. Plante uses a solar-powered bear fence to keep would-be marauding bruins at bay.

Snowy Springs Outfitters

K a l i s p e l l ,   M o n t a n a

A day-long packtrain ride puts you in excellent elk country, just south of Glacier Park.

I F YOU TAKE SHAWN LITTLE'S ADVICE, you'll spring for the air charter and ride a Cessna or Beaver into the depths of the Bob Marshall Wilderness a couple of clicks south of Glacier National Park. The ride takes an hour or so and is a great chance to get the lay of the land. You can also see it up close and all too personal from a saddle on one of Little's well-broken horses. Riding horseback into your base camp can take up to nine hours, and on the trip in, the terrain isn't the only thing you'll get a feel for.

Outfitting primarily for elk, deer and bear, though moose, goat and sheep can make the list if you survive the draw, Snowy Springs runs hunts from five camps in the vicinity of Schafer Meadows. Steep and rugged are overworked words describing Montana's wilderness, but they're apt descriptives nonetheless. From old burns and alder-covered slides to thickly timbered river bottoms and high alpine basins, the landscape is as varied as Mark Twain's weather. Horses will carry you as far as they can. Then it's shanks mare for you. Average bulls carry four points per side or better and about 50 percent of Little's hunters fill their tags. One guide serves two hunters. Distances are deceiving. Shots may stretch out to 400 yards, though 200 is the norm. Wise hunters know how much shooting at steep angles down- or uphill affects point of impact, and they can dismount a horse and mount a rifle in a jiffy if need be.

The season up here begins with archery and bulls calling their cows together. Snowy Springs runs its early-season bowhunts in Area 141, which is closed to rifle hunters until the general season opens in late October. However, in the next unit, 151, there's a one-week either-sex season for elk during the third week of September, and the general season for antlered bulls opens a week later. Bulls will still be in rut and shots may be a little easier to come by than later. This is the time when hunters spend a good deal of time working wallows favored by elk in remote upper basins. Later in the season, after bulls have left their cows, they return to their bachelorhood and occasionally refuse to move unless pushed out of thick cover. Snow comes in mid to late October and really aids hunters in tracking. This is the time when mule deer begin their rut and 4- to 5-point bulls with 24- to 30-inch spreads become more easily hunted. One out of three hunters here takes a nice bull.

VITAL STATISTICS:

Game/Arm/Seasons:
ELK and DEER:
Bow: Early Sept. through mid-Oct.
Centerfire, muzzleloader: Mid-Sept. through late Nov.
Rates:
From $4,200/8 days (includes license)
Accommodations:
TENT CAMPS
MAXIMUM NUMBER OF HUNTERS: 6
Meals: Hearty mountain cooking
Conference Groups: Yes
Guides: Included
Gratuity: $100 to $300
Preferred Payment:
Cash, check
Other Activities:
Canoeing/rafting, fishing, wildlife photography
Getting There:
Fly to Glacier International Airport and rent a car, or take the bush flight for $200 round-trip.

Contact:
Shawn Little
Snowy Springs Outfitters
Box 686
Kalispell, MT 59903-0686
406/755-2137

Tamarack Lodge

T r o y ,   M o n t a n a

Hunt the remote Yaak Valley if you want to know what the West was like 200 years ago.

VITAL STATISTICS:

Game/Arm/Seasons:
ELK and DEER:
Bow: Early Sept. through mid-Oct.
Centerfire, muzzleloader: Late Oct.
through mid-Nov.
MOUNTAIN LION:
Late Nov. through Dec.
BEAR:
Spring, mid-April through mid-May;
fall, mid-Sept. through Nov.

Rates:
DEER and ELK:
Bow from $3,335/6 days; firearms
$3,835/7 days (includes combo
license)
MOUNTAIN LION $3,200/3 days
Bear $2,000/6 days

Accommodations:
MODERN LOG LODGE
NUMBER OF ROOMS: 7 WITH PRIVATE BATH
MAXIMUM NUMBER OF HUNTERS: 22

Meals: Near gourmet, family-style

Conference Groups: Yes

Guides: Included

Gratuity: 10%

Preferred Payment:
Cash, MasterCard, Visa, check

Other Activities:
Bird hunting, fishing, sporting clays,
wildlife photography

Getting There:
Fly to Spokane or Kalispell and rent a
car, or make arrangements for the
lodge shuttle to pick you up at $500
round-trip for up to five persons and
gear.

Contact:
Bill McAfee
Tamarack Lodge
32855 S. Fork Rd.
Troy, MT 59935
406/295-4880
Fax: 406/295-1022
e-mail: tamarack@libby.org
Web: www.libby.org/tamarack

THE YAAK VALLEY high in the northwest-ernmost valley of Montana may, indeed, be the last best place in the Lower 48. Odds are you're not going to come to this place on your way to anywhere else. The region is a healthy 100 miles from any town with a stoplight or two. Even if tourism development continues at its rampant pace, it will be a millennium before this area sees its first fast-food joint. That's why Bill McAfee and his wife Judy built their handsome and luxurious Tamarack Lodge here.

In the fall, needles of the pine-like tamarack tree glow as gold as aspen. That's the time to hunt deer and elk in the Purcell Mountains of the Kootenai National Forest. This corner of the state lacks the steep ups and downs found far-ther south. Heavy forest rolls over the hills and up mountains that rise no farther than 6,500 feet or so. Logging has created clear-cuts thick with new growth, and pocket-like meadows of grass are scattered among the trees.

This heavy cover allows whitetail bucks to reach considerable size. A 140-to 160-class whitetail is a very real possibility here. Closing miles of logging road has dramatically reduced hunting pressure and created swaths of grassy habitat. Over the past few years, guides have found that rattling, grunt tubes, scent and still-hunting the clear-cut edges produce trophies. To reach your hunting area, you'll roll out of bed, breakfast, gear up and climb aboard the horse-drawn wagon a couple hours before sunup. You'll head for the top of a drainage and hunt through it and into another, where you'll meet the wagon at dark for the ride back to the lodge.

Archers seeking a Pope and Young-class buck have a better-than-average chance here and often find themselves face to flank with a bull elk. You can hunt both species during September's archery season. Rifle hunters often encounter elk during deer hunts in October and November. Hunter success for whitetails is 80 per-cent; for elk, 40 percent; for mule deer, 90 percent, though the numbers of hunters seeking mulies is small. After deer and elk seasons, mountain lions averaging 150 pounds take the spotlight, and in the spring there are bear in all color phases.

Tamarack lodge sits on 150 acres with 3,000 feet of the South Fork of the Yaak River flowing across the nearby meadow. All rooms have private baths, and meals are as tasty as they are filling. After dinner, soak in the hot tub or lounge by the fire until Morpheus sends you to your room to dream.

Under Wild Skies Lodge & Outfitters

P h i l i p s b u r g ,   M o n t a n a

To find an elk, follow the seasons.

VITAL STATISTICS:

Game/Arm/Seasons:
ELK, DEER:
Bow: Early Sept. through mid-Oct.
Centerfire: Mid-Oct. through late Nov.
BEAR:
Centerfire: Mid-April through May
ANTELOPE:
Centerfire: Mid-Oct.

Rates:
ELK, DEER from $1,800 /6 days
(bow); $2,000/6 days (rifle)
BEAR $1,500/6 days
ANTELOPE $950/3 days (one-on-one)

Accommodations:
MODERN LOG LODGE AND TENTS
NUMBER OF ROOMS: 10 WITH PRIVATE BATH
MAXIMUM NUMBER OF HUNTERS: 8 (4 PER TENT CAMP)

Meals: Swiss chicken, smoked brisket, wild game

Conference Groups: Yes

Guides: Included

Gratuity: Hunter's discretion

Preferred Payment:
Cash, company check

Other Activities:
Biking, bird hunting, bird watching, boating, fishing, swimming, waterfowling, wildlife photography

Getting There:
Fly to Butte and rent a car, or take the lodge van for free.

Contact:
Vaughn Esper
Under Wild Skies
Lodge & Outfitters
Box 849
Philipsburg, MT 59858
406-859-3000
Fax: 406/859-3161
e-mail: underwildskies@juno.com

THE ANACONDA PINTLER Wilderness is located southwest of its namesake town of copper-mining fame and is some of the toughest country in the state. The Continental Divide staggers through the wilderness where mountain peaks approach 11,000 feet. Heavily forested, there's more up and down than sideways to this country, but the combination of near inaccessibility, heavy timber and an occasional grassy meadow makes it tough to beat if you're an elk or an elk hunter.

Vaughn Esper runs two kinds of hunts in this country. First and foremost are wilderness hunts from seven tent camps scattered through units 211, 214 and 321 and surrounding Beaverhead and Deer Lodge national forests. Just where you'll hunt in these 300,000 acres depends on the weather. If it's warm, you'll hunt high. If it's been snowy, likely the elk are a little lower. In any event, you'll ride up out of camp well before sunup to the general vicinity for the day's hunt. The horses do most of the hard work, but after you've left them tethered, you'll head off on foot, glassing and walking and glassing some more until you see a bull. You may circle back to where you left the horses, or the horses may be moved to a new spot where you'll meet them. On these hunts, there's a 45 percent chance of taking an elk. Most of the elk harvested here are 5x5s, though anything from spikes on up is legal.

If the backcountry gets snowed in, then you'll have to suffer through hunting out of the lodge. And what a lodge! Near the end of 12 miles of gravel road and constructed of honey-toned log, the lodge and its two guesthouses sit on a little bench overlooking a pair of ponds where elk and deer come to drink. The Espers live in the lodge all year so they know the patterns of elk and deer movement in the region. Via 4WD, horseback or foot, you'll leave camp early for your hunting area. Because ranch hunts typically take place later in the season, the success rate here on elk and whitetails averages about 25 percent. The bulls that are taken, however, tend to be pretty good, and the percentage on whitetails taken would be much higher if most hunters were not so intent on taking elk While tent camps only take up to four hunters, groups of six to eight may hunt from the lodge.

You'll also find spring bear hunting from the lodge and a great fall antelope hunt on a 20,000-acre private ranch near Broadus on Route 212 in southeastern Montana. Antelope hunting in the state is on a lottery basis, but the odds of being drawn for the Esper's area are better than 90 percent.

E.W. Watson & Sons Outfitting Inc.

Townsend, Montana

Hunt the Madison Range out of a tent camp or ranch for big bulls and bucks.

VITAL STATISTICS:

Game/Arm/Seasons:
ELK and DEER:
Bow: Early Sept. through mid-Oct.
Centerfire: Late Oct. through Nov.

Rates:
ELK and DEER:
Archery $3,500/7 days
Centerfire from $3,300/6 days

Accommodations:
TENT CAMPS AND CABINS
MAXIMUM NUMBER OF HUNTERS:
RANCH: 4; BACKCOUNTRY 6

Meals: Family-style

Conference Groups: No

Guides: Included

Gratuity: $100

Preferred Payment:
Cash, certified check

Getting There:
Fly to Bozeman and you will be met
by a representative of the camp.

Contact:
Edwin Watson,
E W Watson & Sons
Outfitting Inc.
7837 US Hwy. 287
Townsend, MT 59644
1-800 654-2845
406-266-3741
Fax: 406/266-4498
e-mail: ewwatson@initco.net

WITH EIGHT YEARS in the outfitting business, Ed Watson is earning an enviable reputation for putting hunters on respectable bulls and bucks. He has been able to cater to the needs of hunters of various abilities at his traditional tent camp and his private ranch. Both make use of the Madisons, that range of 11,000-foot peaks separating the Madison and Gallatin rivers in southwestern Montana. Most of the Madison Range has been designated the Lee Metcalf Wilderness. Slopes rise first in a series of benches maintained as pasture, but soon they steepen and give way to low ridges separated by little bright-water valleys of willow and lush grass. Climbing still, the valleys narrow and their flanks take on the heavy forest of lodgepole pine, which grades upward into firs and spruce. Above the forest rise the treeless peaks, which are sometimes snow-capped year-round.

It is good range for elk. Come winter they take cover in the little brush-filled draws and take feed where they can find it in the fringes of lowland pastures. In fall, as snows crust the treeless heights, elk slowly filter down through the forest. During the rut, bugling is as productive as it is everywhere and archers score well on 5x5 bulls. Hunters equipped with medium magnums of 7mm Rem. or .300 Win. have ample opportunity to stretch the legs of their cartridges. While most shots are in the 100- to 200-yard range, some demand 400-yard accuracy. Late-season hunting, which is mostly spotting and stalking, is a true test of shooter's skill. Chances of scoring on a 4x4 or better mule deer are reasonable, as well. Overall success rates run around 75 percent.

Watson believes in personal service. That's why all his hunts are based on one guide per hunter. Pack trips up into the St. Joe camp depart from Ennis and require a three-hour ride. The tent camp is well appointed by most standards, with floored tents covered with indoor-outdoor carpeting. There's also a shower tent next to the cook tent. Each morning you and your guide will head up and out to glass and stalk your way back to camp by nightfall. The Jumping Horse Ranch camp, located farther down the mountains, is a very good alternative for hunters who may not have the physical conditioning demanded by the backcountry hunts. Handicapped hunters are welcome. Here too, there's always the option of hunting afoot or on horseback, or from stands placed above game trails. Rather than wall tents, hunters on the ranch stay in comfortable cabins at the end of a skinny dirt road. Success here is better than in the backcountry, with everyone taking either bulls or whitetail bucks.

Wildlife Adventures Inc.

V i c t o r ,   M o n t a n a

Try a one-on-one hunt to improve your odds for success.

VITAL STATISTICS:

Game/Arm/Seasons:
<u>ELK and DEER:</u>
Bow: Sept.
Centerfire, muzzleloader: Idaho, Oct.;
Montana, Nov.
<u>MOUNTAIN LIONS:</u>
Centerfire, muzzleloader: Dec.
through March
<u>BEAR:</u>
Centerfire, muzzleloader: Late April
through May
Rates:
ELK, DEER, BEAR:
Idaho: From $3,250/7 days
Montana: From $1,535/5 days
LION from $2,500/10 days
Accommodations:
WALL TENTS OR LODGE
NUMBER OF ROOMS: 6 WITH PRIVATE BATH
MAXIMUM NUMBER OF HUNTERS: 8
Meals: Game hens, stews, ham,
beef
Conference Groups: Yes
Guides: Included
Gratuity: $100 to $200
Preferred Payment:
Cash, American Express, check
Other Activities:
Antiquing, biking, bird hunting, bird
watching, boating, canoeing/rafting,
fishing, golf, riding, skiing,
swimming, waterfowling, wildlife
photography
Getting There:
Fly to Missoula and a representative
from the lodge will meet you.

Contact:
Jack Wemple
Wildlife Adventures Inc.
1765 Pleasant View Dr.
Victor, MT 59875
888/642-1010 or
406/642-3262
Fax: 406/642-3462
e-mail: selwayl@aol.com
Web:
www.huntinfo.com/wildlifeadven.htm

BECAUSE ELK POPULATIONS are up, your chances of killing a bull are better than ever. But a lot of hunters handicap themselves by not opting for a one-on-one hunt. That's the word from Jack and Shirley Wemple who've been running this outfitting service for nearly 30 years. Think about the economics of it. On a typical two-hunters-with-one-guide hunt, you and your buddy swap off. Half of the time the guide's positioning you for a shot and the other half, it's your buddy. In addition, it's considerably more difficult for a guide to serve two hunters, even if they are perfectly matched in terms of physical ability and mental attitude, than it is to meet the needs of one. You might look at it this way: one guide and a hunter is a team; two or more hunters per guide and you've got a committee.

Though they like one-on-one hunting, Jack and Rick Wemple and their guides are quite adept at serving the needs of two hunters. The Wemples run hunts in the rugged Lolo zone, in Idaho hunting Unit 12 of the Selway Bitterroot Wilderness and in the Bitterroot and Lolo national forests of Montana. The Idaho hunts are in some of the roughest country imaginable. Three tent camps are located high in the Storm Creek drainage and surrounding area. Densely forested, shots are quick and reasonably close. You won't find many opportunities for 200- to 300-yard kills in this neck of the woods. Archers get first crack at elk during September, the bugling season. Rifle hunters follow in October and can take advantage of tracking snows. From camp, you'll ride anywhere from 15 minutes to an hour or more from camp in the pitch-dark of early morning, then dismount to hunt on foot. Most bulls that come out of this area are 6x6s and one out of every two hunters goes home with a trophy.

Montana hunts operate out of the Wemple's guest ranch five miles west of Victor on the eastern slope of the Bitterroots. From the comforts of the ranch, you'll hunt public lands throughout the entire 100x20-mile valley. Guided archery hunts are conducted in September, and in November rifle hunters have at it. By then, elk are moving down out of the high timber, and if you are lucky you'll connect with a 5x5. Hunter success is lower, however, than on the Idaho hunts. Lion hunts and spring bear hunts are also run from the ranch.

World Class Outfitting Adventures

Arlee, Montana

Go way back, and hunt the largest outfitting area in the state of Idaho.

VITAL STATISTICS:

Game/Arm/Seasons:
ELK, DEER, LION:
Bow, centerfire, muzzleloader:
Mid-Sept. through mid-Nov.
BEAR:
Bow, centerfire, muzzleloader:
Spring, mid-April through mid-June;
fall, mid-Sept. through late Oct.

Rates:
ELK/DEER/BEAR/LION combo
from $4,505/8 days
Trophy ELK/DEER combo $3,500/7 days
Trophy DEER $3,500/7 days
LION $3,495/7 days
BEAR $2,495/7 days (spring)

Accommodations:
WALL TENTS
MAXIMUM NUMBER OF HUNTERS: 8

Meals: Family-style cooking; cook for yourself at drop camps

Conference Groups: Yes

Guides: Included

Gratuity: Hunter's discretion

Preferred Payment:
Cash, MasterCard, Visa, check, money order

Other Activities:
Bird hunting, bird watching, fishing, hiking, wildlife photography

Getting There:
Fly to Missoula, rent a car and drive to the base camp, or a van from the camp will transport you for $100 round-trip.

Contact:
Jason Clinkenbeard
World Class
Outfitting Adventures
Box 351
Arlee, MT 59821
406/726-3829
Fax: 406/726-3466
e-mail: wcoainid@aol

WORLD CLASS OUTFITTING, operating in the legendary Selway-Bitterroot Wilderness of Idaho, has a pretty special thing going. In a nutshell, they operate in the state's largest outfitting area, hunting nearly 300 square miles from 12 reserved camps 10 to 22 miles deep in the wilderness. The only access to these camps is by mule or foot. For the hunter who really wants to get back into the thick of it, hunting either with a guide or out of a drop camp on his own, this is the place!

According to owner Jason Clinkenbeard, "Inaccessibility to this area leads to low hunting pressure, outstanding resident elk herds, terrific bull-cow ratios (25 to 100, when last surveyed), and virtually undisturbed wildlife and habitat." The Selway-Bitterroot has a huge elk herd, with many trophy-sized bulls. Hunts can be combined with white-tailed and mule deer and black bears, if you wish.

On the first three hunts, guides take advantage of the bulls being in rut and try to bugle them into bow or rifle range (the Selway is one of the few areas left in the U.S. where rifles are allowed during the bugle season). Later, when the rut is pretty much over, guides concentrate on going after wise old trophy bulls that know the score when it comes to bugling. Weather is colder at this time, as the season stretches into November, but snow on the ground will let you follow tracks of a big bull deep into the lodgepole pine where he might be hiding.

Deer hunting, both whitetails and mulies, is also prime during the November rut. Mulies favor higher elevations; whitetails like it down lower. Lions can also be hunted into November. And when it comes to big cats, this area has produced some huge ones. Different color-phase black bears are also abundant here, although you can only hunt them from September into October (and then again in spring).

In addition to the normally scheduled backcountry hunts, World Class offers special late-season combo hunts for elk and deer out of the Paradise base camp. This is a comfortable wall-tent camp with hot showers, good food and inviting campfires. Guides will help you find the animals you're looking for, usually along the Selway River.

World Class also runs drop camps for experienced hunters and outdoorsmen who don't need cooks and guides. Clinkenbeard's outfit will pack your party and gear into the camps on mules and horses (they don't leave the animals, as you're already smack in the middle of prime game country).

WTR Outfitters

O v a n d o ,   M o n t a n a

Hunt one of three camps for elk in the Bob Marshall Wilderness.

VITAL STATISTICS:

Game/Arm/Seasons:
ELK and DEER:
Bow: Early through mid-Sept.
Centerfire: Mid-Sept. through late Nov.

Rates:
From $3,000/9 days

Accommodations:
TENT CAMP
MAXIMUM NUMBER OF HUNTERS: 6

Meals: Steak, salads, desserts

Conference Groups: No

Guides: Included

Gratuity: 10 to 15%

Preferred Payment:
Cash, check

Other Activities:
Fishing, wildlife photography

Getting There:
Fly to Missoula and you'll be met at no charge.

Contact:
Jack Hooker
White Tail Ranch Outfitters
520 Cooper Lake Rd.
Ovando, MT 59854
406/793-5666

THOUGH THIS MORNING'S RIDE from camp has taken you and your guide to the head of the drainage, it seems as if you've been climbing all day. You didn't mind it much, though, because you've been seeing game. There was that small group of four cows and the bull that trailed behind. Looked promising through the glasses so you slid off the ridge you were on, crossed the creek and worked you way up to get a closer look. The bull was there, but he was only a 4x4 and you weren't ready to settle for that. Not on the third morning of your hunt. So you climbed to the top of the ridge, ate a sandwich and continued to follow the ridge up. Your guide wanted to check out a little basin where bulls sometimes compete for unbred cows. From the divide, you could see a fair herd but it was two, maybe two and a half miles away. The sun was headed down over the Mission Range to the west and there was almost time to make it back to camp before pitch-dark.

But then you'd have to climb back up here in the morning, and even if you left at 4 a.m., it'd be midmorning before you made it. What the hell — you've got water, half a sandwich, a candy bar, and miracle of miracles, the guide pulls out a tiny gas stove, a couple of bi-metal cups, a tin pot and, lo and behold, two packs of freeze-dried beef stroganoff. There's also tea, and a space blanket.

Presto. Spike camp! The guide radios the main camp and tells them you're spending the night up on the ridge so you can get up and stalk those elk in the morning. Your guide has no more fondness for complete misery than the next guy, but if the weather's not overly severe, he'll do anything to avoid wasting time climbing down and then back up that ridge.

WTR runs three camps: one nine miles, one 16 miles and one 22 miles into the Bob Marshall Wilderness north of Lincoln. Terrain is steep and rocky, forested and broken by clearings. You'll find patches of new forest, regenerating after the 1998 forest fire, near the 16-mile camp that's not far from the Continental Divide. If you go all the way into Danaher Creek, the camp 22 miles from the trailhead, you'll find that the landscape is not too difficult, but that vegetation is, in a word, thick. This is where big mule deer hold court. Bucks are usually 4x4s or better and bull elk run in the 5x5 range. Hunter success is about 50 percent on any elk, mule deer, or whitetails hunted lower down the mountains.

Circle E Outfitters

L o g a n ,   U t a h

The odds are you'll get your bull if you hunt in northern Utah.

VITAL STATISTICS:

Game/Arm/Seasons:
ELK (Utah and Wyoming):
Bow: Sept.
Centerfire: Oct.
DEER (Utah and Wyoming):
Bow: Sept.
Centerfire: Sept. through Oct.
ANTELOPE (Wyoming):
Centerfire: Sept.
MOOSE (Wyoming):
Bow, centerfire: Sept.
Rates:
ELK $2,500/5 days
DEER $1,600/5 days
ANTELOPE $900/3 days
MOOSE $2,800/7 days
Accommodations:
WALL TENTS WITH ELECTRICITY AND RUNNING WATER
MAXIMUM NUMBER OF HUNTERS: 10
Meals: Hearty Western fare
Conference Groups: No
Guides: Included
Gratuity: Hunter's discretion
Preferred Payment:
Cash, cashier's check
Other Activities:
Fishing, wildlife photography
Getting There:
Fly to Jackson, Wyoming, or Salt Lake City, Utah, and be picked up by a representative of the outfitter for an additional $100.

Contact:
Randy Eames
Circle E Outfitters
767 East 600 South
Logan, UT 84321
453/753-5565

WAY BACK IN THE 1800S, elk herds were down across the West. In fact, if it weren't for national parks such as Yellowstone, there were hardly any elk to speak of. The Utah Fish and Game people recognized their state had a problem, and in 1913 decided to do something about it, importing wapiti from Yellowstone. Shipped to the state in boxcars by rail, the elk were released in Fishlake National Forest, Mt. Nebo, Logan Canyon, Manti Mountain, Mt. Timpanogos and the Oquirrhs. This, to supplement the herd still hanging on in the Uintas.

By 1925 the elk had multiplied sufficiently so that limited hunting seasons were opened on the Cache National Forest east of Logan. Hunting was later allowed in the other areas where elk had been transplanted. And the rest, as they say, is history. Today, elk numbers are running high throughout the state. Circle E offers two elk hunts in the state, the first a limited-entry elk hunt in northern Utah. Your odds of drawing a tag here are maybe 35 percent, but if you do draw one, you'll be on a hunt that has had a 100 percent success rate for the past six years.

The second hunt by Circle E is on their 20,000-acre ranch in north-central Utah, outside of Logan. This hunt is also done from 4WD vehicles and on foot. Hunters stay in comfortable wall tents on this hunt, which puts them right near the game.

Circle E also operates in the Bridger-Teton Forest in western Wyoming, offering archery elk hunts in September, right when the rut is in full swing; and then, later, rifle hunts for bulls that can score 320 and up. Deer, moose and black bear hunts can also be arranged, as can antelope hunts on the nearby prairies.

H&H Hunting

Salem, Utah

Guaranteed permits and access to trophy areas let H&H put clients on monster mulies, elk, moose and more.

VITAL STATISTICS:

Game/Arm/Seasons:

DEER:
Bow: Late Aug. through early Sept.
Centerfire: Mid through late Oct.
Muzzleloader: Late Oct. through early Nov.

ELK:
Bow: Early through mid-Sept.
Centerfire: Early Sept. through mid-Oct.
Muzzleloader: Mid through late Oct.

MOOSE:
Centerfire: Late Sept. through late Oct.

Rates:
DEER, ELK, MOOSE $3,000/5 days

Accommodations:
RANCH HOUSE, TRAILERS, MOTELS, TENTS; VARIES WITH HUNT LOCATION
MAXIMUM NUMBER OF HUNTERS: 6

Meals: Steaks, roasts, potatoes, veggies, desserts

Conference Groups: No

Guides: Included

Gratuity: $200 to $700

Preferred Payment:
Cash, check (for deposit only)

Other Activities:
Bird hunting, fishing, waterfowling

Getting There:
Fly to Salt Lake City, Utah, or Ely, Nevada, rent a car, or be picked up by a representative of the outfitter for an additional $50 to $200.

Contact:
Bruce or Craig Hubbard
H&H Hunting
Box 574
Salem, UT 84653
801/423-1142
Fax: 801/423-3259

BASED OUT OF SALEM, UTAH, H&H Hunting is right near the border of the Uinta National Forest, home to trophy mule deer, bear, elk and some pronghorn. But hunting on public land isn't H&H's only gig. With private leases all over Utah, Wyoming and Nevada, and guaranteed landowner permits on a lot of spreads, H&H can take client hunters to top spots for mule deer and elk, in particular, but also for antelope, shiras moose, black bears and lions.

"We put an emphasis on quality hunts for trophy animals," says Craig Hubbard, co-owner of H & H with his father, Bruce. "We have guaranteed permits through the landowners, we have access to the land and we can put our clients on the game."

Hubbard spends a good deal of his off-season scouting H&H's hunting leases, studying the game, and finding where the truly big animals are located on a given tract. When the season approaches, he'll take his guides with him and follow the animals with them so they know what they're after as well.

"Of course, most of our guides have been with us for more than five years, so they pretty much know the score anyway," Hubbard concludes.

Depending on what you're hunting, and whether you're hunting Utah, Nevada or Wyoming, on private or public land, accommodations vary greatly. In Nevada, most clients stay in either a ranch house or wall tents; in Utah, it could be a cabin, tent or trailer.

"Most of our clients are repeat customers," says Hubbard. "They know that sometimes they won't be staying in the plushest place in the world. On the other hand, they know that we hunt some of the best trophy spots around, and that we can get them the game.

"Just as an example, on 13 mule deer hunts in 1995, our hunters took 10 book bucks. In '95 and '96, we took three each (and those were drought years). In '97, we took five. The herd has been healthy the past few years, so we anticipate more trophy racks this year and next." Average spreads go 25 inches or so for 4x4s, though last year one hunter took a 36-incher. And that doesn't even touch on the elk and moose hunts, where last year one hunter with a landowner tag took a record-book moose in Utah.

Black bear and lion hunts with hounds are also available. Just take your pick of options.

Pines Ranch Outfitters

Spanish Fork, Utah

If you're after a lion, look no further.

VITAL STATISTICS:

Game/Arm/Seasons:
MOUNTAIN LION:
Bow, centerfire, muzzleloader: Dec. through April
BOBCAT:
Bow, centerfire, muzzleloader: Nov. through Feb.
ELK:
Bow, centerfire, muzzleloader: Sept. through Oct.
DEER:
Bow, centerfire, muzzleloader: Nov.
Rates:
$2,500/5 days
$3,000/7 days
Accommodations:
RUSTIC FARMHOUSE
NUMBER OF ROOMS: 4
MAXIMUM NUMBER OF HUNTERS: 4
Meals: Chicken, steaks, meat loaf, Italian dishes
Conference Groups: No
Guides: Included
Gratuity: 10%
Preferred Payment:
Cash, money orders
Other Activities:
Bird hunting, bird watching, fishing, golf, hiking, skiing, tennis, wildlife photography
Getting There:
Fly to Salt Lake City, Utah, and the lodge van will meet you.

Contact:
Scott Swenson
Pines Ranch Outfitters
HC 13, Box 460
Fairview, UT 84629
801/873-3206
Fax: 801/873-3369

TO MANY, THE MOUNTAIN LION represents the wilderness. Stealthy, nocturnal and swift, it's a shadow of the forests. People sometimes live their whole lives in lion country without actually seeing one.

Hunting cougars with dogs is perhaps the most exciting form of hunting. The trick is to do it on snow, riding along in a vehicle with the dogs in the back until a track is crossed. Then you release the hounds, who quickly pick up the hot track and go barreling off into the woods with you in hot pursuit. Is there anything more exciting than running after a pack of hounds, listening to them baying as they follow a track, their sounds echoing up from some rocky, brush-choked canyon bottom? If you can stay with them as they follow the cat—and hopefully it's a big tom, if you've read his tracks correctly—you'll eventually come to a spot where they've treed him, waiting for you to either take him or pass on him for another, on another day.

Most hunters prefer rifles of .30 caliber and larger for this type of hunting, although many also use .38 and .44 caliber handguns.

No matter what you prefer to shoot, Pines Ranch Outfitters can put you onto a big cat. "We specialize in mountain lion hunting," says owner Scott Swenson. "We have a stable population of mountain lions in our area (35 minutes south of Provo), with permits available. In fact, there are so many that we can be selective, taking only mature toms. We hunt from snowmobiles, 4x4 pickups or horses, whichever the weather dictates. In the past eight years our success rate has been over 95 percent, with six Boone & Crockett cats."

Swenson also points out that there are excellent elk and deer populations in his area, although it's a limited-entry area and permits can be difficult to obtain (the Uinta and Manti-Lasal national forests are both nearby). Swenson can get his hands on a number of landowner permits, however.

The ranch itself is situated on 320 acres, with a mile of creek fishing and hiking available to hunters who have already filled their tags. Each hunter has his own bedroom and bathroom, with the rustic lodge itself having a 52-inch screen television, satellite dish, pool table and other amenities. Meals include chicken, steak, spaghetti and lasagna, with special diets available to those who arrange in advance.

[R O C K Y   M O U N T A I N S]

7-D Ranch

C o d y ,   W y o m i n g

Once inhabited by gold prospectors, this area north of Yellowstone is now home to big bull elk and mule deer.

SETTLERS CALLED IT the Sunlight Basin because only the rays of old Sol and a few wandering Nez Perce could find their way into this bowl hidden deep in the Beartooths north of Yellowstone National Park. Then, the high mountain meadows were thick with elk and mule deer. Lower down lived moose, bison and bear. Among the craggy peaks of the Absarokas were bighorn sheep and mountain goats. A creek drains the basin, rushing through a flat valley before tumbling down into a tight little canyon above its junction with the Clarks Fork of the Yellowstone. Pioneers prospected their way up the creek, finding gold at the head of the valley, but the mines they established, like the fledgling town of Lee City, are long played out. Remaining are valley-bottom ranches and fields thick with verdant grasses where elk and mule deer come to feed.

Just above Strawberry Gulch is Marshall Dominick's 7-D Ranch. During the summer, families vacation in his pine log cabins. They ride his horses up into the backcountry to catch cutthroat trout in the headwaters of Sunlight Creek. Evening programs feature naturalists, historians or musicians. Come fall, the drill changes. Archery season for elk opens on Sept. 1 and high meadows ring with the guttural whistles of rutting elk. The first three weeks of October catch the end of the rut. This is when the winter's first major snows push elk out of their high summer ranges. A late horseback hunt, normally with heavy snow, is usually held in the last half of November into early December. For this hunt, though, you must be drawn or purchase a "Governor's Tag." Big bulls—6x6s scoring 300 to 350—are reasonably easy to come by during this hunt. And hunting them is something less than arduous. Hunts for deer and antelope, down in the plains east of Cody, are also available. All hunts are based on one guide per hunter.

Elk hunting is the mainstay at this ranch, though bighorn sheep and mule deer are hunted in Sunlight Valley as well. Early in the season, hunters ride into Gravel Bar Camp in the North Absaroka Wilderness and hunt on foot or horseback from there. Set in a swale between alpine ridges, a cluster of floored wall tents as well as a dining tent make up Gravel Bar Camp. When snow becomes too heavy, operations shift to the main ranch. Log cabins with woodstoves and private baths are welcome indeed after a day's hunt in the cold winter woods. Meals are served in the main lodge where the open fire crackles all day long.

VITAL STATISTICS:

Species/Arm/Seasons:
ANTELOPE:
Bow, centerfire, muzzleloader: Early through mid-Oct.
DEER:
Centerfire, muzzleloader: Mid-Oct. through mid-Nov.
ELK:
Bow: Sept.
Centerfire, muzzleloader: Early through late Oct.; late Nov. through early Dec.
BIGHORN SHEEP:
Bow, centerfire, muzzleloader: Sept.
Rates:
ANTELOPE, DEER $1,900/5 days
ELK $4,000/10 days
BIGHORN SHEEP $5,000/15 days
Accommodations:
LOG LODGE, TENT CAMP
MAXIMUM NUMBER OF HUNTERS: 4
Meals: Great family fare
Conference groups: No
Guides: Included
Gratuities: Hunter's discretion
Preferred payment:
Cash or check
Other activities:
Fishing, hiking, snowshoeing, cross-country skiing, snowmobiling, wildlife photography
Getting there:
Fly to Cody, Wyoming, and be met by a van from the ranch.

Contact:
Ward Dominick
7-D Ranch
Sunlight Basin
Box 100
Cody, WY 82414
307/587-3995
Web: www.7dranch.com

Allen's Diamond Four Ranch

L a n d e r ,   W y o m i n g

At the end of this winding road are elk and moose and Western hospitality.

VITAL STATISTICS:

Game/Arm/Seasons:
ANTELOPE:
Bow, centerfire, muzzleloader: Late Sept. through late Oct.
DEER:
Bow, centerfire, muzzleloader: Mid-Oct.
ELK:
Bow: Sept.
Centerfire, muzzleloader: Early to mid-Oct.
MOOSE:
Bow, centerfire, muzzleloader: Oct.
SHEEP:
Bow, centerfire, muzzleloader: Mid-Aug. through mid-Oct.
Rates:
ANTELOPE $1,100/3 days
DEER $1,600/4 days
ELK from $2,950/8 days
MOOSE $3,450/10 days
SHEEP $4,500/12 days
Accommodations:
LOG CABINS AND TENT CAMPS
MAXIMUM NUMBER OF HUNTERS: 6-8
Meals: Very hearty family cooking
Conference Groups: No
Guides: Included
Gratuity: 15%
Preferred Payment:
Cash, check
Other Activities:
Fishing, wildlife photography
Getting There:
Fly to Casper or Jackson, rent a car and drive to the ranch.

Contact:
Jim Allen,
Allen's Diamond Four Ranch
Box 243
Lander, WY, 82520
307/332-2995
Fax: 307/332-7902

THE ROAD TO LANDER is flat. But off to the west, rises the Wind River Range, a serrated and snowcapped string of peaks rising cold and gray from forests of lodgepole pine, fir and spruce. The valley is a good mile below the mountain crest, though you're not aware of the elevation until you turn left from Hwy. 287 and begin the climb to the ranch. The road, a single lane with wide spots, zigzags up the flank of a 2,000-foot hill of grass. You have no sense of how much altitude you've gained until you reach the first switchback and see all of eastern Wyoming spread before you. At the top of the pass the road splits, the left fork heading for Dickinson Park on the threshold of the Popo Agie wilderness. Here, you plunge into heavy forest only to emerge in the broad meadows of the park. Above the park rise the Bears Ears and a number of other peaks, the height of land that you've only begun to reach.

Jim and Mary Allen have operated the ranch here for more than a quarter of a century. In summer, it's alive with strings of horseback packers bound for alpine lakes rich with native cutthroat and wild rainbows, brookies and browns. Come fall, hunters take over. Then, when aspens flame and shed their leaves, the quarry is elk, bighorn sheep and moose. From the ranch, you'll ride a dozen or more miles up and into the Popo Agie, heading for little alpine draws used by elk and moose. Jim runs a pair of pack-in camps at the foot of the highest mountains. From those tents complete with wooden floors and stoves, you'll hunt afoot or on horseback as the vagaries of the game dictate. Rarely are there more than six hunters in camp. While hunters sport gear of fleece and Dry-Plus and carry scoped bolt-actions chambered for magnums in 7mm, the .30s and .338s (bows, too, of course), hunting here has all the rigorous charm of hunting a century ago. You'll leave camp each morning before sunup, riding until you can ride no more, and then climb, spot and stalk. Bugling can bring in big bulls during the rut, which spans bow and rifle seasons.

Along with high-country horseback hunts, Jim also runs deer and antelope hunts from his ranch in the low foothills of the Wind River Range. Deer terrain is open and rocky with canyons and little forest; antelope range is gentle in comparison. In any event you'll do a lot of walking, glassing and staking. If you're not in great shape when you come, you will be when you leave.

[R O C K Y   M O U N T A I N S]

Bear Track Inc.

B u f f a l o ,   W y o m i n g

Go for antelope and mule deer at exclusively leased, well-managed ranches.

VITAL STATISTICS:

Game/Arm/Seasons:
ANTELOPE and MULE DEER:
Bow: Sept.
Centerfire, muzzleloader: Oct.

Rates:
ANTELOPE from $1,395/3 days
MULE DEER $2,695/5 days (Sept. bow); $2800/5 days (Oct. rifle)
ANTELOPE/MULE DEER combo $2,995/5 days (Oct. rifle)

Accommodations:
MODERN RANCH-STYLE BUNKHOUSE
NUMBER OF ROOMS: 6
MAXIMUM NUMBER OF HUNTERS: 22

Meals: Turkey, ham, chicken, steak with all the trimmings

Conference Groups: No

Guides: Included

Gratuity: $50 per animal

Preferred Payment:
Cash, check

Other Activities:
Bird hunting, bird watching, fishing, wildlife photography, varmint hunting

Getting There:
Fly to Sheridan, Wyoming, rent a car and drive to the lodge.

Contact:
Peter J. Dube
Bear Track Inc.
885 US 16 West
Buffalo, WY 82834
307/684-2528
e-mail: pdube@vcn.com

OPERATING out of a modern ranch-style bunkhouse on the outskirts of Buffalo, Bear Track's owner Pete Dube and his guides take hunting clients on private ranches throughout the northeast corner of Wyoming. Dube leases hundreds of thousands of acres on 15 to 20 ranches each year, and is thus able to manage each property carefully, making sure no one area is overhunted and that the quality of mule deer and antelope on each is maintained.

Dube employs 10 to 12 guides, so each of the hunters at Bear Track gets a lot of attention. Most hunts are two hunters with one guide, although one-on-one hunts are available.

This is exciting hunting, taking you through rimrock country, up and down gullies and mesas and across flats and prairies. If you're in shape, you will get in range of a good-sized mule deer buck (average is 4x4 with 25-inch spread) and pronghorn of 13 inches plus. And even if you're not in great shape, Dube's guides will drive you in a vehicle to areas where the walking isn't as tough.

Coyotes are a bonus for hunters here. And if you get your mulie and prong-horn, Dube also knows of some great prairie dog towns nearby. Bring a fishing rod, too, as some of the area's trout streams aren't so bad!

Meals back at the ranch are good and hearty, with turkey, ham, chicken, roast beef and even salmon featured. Just save room for some of the major desserts that Dube's wife Carey oversees in the kitchen each night.

Big Rock Outfitters

Jackson Hole, Wyoming

Hunt for trophy bulls in the middle of Wyoming's largest elk concentration.

VITAL STATISTICS:

Game/Arm/Seasons:
ELK:
Bow: Early through late Sept.
Centerfire: Late Sept. through late Oct.
MULE DEER:
Bow: Early though late Sept.
Centerfire: Early Sept. through late Oct.
BIGHORN SHEEP:
Bow, centerfire: Early Sept. through late Oct.
MOOSE:
Bow, centerfire: Late Sept. through late Oct.

Rates:
ELK, MULE DEER $2,500/7 days
BIGHORN SHEEP $5,000/10 days
MOOSE $3,000/7 days

Accommodations:
TENTS
MAXIMUM NUMBER OF HUNTERS: 6
Meals: Steaks, ribs, chicken, chops, salads, veggies
Conference Groups: No
Guides: Included
Gratuity: $100
Preferred Payment:
Cash, check
Other Activities:
Bird watching, fishing, hiking, wildlife photography
Getting There:
Fly to Jackson Hole, Wyoming, and be met by the outfitter.

Contact:
Randy Engler
Big Rock Outfitters
1079 County Road 119
Thayne, WY 83127
307/883-3226

JACKSON HOLE harbors the largest elk herd in North America, reaching up to 12,000 animals on the National Elk Refuge itself. The numbers top 30,000 including areas surrounding Jackson Hole. And sitting smack in the middle of all these elk is Big Rock Outfitters.

Pack trips are Big Rock's strong point. Hunters ride three hours by horse from a trailhead to a comfortable wall tent set-up deep in the Gros Ventre Wilderness, on the banks of Flat Creek. The camp has sleeping tents, a shower tent and a large, warm dining tent where hearty meals are served early in the morning and at night. (Meals in camp include steak, ham, ribs, roast beef, chicken, pork chops, salads, rolls, veggies, pies and cakes—just what you need to put back the pounds you lost after hiking around the mountains all day.) Most hunters take bag lunches and eat on the trail.

With knowledgeable guides who know the area well, Big Rock's kill ratio has been 75 to 80 percent on elk for the past four years. Early archery hunts start in September, when bulls are bugling. Smart hunters bugle back, trying to lure a 5x5 or better into range. The key to calling is to not call too much, especially once a bull is coming in. There, a few soft cow calls might be all you need to convince him to come the few extra yards into bow range. Most archers use bows with a minimum draw weight of 60 pounds.

Later, when the bugling season is over and rifle seasons begin, it becomes more a matter of glassing the ridges for elk movement than trying to get in front of the herd in an ambush spot before it moves through. Bugles can work on occasion at this time, but smart hunters rely even more on cow calls. While bull elk only bugle for a certain short period during the year, cows call all year, talking with other cows, communicating with their offspring and just staying in touch with the herd. A bull that hears a soft cow call won't suspect anything out of the ordinary. Cow calls are also good to help you mask any noises you might make as you move through the woods.

Big Rock also hunts mule deer, bighorn sheep and moose, the latter two being on a lottery permit system. Black bear hunts are offered in May and in January.

Bliss Creek Outfitters

C o d y ,   W y o m i n g

A 22-mile ride into the Washakie Wilderness will take you to a first-rate elk camp in prime game country.

VITAL STATISTICS:

Game/Arm/Seasons:

ELK:

Bow: Early through late Sept.
Centerfire: Early Oct. through mid-Dec.

MOOSE:

Bow: Early through late Sept.
Centerfire: Early Oct. through mid-Nov.

BEAR:

Bow: Mid through late April
Centerfire: Early Oct. through mid-Nov.

BIGHORN SHEEP:

Bow: Mid through late Aug.
Centerfire: Early Sept. through late Oct.

Rates:

ELK from $3,400/ 9 days
MOOSE $4,200/9 to 10 days
BEAR $2,100/7 days
BIGHORN SHEEP $4,700/10 days

Accommodations:

WALL TENTS
NUMBER OF ROOMS: 8; 6 w/PRIVATE BATH
MAXIMUM NUMBER OF HUNTERS: 8

Meals: Steaks, roasts, fried chicken, pork shops, turkey

Conference Groups: No

Guides: Included

Gratuity: Hunter's discretion

Preferred Payment:
Cash, MasterCard, Visa, check

Other Activities:
Wildlife photography

Getting There:
Fly to Cody, Wyoming, and take the hotel shuttle at no extra charge.

Contact:
Tim Doud
Bliss Creek Outfitters
326 Diamond Basin Rd.
Cody, WY 82414
307/527-6103
Fax: 307/527-6523
e-mail: bliss@wave.park.wy.us
Web:
www.http://iigi.com/os/guides/wyomi
ng/bliss/bliss.htm

I F THE IDEA OF RIDING A HORSE through 22 miles of the West's most incredible scenery in a wilderness area where no motorized vehicles are allowed, then consider booking a hunt with Tim Doud's Bliss Creek Outfitters. Doud's outfit hunts the mountains of the Washakie Wilderness in the Shoshone National Forest, with camp set up along a pretty little mountain stream named after horse thief Jack Bliss, gunned down by lawmen in 1892 and buried along its banks. Legend has it that his ghost still rides a restless gray gelding in the meadows below camp.

Today's hunters, of course, don't have to worry about getting their horse stolen by Bliss. In fact your horse, along with everything else on this hunt, is well cared for by Doud and his crew. This is a tightly run, well-tended tent camp smack in the middle of prime elk country.

Doud caters to both bow and rifle hunters. A bowhunter himself, he knows what it takes to put a client within point-blank range of trophy-class big game. You'll arise way before dawn, have a hearty breakfast, then ride off into the mountains where you'll dismount and start bugling for bull elk. Many first-time elk hunters aren't quite ready for the sight and sounds of a rut-crazed bull crashing into view, ripping up saplings as if they were toothpicks, ready to find you and rip you to shreds too.

"Our problem usually isn't getting shooting chances," Doud says. "Our problem is having hunters who don't get rattled and miss their shots."

After bow season, rifle hunters usually get in on the tail end of the bugling season. Hunts after that are glass-and-stalk affairs, climbing high and glassing the hills and ridges for moving bulls.

Doud also runs mule deer hunts out of his Bliss Creek camp and on National Forest Service land around Cody, depending on weather conditions and the deer migrations. If you draw a sheep tag, he'll also take you for sheep out of his base camp or, if need be, a spike camp. Then, in spring, he runs black bear hunts in the Bighorn Mountains. These take place out of a pack-in tent camp, a six-mile horseback ride from the nearest road. You hunt over baits at 6,000 to 9,000 feet where your chances of seeing a bear are 100 percent. Then it's up to you.

To reach Jim Allen's Diamond Four Ranch near Lander, Wyoming, you'll climb until you think your car will die. Once on top you'll enter a world of forests and meadows with elk and moose. Cabins are sturdy, comfortable and clean.

Riding across a meadow stream deep in the Absarokas, guide and hunters return from a successful hunt with Hidden Creek Outfitters out of Cody, Wyoming.

[R O C K Y   M O U N T A I N S]

Crystal Creek Outfitters

J a c k s o n   H o l e ,   W y o m i n g

Hunt with one of the oldest, most experienced outfits in Wyoming.

VITAL STATISTICS:

Game/Arm/Seasons:
ELK, MULE DEER, BIGHORN SHEEP, MOOSE:
Bow, centerfire, muzzleloader: Sept. through Nov.
BEAR:
Bow, centerfire, muzzleloader: Spring, May through June; fall, Sept. through Nov.

Rates:
ELK $2,600/8 days
MULE DEER $2,600/8 days
BIGHORN SHEEP $4,500/10 days
MOOSE $3,000/10 days
BEAR $2,000/7 days (spring)
BEAR/ELK/DEER combo $4,100/10 days

Accommodations:
LODGEPOLE TENTS
MAXIMUM NUMBER OF HUNTERS: 8

Meals: Roast beef, steaks, chicken, pork chops, potatoes, veggies, salad

Conference Groups: Yes

Guides: Included

Gratuity: From $25 to $300

Preferred Payment:
Cash, cashier's check

Other Activities:
Bird hunting, bird watching, fishing, wildlife photography

Getting There:
Fly to Jackson Hole, rent a car and drive to the base camp, or be picked up at the airport by a representative of the outfitter.

Contact:
Gap Puchi
Crystal Creek Outfitters
Star Rt., Box 44A
Jackson Hole, WY 83001
307/733-6318

THE TETONS ARE SIMPLY AWESOME. Soaring to almost 14,000 feet, they dominate the horizon in western Wyoming, eastern Idaho and virtually all points north and south. At the base of the Grand Tetons, below sprawling Jackson Lake and diminutive Jenny Lake, lies the bustling tourist town of Jackson Hole. Here, visitors from all over the globe come to visit Teton and Yellowstone national parks, to shop in town, to see the elk-antler archways and to maybe down a cold one at the Silver Dollar Bar. Hunters in the know come here for elk.

Crystal Creek Hunting Camps, comprising one of the largest hunting territories in this part of Wyoming, operates from three camps. Base camp, which is on the Gros Ventre River at 7,000 feet and can be driven to by vehicle, consists of a log cabin for dining and socializing, and trailer houses as bunkhouses. The two high camps are in the Gros Ventre Mountains, the first on Crystal Creek, at 8,100 feet, the second on Jagg Creek, at 8,600 feet. Both are 17 miles by horse from base camp. Hunters stay where the elk are, which is usually near the high camps.

Each morning starts with the aroma of fresh brewing coffee, eggs and bacon drifting through the brisk mountain air. Afterwards, you'll ride up into the mountains, headed to likely ambush spots. The sure-footed mountain horses will take you into some really tough terrain where you eventually have to dismount and start hiking, listening for bugling bulls, glassing the draws below you and the ridges above. If you hear or spot a good bull, then the hunt is really on, with you and your guide scrambling to get within range, to somehow get ahead of an animal that may weigh 600 to 800 pounds with a rack like a rocking chair. If you're fortunate enough to get within range, then the question is can you get a steady rest, can you keep your heart from pounding for a few minutes so you can make a clean shot at that trophy of a lifetime?

Gap Puchi's Crystal Creek Outfitters can arrange bow, rifle or muzzleloader hunts for elk, mule deer, bighorn sheep and moose in the fall, or for black bear in the spring. Gap has been in the business for almost 50 years, and employs up to five guides who have worked with him, on average, 10 years. They know their stuff; and if you draw the right tags, which they'll help you apply for, they can guide you to the big game animals you have always wanted.

Darby Mountain Outfitters

Big Piney, Wyoming

Hunting an isolated spot in Wyoming, this outfit specializes in huge mulies.

VITAL STATISTICS:

Game/Arm/Seasons:
ELK:
Bow: Early through late Sept.
Centerfire, muzzleloader: Mid through late Oct.
BIGHORN SHEEP:
Bow: Mid through late Aug.
Centerfire, muzzleloader: Early Sept. through late Oct.
MOOSE:
Bow: Mid through late Sept.
Centerfire, muzzleloader: Early through late Oct.
MULE DEER:
Bow: Early though mid-Sept.
Centerfire, muzzleloader: Mid-Sept. through mid-Oct.
ANTELOPE:
Bow: Late Aug. through mid-Sept.
Centerfire, muzzleloader: Early Sept. through late Oct.
BLACK BEAR:
Bow, centerfire: Spring, early May through mid-June; fall, Early Sept. through late Oct.
MOUNTAIN LION:
Bow, centerfire, muzzleloader: Early Sept. through late March
Rates:
ELK $2,500/ 9 days (centerfire); $2,100/7 days (bow)
BIGHORN SHEEP $3,600/10 days
MOOSE $2,500/7 days
MULE DEER $1,800/7 days
ANTELOPE $1,000/5 days
BLACK BEAR $1,500/7 days
MOUNTAIN LION $2,500/7 days
Accommodations:
WALL TENTS
MAXIMUM NUMBER OF HUNTERS: 8
Meals: Beef, chicken, pork chops, veggies, desserts
Conference Groups: No
Guides: Included
Gratuity: 10 to 15%
Preferred Payment:
Cash, check
Other Activities:
Biking, boating, fishing, horseback trips, snowmobile trips, wildlife photography

CHUCK THORNTON and John Harper, owners of Darby Mountain Outfitters in southwestern Wyoming, have been in the business for 23 years. They run a small camp, and specialize in big mule deer and elk.

"We keep our operation small, because we want to keep it personable," says Thornton. "Hunting is more than just harvesting a game animal," he continues. "It's camaraderie and good times that draw people back. We are also fortunate in that our area is pretty isolated, and not overpopulated with hunters."

Darby Mountain hunts primarily in the Wyoming Range of the Bridger-Teton National Forest, where elevations soar to 11,000 feet. Hunts are generally one guide per two hunters, on foot, by horse or 4WD in all types of terrain. All hunts are conducted out of comfortable wall tents, with three hunters per tent.

Hunters ride to spike tents, then get up early each morning and head into the hills. Your chances of getting a big bull elk are good here, especially since hunting pressure is light. Even better, this is big mule deer country, with 4x4s and 5x5s common. Don't be surprised if you see nontypical racks, either. One hunter, a Dr. B.L. Harper, hunting in Region H, recently took a 31-inch mulie with 8 points on one side and 10 on the other. This with a .257 Weatherby Magnum topped with a 3-9X Leupold scope, and using 100-grain Noslers.

"Thornton has an attitude and desire to please," said Harper.

Sig Dietrich, another hunter who has hunted with Thornton, agrees. "We saw plenty of big game and had adequate opportunities to score," he said. "Not only that, but these people (Darby) are very sensitive to hunter needs, and I respect them for their hunter savvy."

Thornton's outfit hunts not only elk and deer, but bighorn sheep, moose, antelope, black bear and mountain lions. All hunts take place out of spike camps except antelope, which are run out of the base camp.

Getting There:
Fly to Jackson Hole or Rock Springs, Wyoming, or Salt Lake City, Utah, rent a car and drive to the base camp, or be transported by the outfitter for $100 from Jackson Hole and Rock Springs, or $200 from Salt Lake City.

Contact:
Chuck Thornton
Darby Mountain Outfitters
Box 477
Big Piney, WY 83113
307/386-9220 or
307/276-3934

Darwin Ranch

J a c k s o n ,   W y o m i n g

Hunt out of a special ranch in the Bridger-Teton National Forest.

VITAL STATISTICS:

Game/Arm/Seasons:

ELK:
Bow: Early Sept. through early Nov.
Centerfire: Late Sept. through early Nov.

MOOSE:
Bow, centerfire: Early Sept. through early Nov.

MULE DEER:
Bow: Early Sept. through late Oct.
Centerfire: Mid-Sept. through late Oct.

Rates:
ELK, MOOSE, MULE DEER
$2,600/7 days; $2,800/8 days

Accommodations:
RUSTIC LOG CABINS
NUMBER OF ROOMS: 8; 4 W/PRIVATE BATH
MAXIMUM NUMBER OF HUNTERS: 6

Meals: Leg of lamb, lasagna, oriental ginger beef

Conference Groups: Yes

Guides: Included

Gratuity: $50 to $200

Preferred Payment:
Cash, check

Other Activities:
Bird watching, fishing, hiking, wildlife photography

Getting There:
Fly to Jackson Hole, rent a car and drive to the ranch.

Contact:
Loring Woodman
Darwin Ranch
Box 511
Jackson, WY 83001
307/733-5588
Fax: 307/739-0885

ACCORDING TO RECENT STATISTICS, more than 12,000 elk winter on the National Elk Refuge just outside of Jackson Hole. Add another 6,000 or so animals to that, and you have a total of 17,000-plus wapiti in the Jackson elk herd. In spring, these animals disperse, heading north to calving grounds in Grand Teton and Yellowstone national parks and the surrounding national forests.

Hunters who hunt in the Jackson Hole region have never had it so good. In this part of the West, hunters no longer ask themselves if they're going to take an elk this season; rather, the question is, which one? If you're after a trophy, the Darwin Ranch can put you in a position to find and take the bull you want.

Twenty-two miles inside the Bridger-Teton National Forest, the Darwin Ranch is on a 160-acre inholding. Hunters staying at the ranch thus have an opportunity to hunt unpressured land that is teeming with elk. Success rates at the ranch have run at least 74 percent since 1986 and have risen to 100 percent in the past few years.

This is gorgeous, untrammeled country. Hunters ride out from the ranch early each morning, heading to nearby ridges that soar to 10,000 feet, with views of the Wind River and Teton ranges in the distance. Depending on the conditions and the animals you're hunting (Darwin hunts not only elk, but mule deer and moose as well), you may stay in an area all day or you might ride to another area, drainage or meadow for the evening hunt. On warm, sunny days, the elk like to bed down in the dark, cool timber, where it's practically impossible to sneak up on them. Then it's mostly a matter of figuring out where they are and waiting patiently until the wind is right and the bulls are up and bugling at the tail end of the day.

At dark, you'll ride back to the ranch, hopefully followed by packhorses loaded down with elk quarters. You'll take a shower in your rustic log cabin, then saunter over to the old but elegant main lodge for a sumptuous dinner that may include roast leg of lamb, lasagna or oriental ginger beef. After dinner, and especially if you've been bowhunting in early September, you may unlimber your fly-rod and fish for cutthroat trout in the Gros Ventre River, which flows a mere 50 feet from the lodge.

Dodge Creek Ranch

Rock River, Wyoming

This is a family-run business that specializes in tailoring your hunt to your needs.

VITAL STATISTICS:

Game/Arm/Seasons:
ELK:
Bow: Sept.
Centerfire: Late Oct. through late Nov.
ANTELOPE:
Bow: Sept.
Centerfire: Late Sept. through Oct.
DEER:
Bow: Sept.
Centerfire: Late Sept. through late Oct.
BIGHORN SHEEP:
Centerfire: Sept. through Oct.

Rates:
ELK $2,640/7 days
ANTELOPE $900/3 days
DEER $2,200/5 days
BIGHORN SHEEP $4,400/7 days

Accommodations:
RANCH HOUSE OR CABIN (VARIES BY HUNT LOCATION)
NUMBER OF ROOMS: 3
MAXIMUM NUMBER OF HUNTERS: 6

Meals: Meat and potatoes, veggies, salads

Conference Groups: No

Guides: Included

Gratuity: Hunter's discretion

Preferred Payment: Cash, check

Other Activities:
Fishing, wildlife photography

Getting There:
Fly to Cheyenne, Wyoming, or Denver, Colorado, rent a car and drive to the ranch.

Contact:
Jerry or Evelyn Kennedy
Dodge Creek Ranch
402 Tunnel Rd.
Rock River, WY 82058
307/322-2345

J ERRY KENNEDY, owner of the Dodge Creek Ranch, has been hunting the Laramie Peaks area for most of 35 years now, guiding hunters after elk, mule deer and bighorn sheep in the higher elevations, and antelope down low. Located in southeastern Wyoming, an area that a lot of hunters overlook for regions with more glamorous names, Kennedy specializes in small groups and takes great pride in giving close personal attention to each client.

"We aim to give everyone an enjoyable hunt," he says. "The emphasis is on having a quality wilderness experience, not just on killing an animal."

Kennedy hunts a combination of areas for elk, deer and sheep. "We mostly hunt the Peaks area, but it's a combination of national forest land (Medicine Bow), private leases and Bureau of Land Management land. Of course, we hunt some state land as well."

Elk are generally hunted right out of the modern ranch, with hunters leaving in the morning either by vehicle or on foot. "You can step out the door and be in the wilderness," Kennedy notes. Kennedy says he prefers not to do much bugling, even in the early bow season. "A lot of big bulls know the score or they wouldn't have gotten so big, and they'll take off if you start bugling. I'd rather let them do the talking and try to sneak up on them silently."

Deer and sheep are usually hunted in semi-wilderness areas out of a 24x30-foot cabin Kennedy has up in the mountains. Antelope hunting takes place on the main ranch and on almost 10,000 acres of private leases in the area.

"So long as you draw your tags, we can help you get your game," he concludes. "Just make sure you bring enough clothing so you can deal with everything from really hot to really cold weather. It also helps if you've practiced with your rifle and know how to shoot straight. A lot of people ask me what calibers they should bring along, but to be honest, shot placement—not caliber—is what makes the difference most of the time."

Ron Dube's Wilderness Adventures

W a p i t i ,   W y o m i n g

Hunt the Washakie Wilderness for unpressured bull elk.

VITAL STATISTICS:

Game/Arm/Seasons:

ELK:
Bow: Early Sept.
Centerfire: Early Sept. through mid-Oct. and early through late Nov.
SHEEP:
Centerfire: Early Sept. through mid-Oct.
MOOSE:
Bow: Early Sept.
Centerfire: Early Sept. through mid-Oct.
MULE DEER:
Centerfire: Late Oct. through early Nov.

Rates:
ELK from $1,500/3 days
SHEEP $5,000/10 days
MOOSE $4,000/8 days
MULE DEER $2,550/7 days

Accommodations:
WALL TENTS
MAXIMUM NUMBER OF HUNTERS: 8

Meals: Steak, chicken, ham, turkey, roast beef, lasagna, ham

Conference Groups: No

Guides: Included

Gratuity: $200

Preferred Payment:
Cash, check

Other Activities:
Bird watching, fishing, wildlife photography

Getting There:
Fly to Cody, Wyoming, overnight at the Irma Hotel and be picked up by a representative of the outfitter in the morning.

Contact:
Ron Dube
Ron Dube's Wilderness Adventures
Box 167
Wapiti, WY 82450
307/527-7815
Fax: 307/527-6084
e-mail: dube@huntinfo.com
Web: www.huntinfo.com/dube

RON DUBE HAS A SAYING: "Luck is the result of preparation meeting opportunity." Roughly translated, it means you make your own luck. Hunt with Dube and you'll know why he says that. When it comes to preparation, he has no peers. And when you're in the mountains with him chasing bugling elk, he'll make sure you get your opportunity.

Dube has a tent camp set up in the Washakie Wilderness, almost 25 miles by horse from the trailhead. The ride in is worth the price of the trip itself. Riding through thick lodgepole pine groves, crossing raging streams, climbing up and over ridges, trotting through lush alpine meadows, you'll see parts of the West that few people have seen. And it's unchanged since the days of the mountain men.

Elk are plentiful in this area. You'll awaken around 4 a.m., have breakfast in the cook tent with the other hunters in camp, then ride out with your guide to an area where he no doubt has heard bulls bugling. When you hear one, you'll dismount and start hiking, trying to set up in an area where you can call him into range for a clean shot. If you hunt after the bugling season is over in September, then hunting is more a matter of riding to the ridges and glassing, looking for moving animals. If you see a bull you want, then the stalk is on—and it may last for hours and cover many miles, depending upon where that bull is headed.

All Dube asks is that you try to get in reasonable shape before your hunt, as you will be doing a lot of hiking in thin mountain air. And he likes you to be able to shoot straight.

"We prefer .30 caliber rifles," he says, "the bigger the better, but the 7mm Rem. Mag. with 165-grain bullets is fine. I shoot a .300 Win. Mag. with 180-grain Federal Premiums. Just don't bring a rifle that causes you to flinch. A .270 with 150-grain bullets or a .30-06 with 180-grain bullets that you can shoot well is better than a .338 Mag that you can't shoot."

Dube also runs bighorn sheep hunts in this area, and there are some big, full-curl rams around. All you have to do is draw the tag—no mean feat. He'll also take you for moose (draw a tag!) and big mulies.

Gary Fales Outfitters

Cody, Wyoming

Hunt the back of beyond for elk and deer on the fringe of the great Yellowstone.

VITAL STATISTICS:

Game/Arms/Season:
DEER:
Bow, centerfire, muzzleloader: Nov. through mid-Dec.
ELK:
Bow: Early Sept.
Centerfire, muzzleloader: Oct.
SHEEP:
Bow, centerfire, muzzleloader: Late Aug. through Oct.

Rates:
DEER from $1,850/5 days
ELK from $2,900/7 days (archery);
$3,800/7 days (rifle)
SHEEP $4,500/7 days

Accommodations:
TENTS
MAXIMUM NUMBER OF HUNTERS: 6
Meals: Prime rib, fried chicken and the works
Conference Groups: No
Guides: Included
Gratuity: Hunter's discretion
Preferred Payment:
Cash, credit cards (no AMEX), checks
Other Activities:
Boating, fishing, riding, snowmobiling
Getting There:
Fly to Cody and you will be met by the lodge van.

Contact:
Gary Fales
Gary Fales Outfitters
2768 North Fork Rd.
Cody, WY 82414
307/587-3747
Fax: 307/527-5014
e-mail: rimrock@wyoming.com
Web:
www.westwyoming.com/rimrock

YOU KNOW THE OLD WAG: "There are lies, damn lies and statistics." Well, here are some numbers from Gary Fales. "In 1997, we hunted 37 clients who took 34 elk." That, he says, is a little better than the general hunter success rate of 85 percent that he reports. For more than 35 years Fales has been operating camps on Thorofare Creek and over in the Boulder Basin area near the Shoshone River.

Rising in a rugged band of 12,000-foot mountains of the Absaroka Range in northwest/central Wyoming, Thorofare Creek is a tributary of the Yellowstone River. The creek flows west from its headwaters, and at the confluence of Woody Creek, Fales' dad first pitched an outfitting camp in the 1960s. He had help in choosing the spot from Buffalo Bill's grandson, and it's served the Fales well over the years. Not only is the country consistently productive for elk because they migrate through as winter drives them out of the high country, but its peaks contain good populations of bighorn sheep. (The Wyoming license is harder to get than a trophy ram. The former requires patience; the latter, great shooting ability plus physical conditioning.) Well off the beaten path, the tent camp that Fales runs is as secluded as it is well run.

The second camp, Boulder Basin, is a handful of miles southeast of the hamlet of Valley, aptly named because it lies deep in the trough that the South Fork of the Shoshone River has carved through the Absarokas. The camp lies in a sloping valley at about 9,000 feet. The trail down to the river is steep; ridges above the camp top out at 11,000 feet and more. This camp also traces its lineage to a friend of Buffalo Bill. Terrain is tough in spots, but in others it's a bit more open. The elk population has proven consistently good since Fales took over operation of the camp in 1987.

To hunt in this area, you need to be drawn for a license. Aware of the vagaries of the draw, Fales and other outfitters always overbook by charging a minimum fee—less than 10 percent of the cost of the hunt—to place a reservation. Normally this works out fine because about one out of three who apply get their choice. Once in a while statistics fail, and more hunters than usual draw tags for their first choice. Hunters have the following options: negotiate another date with the outfitter, book with another outfitter, or decline the license and accumulate preference points. The draw is a wacky system.

Full Circle Outfitters Inc.

M e e t e e t s e ,   W y o m i n g

The Absarokas are loaded with big game, and the well-equipped hunter has the best chances for success.

VITAL STATISTICS:

Game/Arm/Seasons:
ELK:
Bow: Early through late Sept.
Centerfire: Mid through late Oct.
MULE DEER, ANTELOPE:
Bow: Early through late Sept.
Centerfire: Early through late Oct.
BIGHORN SHEEP, MOOSE:
Bow: Mid-Aug.
Centerfire: Early Sept. through late Oct.
BEAR:
Call for type and time of hunt and rate
Rates:
ELK from $3,000/7 days
MULE DEER $3,000/7 days
ANTELOPE $1,800/5 days
BIGHORN SHEEP $5,000/10 days
MOOSE $3,500/7 days
Accommodations:
WALL TENTS
MAXIMUM NUMBER OF HUNTERS: 10
Meals: Hearty fare served family-style
Conference Groups: No
Guides: Included
Gratuity: $200
Preferred Payment:
Cash, check
Other Activities:
Bird watching, fishing, hiking, wildlife photography
Getting There:
Fly to Yellowstone Regional Airport, rent a car and drive to Meeteetse, or fly to Cody, Wyoming, and be picked up on the morning of the first day of the hunt.

Contact:
Buck or Shelly Braten
Full Circle Outfitters Inc.
548 Rd. 3LE
Meeteetse, WY 82433
307/868-2323
Fax: 307/868-2383

FULL CIRCLE, based in Meeteetse, offers both pack-in and ranch hunts. The pack-in camp is located in the Washakie Wilderness, 40 miles west of Meeteetse. Hunters are picked up in Cody at 6 a.m. and driven to the Jack Creek trailhead, where cowboys with horses meet up with hunters for the ride into camp. The three-mile ride into camp, through some of the most awesome scenery in the West, will put you into prime elk, mulie, bear and lion country. Hunters stay in roomy wall tents with woodstoves.

If you wish, you can also hunt Full Circle's Ranch for whitetails, mulies and pronghorn. At the ranch, you live in the lap of luxury, taking a dip in the indoor pool after a hard day afield, then dining on home-cooked meals.

No matter which hunt you choose, owner Buck Graten has these tips on equipment. "Fall conditions in Wyoming can range from shirt-sleeve temperatures to downright cold," he says. "And well-planned packing will add to the success and enjoyment of your hunt. We suggest that you bring all that you need to be comfortable." That includes the following:

- *Good sleeping bag for pack-in hunts, rated to below 0°F, plus a pillow.*
- *Lightweight, waterproof hunting boots.*
- *Cold-weather, waterproof pack boots.*
- *Cold-weather jacket, cold-weather coat.*
- *Light leather gloves, cold-weather gloves.*
- *Warm-weather brimmed hat or cap.*
- *Cold-weather cap with earflaps.*
- *Sneakers or camp shoes.*
- *Blue jeans or wool pants.*
- *Wool or flannel shirts, sweaters.*
- *Polypropylene or Thermax long johns.*
- *Plenty of wool socks and underwear.*
- *Rainsuit, top and bottom.*

- *Frameless daypack or fanny pack.*
- *Washcloths, towels, soap.*
- *Shaving kit, toothbrush, etc.*
- *Aspirin, sunscreen, Chapstick, etc.*
- *Flashlight and extra batteries.*
- *Canteen, binoculars, hunting knife.*
- *Compass, lighter, sunglasses.*
- *Camera and plenty of film.*
- *Licenses and conservation stamps.*
- *Rifle and three boxes of ammunition.*
- *Fluorescent orange vest and/or cap.*
- *Bow and two dozen arrows, broadheads.*
- *Camouflage clothes, headnet or face paint.*

That's a good list to keep, no matter where you hunt in the West.

Great Rocky Mountain Outfitters

Saratoga, Wyoming

Hunt for elk, mule deer and antelope in an unpressured trophy environment.

VITAL STATISTICS:

Game/Arm/Seasons:
ANTELOPE:
Centerfire: Mid-Sept. through late Oct.
Muzzleloader: Mid through late Sept.
DEER:
Centerfire: Early through mid-Oct.
ELK:
Bow: Early through late Sept.
Centerfire: Early Oct. through early Nov.
MOUNTAIN LION:
Centerfire; Early Sept. through early Jan.

Rates:
Antelope $850/2 days
Deer $3,000/5 days
Elk $4,750/5 days
MOUNTAIN LION $3,000/5 days
Combination hunts are also available

Accommodations:
MODERN RANCH BUNKHOUSE
NUMBER OF ROOMS: 4, 3 WITH PRIVATE BATH
MAXIMUM NUMBER OF HUNTERS: 12

Meals: Family-style cooking
Conference Groups: Yes
Guides: Included
Gratuity: 15%
Preferred Payment:
Cash, American Express, Discover,
MasterCard, Visa, check
Other Activities:
Bird hunting, canoeing/rafting,
fishing, waterfowling
Getting There:
Fly to Denver or Laramie, rent a car
and drive to the lodge, or take the
lodge van for an extra charge of
between $50 to $150.

Contact:
Robert Smith
Great Rocky Mountain
Outfitters
Box 1636
216 E Walnut St.
Saratoga, WY 82331
307/326-8750
Fax: 307/326-5390
e-mail: GRMO@union-tel.com
Web:
iigi.com/os/wyoming/grmo/hunting.htm

ROBERT SMITH has a great deal going on in south-central Wyoming, about 130 miles west of Laramie. You see, Smith, who has been guiding hunters in this region since 1981, has exclusive hunting rights on Elk Mountain Ranch. And Elk Mountain is special. Shaped like a volcanic crater, it provides ideal habitat for both elk and deer, which not only summer there, but often winter there as well. It's the northernmost mountain in the Snowy Range Mountains, and its base is totally enclosed by private land. There is no national forest land on the mountain, and the public has no access to any of the lands.

What this means to Smith's clients is that they can hunt 72 square miles of prime, unpressured hunting land. The game is carefully managed here, too, as hunters only take a certain number of bulls a year—preferably 6x6s or better, according to Smith. An average of 30 cows are also culled from the herd annually to maintain a 60 percent cow/40 percent bull ratio in the herd.

Mule deer hunts are managed in the same manner. "We ask our hunters to shoot only large 4x4s or better," states Smith. "This means we've got a lot of 150-class bucks on the property."

Ultimately, by running only two to four hunters on the ranch at one time, Smith is able to get most clients the animals they're seeking. "Assuming a hunter can hunt, is in reasonably good shape, and can hit his target, hunter success should be 100 percent."

The terrain itself is rugged, with elevations ranging from 7,300 to 11,000 feet. Hunters will find themselves hiking across sagebrush flats, aspen draws and canyons, and through steep, rugged pine forests — whatever it takes to reach the game, in other words.

After a tough day in the woods after elk, deer or antelope on the flats, hunters are picked up in four-wheelers and ferried back to the lodge, which is a modern ranch bunkhouse with private bath and laundry. Meals are prepared by the cook and served family-style in the adjacent cookhouse.

Haderlie's Tincup Mountain Guest Ranch

F r e e d o m ,   W y o m i n g

Surrounded by national forests, this ranch specializes in big bull elk and mule deer.

VITAL STATISTICS:

Game/Arm/Seasons:
ELK:
Bow: Late Aug. through late Sept.
Centerfire, muzzleloader: Late Oct. through early Nov.
DEER:
Bow: Late Aug. through late Sept.
Centerfire, muzzleloader: Early through late Oct.

Rates:
Archery ELK, DEER $1,250/5 days
Rifle ELK from $1,500/5 days (spikes and cows)
Rifle ELK $2,500/9 days (bulls, 7 days of hunting)
Rifle DEER from $1,375/5 days

Accommodations:
RUSTIC LOG CABIN AND TENTS
NUMBER OF ROOMS: 2
MAXIMUM NUMBER OF HUNTERS: 6 IN CABIN, 18 IN TENTS

Meals: Steak, potatoes, salads
Conference Groups: No
Guides: Included
Gratuity: Hunter's discretion
Preferred Payment:
Cash, MasterCard, Visa, check
Other Activities:
Bird hunting, bird watching, fishing, hiking, horseback riding, wildlife photography
Getting There:
Fly to Jackson, Wyoming, rent a car and drive to the lodge, or take the lodge van for $30 per person.

Contact:
David Haderlie
Haderlie's Tincup
Mountain Guest Ranch
Hwy. 34 #5336
Box 175
Freedom, WY 83120
1-800 253-2368 or
208/873-2368
Fax: 208/873-2369
e-mail: htmgr@cyberhighway.net
Web: www.silverstar.com/htmgr

LOCATED IN THE HEART of the Rockies on the Idaho-Wyoming border, the Tincup Guest Ranch is surrounded by three national forests: the Bridger-Teton, the Caribou and the Targhee. Hunters and non-hunters alike find the Caribou of interest. It was home to a number of gold-mining towns from the 1860s through the 1930s. Hunters riding through still find relics from the days when prospectors roamed the hills.

While the gold is played out, the area's rich with game: elk, mule deer, some shiras moose and black bears. Run by David and Lorie Haderlie, Tincup focuses on big mule deer and elk. All hunts are conducted on the national forests in Idaho, with hunters staying either in a cabin at the main ranch or at a pack-in camp with wall tents and woodstoves back in the mountains. Horses, tack, food, cook and a guide for each two hunters are part of the deal, as is field care of meat and trophies.

This is classic Western hunting. In the early archery season, which runs from the end of August well into September for both deer and elk, bowhunters ride off into the mountains well before sunup, setting up at likely spots, listening for bugling bulls, then calling back to them, trying to bugle them into range. If they come close but don't get in the range of your bow (for most people, that's 40 yards maximum), try some soft cow calling to pull them in those few extra yards. You'll be surprised how well cow calls work.

Later, when rifle season opens in October, hunters are more likely to glass a big bull then stalk it. Quality high-power binoculars (10x40) and a strong, high-quality spotting scope are important, aiding you in judging a bull from a distance before you start another long hike in the thin mountain air.

The same applies to mule deer in this region. They're apt to be way high at this time, and you'll be doing a lot of climbing to find the one you want. As the seasons move along, though, and bad weather hits the high country, the deer will start to migrate to lower elevations, where you can ambush them along their traditional routes. Haderlie has been in this business almost 30 years, and he and his guides know where to post you.

The lodge is a welcome sight at the end of the day, featuring two guest rooms and six beds, plus a comfortable living room area. Dinners are family-style, featuring steak, Dutch oven potatoes (one of Tincup's specialties), salads, and too many desserts. Tent camp food is of the same caliber; only, better since it's prepared deep in the backcountry.

Hidden Creek Outfitters

C o d y ,   W y o m i n g

Every hunter owes it to himself to try this kind of trophy elk safari.

VITAL STATISTICS:

Game/Arm/Seasons:

ELK:
Bow: Late Aug. through early Sept.
Centerfire: Early Sept. through mid-Oct.
DEER:
Centerfire: Early Oct. through late Nov.
ANTELOPE:
Centerfire: Early Oct. through early Nov.
SHEEP and MOOSE:
Bow: Mid-Aug. through mid-Oct.
Centerfire: Early Sept. through mid-Oct.
MOUNTAIN LION:
Bow and centerfire: Early Dec. through early April

Rates:
ELK or ELK/DEER combo $4,500 /8 days
DEER or ANTELOPE $2,250/5 days
DEER/ANTELOPE combo $2,500/5 days
SHEEP or MOOSE $5,500/9 days
MOUNTAIN LION $2,850/5 days

Accommodations:
WALL TENTS
MAXIMUM NUMBER OF HUNTERS: 8
Meals: Steak, chicken, pork chops, Italian and Mexican dishes
Conference Groups: No
Guides: Included
Gratuity: $100 to $200
Preferred Payment:
Cash, MasterCard, Visa, check
Other Activities:
Bird watching, fishing, hiking, horseback riding, wildlife photography
Getting There:
Fly to Cody, Wyoming, and be picked up by a representative from Hidden Creek.

Contact:
Bill Perry
Hidden Creek Outfitters
Box 1203
Cody, WY 82414
307/527-5470
Fax: 307/527-5470
e-mail: hiddencr@wave.com
Web: //hiddencr.wavenet.com

FOR A TRUE WILDERNESS HUNT, it's tough to beat a packtrain trip into the Thorofare region off the southeastern corner of Yellowstone Park. This is backcountry hunting at its best, the kind our forefathers did. The 25-mile horseback ride into camp from the trailhead along the South Fork takes nine hours through some of the most incredible scenery in the West. Camp, in a designated wilderness area, consists of wall tents with wood-stoves. Hunters wake up at 4 each morning, saddle up, then ride out of camp to bugle for bull elk. If one answers, you hobble your horses and start walking, hoping to set up for an ambush. Hunters generally have to hike at least five miles a day through thin mountain air, but your chances of getting a bull in this elk-rich region are great. Bulls with 5x5 and 6x6 are fairly common here, and once in awhile someone even takes a big 7x7 animal.

The key to success on these hunts is to get into decent shape and practice with your bow or rifle until you can shoot well. Most hunters go with a .30-06 or larger, zeroed in three inches high at 100 yards. Shots can be long, out to 300 yards, although most are under 100, especially in the early bugling season when the bulls hear your calls and come looking for you. Later, hunters set up for bulls migrating out of the high country.

Guide Bill Perry and his crew guide six to eight hunters per week. And they will put you within range of a good elk at some point during your eight-day hunt; then it's up to you. They'll also take you for mule deer, antelope, shiras moose, bighorn sheep, black bear and mountain lion, if you've got the permit.

Food on this trip is sumptuous, with steaks, chops, chicken, Italian and Mexican cuisine all on the menu. You eat a lot of it, too, as you'll burn up the calories hiking after that trophy of a lifetime.

[ROCKY MOUNTAINS]

K-Z Guest Ranch & Outfitters

C o d y ,   W y o m i n g

Elk, deer, moose and sheep, deep in the Absarokas.

WITH A COMFORTABLE modern lodge, seven guest cabins and two tent camps in the North Absaroka Wilderness just east of Yellowstone National Park, K-Z—owned by the Barnett family—can accommodate 12 hunters per week (or about 65 per season) in this game-rich part of the West. Moose, deer, sheep, goat and elk are all available here, with the majority of K-Z's clients concentrating on elk that migrate out of Yellowstone Park, headed for the Sunlight winter range.

On the first morning of the seven-day hunt, some of K-Z's hunters saddle up and ride out from the lodge, headed for one of the two tent camps from which they'll hunt for the week. Others may stay at the ranch itself, hunting out of there instead. Especially in the early season, hunters in either case should bring clothing for hot or cold weather, as the temperatures can change quickly and drastically at this time of year.

Getting a trophy bull in this territory can require work, with hunters having to ride or hike through gullies and gulches, up and down mountains, and over fallen trees and crags. Late hunts can be especially challenging, as the snow is often deep at the end of November and beginning of December, and reaching the tent camps can be difficult if not impossible. The bulls aren't bugling then, either, but if you can set up along one of the migration routes, your chances of success are high.

Meals are sit-down, family-style affairs at the lodge, and you can order vegetarian or salt-free if you let the Barnetts know ahead of time.

VITAL STATISTICS:

Game/Arm/Seasons:
ELK:
Bow: Sept.
Centerfire: Early through mid-Oct. and mid-Nov. through early Dec.
DEER:
Centerfire: Mid-Oct. through early Nov.
SHEEP and GOAT:
Centerfire: Begins Sept. 1
MOOSE:
Centerfire: Begins Oct. 1
Rates:
ELK from $2,200/ 7 days
DEER $1,500/7 days
SHEEP $3,500/10 days
GOAT $3,000/8 days
MOOSE $2,200/6 days
Accommodations:
CABINS AND TENTS
NUMBER OF ROOMS: 7 CABINS WITH PRIVATE BATHS
MAXIMUM NUMBER OF HUNTERS: 12
Meals: Family-style meals
Conference Groups: Yes
Guides: Included
Gratuity: $50 to $100
Preferred Payment:
Cash, Discover, American Express, MasterCard, Visa, check
Other Activities:
Bird watching, boating, canoeing/rafting, fishing, hiking, swimming, wildlife photography
Getting There:
Fly to Cody, Wyoming, or Billings, Montana, and either rent a car and drive to the lodge or be met by a van from the lodge.

Contact:
Dawna Barnett
K - Z Guest Ranch
& Outfitters
Box 2167
Cody, WY 82414
307/587-4410
Fax: 307/527-4605

Western Wyoming Trophy Hunts

Cora, Wyoming

The oldest family-tenured outfitter in Wyoming has access to incredible elk and deer hunting.

VITAL STATISTICS:

Game/Arm/Seasons:

ELK:
Bow: Early through late Sept.
Centerfire, muzzleloader: Late Sept. through late Oct.

MULE DEER:
Bow: Early through mid-Sept.
Centerfire, muzzleloader: Late Sept. through early Oct.

ANTELOPE:
Bow, centerfire, muzzleloader: Mid-Sept. through mid-Oct.

SHIRAS MOOSE:
Bow: Early Sept. through late Oct.
Centerfire, muzzleloader: Mid-Sept. through late Oct.

BIGHORN SHEEP:
Bow: Early Aug. through mid-Sept.
Centerfire, muzzleloader: Mid-Aug. through mid-Oct.

Rates:
ELK from $2,800/6 days (ranch hunt); from $3,500/7 days (camp hunt)
MULE DEER from $2,000
ANTELOPE from $1,000/3 days
SHIRAS MOOSE $3,000/6 days
BIGHORN SHEEP from $4,500/9 days

Accommodations:
RANCH HOUSE AND TENTS
NUMBER OF ROOMS: 10 IN RANCH HOUSE, TENTS
MAXIMUM NUMBER OF HUNTERS: 19 RANCH HOUSE, 8 TENTS

Meals: Steaks, roast beef, chicken, casseroles

Conference Groups: Yes

Guides: Yes

Gratuity: 5 to 10%

Preferred Payment:
Cash, Discover, MasterCard, Visa, check

Other Activities:
Fishing, wildlife photography

Getting There:
Fly to Jackson Hole, Wyoming, rent a car and drive to the lodge, or be picked up by the lodge van at no additional cost.

CONTACT:
Levi Lozier
Western Wyoming Trophy Hunts
Box 100-SA
Cora, WY 82925
1-800/822-8466
Fax: 307/367-6260
e-mail: llozier@wyoming.com
Web: www.huntinfo.com/wwth/

"ELK HUNTING is our bread-and-butter occupation," says Levi Lozier of Western Wyoming Trophy Hunts. "With a 65-day-long season, beginning with archery hunts in early September, we offer hunters a choice or combination of 10 different elk hunts and dates." These include an early archery hunt, a combo bow/rifle hunt, a rifle bugle hunt, a late hunt for trophy bulls and more. The key to Lozier's success, however, is in his statement about being "uniquely located."

Western Wyoming, you see, operates from and maintains two backcountry elk camps, each permitted by the U.S. Forest Service, inside the inaccessible and remote 893,000-acre Bridger Wilderness, on the western slope of the Wind River Mountains, 50 miles southeast of Jackson Hole. Western Wyoming also hunts from the Loziers' Box "R" Ranch, which is the only deeded land in the state bordering the Bridger Wilderness. Homesteaded in 1900 and located in a remote mountain valley surrounded on three sides by national forest land, the ranch is the base for superb antelope, elk, shiras moose and mule deer hunting.

Add to all this the fact that this is the oldest family-tenured hunting business in Wyoming, active through five generations since 1898, and you get the picture. Lozier's outfit knows this business well. Consider their success rates over the years: elk—74 percent, mule deer—68 percent, antelope—95 percent, sheep—91 percent and shiras moose—93 percent. The majority of hunts are for deer, elk and antelope, as sheep and moose are on a lottery system. It's rare for the outfit to get more than four sheep or four moose hunters per year.

Depending on what you're hunting, and when, elk, deer and moose hunts are conducted either out of the wilderness tent camps or the ranch. Sheep are hunted only out of camps; antelope are hunted solely from the ranch. If you do hunt out of the ranch, be prepared to be treated like a king. With 10 guest rooms and 19 beds, business conveniences such as telephone/fax/copier, and a dining room serving the likes of enchiladas, casseroles, chicken, steak, roast beef, corned beef, and all the fixings, you'll feel right at home, just as the Loziers have for 100 years.

Whitetail Creek Outfitters

H u l e t t ,   W y o m i n g

A guaranteed hunt for whitetails in the heart of the West.

VITAL STATISTICS:

Game/Arm/Seasons:
DEER and ANTELOPE:
Bow: Early through late Sept.
Centerfire, muzzleloader: Early Oct. through late Nov.
ELK:
Centerfire, muzzleloader: Mid through late Oct.
Rates:
DEER from $2,250/5 days
ANTELOPE from $1,350/5 days
Combo hunts are also available
Accommodations:
RUSTIC RANCH HOUSE
NUMBER OF ROOMS: 10
MAXIMUM NUMBER OF HUNTERS: 16
Meals: Family-style buffet
Conference Groups: Yes
Guides: Included
Gratuity: $100 per week
Preferred Payment:
Cash MasterCard, Visa, check
Other Activities:
Antiquing, biking, bird watching, boating, fishing, swimming, wildlife photography
Getting There:
Fly to Rapid City, South Dakota, and take a shuttle flight, or rent a car and drive to the lodge. For $100 round-trip a van from the lodge will meet you at the airport.

Contact:
Ray Hulse
Whitetail Creek Outfitters
Box 279
Hulett, WY 82720
307/467-5625

LOCATED JUST WEST of the Black Hills National Forest in the northeastern corner of Wyoming, the Tumbling T Ranch offers some of the best white-tailed deer hunting in the state. Why? Because before Whitetail Creek Outfitters bought it back in 1994, the ranch had little or no hunting pressure. There were a lot of old bucks around, many of which had never even seen a hunter.

The ranch borders the national forest, and owner Ray Hulse plants crops to attract the deer onto the 4,000 acres that he owns, while also maintaining several feed locations that he supplements with grain and mineral blocks.

Hunting here is pure Western hunting, with rimrocks, deep canyons and vast meadows. The only thing is, you're mostly hunting for whitetails (though antelope and mulies are available). Hulse sends his guided hunters onto his own ranch, and also leases hunting rights to more than 200,000 acres covering 19 ranches in three separate Wyoming hunt regions. Hunters still-hunt, rattle or hunt from blinds that overlook feeder locations, with many bucks going in the 125 Boone & Crockett range, and a few into the 150s! Bow, rifle and blackpowder hunters are all welcome.

The lodge is roomy and comfortable, able to accommodate 16 hunters—six in the lodge, 10 in adjoining cabins. Meals are buffet-style, guaranteed to keep you fueled for the next day. And if you don't see a suitable buck the next day, or any other time during your trip, don't worry: Hulse guarantees a shooting opportunity at a quality buck at some point during your trip or you'll get a free trip the next year. Now that's something not many outfitters are confident enough to offer!

WyCon Safari Inc.

Saratoga,   Wyoming

The Medicine Bow Forest is home to trophy mule deer, elk and black bear. Antelope on the nearby prairies also go big in this part of Wyoming.

VITAL STATISTICS:

Game/Arm/Seasons:
MULE DEER AND
(UTAH AND WYOMING) MOOSE:
Bow: Early Sept. through late Oct.
Centerfire: Early through late Oct.
ANTELOPE:
Bow: Mid-Aug. through late Sept.
Centerfire: Early Sept. through late Oct.
Muzzleloader: Mid-Aug. through late Sept.
ELK:
Bow: Early Sept. through late Sept. (bull)
Centerfire: Early through late Oct. (bull); early Oct. through late Dec. (cow)
SHEEP:
Bow: Mid-Aug. through late Sept.
Centerfire: Early Sept. through mid-Oct.
Rates:
MULE DEER from $1,895/3 days
ANTELOPE from $700/2 days
ELK from $2,600/ 6 days
MOOSE $3,200/7 days
SHEEP $3,500/10 days
Combo hunts are also available
Accommodations:
MODERN LODGE
NUMBER OF ROOMS: 4
MAXIMUM NUMBER OF HUNTERS: 12
Meals: Bacon and eggs, French toast, beef, vegetables and potatoes
Conference Groups: No
Guides: Included
Gratuity: $50 to $100
Preferred Payment:
Cash, traveler's check
Other Activities:
Biking, boating, fishing, float trips, hiking, horseback riding, prairie dog shoots
Getting There:
Fly to Laramie, rent a car and drive to the lodge.

Contact:
Wynn G. Condict
Wycon Safari Inc.
Box 1126
Saratoga, WY 82331
307/327-5502
Fax: 307/327-5332

WYNN CONDICT makes no bones about it. If you hunt with his WyCon Safari Inc., you are going to get your chance at a trophy antelope, mule deer or elk. There's a catch, though. You've got to be in decent physical shape (no, you don't need to be an Olympic athlete); you should be able to ride a horse (although you can hunt out of a Suburban, if you wish); and you have to be able to shoot straight.

"I can't emphasize enough the importance of practicing with your rifle," says Condict. "You should practice close off-hand shots and long-range shots of 200 to even 600 yards. Practice shooting without a dead rest, such as off your knee or sitting down, for sometimes there isn't a rest around and you have to make a quick shot. I tell my clients that they ought to shoot their gun at least 100 times a month prior to the hunt."

What Condict says makes sense. If you're going to plunk down your hard-earned money, and do a lot of hard riding and hiking in the mountains to get a chance at a trophy animal, the last thing you want to do is miss. "We all work hard to get our hunters chances at the game they want," Condict concludes. "But each year some of the largest trophy animals get away because of the hunter's shooting or physical abilities."

Enough said. Get in shape, and know how to shoot. And you'll get your chances in the area that Condict hunts, which is south-central Wyoming, 90 miles west of Laramie, near the Colorado line. Hunts for antelope up to 16 inches (the average trophy buck is 14), mule deer (average spreads are 22 to 28 inches), elk ("We run 50 to 100 percent kill rates") and black bears (average size is 250, though bruins up to 450 pounds are taken each year) take place in the sprawling Medicine Bow National Forest, as well as on a number of private ranches, including Condict's. His ranch, in fact, gets a lot of elk movement once the animals start feeling pressure on nearby BLM land.

The ranch itself has a modern log cabin with four guest rooms accommodating up to 12 hunters (three per room). Meals are guaranteed to fill: roast beef with vegetables and potatoes is a favorite, as is the French toast breakfast. Don't forget to take along your flyrod, too. The trout fishing is first-rate in the North Platte and Encampment rivers. Bowhunters, who start in August for antelope and in September for deer and elk, can really get some trophy trout if they fill their hunting tags early.

Wyoming Trophy Outfitters

C a s p e r ,   W y o m i n g

This family-run operation can put you into some of the finest antelope in the state.

ESTLED IN THE ROLLING prairie outside of Casper, Wyoming, Trophy Outfitters offers elk, mule deer and antelope hunts. All three open in early September, and you can hunt them all if you get the permits (there is a limited quota for elk).

Some of Wyoming's largest antelope herds are in the Casper area, and your chances of getting a 14-inch-plus buck are good. A September hunt coincides with their rut, which makes for an exciting hunt. The general scenario is to get to your hunting area by 4WD, then start glassing. If you spot a good-sized buck, you and your guide begin your stalk. The land may appear flat at first, but you'll find that there are many draws to hide you as you try to get in range. Most hunters prefer flat-shooting .270s for this type of hunting, with 150-grain bullets.

Trophy Outfitters also has several areas for hunting mule deer. Most are on private ranches, and you can go with a 4WD or a horse, your choice. The chances of getting a deer with a 4x4 or better rack are good in this region. Unlike some parts of the West, where mule deer herds are on the decline, this area's herd has remained relatively steady. This is tough terrain, mostly rimrocks and canyons, and the fit hunter who can move quickly has a better chance of getting that big buck he spotted with his 10x40 binoculars from half a mile away.

Elk are available on leased ranches in the area, but if you don't draw a tag, don't worry. Owners Sharon and Randy Brown can help you get a license for an area in Jackson, which is where the Yellowstone herd migrates each fall. That hunt starts in November.

Hunters have a choice of accommodation with the Brown's operation. For those who like to end up in a town after a day of hunting, Trophy Outfitters will arrange for a motel in Casper. Your guide will pick you up each morning at the motel and, after breakfast, you'll head to your hunting area. The other option is to stay at a cabin on the ranch. The cabins have beds, propane and wood heat, and are a stone's throw from the main house, where meals featuring Swiss steaks, roast chicken, ham and barbecued pork chops are served up in sumptuous portions.

VITAL STATISTICS:

Game/Arm/Seasons:
ANTELOPE:
Centerfire: Early to mid-Sept.
DEER:
Centerfire: Early Sept. through mid-Oct.
ELK:
Centerfire: Early Sept. through early Oct.

Rates:
ANTELOPE from $875/2 days
DEER from $1,225/3 days
ELK from $2,200/5 days

Accommodations:
LOG CABINS OR TOWN MOTELS
NUMBER OF ROOMS: 3
MAXIMUM NUMBER OF HUNTERS: 24

Meals: Steaks, chicken, ham

Conference Groups: Yes

Guides: Included

Gratuity: Hunter's discretion $50 to $200

Preferred payment:
Cash, check

Other Activities:
Biking, fishing

Getting There:
Fly to Casper, Wyoming, and you will be met by representative of the lodge.

Contact:
Sharon Brown
Wyoming Trophy Outfitters
Box 1981
Casper, WY 82602
307/234-1411 or
307/234-6167

THE WEST

ARIZONA, CALIFORNIA, NEVADA, NEW MEXICO, OREGON, WASHINGTON

WRAPPING AROUND the southern tip of the Rockies and swinging up the Pacific Coast, these six states offer their own brands of hunting. New Mexico and Arizona are fabled for elk, mule deer, sheep and mountain lions. California has its blacktails, while Roosevelt elk and blacktails roam the lush forests and canyons of Oregon and Washington. And Nevada, often overlooked by hunters going West, offers opportunities not only for big mule deer, but for bears and lions as well. Terrain varies tremendously from the dry mountains and gulches of the southern deserts to the lush rain forests of the Olympic peninsula to the rolling grain fields of western Washington. Outfitters are fairly numerous but hunting lodges are not. Motels and restaurants provide room and board, and horses or 4x4s carry hunters to the trailhead.

L o d g e s :

ARIZONA
1 SHEEP LTD.

CALIFORNIA
2 ROCK SPRINGS RANCH & LODGE

NEVADA
3 ELKO GUIDE SERVICE
4 MUSTANG OUTFITTERS

NEW MEXICO
5 BLUE MOUNTAIN OUTFITTERS
6 DOUBLE J OUTFITTERS
7 ROSS JOHNSON GUIDE & OUTFITTERS
8 TIMBERLINE OUTFITTERS
9 UNITED STATES OUTFITTERS, INC.

OREGON
10 THE BIG K GUEST RANCH

WASHINGTON
11 BEARPAW OUTFITTERS
12 LAKE QUINAULT OUTFITTERS

References:

HUNTING WILD BOAR IN CALIFORNIA
by Bob Robb
P.O. Box 1296
Valdez, AK 99668
fax 907/835-4738

PACIFIC BIG THREE
by Cork Graham
Dragon Press Publishing
723 Camino Plaza, #160
San Bruno, CA 94066; 650/595-4346

Resources:

ARIZONA GAME AND FISH
DEPARTMENT
2221 W. Greenway Rd.
Phoenix, AZ 85023
602/942-3000
Web: www.gf.state.az.us

CALIFORNIA DEPARTMENT OF
FISH & GAME, WILDLIFE AND
INLAND FISHERIES DIVISION
1416 9th St., Box 944209
Sacramento, CA 95814
916/653-7664
Web: www.dfg.ca.gov

NEVADA DIVISION OF WILDLIFE
Box 10678, Reno, NV 89520
775/688-1500
Web: www.state.nv.us/cnr/nvwildlife

NEW MEXICO DEPARTMENT OF
GAME AND FISH
Box 25112, Santa Fe, NM 87504
800/862-9310, 505/827-7911
Web: www.gmfsh.state.nm.us

OREGON DEPARTMENT OF
FISH AND WILDLIFE
Box 59, Portland, OR 97207
503/872-5268
Web: www.dfw.state.or.us/

WASHINGTON DEPARTMENT OF FISH
AND WILDLIFE
600 Capitol Way North
Olympia, WA 98501-1091
360/902-2515
Web: www.wa.gov/wdfw/

Sheep Ltd.

Kingman, Arizona

As you'll discover, hunters can go after much more than sheep with this outfit.

FORMED IN 1994 by hunter/conservationist Jerry Fletcher and outfitter/guide Larry Heathington, Sheep Ltd. is aimed at the serious sheep hunter, one who is looking for an exceptional trophy, plus the hunt of a lifetime. Sheep Ltd. now runs hunts not only in Heathington's native Arizona, but in other states throughout the West, plus Mexico. They guide for desert bighorn and Rocky Mountain sheep, plus mule deer, Coues deer, antelope, black bear and elk.

Most of these hunts run from a week to 15 days, with sheep taking longer than the other animals due to the hard hunting involved. But everything is included. In the Mexican desert bighorn sheep hunt, for example, the hunt includes an American advisor, Mexican guides, camp personnel, horses, meals, beverages, lodging, trophy care, firearms permits, and consular letters. Of course, the price on this one is $50,000, so you are indeed treated like a king.

For more affordable hunts, you might try a five-day guided hunt in Arizona for a trophy antelope. Costing about $3,500, this hunt takes place in northern Arizona, where seven of the top 10 heads listed in Boone & Crockett have been taken.

Depending on where your hunt takes place, you'll stay in a tent, trailer or motel. Meals are always good and hearty, with meat and potatoes the main fare, and sumptuous desserts capping everything off. As sheep hunters know, you burn a lot of calories chasing animals around the mountains. Best to refuel as best you can whenever you have the opportunity.

Rock Springs Ranch & Lodge

P a i c i n e s ,   C a l i f o r n i a

This is California blacktail hunting at its finest.

VITAL STATISTICS:

Game/Arm/Seasons:
BLACKTAIL DEER:
Centerfire: Early Aug. through late Sept.
WILD BOAR:
Centerfire: Early May through late June
Rates:
BLACK-TAILED DEER $1,500/3 days
WILD BOAR $630/2 days
Accommodations:
CEDAR LODGE AND GUEST HOUSES
NUMBER OF ROOMS: 6 IN LODGE, 6 IN GUEST HOUSES
MAXIMUM NUMBER OF HUNTERS: 30
Meals: Barbecued chicken, paella, salmon, pork loin
Conference Groups: Yes
Guides: Included
Gratuity: Hunter's discretion
Preferred Payment:
Cash, MasterCard, Visa, check
Other Activities:
Bird hunting, hiking, wildlife photography
Getting There:
Fly to San Jose, rent a car and drive to the ranch, or be picked up by the lodge van for an additional $100.

Contact:
Ken or Nola Range
Rock Springs Ranch & Lodge
11000 Old Hernandez Rd.
Paicines, CA 95043
1-800/209-5175 or
408/385-5242
Fax: 408/385-5270
e-mail: covey@sirius.com
Web: RSLODGE (currently being designed).

COVERING ALMOST 19,000 ACRES of prime game habitat, including oak chaparral, river bottoms, abandoned farmland and fields planted in rye and wheat, Rock Springs is an Orvis-endorsed wingshooting lodge. Only 75 miles south of San Jose, it also happens to offer excellent hunting for black-tailed deer and wild boar.

European wild boar were introduced into the Carmel Valley back in 1923. By the 1950s they had migrated east, with feral domestic hogs and established themselves in San Benito County (where Rock Springs is located). Their numbers have been increasing ever since, and hunters find them a real challenge to hunt. All hunting on the ranch is spotting and stalking, with no dogs. Most boars are in the 175-pound range, though enough boars over 200 pounds are taken to make things interesting.

Black-tailed deer, on the other hand, have been native to this area since before settlers arrived. Good blacktails taken off the ranch may hit 130 pounds, with racks of 3x3 common (although the occasional 4x4 is shot). This is fun hunting, with hunters climbing the deep canyons along the valley of the San Benito River, looking for blacktails bedded under low vegetation. Elevations range from 1,500 feet along the river to 4,000-foot peaks, so be prepared to do a lot of climbing and glassing. Most hunters use rifles they would use for mule deer (the blacktail's cousin) and whitetails.

No matter what you're hunting at Rock Springs, you'll return at the end of the day to incredible accommodations. Hunters stay in the main lodge or the nearby guest house, with meals prepared by a professional chef at the lodge. With a warm cedar interior, high-beamed ceilings, stone fireplaces and four private bedrooms, the lodge provides an atmosphere of comfort. A covered deck wraps around two sides and includes a built-in stone barbecue. Relax on the deck after a long day afield, taking in the view of the valley; or take a soak in the spa. You'll be pampered either way; just the thing you need to get you ready for the next day of hiking and glassing for blacktails.

Elko Guide Service

E l k o ,   N e v a d a

───

There are some diamonds in the rough in northeastern Nevada.

VITAL STATISTICS:

Game/Arm/Seasons:
MULE DEER:
Bow: Aug.
Centerfire: Oct.
Muzzleloader: Sept.
ELK:
Centerfire: Nov.
ANTELOPE:
Centerfire: Aug.
MOUNTAIN GOAT:
Centerfire: Sept. through Oct.
BIGHORN SHEEP:
Centerfire: Nov.

Rates:
MULE DEER $2,500/7 days (centerfire, muzzleloader); $1,250/4 days (bow)
ELK $2,000/7 days
ANTELOPE $750/7 days
MOUNTAIN GOAT $2,500/7 days
BIGHORN SHEEP from $2,000/7 days

Accommodations:
RUSTIC LOG CABIN AND TENTS
NUMBER OF ROOMS: 4; 1 WITH PRIVATE BATH
MAXIMUM NUMBER OF HUNTERS: 8

Meals: Ranch-style cooking

Conference Groups: No

Guides: Included

Gratuity: Hunter's discretion

Preferred Payment:
Cash, check

Other Activities:
Bird hunting, bird watching, boating, canoeing/rafting, fishing, hiking, waterfowling, wildlife photography

Getting There:
Fly to Elko, Nevada, rent a car and drive to the ranch or be met by a representative of the ranch.

Contact:
Bill Gibson
Elko Guide Service
Ruby Crest Ranch
HC30, Box 197 #13
Elko, NV 89801
702/744-2277
Fax: 702/744-2229

IF YOU'VE DRIVEN ACROSS UTAH, you know what a desert really is. Heading across the Great Salt Lake Desert, passing through the Bonneville Salt Flats, your eyes beet-red from staring into the setting sun, you begin to think that the endless stretch of bright white sand will never end. You'll no doubt hit more of the same when you cross the Nevada line, right?

Not! Once you enter Nevada, it's almost as if you've stepped onto another planet. And while Interstate 80 will take you through more desert flats, you'll also pass through some incredibly beautiful mountain ranges. You'll hit the Pequop Mountains first, then there's the Humboldt Range, the Butte Mountains, the Independence Mountains, the Tuscaroras and, south of Elko, the Diamond Mountains.

Bill Gibson's Elko Guide Service operates in those mountains. And, depending on what types of tags you draw (all big game tags are awarded through a computer draw), Gibson will take you after elk, antelope, mountain goats, desert bighorns, or monster mule deer. Bow season starts in August for mulies, muzzleloading comes in September, but for the really big boys, October is when you want to go.

There's some rough weather at this time of year, and if you think the trophy mulies are going to be driven down by a little snow, forget it. They'll stay up high, not wanting to budge until the really nasty stuff forces them to. Smaller bucks might move, but the big bucks have a few hunting seasons under their belts and they know that moving down early will only expose them to danger.

Hunters ride out of camp early each morning, heading high for deer. But don't worry, the beauty of the terrain will keep your energy level high. Snow-capped peaks, sweeping desert valleys, junipers galore, groves of quaking aspens dancing in the wind make striking panoramas. This is God's country.

It's also Gibson's country, at least for the past 23 years. He and his guides will take you to the ridges where the bucks are, glass for you using big 10x50 binoculars and help you find the trophy mulies, many of which are 5x5 and heavier than 175 pounds. Shots can be long in these mountains, as it's tough to sneak really close to a wary buck. But if you've practiced those 200-yard-plus shots with your .270 or .280, you've got a chance.

At the end of the day you'll ride your horse back to your cabin, then amble over to the ranch house for some home cooking served family-style. And then you can tell everyone about that nice 5x5 you came riding in with.

Mustang Outfitters

Round Mountain, Nevada

Lion hunting is a passion with this outfit in central Nevada.

KAREN STAHL, CO-OWNER OF Mustang Outfitters with husband Jim, loves mountain lion hunting as much as anyone. If you've never been on a lion hunt, or if you're curious about it, Karen can convey the excitement of the hunt.

"I was running down a steep mountain draw through the thick pinion and junipers, hoping to retrieve a video camera while the tom was still in the tree, when I heard the howling of the hounds change from a tree howl to a chase howl. I turned back uphill and there was the big male lion charging right down the draw, straight at me! I jumped behind a tree, hoping the lion wouldn't take a defensive swipe at me with his razor-sharp claws, and luckily he turned and sped past me on the uphill side. My heart was pounding!" From fall until spring, Karen follows her passion, chasing lions with clients.

Mustang Outfitters specializes in mountain lion hunts in Kingston Canyon, in the heart of central Nevada's lion country, but that's not all they hunt. Big mule deer, bighorn sheep and antelope hunts are also offered by Mustang.

"I hunt three wilderness areas," says Jim Stahl. "Most hunts are pack-in on horseback and mules. Antelope is by truck, however."

Stahl's hunts generally take place near the middle of the state. His deer hunts occur within the Arc Dome, Alta Toquima and Table Mountain wilderness areas; elk are hunted in the Table Mountain Wilderness Area, on the south end; and sheep are hunted in the beautiful and rugged Alta Toquima Wilderness Area, with base camp at 10,000 feet.

"Nevada is on a draw and bonus point system," he continues. "Mule deer and antelope are fairly easy to draw. Elk and desert bighorn sheep are tougher. Mountain lion tags may be bought over the counter."

In the past few years, Stahl has had 100 percent success on elk, mule deer, antelope and desert bighorns. He generally runs about 85 percent success with lions on snow, and 35 percent on bare ground.

[W E S T]

Blue Mountain Outfitters

B e l e n ,   N e w   M e x i c o

Big antelope abound in New Mexico; the elk and mule deer hunting isn't too bad, either!

VITAL STATISTICS:

Game/Arm/Seasons:
ELK:
Bow: Early through mid-Sept.
Centerfire: Early Oct. through early Nov.
Muzzleloader: Early through late Oct.
MULE DEER:
Bow: Early through mid-Jan.
Centerfire: Early through mid-Nov.
ANTELOPE:
Bow: Mid-Aug.
Centerfire: Late Sept.
Rates:
ELK $1,950/6 days (bow); $2,600/5 days (centerfire)
MULE DEER $1,800/8 days (bow) or 5 days (centerfire)
ANTELOPE $1,500/5 days (bow) or 3 days (centerfire)
Accommodations:
WALL TENTS
MAXIMUM NUMBER OF HUNTERS: 6
Meals: Steak, fried chicken, roast beef, Italian food
Conference Groups: No
Guides: Included
Gratuity: $100
Preferred Payment:
Cash, check
Other Activities:
Wildlife photography
Getting There:
Fly to Albuquerque. Transportation to and from Albuquerque is provided by the outfitter.

Contact:
Bob Atwood
Blue Mountain Outfitters
Box 697
Belen, NM 87002
505/864-6867

THE QUESTION OF HOW FAST an antelope can really run will never be settled to anyone's satisfaction. All will agree, however, that the pronghorn can run faster for longer distances than any other mammal in the Western Hemisphere. They have been known to keep pace with cars barreling down highways at 65 mph, if that's any clue.

Pronghorns also have incredible eyesight, able to spot movement out to 500 yards and beyond. The key to taking a pronghorn is to spy him from a long distance, glass his horns (13 inches is decent), then figure out a route that will get you into rifle range before he sees you again. More than a few antelope are shot at ranges longer than 300 yards.

Bob Atwood of Blue Mountain Outfitters knows a few things about antelope. He's been hunting them since he was 11 years old, and has been guiding for them for the past 12 years.

"Hunting these beautiful speedsters is a whole lot of fun," he says. "We have exclusive hunting rights on a private ranch. In the past, all of our rifle hunters have taken bucks with horns at least 15 inches long. This particular hunt is not physically demanding, either. It's a nice, relaxing, no-pressure type of hunt. And for the bowhunter, this ranch is an excellent place to take a record buck."

Atwood doesn't hunt just pronghorns, though. He runs a rifle mule deer hunt on national forest land in southwest New Mexico at the end of October. He also runs bow and muzzleloader hunts for big mulies, plus bow and rifle elk hunts.

"On the first muzzleloader hunt we drive to camp, then hunt with horses and on foot. On all of the other hunts we drive to camp, then use four-wheel-drives to get to various locations and hunt on foot. We have had very consistent success on our elk hunts, and the majority of our hunters have had a chance to take a mature bull."

Blue Mountain is a small, family-run business that prides itself on personalized service. Camps, set up where the game is found, consist of waterproof wall tents equipped with cots, mattresses, heaters and lanterns. Meals are prepared and served in the cook tent, starting with a big breakfast early in the morning, followed by field lunches, and capped off with delicious dinners that run the gamut from rib eye steaks, fried chicken, pork chops, spaghetti and roast beef, with all the fixin's. Fresh desserts are served nightly.

Double J Outfitters

A p a c h e   C r e e k ,   N e w   M e x i c o

Oh, give me a home where the elk always roam.

ELK WERE PUT ON THIS GREEN EARTH, according to ranchers in west-central New Mexico, for the sole purpose of eating tender shoots of new wheat. It takes a lot of hay to feed a 1,200-pound bull, and there's nothing like a bull with an appetite to lay waste to a field of grain. The old strategy of planting a little for the elk and more for the rancher doesn't work anymore. Why? Because there are more elk than farmers, and guess which is multiplying faster?

All this is by way of introducing Jimmy and Jenny Heap, whose family runs the 2,300-acre NH Ranch on the flanks of 8,900-foot Apache Mountain deep in the Gila National Forest. Where once they grazed 1,200 cattle, a herd of 700 elk now roams. Once reserved strictly for family and friends, today the ranch takes between 24 and 30 hunters per season, averaging between four and eight hunters per hunt. No centerfire rifles are allowed; it's bow and blackpowder throughout the season. That means you're likely to have a very close encounter with a bull. Jimmy is committed to maintaining a trophy experience. Guests are encouraged to pass up bulls of less than six points per side. Most, as you'd expect, comply.

In this area where snowfalls are relatively light and short-lived, elk have little incentive to herd up and migrate. They live where they eat and eat where they live. And after they've been reminded that there are humans about, the bulls begin to drift deeper into the forest. Jimmy uses whatever means of transportation necessary — be it horseback, four-by-four or hiking — to get hunters to where the bulls are. Archers hunt for two weeks in September; muzzleloaders get two weeks in October and one in mid-November. Over the long haul, hunter success rates average right around 50 percent, but in recent years it's been a little higher. Elk licenses are available via lottery and nonresidents have about a 30 percent chance of being drawn. Also available, albeit for a price, are guaranteed landowner permits. Shelling out about $3,000 along with the price of the hunt, guarantees a nonresident a chance at one of these big bulls.

Not only the reasonable terrain, the high number of elk and good success rates commit Double J to hunters, but so, too, do the creature comforts. You'll stay in the Heap's farmhouse or in nearby guest cabins. Meals are comfortable affairs where everyone sits down to fajitas, steaks, green chili or whatever guests want (with some advance notice). Hunting here is like coming to visit a favorite cousin who you don't see as often as you'd like.

[W E S T]

Ross Johnson Guide & Outfitters

M a g d a l e n a ,   N e w   M e x i c o

For record-class bulls and bucks, look no further.

VITAL STATISTICS:

Game/Arm/Seasons:

ELK:
Bow: Early through late Sept.
Centerfire: Late Oct.
Muzzleloader: Mid-Oct.
COUES and MULE DEER:
Bow: Sept. and Jan.
Centerfire: Nov.
Muzzleloader: Sept.
ANTELOPE:
Bow: Aug.
Centerfire: Oct.

Rates:
ELK from $3,800/5 days
COUES DEER $3,000/3 days
MULE DEER from $2750/5 days
ANTELOPE from $2,000/2 days

Accommodations:
RANCH HOUSES
NUMBER OF ROOMS: VARIES
MAXIMUM NUMBER OF HUNTERS: 5 PER CAMP

Meals: Italian, Mexican, American
Conference Groups: No
Guides: Included
Gratuity: 10%
Preferred Payment:
Cash, MasterCard, Visa, check
Other Activities:
Wildlife photography
Getting There:
Fly to Albuquerque, rent a car and drive to the camps.

Contact:
Susan Johnson
Ross Johnson Guide & Outfitters
Box 26
Magdalena, NM 87825
505/772-5997
Fax: 505/722-5998

NEW MEXICO OFFERS a variety of fine hunting, from the picturesque high desert to the majestic timberline. It's extremely game-rich country, too, with not only elk, deer and antelope, but bear, lion, javelina, turkey, coyotes and a menagerie of small animals.

Ross Johnson's outfit offers a choice of archery, muzzleloader or rifle on all of its hunts, and has many years experience in each. Each hunt has distinct characteristics, be it an archery elk hunt when the bulls are bugling at sunset, or a muzzleloader or rifle hunt in the thick timber after the rut.

Based in Magdalena, 100 miles or so south of Albuquerque, and hunting private ranches and public lands such as the Cibola National Forest, Johnson's outfit has placed numerous trophies in the Safari Club International (SCI) record books. Last year, for example, Archie Nesbitt of Alberta, Canada, and his guide bugled a huge bull to within 23 yards, an easy shot for the bowhunter. That huge bull scored 413 SCI! Other book bulls included a 361 SCI animal taken with a muzzleloader by Steve Topagna of Reno, Nevada, and a 463 SCI bull taken by Ken French of Morrilton, Arkansas.

Johnson says that his most successful rifle elk hunting takes place on the Pueblo of Acoma. The genuine hospitality of the Pueblo of Acoma people, the enchantment of the reservation's mesa tops and its deep-seated traditions along with the opportunity to hunt record-book bulls during the rut, make this one of Johnson's finest hunts. The hunts start with a tour of the magnificent Sky City, followed by a trip to the top of the mesa for five days of hunting. The lush meadows and abundant ponds of the mesa tops have attracted an increasing number of elk over the years, and Johnson's hunters annually take Boone & Crockett-plus bulls off the reservation each season.

Johnson Guide and Outfitters doesn't just hunt elk, however. They also run trophy antelope hunts in the vast plains and open country in the Magdalena area. These hunts usually take place on weekends at the end of September. In November, Johnson guides mule and Coues deer hunters. "Between the new private ranches that we now hunt and the limited-draw areas that are producing more big bucks every year, we will be harvesting some tremendous deer," he predicts.

Most of these hunts are physically demanding, so it pays to get in shape before you go. Lodging is provided in four ranch houses in the area, three to four hunters per camp. Food is good and hearty, featuring a variety of Mexican, American and Italian cuisine.

Timberline Outfitters

Luna, New Mexico

Hunt the Gila for mammoth elk and big mulies; or head south of the border for desert bighorns and Coues deer.

VITAL STATISTICS:

Game/Arm/Seasons:

ELK:
Bow: Sept.
Centerfire, muzzleloader: Oct. through Nov.
MULE DEER, COUES DEER:
Bow: Sept. through Dec.
Centerfire: Dec. through Jan.
BIGHORN SHEEP:
Bow, centerfire, muzzleloader: Dec. through March
ANTELOPE:
Bow: Aug.
Centerfire: Sept.
BEAR:
Bow, centerfire, muzzleloader: Aug. through Oct.
MOUNTAIN LION:
Bow, centerfire, muzzleloader: Dec. through March

Rates:
ELK from $2,500/5 days
MULE DEER from $2,500/3 days
COUES DEER $3,000/7 days
BIGHORN SHEEP $4,500/10 days
ANTELOPE $2,500/5 days
BEAR $2,800/7 days
MOUNTAIN LION $2,500/5 days

Accommodations:
RANCH HOUSES, TENTS
NUMBER OF ROOMS: VARIES
MAXIMUM NUMBER OF HUNTERS: 12

Meals: Steaks, ham, potatoes, salads, pies

Conference Groups: Yes

Guides: Included

Gratuity: $100 to $200

Preferred Payment:
Cash, check

Other Activities:
Biking, bird hunting, hiking, waterfowling, wildlife photography

Getting There:
Fly to Albuquerque or Phoenix, rent a car and drive to the ranch, or be met by a representative of the outfitter for an additional cost.

Contact:
Perry Hunsaker
Timberline Outfitters
Box 38
Luna, NM 87824
602/988-9654
Fax: 602/988-3292 or
505/547-2413
off-season:
19831 E. Warner Rd.
Higley, AZ 85236
602/988-9654
Fax: 602/988-3292

IMAGINE HOW BOWHUNTER Bob Lemberger felt. On the first morning of the first day of his hunt with Timberline Outfitters, his guide Joel woke him at 4 a.m. and, after a hearty breakfast, took him in a 4x4 pickup to a favorite spot for bull elk in New Mexico's Gila National Forest. The two men left the truck along a dirt road and started a two-mile hike. They were criss-crossing ridges when Joel suddenly stopped and pointed. There, in a narrow meadow, were three cows and a respectable bull working their way toward the hunters. The animals kept coming. Lemberger nocked an arrow. The bull got closer and closer, eventually stopping at 25 yards behind two small scrub pines that blocked any shot. Lemberger went to full draw, waiting for the 5x5 to take just one more step. The bull fled instead.

Such is elk hunting, especially when you hunt with a bow. But if you hunt with Perry Hunsaker's outfit, you'll get more than one chance. Later in the week, hunting with Hunsaker himself, Lemberger worked another. Three bulls were bugling from high up, and the two hunters put on a classic stalk ending up in below the bulls. With Hunsaker bugling, Lemberger readied himself and waited. Closer, closer came the bugling bull. Lemberger nocked an arrow on his Martin Firecat and chose a shooting lane. The ivory-white tines of an enraged bull were coming right at him! Lemberger drew. A branch snapped. There he was not six yards away, nostrils wet flared, neck extended and swollen. So close, but the angle was wrong — a head-on shot. Only one small zone could be fatal: just above the breastbone at the base of the neck. He release the arrow, and the bull, a massive 6x7 that eventually scored 362, ran 25 yards before collapsing.

Bowhunters aren't the only ones who get turned on by hunting with Hunsaker, as he guides firearms hunters as well. And in this part of the Gila, there's game galore besides elk — mule and Coues deer, antelope, black bear and lions. Hunsaker also hunts parts of Arizona, as well as Mexico (desert bighorns, javelina, mule deer, Coues deer and upland birds).

If you hunt the Gila, you'll stay in a heated bunkhouse and eat dinners, ham, green beans, hot rolls and desserts that include cherry pie like mom only dreamed of baking (all courtesy of Brenda Hunsaker).

United States Outfitters, Inc.

T a o s ,   N e w   M e x i c o

Let George handle the paperwork...and the guiding!

VITAL STATISTICS:

Game/Arm/Seasons:

ELK:
Bow: Sept.
Centerfire: Oct. through Dec.
Muzzleloader: Sept. through Dec.
MULE DEER:
Bow: Sept.
Centerfire, muzzleloader: Nov.
ANTELOPE:
Bow, centerfire, muzzleloader: Sept.
BIGHORN SHEEP:
Bow: Sept. through Oct.
Centerfire, muzzleloader: Oct. through Dec.
MOOSE:
Bow: Sept.
Centerfire, muzzleloader: Oct.

Rates: (for draw hunts guided by United States Outfitters)
ELK, MULE DEER, BIGHORN SHEEP, MOOSE $2,950/5 days
ANTELOPE from $1,950/3 days

Accommodations:
FARMHOUSES, RANCH HOUSES, TENTS, TRAILERS, MOTELS (VARIES WITH HUNT AND LOCATION)
NUMBER OF ROOMS: VARIES
MAXIMUM NUMBER OF HUNTERS: LODGES 28, TENT CAMPS 60

Meals: Near-gourmet Western fare
Conference Groups: Yes
Guides: Included
Gratuity: $200 to $300
Preferred Payment:
Cash, MasterCard, Visa, check
Other Activities:
Fishing, wildlife photography
Getting There:
Hunters are responsible for their own transportation to the arranged pick-up area, although airport pickup is available.

Contact:
George Taulman
United States Outfitters, Inc.
Box 4204
Taos, NM 87571
1-800/845-9929
Fax: 505/758-1744
e-mail: www.huntuso.com
Web: www/huntuso.com

GEORGE TAULMAN had a unique concept about outfitting, and in 1986 he began to make it a reality. Back then he started United States Outfitters, an outfitting service that hunted for trophy elk, antelope and mule deer on private ranches in New Mexico. Then, in 1991, he started up his Professional Licensing Service, which applies for trophy licenses in all of the Rocky Mountain states, plus Alaska, Kansas and a few others.

The deal is this. Suppose you want to hunt for trophy bighorn sheep, or whitetails, or elk, or whatever. You call Taulman's group, tell them what you want to hunt, and he'll work out an arrangement whereby he puts your name into the big game lotteries in the states that you'd like to hunt.

"We deal strictly with quality, trophy hunts," says Griz Montoya, who's been working with Taulman for years. "We don't apply for tags in areas where the trophy quality is not there."

So, at one time, you could have Taulman applying for bighorn sheep tags in five different states, moose in two others and elk somewhere else ("We mostly apply in New Mexico for elk, because that's where the true trophies are," says Montoya.). If you don't draw a tag, nothing's lost except the application fee. Unless you tell him otherwise, Taulman will apply for you again the following year. And he'll keep doing it until you've built up enough credits so that, eventually, you draw your tag.

Once that's done, you can either go hunt on your own, provided you're allowed to hunt without a guide in the area you've drawn for. Or Taulman will help you set up your hunt. With a network of first-rate guides across the country, and also leasing hundreds of thousands of private acres across the West, Taulman can make sure you're in the right place with the right people. And if you draw a tag in Arizona or New Mexico, he or one of his people will probably guide you personally.

Elk, mule deer, bighorn sheep, desert sheep, antelope, black bears, mountain goats, Dall sheep, shiras moose, ibex/oryx, Coues deer and whitetail deer: Take your pick, and U.S. will make it happen.

The Big K Guest Ranch

Elkton, Oregon

Primarily a fishing operation, the Big K offers a few special hunts for blacktails and elk.

VITAL STATISTICS:

Game/Arm/Seasons:
BLACK-TAILED DEER:
Bow: Late Aug. through late Sept.
Centerfire: Early Oct. through early Nov.
Muzzleloader: Mid through late Nov.
ELK:
Bow: Late Aug. through late Sept.
Centerfire: Mid and late Nov.
Muzzleloader: Early Dec.
TURKEY:
Bow, centerfire: Mid-Apr. through May

Rates:
BLACK-TAILED DEER $2,395/5 days
ELK $2,950/5 days
TURKEY $950/2 days

Accommodations:
LOG CABINS
NUMBER OF ROOMS: 20, ALL WITH PRIVATE BATH
MAXIMUM NUMBER OF HUNTERS: 2 OR 3

Meals: Excellent Western cuisine

Conference Groups: Yes

Guides: Included

Gratuity: 15% to 20%

Preferred Payment:
Cash, check, credit cards

Other Activities:
Biking, bird watching, fishing, riding, swimming, wildlife photography

Getting There:
Fly to Eugene and rent a car, or have the lodge pick you up for $50 each way.

Contact:
Kathie Williamson
The Big K Guest Ranch
20029 Hwy. 138 W.
Elkton, OR 97436
1-800/390-2445
Fax: 541/584-2395
e-mail: aparrish@jeffnet.org
Web: www.big-k.com

O N ITS WAY TO THE SEA, the lower Umpqua writhes like a snake as it cuts through the gentle foothills between the Coast and Cascade ranges. The terrain is gentle, or reasonably so, capped with heavy stands of fir, with wide swaths of open meadow. It is prime territory for Columbia black-tailed deer. With a range that stretches from northern California to northern British Columbia, this close relative of the mule deer is smaller than its Rocky Mountain cousin, standing only about three feet at the shoulder. A big one will weigh 150 pounds on the hoof. And it is the only mulie with a pure black tail. Racks fall into two categories: the typical mule deer bifurcated spread with three or four points per side along with a small eye-guard, and the so-called "Pacific buck" which hunter/writer Craig Boddington says many hunters ignore. Why? Only two points per main beam, but the main beams may reach 18 inches in length with a spread of 20 inches. That's a trophy in anyone's book.

Blacktail hunting in Oregon is a challenge. Cover is thick. Still-hunting can work, but glassing and stalking at dawn and dusk will give you a better opportunity. Areas where meadows meet woods offer the best chances. The difficulty is in finding high ground so you can glass them before planning a stalk. Stand hunting is actually a better option, if you can figure out the routes blacktails are using. The challenges in blacktail hunting lead many to forego it entirely, or hunt on private land where there is less pressure.

While almost exclusively an angling lodge specializing in smallmouth bass, steelhead, shad and salmon, the Big K offers two or three hunts per season for blacktails on its 25,000-acre spread five miles south of Elkton. The same number of hunts are available for elk as well. You'll arise from your fully appointed cabin or room in the lodge (private baths), breakfast heartily, and head out for the day's hunt in a 4WD with your guide. Upon reaching the trailhead, you'll shoulder your rifle and daypack and hustle to the vantage point you want to be glassing from as dawn breaks. From there it's a matter of spotting and stalking or sitting and waiting for a blacktail or elk to come through. During the elk rut, Big K guides bugle and call. This is not a large operation. Everything is tailored to the abilities and interests of the hunters. Every hunter has a personal guide.

Bearpaw Outfitters

C o l v i l l e ,   W a s h i n g t o n

Hunt prime game territory in three states for deer, elk, bear and lion.

VITAL STATISTICS:

Game/Arm/Seasons:

MULE DEER:
Bow: Late Aug. through late Sept.
Centerfire: Early Sept. through late Oct.
Muzzleloader: Mid through late Nov.

ELK:
Bow: Late Aug. through late Sept.
Centerfire: Late Oct. through early Nov.
Muzzleloader: Mid through late Nov.

WHITETAILS:
Bow: Early-Sept. through mid-Dec.
Centerfire: Mid-Oct. through mid-Nov.
Muzzleloader: Early to mid-Oct.

COUGAR:
Bow, centerfire, muzzleloader: Early Nov. through Mar.

BEAR:
Bow, centerfire, muzzleloader: Early Aug. through late Oct.

TURKEY:
Bow and shotgun: Mid-Apr. through mid-May

Rates:
MULE DEER: $1,900/4 days (one-on-one hunt)
ELK: From $1,900/5 days
WHITETAIL: $1650/5 days
COUGAR: $2,000/4 days
BEAR: $1,250/5 days
TURKEY: From $600/2 days

Accommodations:
GUEST HOUSE, LODGE, WALL TENTS
NUMBER OF ROOMS: LODGE 4,
GUEST HOUSE 1
MAXIMUM NUMBER OF HUNTERS: 12

Meals:
Roast beef, potatoes, chicken, salads

Conference Groups: No

Guides: Included

Gratuity: $20 to $100

Preferred Payment:
Cash, check, credit cards

Other Activities:
Biking, bird hunting, bird watching, boating, canoeing/rafting, fishing, horseback riding, skiing, waterfowling, wildlife photography

Getting There:
Fly to Spokane and rent a car, or be transported by a representative of the lodge for $150 round-trip.

Contact:
Dale Denney
Bearpaw Outfitters
345 Hwy. 20 E #A
Colville, WA 99114
509/684-6294
Fax: 509 684-6400
Web:
www.huntinfo.com/bearpaw.htm

UNTING THREE DIFFERENT STATES may seem like a daunting task to most, but not to Dale Denney of Bearpaw Outfitters. He's been in the business for more than 20 years now, knows this part of the world well and knows the game even better.

In southeastern Idaho, Denney's hunters go after record-class mule deer and trophy bull elk. Mountain lion populations have been on the increase in that area too, and the hunting is better than ever. Hunt this part of Idaho, and you can range through most of units 73, 74, 75, 77 and 78.

In northern Utah, Bearpaw can put you into trophy mulies, elk and cougars. Waterfowl hunting is also available to Denney's clients here. His leased ranches offer an especially high, well-balanced deer population, with a good chance for a big buck.

Northeastern Washington is where Denney's lodge is located. There, he offers both guided and unguided hunts for whitetails, bears, turkeys, elk, moose, grouse, sheep, mule deer, cougars, predators and waterfowl. And if that isn't enough for you, there's also good fishing nearby.

Four-on-one, two-on-one and one-on-one hunts are available through Bearpaw. And if you hunt out of the lodge, expect a modern, clean operation run by good people who like to have some fun. Just be prepared for good food and lots of it at the end of the day. Roast beef with mashed potatoes, fried chicken and corn, and all the salad you can eat will fuel you up for the next day.

Lake Quinault Outfitters

P o i n t   A n g e l e s ,   W a s h i n g t o n

*Guided or unguided hunts for
bull elk in the Olympic Mountains.*

VITAL STATISTICS:

Game/Arm/Seasons:
ELK:
Bow: Early through mid-Sept.
Centerfire: Early through mid-Nov.
BEAR:
Bow, centerfire, muzzleloader: Early
Aug. through mid-Nov.
Rates:
From $500 to $2,100 per week
Accommodations:
TENTS
MAXIMUM NUMBER OF HUNTERS: 40
Meals: Varied Western fare
Conference Groups: Yes
Guides: Included
Gratuity: Hunter's discretion
Preferred Payment:
Cash, Discover, MasterCard, Visa,
check
Other Activities:
Bird watching, fishing, hiking,
wildlife photography
Getting There:
Fly to Port Angeles and a van from
the outfitter will pick you up.

Contact:
Bruce Deane
Lake Quinault Outfitters
310 W. 6th
Port Angeles, WA 98362
360/452-8742
Fax: 509/533-0302
e-mail: bdeane@ior.com
Web: www.diocom/quinault
off-season:
Box 496
Aminy Heights, WA 99001
509/623-2076
Fax: 509/533-0302

O PERATING IN THE beautiful Olympic Mountains under a permit from the U.S. Forest Service, Lake Quinault Outfitters runs a number of elk and black bear hunts, with elk season opening Sept. 1 for bowhunters and continuing into mid-November for rifle hunters. Bear season runs from Aug. 1 into mid-November for bow, modern firearm and muzzleloader.

According to owner Bruce Deane, "We offer special deluxe hunts with two hunters per one guide. Our cook/guide will handle the camp and help you find the elk. We restock your camp daily with fresh fruits and vegetables and prepare delicious, hearty meals for you at the end of the day."

Quinault also offers two types of unguided drop camps. The first, the most affordable, is a tent camp way back in the Olympic Forest. "We just pack you and your gear in and out," says Deane. "We consider this a good deal for hunting groups who want to get away from the crowds without having to pack gear or game very far. The price includes use of tent, woodstove, ax, shovel, saw and water jugs.

"Our other drop camp has a bit more, including a tent in a site chosen to place you near game, a day's worth of cut wood, ax, water, shovel, cookstove with propane, complete kitchen, ice chest, cots and lantern."

They'll get you there; then it's up to you to go out and find your elk. It's an ideal hunt for someone who's already hunted elk a few times and wants to try it on his own, one-on-one with one of North America's most majestic game animals.

INDEX